BETWEEN TRADITION AND MODERNITY

New Perspectives
Jewish Life and Thought

BETWEEN TRADITION AND MODERNITY

*Haim Zhitlowski, Simon Dubnow,
Ahad Ha-Am, and the Shaping of
Modern Jewish Identity*

DAVID H. WEINBERG

HOLMES & MEIER
New York / London

Published in the United States of America 1996 by
Holmes & Meier Publishers, Inc.
160 Broadway
New York, NY 10038

Epigraph translated by David. H. Weinberg and printed with permission of Dvir Publishing.

Design by Robert Sugar

This book has been printed on acid-free paper.

Library of Congress Cataloging-in-Publication Data

Weinberg, David H., 1945–
    Between tradition and modernity : Haim Zhitlowski, Simon
Dubnow, Ahad Ha-Am, and the shaping of modern Jewish identity /
David H. Weinberg.
      p.   cm. — (New perspectives)
    Includes bibliographical references and index.
    ISBN 0-8419-1355-2 (cloth : alk. paper)
    1. Jews—Identity. 2. Jews—Politics and government.
3. Zhitlowsky, Chaim. 1865–1943. 4. Dubnow, Simon. 1860-1941.
5. Ahad Ha'am, 1856-1927. 6. Jews—Cultural assimilation—
Russia—History—19th century. I. Title. II. Series: New perspectives
(Holmes & Meier)
DS143.W39   1996
305.892'4—dc20   96-11218
                                                CIP

Manufactured in the United States of America

CONTENTS

Under a constellation whose name we do not know and amidst mounds of ruins
We were born again in our old age as children who have returned to our people in darkness;
Reared from our youth in shadows
With trembling upon the graves of our fathers,
We searched for the meaning of life with all our innermost being.
And each of us with a divine candle in his heart
Went out at twilight to seek his star.
And the hour was one of chaos, an hour of confused parameters,
Of beginnings and ends, of destruction and building, of old age and youth.
And we, the transitional children, whether knowingly or not,
Together bowed down before and acknowledged the two possibilities;
And suspended in the middle between these two magnetic poles
All of the blocked feelings in our hearts cried out for a prophet:
A true prophet who would touch the innermost reaches of our hearts and who would
      come and illuminate his star from above,
And his spirit would be the source for all the feelings that were trapped in many hearts as
      vague dreams,
And still our hope remains enclosed in a fog,
And still we wander despairingly and with little faith, lost at the crossroads and ask:
Where shall we go?

A selection from the poem "To Ahad Ha-Am,"
written by Haim Nahman Bialik in 1903

PREFACE

THIS WORK began more than a decade ago as an investigation of secular Jewish ideology in the modern era. For a long time I have been intrigued for both personal and scholarly reasons with the varying ways that Jews have sought to fashion a personal and collective identity divorced from its traditional religious base. I was especially fascinated with the role of Jewish leadership in the modernization of Jewish life. What were the factors that led to the transformation of communal authority from the *rav* or traditional rabbi, whose primary role was to teach and to interpret religious law, to the contemporary Jewish leader, including the modern rabbi, who is mainly concerned with the unity of the community and the shaping of its collective future? In my enthusiasm, I intended to cover no less than four geographical areas — eastern and western Europe, America, and Israel. I was convinced that a general survey would shed light on the modernization of world Jewry in the nineteenth century while at the same time offering insight into strategies for the survival of Jewish communal life in the future.

Unfortunately, the task soon proved to be overwhelming and I was forced to abandon the project. For a while, I tried to put the study out of my mind by immersing myself in other topics in modern Jewish history. Yet the issue that originally had fired my imagination refused to go away: the problematic of creating a Jewish identity in an era of transition from traditional to modern life. After much soul-searching and frequent proddings from colleagues, I returned to my project a chastened scholar. Winnowing down my original encyclopedic proposal to manageable size, I decided to focus my study on three remarkable individuals — Haim Zhitlowski, Simon Dubnow, and Ahad Ha-Am — who attempted to grapple with this task in the context of late nineteenth-century Russia. I chose these three thinkers because they illustrate the complexity of both the process of Jewish identity formation and the development of an appropriate leadership to guide the Jewish community in its transformation from tradition to modernity. Specifically, their experiences demonstrate that the secularization of modern Jewish life was marked by a long transitional period in which religious ideals and values continued to hold sway long after individuals had rejected the theological beliefs that had originally given them meaning. Their writings also helped me to recognize that the formation of a modern cadre of leaders within the Jewish community contained a similar transitional phase in which elements of traditional rabbinic authority and modern professional expertise were often intertwined. In contrast to what I had originally assumed, I began to realize that a central element in what is generally called secular Jewish thought in the modern era has often consisted of an attempt to recapture rather than to deny the spiritual in Jewish life.

Though I do not claim to have written the definitive study of Jewish identity formation in eastern Europe at the end of the nineteenth century, I hope that at the least I will have introduced the English-reading public to three individuals who are undeservedly ignored in our own era. For despite the time-bound nature of their programs and the yawning abyss of the Holocaust that separates us from pre-war European Jewry, the voices of Zhitlowski, Dubnow, and Ahad Ha-Am resonate across the generations. Their quest to confront the challenge of living in the Diaspora — how to balance Jewish and general loyalties and commitments in an era of significant transformations in both Jewish and non-Jewish society — is as relevant today as it was a century ago. In a more general sense, their perceptions can offer modern Jews, whose personal and collective Jewish identity is often no more than a symbolic or aesthetic experience, a conceptual framework to understand and to identify with the Jewish past, present, and future.

A word must be said about the sources used in the book. I make no pretense of having written an exhaustive study. For a variety of reasons, I did not read all of the writings of the three individuals. In particular, I chose not to examine the archives of Zhitlowski, Dubnow, and Ahad Ha-Am that are to be found in New York and Jerusalem. Instead, I decided to concentrate upon collected works — correspondence, autobiographies, articles, literary essays, and historical studies — that the three authors themselves considered most reflective of their own viewpoints and philosophies. In cases where significant works were unavailable to me, I have relied upon scholarly secondary sources. All three individuals were autodidacts who treasured the written word and who invested as much time and energy in the preparation of personal correspondence and newspaper articles as in the publication of their more formal scholarly pieces. The writings of Zhitlowski, Dubnow, and Ahad Ha-Am are also deeply personal and reveal much about their own intellectual development. At the same time, they reflect in microcosm the spiritual development of Russian Jewish intellectuals as a whole at a crucial point in modern Jewish history. The result is an overview of a distinctive generation of Jewish nationalist intellectuals in late-nineteenth-century Russia rather than a detailed study of the life or thought of any one of the individuals.

My transliterations of Yiddish words are based upon the method developed by the YIVO Institute for Jewish Research. I have adopted a modified form of the Library of Congress's guidelines for Hebrew transliteration as contained in Paul Maher's *Hebraica Cataloging: A Guide to ALA/LC Romanization and Descriptive Cataloging* (Washington, D.C.: Library of Congress, 1987). Where appropriate, I have been faithful to the transliterations of titles as noted in original works, even when they contradict the YIVO and Library of Congress guidelines. This is especially true of Yiddish newspapers, which often adopted Germanic renderings of their names on their mastheads. Readers should also note differing spellings of individual's names, especially in the Bibliography. Here too I have followed the citation of the author in the original work. My intention, as always, is to enable the interested reader to more easily search out the source in a library or archive catalogue.

In the course of my research which spanned three continents, I have been aided by many librarians and scholars. In particular, I wish to thank the members of the Institute of Contemporary Jewry at the Hebrew University for inviting me to be a Visiting Fellow during my sabbatical year in 1985–86. From my perch high atop Mount Scopus, I could feast my eyes on the Judean hills and the Old City. It was not always easy to concentrate on my reading, yet the intense Jewish experience that is Jerusalem spurred me on in my research and writing. I am also indebted to Zachary Baker and Dina Abramowicz of the YIVO Institute and to the staff of the Jewish Room of the New York Public

Library who helped me to retrieve (and at times to decipher) microfilms and yellowed pages of newspapers and journals from a forgotten era. I am grateful to Dvir Publishing House for granting permission to reproduce the photograph of Ahad Ha-Am and to reprint the epigraph by Haim Nahmam Bialik. Among the many scholars in Russian Jewish history who provided me with constructive suggestions were Rina Poznanski, Alexander Orbach, Jonathan Frankel, and John Klier. Needless to say, I bear all responsibility for any errors that appear in the text.

Over the course of the past ten years, I have been privileged to present my preliminary findings in public lectures at a number of distinguished colleges and universities, including University College London, the Hebrew College in Boston, the University of Michigan, the University of Pennsylvania, and the University of Wisconsin. Generous grants from Bowling Green State University, the Memorial Foundation for Jewish Culture, the Lucius N. Littauer Foundation, and the Alex Silberman Foundation allowed me to travel to libraries. I also wish to thank the Department of History at Bowling Green State University whose continuing support enabled me to complete my study. Finally, I deeply appreciate the assistance of my editor at Holmes & Meier, Sheila Friedling, who gently prodded me to persevere in my study and who helped to expedite its publication.

As always, my wife Judy has been a patient and supportive helpmate in my research and writing. Over the years, my children, Joshua and Rachel, learned to gracefully accept my frequent absences from home on research trips. As they have matured, they have also grown to appreciate the importance of their father's commitment to the study of Jewish history.

I come to this study not as a Russian Jewish historian nor as a historian of Russia, but as a scholar with strong interests in both the Jewish and general European experience in the modern era. As more than one observer has noted, Russian Jewish historiography has been largely framed by scholars writing over a century ago. The tragic destruction of European Jewry during World War II and the systematic elimination of Russian Jewish cultural life under the Soviet regime have meant that until recently, there has been little effort to reassess classical formulations of the Russian Jewish past. I trust that in its own small way my study will contribute to the ongoing process of reinterpretation that enriches the understanding of Russian Jewry at a crucial point in its modern historical development.

BETWEEN TRADITION AND MODERNITY

INTRODUCTION

The Transitional Generation

THE CENTRAL theme of the historiography of nineteenth-century Russian Jewry has been the community's radical transformation from a society steeped in the tenets of rabbinic Judaism to an activist and self-assertive collectivity — from a "world of piety" to a "world of politics," as one writer has cogently described it.[1] Though recognizing the groundwork laid by the Haskalah, or Jewish Enlightenment, in the early nineteenth century, scholars generally have focused their attention on a sudden and dramatic shift in Russian Jewish attitudes and behavior at the end of the century. The triggering mechanism, according to this view, was the pogroms of 1881–82, which in demonstrating the vulnerability of the community and the impotence of its traditional leadership, led to the establishment of movements of "autoemancipation" such as Bundism, Zionism, and mass emigration to America. As such, the development of a modern Russian Jewish consciousness, like the modernization of Jewry in general, has been viewed as essentially a response to external forces.[2] Scholars have also contended that, in contrast to the experience of western European Jewry where changes in Jewish consciousness remained within the communally acceptable perimeters of religious thought and activity, the modernization of Jewish consciousness in Russia was radical and irreversible, involving both a deliberate rejection of the authority structure and value system of traditional communal life and the positing of distinctive new activist forms of thought and behavior.[3]

1

Such a view is far too simplistic and needs to be refined. Without denying the dramatic impact of the events of 1881–82 upon Russian Jewish consciousness, one must nevertheless recognize both the deeply rooted nature of the demand for change and the powerful pull of traditional Jewish culture within East European Jewish society. Far from a sudden and desperate response to an externally imposed crisis, the process of ideological and political modernization among Russian Jews was in actuality gradual and complex, extending over a number of generations and characterized by a long period in which adherence to and rejection of Jewish tradition existed side by side within the community and often within the consciousness of individuals themselves. Rather than initiating change, the pogroms and their aftermath served as a catalyst that accelerated the movement toward a reassessment of the nature of Jewish life which had begun decades before. Even in the crucial period of the 1880s and '90s, calls and proposals for Jewish modernization reflected an interweaving of themes of continuity and change as intellectuals grappled with the daunting task of creating an appropriate cultural and philosophical framework to guide an ancient people into the modern age.

The purpose of this study is to examine the attitudes and activity of Haim Zhitlowski, Simon Dubnow, and Ahad Ha-Am (Asher Ginsberg) — three representative figures of a crucial but often neglected generation of Russian Jewish intellectuals in the late nineteenth and early twentieth centuries who acted as a bridge between religious tradition and the secularizing tendencies of the modern era. In a remarkable way, these three thinkers reflected in their own lives the significant changes that the Russian Jewish community as a whole underwent in the nineteenth century in its movement from religious orthodoxy through the Haskalah and finally to secular nationalism and political activism. In responding to these developments, Zhitlowski, Dubnow, and Ahad Ha-Am attempted to forge a distinctive personal and collective identity based on a synthesis of traditional concerns with ethics, communal solidarity, and spiritual commitment and modern longings for sovereignty, material progress, and intellectual and cultural development.

My examination of the life and thought of members of this distinctive group of thinkers stems from a strong belief that the end of the nineteenth century was as much an age of profound soul-searching as of activism for Russian Jewish intellectuals. Spurred by long-term developments such as declining religious belief among the Jewish masses and the growing alienation of intellectuals from Jewish life, and often dismissive of what they regarded as the community's emotional responses to the immediate realities of pogroms and economic immizeration, young thinkers emerged in the 1880s and '90s who searched for a new Jewish raison d'être that would ensure collective survival and growth in the future. The challenge was twofold. On the one hand, there was the need to build a strong Jewish collective consciousness that would reconcile freethinking Jews with the deeply rooted values and beliefs of Jewish life. On the other, there was the challenge of developing a collective identity that would enable Jews to participate in the modern world despite the absence of the objective conditions of territory and sovereignty that characterized nation building in the nineteenth century. The solutions ultimately proposed by Zhitlowski, Dubnow, and Ahad Ha-Am — agrarian socialism and Yiddishism, communal autonomy in a multinational state, and cultural revival in Palestine, respectively — though eventually giving way to more dynamic and aggressive ideologies and movements, reflect the melding of the past with the present that typifies an intellectual community in transition.

All three thinkers shared in what the historian Robert Wohl has described as "generational consciousness," that is, a common frame of reference that "provides a sense of rupture with the past and that will later distinguish the members of the generation from those who follow them in time."[4] Chronologically, Zhitlowski, Dubnow, and Ahad Ha-Am can be seen as reflecting a critical period in the modernization of Russian Jewry characterized by a movement away from the philosophical and literary abstractions of the Haskalah that had dominated Jewish thought since the 1840s and by a new emphasis upon defining concrete strategies for national survival. At the same time, however, all three rejected the pragmatic orientation and militant activism of younger Bundist and Zionist Jewish radicals of the early twentieth century. While criticizing the Jewish Enlightenment's refusal to question the fundamental religious tenets of Judaism, they could not accept the view of the "younger" generation who vehemently denounced the religious heritage of the past and for whom a new Jewish identity would only arise from the struggles of contemporary daily life.   Nor did they generally share the concerns of the radical individualists and political activists with the larger world outside the Jewish community.   Reflecting their deeply rooted ties to religious and cultural traditions despite their often bitter criticism of established Jewish institutions and leadership, Zhitlowski, Dubnow, and Ahad Ha-Am can be seen as representative of a "transitional generation" that attempted to establish a new Jewish self-consciousness and national agenda while remaining deeply grounded in a respect for the values of ancient Judaism.[5]

In rejecting both the traditionalists' absolute reliance upon the past and the younger generation's obsession with the future as the sole determinant of the present, the three thinkers insisted upon a clear vision of what they regarded as the evolutionary nature of Jewish life.   Despite their emphasis upon process and continuity in human development, Zhitlowski, Dubnow, and Ahad Ha-Am presented a highly eclectic and tendentious view of Jewish history to their readers that pointed to certain periods and Jewish communities as significant, while ignoring others that were deemed to be irrelevant to contemporary Jewish concerns.   In this sense, members of the transitional generation can be said to have pioneered in the selective application of the past to serve the needs of the present and the future — the hallmark of all modern Jewish ideologies and movements.[6]

As reflections of a relatively short-lived intellectual phenomenon, the activities and influence of Zhitlowski, Dubnow, and Ahad Ha-Am were severely circumscribed by the rapidly changing events around them.   Born in the late 1850s and early 1860s, their most intense activity took place at the end of the era of so-called liberal reforms under the reign of Alexander II in the 1880s and the first bold assertions at the turn of the century of a distinctive Russian Jewish consciousness that was not simply imitative of western Jewry. Like pioneering nationalist thinkers in other societies, however, they would soon be overshadowed by activists who would seek to realize their ideals in daily life.[7] By the end of the first decade of the twentieth century, Zhitlowski, Dubnow, and Ahad Ha-Am were already in partial eclipse, their ideas and activities increasingly questioned by a new generation of Jewish socialists and Zionists who sought national renewal beyond the boundaries of the established Russian Jewish community.

The increased globalization of Jewish life at the beginning of the twentieth century only seemed to further demonstrate the growing irrelevance of their proposals and programs. Zhitlowski, Dubnow, and Ahad Ha-Am claimed to speak for the concerns of Jews wherever they lived, yet their purview generally remained limited to Russia and Poland — the source of their generation's support and the model for its plans for the Jewish future. Though the three men traveled extensively throughout the Jewish world, their journeys generally reflected the migratory patterns of East European Jewry at the turn of the century. Even when they settled abroad, their point of reference remained fixed on their homeland.[8] For the most part, western Jewry remained merely a foil for their arguments and polemics against assimilationism. Even less attention was paid to the Jews of the Middle East and North Africa whose culture was seen as derivative of the more "established" European Jewish communities and who were therefore deemed to have only minimal influence upon contemporaneous Jewish life.[9] Not surprisingly, Zhitlowski, Dubnow, and Ahad Ha-Am were unable to respond effectively to the rapid growth of a distinctively "American" Jewish community and the proclamation of the Balfour Declaration after World War I, which turned Jewish attention from East European ideological debates to practical issues of settlement in the newly emerging centers of world Jewry.

Their dreams either shattered or realized in dramatically different ways than they had originally envisioned, some members of the transitional generation like Ahad Ha-Am would not survive the 1920s. Others like Dubnow turned inward during the interwar years to reflect upon their lives or to complete major works that would serve as testaments of their commitment to the Jewish people. Still others like Zhitlowski would join the migration of Russian Jews westward and would seek to realize their prewar ideals in what they mistakenly believed to be the more fertile soil of America.

In the interwar period, one could still find intensive discussions of concerns with agrarian socialism, Diaspora autonomism, and the "Jewish national spirit" among Jews in Poland and in the Soviet Union and to a lesser extent within immigrant Russian Jewish circles in the United States. Yet the visions of a new Jewish society evoked by Zhitlowski, Dubnow, and Ahad Ha-Am could not long withstand the onslaught of world war, the rise of fascism and Nazism, and the growth of a bureaucratic and dictatorial Soviet state. In their declining years, all three were forced to witness the brutal triumph of cruel perspectives and violent policies that they had so bitterly opposed throughout their lives, including state-imposed persecution, ethnic hostility, and class struggle.[10] By the 1930s, proposals for cultural rejuvenation and social transformation seemed to pale beside the immediate and urgent need to seek refuge from Nazi persecution. Those members of the transitional generation who survived to see the rise of the Third Reich could offer only pious hopes that Jewry would emerge from its nightmare with renewed vigor. Ultimately, the gas chambers of the Holocaust destroyed the East European constituency of Zhitlowski, Dubnow, and Ahad Ha-Am and signaled the failure of the humanistic ideals that formed the basis of their ideologies.

Yet viewed in their own era, the perspectives of Zhitlowski, Dubnow, and Ahad Ha-Am clearly reflected the anxieties and hopes of Russian Jewry on the threshold of modernity. The origins of the three thinkers' diverse ideologies can be found in the response of their generation to both the general economic and political crisis affecting the Russian Jewish community and the personal crisis facing young Russian Jewish intellectuals in the latter half of the nineteenth century. As I will examine in Chapter 1, the onset of industrialization, the expansion of communication and travel, and growing social and economic differentiation all played their part in the decline of traditional institutions and values within the Jewish community. The result was a gradual weakening of collective ties, which could be seen first in the inability of traditional leadership to prevent the movement toward Russification on the part of many young Jews and then later, after the collapse of such efforts, in the rise of internal class divisions and the development of sharply contrasting ideological solutions to the problem of Jewish survival.

The writings of Zhitlowski, Dubnow, and Ahad Ha-Am reveal an ongoing concern with the effect on the Jewish community of increased mobility and opportunities for economic advancement and social assimilation during the 1870s and '80s. Their understanding of such developments was generally framed in terms of a loss of faith and loyalty rather than in the collapse of established institutions and structures. This was clearly evidenced in the all-too-familiar stories of youthful rejection of tradition, family, and community in the name of universalism and European culture that dominate the early pages of the memoirs of all three individuals. What emerged from such soul-searching was no mere repudiation of traditional religion, however. To do so would be to sever their ties with deep-seated Orthodox beliefs and institutions that continued to find support among the general Jewish population and that served as the foundations of Jewish collective identity. Projecting their own sentiments upon their peers, Zhitlowski, Dubnow, and Ahad Ha-Am sensed a yearning among self-styled "modern" Jewish intellectuals for a transcendent ideal that would fill the spiritual vacuum created by their alienation from traditional Judaism and would provide a rational justification for their involvement in the struggle to ensure the survival of the Jewish people.

The foundation of their new approach to Jewish life was the ideal of *Bildung*, that is, the importance of self-consciousness and self-awareness as a sign of the cultured individual and as a prerequisite for correct action. Such notions were especially evident in the writings of the Berlin Haskalah and could also be found in Russian intellectual thought of the mid-nineteenth century. The emphasis upon cultured self-awareness also served to separate the transitional generation from younger Zionist and Bundist popularizers and propagandists who saw political activism largely in terms of pragmatic strategies and short-term goals. As proponents of *Bildung*, Zhitlowski, Dubnow, and Ahad Ha-Am sought not only to ensure Jewish existence but to enrich it for both the traditional believer and the freethinker. Far less concerned with the validity of belief, the three thinkers would labor to create an aesthetic Judaism, one which more closely reflected the sensibilities and sensitivities of cultured and sophisticated Europeans in the late nineteenth century. In so doing, they hoped not only to reconcile traditionalists with modern views but also to stem the process of assimilation among Jewish youth.[11]

It was not necessary to acquire a formal education to achieve *Bildung*. Despite the efforts of Zhitlowski, Dubnow, and Ahad Ha-Am to pursue their studies in Russian schools of higher learning, none of them succeeded in earning a degree. In this sense, as well, they stood in between the maskilim (Enlighteners) of the previous generation, for whom the attainment of a diploma was an end in itself, and younger activists who no longer viewed formal education as a prerequisite for participation and leadership in Jewish life. In many ways, the staunch commitment of these transitional thinkers to modernization within the Jewish community served to compensate for their own failure to gain intellectual acceptance in the larger Russian society. The highly selective and piecemeal nature of their education also helps to explain the eclectic nature of their thought, in which ideas borrowed from varying sources and disciplines "cohabited" in essays and speeches, often without clear synthesis or elaboration. In turn, the childhood experiences of Zhitlowski, Dubnow, and Ahad Ha-Am as self-taught intellectuals undoubtedly reinforced their belief in the power of the written word and in the ability of similarly minded Jews who had not received formal higher education to grasp their ideas through thoughtful reflection.

For all their concern with the crisis facing the Russian Jewish community, the three thinkers' quests for unity and direction remained relatively dispassionate and lacked the urgency of both earlier and later generations. Like other Jewish intellectuals whom they encountered, Zhitlowski, Dubnow, and Ahad Ha-Am were far removed from the concerns of the Jewish masses in the Pale of Settlement, the area to which Russian Jews were confined under tsarist rule (see map, p. 35). Products of middle-class families, having left the countryside at an early age to find employment and/or intellectual stimulation in cities like Odessa and St. Petersburg, and experiencing life in western or central Europe, the three individuals rarely fashioned their ideas in response to personal misfortune. Their highly dramatic accounts of their alienation and ultimate return to the Jewish fold certainly reflected the growing awareness among European intellectuals of adolescence as a distinctive and painful stage in human development. Nevertheless, none had experienced the wrenching conflict between traditional fathers and rebellious sons that allegedly characterized both Russian and Jewish middle-class life in the late nineteenth century.[12] All three thinkers had come from homes that already bore the signs of the filtering down of Haskalah ideals to the Jewish population as a whole. Though the parents of Zhitlowski, Dubnow, and Ahad Ha-Am were deeply religious, they were generally open to new ideas and at least tolerated their sons' interest in the works and ideas of both the Jewish and the Russian Enlightenment.

All of these factors combined to create in all three thinkers a distinct approach to intellectual matters, marked by a self-perception of objectivity in contrast to the alleged irrationality and utopianism of their ideological enemies, a deliberate desire to emphasize long-range issues rather than immediate concerns, a certain distaste for the material world, and a reverence for the cerebral. It was for this reason that Zhitlowski, Dubnow, and Ahad Ha-Am generally appeared more concerned with the survival of Jewish values and ideals than with the physical welfare of Jewry. Such attitudes were reinforced by their tendency to view conflicts within Jewish society in terms of competing ideologies and generations rather than as a result of political, social, and economic divisions. In his second volume on the formative years of Zionism, the historian David Vital describes the first generation of Jewish nationalists in terms that could well apply to all three men: "[B]y virtue of their easier circumstances, their education, their habits of mind, and the tremendous impact upon them of influences from outside Jewry — in brief, as members *par excellence* of the modern Jewish intelligentsia — they tended to attach more weight than other sectors of the Jewish population to matters of principle, to argue social issues on an *a priori* basis, and, so far as the world of action was concerned, to wish it to reflect their ideas and principles with the greatest possible accuracy."[13]

The biographies of Zhitlowski, Dubnow, and Ahad Ha-Am also would seem to corroborate Robert Brym's argument in his work on the Jewish intelligentsia in Russia that Russian Jewish activists in the nineteenth century were not rootless and culturally alienated, as is generally assumed.[14] Though Brym deals largely with Jewish revolutionaries, his questioning of the marginality theory as an explanation for Jewish activism has direct relevance to members of the transitional generation as well. Indeed, Brym's discussion of degrees of embeddedness as the major factor in defining the shaping of revolutionary activity only confirms the need to view individuals like Zhitlowski, Dubnow, and Ahad Ha-Am as caught between the traditional Jewish community and the larger non-Jewish world. In contrast to later radicals and revolutionaries who no longer identified with established Jewish perspectives and institutions, members of the transitional generation often found themselves confronting a society whose fundamental values and ideals they sought to recover and reaffirm.

Even the pogroms of 1881–82 did not shake the belief of Zhitlowski, Dubnow, and Ahad Ha-Am that only a calm and reasoned study of the nature of Jewish life through the centuries could ensure the survival of the Jewish people in the modern era. In part, their surprisingly mild response to the attacks upon Jews by Russian peasants can be explained by their analytical and at times even introspective personalities. More significant was the fact that for young men in their early twenties obsessed with issues of personal Jewish identity and having only recently begun to formulate an appropriate response to collective Jewish problems, such events could only be seen as transitory and fleeting. At most, the anti-Semitic outrages of 1881–82 and the government's harsh response forced these young Jews to begin to think seriously about developing a distinctive East European path to modernization. Yet there was no urgency to this quest. Indeed, by the end of the 1880s, reason had begun to replace desperation not only in their writings but in the writings of Russian Jewish nationalist intellectuals as a whole.

Far different was the impact of the pogroms of Kishinev and Odessa in 1903 and 1905 respectively, which not only profoundly shocked a now mature generation but also marked a transformation in Jewish thought and behavior from an emphasis upon identity and culture to a commitment to physical self-defense and practical action in general.[15] Despite their insistence upon the need for Jewish militancy in the face of attack, however, Zhitlowski, Dubnow, and Ahad Ha-Am could not completely dispense with their deep-seated faith in the ultimate triumph of enlightenment over superstition and prejudice. They sincerely believed, in the words of Dubnow, that in spite of all the brutality of the Russian masses, "a more refined culture and lofty education" might ultimately "extirpate the bestiality" of the Black Hundreds.[16] As a result, they played only a small role in the preparations for the mobilization of Russian Jewry against further anti-Semitic acts. Indeed, one senses in their responses the growing realization that they were soon to be eclipsed by a newly emerging generation of activists.[17] For the remainder of their lives, despite their deep concern over the rise of anti-Jewish sentiment and activity in Russia and in Europe as a whole and their occasional support of movements of self-defense, Zhitlowski, Dubnow, and Ahad Ha-Am remained true to their belief that Jewish self-consciousness had to emerge gradually from within the Jewish community and could never arise from a momentary response to threatening forces and pressures from the outside.

In attempting to formulate a modern Jewish ideology, Zhitlowski, Dubnow, and Ahad Ha-Am faced three major tasks that had previously been assumed by traditional Judaism: first, the need to explain and justify Jewish survival in the past; second, the definition of Jewry and of the nature of communal authority in the present; and third, the development of appropriate methods of transmission of belief and loyalty to ensure the Jewish future. Here, as well, they demonstrated their distance from both the Haskalah, which could only meekly challenge the approach of Orthodoxy, and the later generation of activists who would scoff at their efforts, choosing instead to break with the past, limit its audience to a segment of the community, and rely upon militant self-defense to ensure the Jewish future.

Yet how exactly to unravel the intricate weave that bound Jewry to its centuries-old religious traditions? Despite their conviction that Othodox Judaism could no longer command the loyalty of the majority of Jews, Zhitlowski, Dubnow, and Ahad Ha-Am understood that the formulation of a new unifying principle for Jewish identity could not simply involve the replacement of one set of ideas with another. They recognized, as the sociologist of religion Robert Bellah has insightfully written, that belief in religious tradition often is not a matter "of cognitive assent but of faith, trust, and obedience."[18] Whatever their own particular attitudes, all three intellectuals realized that they would have to appeal to Jews much like themselves who were still bound to significant elements of religious tradition.

The key to developing a new Jewish identity grounded in traditional values differed radically from individual to individual. For Zhitlowski, it was the Yiddish language and "progressive" Yiddish culture in general. An eclectic thinker who borrowed liberally from the writings of linguistic nationalists, romantic revolutionaries, and Utopian socialists, Zhitlowski hoped to synthesize the competing demands of nationalism and internationalism into a meaningful and logically consistent collective identity that would allow Jews to participate in the larger society while at the same time maintaining their own distinctive culture and institutions. In so doing, he helped to formulate many of the basic ideas that would later be associated with

Jewish socialism and linguistic nationalism. For Dubnow, the key to forging a new Jewish identity and ensuring the future of the Jewish people lay in the examination of Jewish history and specifically in an understanding of the role of communal institutions. In his view, such a study would not only reinforce the ties of contemporary Jews to the past but would also provide them with the structural tools to create a viable Jewish life in the Diaspora in the modern era. For Ahad Ha-Am, the new Jewish identity would emerge from the Jewish national spirit that was embodied in Jewish culture and in the Jewish people's eternal longing for the Land of Israel. Here again the past and the future merged in the effort to revivify an ancient culture by infusing it with modern ideals and values and in the attempt to create a modus vivendi between centuries-old Jewish communities in the Diaspora and the emerging Jewish settlement (*yishuv*) in Palestine.

In their insistence upon the need for a new Jewish identity, all three men were convinced that only a "scientific" investigation of the Jewish condition through the application of the tools of the social and economic historian, sociologist, and anthropologist would reveal the underlying truths of Jewish life. In their own work and activity, each strived to advance the scholarly study of Jewry and Jewish life. Thus Zhitlowski was instrumental in the development of research into Yiddish language and literature and helped establish institutes of adult Jewish education in America. The preeminent Jewish historian of his day, Dubnow was a founding member of the Yidisher vishenshaftlikher institut (YIVO Institute for Jewish Research) established in Vilna in 1926. Similarly, Ahad Ha-Am took special pride in helping to formulate modern Hebrew writing style and was closely associated with the founding of both the Technion and the Hebrew University in Palestine.

Ironically, the efforts by Zhitlowski, Dubnow, and Ahad Ha-Am to create rational foundations for the Jewish past, present, and future often involved them in contradictions and ambiguities that betrayed the attitudes and beliefs of the society in which they lived. In rejecting a religious explanation for Jewish survival, for example, all three men often employed rigid historicist terms, substituting laws of social and cultural evolution for the Covenant at Sinai and insisting upon the need for what Zhitlowski awkwardly described as "the humanization of religious sancta."[19] In defining Jewry as a collectivity, they relied upon pseudoscientific analyses of race and soul that ignored social and economic divisions and that obviated the need for an in-depth analysis of the nature of Jewish unity. In attempting to describe new forms of Jewish identity in the "unscientific" languages of Hebrew and Yiddish, they often translated accepted German terms literally, thereby confusing both their readership and modern-day researchers.[20] And in the end, for all their insistence upon the need to define Jewish national identity in "objective" psychological and sociological terms, the transitional generation could not shake their deep-seated belief that the core of Jewishness lay in spiritual and ethical ideals that were eternal and independent of outside influences.

Intermingling deeply rooted private concerns with newly affirmed public loyalties to their people, Zhitlowski, Dubnow, and Ahad Ha-Am grew to perceive themselves as modern-day Jewish prophets, reaffirming the basic principles of eternal Judaism in an age of growing social, economic, political, and ideological fragmentation within the community. Believing that, in the words of Ahad Ha-Am, "the salvation of Israel will be brought about by prophets, not by diplomats," they pledged themselves not to succumb to the vagaries of public politics.[21] In this sense, the attitudes and behavior of the transitional generation mirrored those of the leadership of many nascent nationalist movements in central and eastern Europe in the nineteenth century, who saw themselves (and were perceived by others) as moral teachers and guides to spark the cultural reawakening of a downtrodden people.[22] At the same time, Zhitlowski, Dubnow, and Ahad Ha-Am sought to introduce "worldly" concerns into the realm of Jewish intellectual and cultural discourse. As such, they helped to introduce an entire generation of young Jews only recently emerged from the shtetl (small East European Jewish village) and the yeshiva (religious school of learning) to European culture. As one devotee of Ahad Ha-Am remarked in 1900, it was not usual for students to arrive at the yeshiva at the beginning of the academic year with their phylacteries and a copy of the "master's" work *Al parshat derakhim* (At the Crossroads) under their arms.[23]

The identification by each of the individuals with ancient prophets and the prophetic tradition could be seen in other facets of their lives as well. While emphasizing the need for collective consciousness and the national will to survive, Zhitlowski, Dubnow, and Ahad

Ha-Am frequently espoused elitist values. Though often critical of rabbinic leadership for its inability to speak to the needs of a growingly sophisticated generation of Jewish youth, they nevertheless strove to assume the rabbi's mantle of spiritual leadership. Distinctly uncomfortable with mass politics and with political power itself, they generally restricted their public activity to small groups of devoted followers who developed a cult of personality around them and who treated them with almost mystical reverence.[24] As we shall see, Ahad Ha-Am played a crucial role in Hibbat Zion (Love of Zion) and Bnei Moshe (Sons of Moses); Dubnow provided direction for the Society for the Promotion of Enlightenment among Jews in Russia; and Zhitlowski was a central figure in Russian Jewish emigré groups in central Europe. The goal of such circles was not to create a mass movement but to forge an intellectual vanguard charged with developing a new, commonly accepted, sacred tradition. The underlying contradiction between the three individuals' elitism and their demand for collective action found its resolution in the commitment by members of such protomovements to force the masses to be free.[25]

The writings of Zhitlowski, Dubnow, and Ahad Ha-Am attest to their uncertain relationships with the general Jewish population. Publicists rather than philosophers, feuilletonists and essayists rather than polemicists, the three thinkers sought to synthesize the concern of the Haskalah for skillful prose with a commitment to significant and meaningful change. Their preference for articles and essays rather than scholarly monographs reflected a shaky compromise between their emphasis on intellectualism and their growing recognition of the need to "go to the people" in an era before the rise of political parties. Not surprisingly, therefore, the writings of Zhitlowski, Dubnow, and Ahad Ha-Am often combined scholarly research with homiletics, and mingled rigorous methodology with pseudoscientific preachments and speculations. Neither academicians nor politicians, they represented the first generation of professional Jewish writers who arose in response to the felt need on the part of the growing segments of the population for an explanation for the changes taking place both within and outside the Russian Jewish community. It was a precarious life, marked by bitter quarrels with publishers on the verge of bankruptcy, gnawing uncertainties over the nature and extent of their audience, and constant fears of not earning enough money to feed their families.[26]

Despite their commonly held underlying assumptions about the nature of Jewish life, Zhitlowski, Dubnow, and Ahad Ha-Am each maintained an exclusivist posture. Like Erik Erikson's young Martin Luther, each viewed the world in "totalistic" terms that made "every matter of differences a matter of mutually exclusive essences; every question mark a matter of forfeited existence; every error or oversight, eternal treason."[27] Such a position was important not only in establishing clear differentiations among competing perspectives within the Jewish community but also in defining a distinctive Jewish approach that was not imitative of the larger society. The fact that the three men's espousal of an authentic Jewish identity was often framed in absolutist terms, with little allowance for conciliation and compromise, reflected both the impassioned nature of their beliefs and their unconscious desire to fill the vacuum left by the decline in autocratic religious authority and leadership. Such attitudes extended beyond intellectual debates within the Jewish community to the community's perceptions of the larger society. Unlike western European Jews who lived with a variety of personal and collective identities and loyalties, East European intellectuals of the transitional generation generally insisted that only Jewish life had meaning and significance. Persons and activities outside the Jewish totality were simply dismissed as unimportant or irrelevant.[28]

Not surprisingly, therefore, Zhitlowski, Dubnow, and Ahad Ha-Am often bitterly attacked rivals in the Zionist and Jewish socialist movements who emerged to challenge their arguments and authority. In particular, they denounced Zionist leaders like Theodor Herzl and Max Nordau as utopian dreamers and self-aggrandizing megalomaniacs with little rootedness in the authentic values of Judaism. Like the "false" prophets and tyrannical biblical kings who arose in the past to save the Jewish people, such self-appointed leaders were demagogues who manipulated and in turn were manipulated by ephemeral events, individuals swayed by the masses but ultimately insensitive to their true needs. In place of what they regarded as these modern variants of religious messianism and selfish egotism, Zhitlowski, Dubnow, and Ahad Ha-Am emphasized the collective fate of the Jewish people and its ultimate redemption through a dispassionate contemplation of traditional spiritual values.[29] While retaining a deep attachment to the concept of Zion, they could not accept the uprooting of the East European community as a solution to the "Jewish problem." In voicing such skepticism, the three individuals also stood in opposition to the zeitgeist of imperialism — especially its emphasis on open spaces and the virtue of colonization — that clearly influenced Zionists, territorialists, and immigrants to America. Suspicious of ideologies and movements that denied the rootedness of East European Jewish settlement, Zhitlowski, Dubnow, and Ahad Ha-Am emphasized the viability or at least inevitability of the continued existence of Jewish life in the Diaspora.

An attitude of totalism also informed their attitudes toward Jewish modernization in the West. As "unemancipated" Jews whose perspective on the larger society was largely shaped by their own early bitter experiences in attempting to gain admittance to Russian schools, Zhitlowski, Dubnow, and Ahad Ha-Am perceived most forms of Jewish integration not as a natural process but as assimilationism, that is, a deliberate act of national suicide. Unlike western Jewry, the "Jewishness" of the three thinkers preceded rather than resulted from their renewed national identity. Unlike western Jews, they remained unconvinced that Jewish participation in non-Jewish society would end anti-Semitism. Zhitlowski, Dubnow, and Ahad Ha-Am saw British, French, and German Jews as slavish imitators of western values and ideals that denied the uniqueness of Jews and ultimately endangered Jewish physical and cultural survival. Although sharing many of the philosophical attitudes of liberal Jews in Germany, they rejected all programs of religious reform, which they claimed ignored Jewish nationality and mimicked Christian practice in a desperate attempt by individuals to gain acceptance into the larger society. Stressing collective rather than individual needs, they were less concerned with the alleged unscientific nature of Orthodoxy than with its irrelevance to the immediate issue of Jewish national survival.[30]

Nor were Zhitlowski, Dubnow, and Ahad Ha-Am impressed with the emergence of Jewish nationalist sentiment among western Jews at the end of the nineteenth century. Such transformations in Jewish loyalty and commitment, they argued, only occurred after the failure of British, German, and French Jews to gain acceptance as free and equal citizens of their countries. As such, they were seen as self-serving rather than sincere reevaluations of the position of Jewry in modern society. In order to have significance for future generations, the three thinkers maintained, the modernization of Jewish life had to be understood as an internal necessity for the people as a whole, not a personal accommodation to the external society. Such an understanding existed only among Jews of Russia and Poland. For the transitional generation, both the problem of and solution to Jewish life in the modern era were quintessentially East European in nature.

Unlike western Jewish nationalists, Zhitlowski, Dubnow, and Ahad Ha-Am envisioned a future society that would not simply appropriate western values such as individualism, competition, and pluralism. Indeed, in their zeal to disassociate themselves from what they regarded as the French and German Jew's wholesale acceptance of western culture, transitional thinkers at times seemed to adopt the views of their Orthodox opponents; hence their emphasis upon the importance of collective memory and tradition and the role of deeply rooted ideals in maintaining collective identity. Ultimately, however, their attack upon western Jewish ideals did not rest upon a preemancipationist defense of Jewish tradition. Indeed, in their hostility toward what they regarded as the western Jew's naive assimilationism, blind cosmopolitanism, and disdain for the past, Zhitlowski, Dubnow, and Ahad Ha-Am can be said to have foreshadowed the post-emancipation perspective of later Russian Jewish political movements such as Bundism and Zionism — an aggressive posture that sought not so much to embrace modernizing ideas and institutions as to adapt them to the needs of the collectivity.

The extreme suspicion with which Zhitlowski, Dubnow, and Ahad Ha-Am viewed developments in the Jewish communities of the West owed much to the significant differences in the social context of the assimilation of western and East European Jewry in the nineteenth century. In countries like England, France, and Germany, the development of new forms of Jewish identification arose in a situation of competing religions, the loss of Jewish communal authority, and increased material well-being. More often than not, what emerged was a sense of "Jewishness," a vague sentiment of personal attachment to religious ritual and family traditions that reflected the day-to-day interaction with the larger society. In this sense, assimilation was often an unconscious accompaniment to social and economic integration.

In eastern Europe, on the other hand, the modernizing tendencies that had facilitated cultural and social assimilation in the West were delayed. When they finally began to appear at the end of the nineteenth century, they often brought economic dislocation and political persecution. For much of the century, assimilation, if it was possible at all, represented a direct threat to traditional Jewish leadership and necessitated a deliberate and often desperate attempt to find a home in a generally hostile larger society. As a result, the individual who attempted to integrate into Russian society invariably chose to remove himself from the established Jewish community. No wonder that the vision of a massive exodus from the community, whether through assimilation or emigration, disturbed individuals like Zhitlowski, Dubnow, and Ahad Ha-Am.

The result was that in contrast to western Europe, the assertion of a modern Jewish identity in Russia was necessarily defensive and deliberate, involving as it did the multiple challenges of justifying change to a traditionalist population, countering assimilationist models of western Jewry that were deemed to be destructive of the Jewish future, and fending off anti-Semitic assaults from the larger society and governmental authority. Most important, given the geographical and economic concentration of Russian Jewry as well as the limited opportunities for individual integration, the creation of a new Jewish identity generally rested on collectivist rather than individual concerns. The breakdown of Judaism in Russia in this context necessarily meant more than a simple loss of faith. Its collapse signaled the disintegration of a whole complex of behavioral and attitudinal norms that had been reinforced over the centuries by communal pressure and example. For all these reasons, the assertion of a modern Jewish identity in eastern Europe was invariably linked to the question of national existence.

As noted earlier, the programs of the transitional generation reflected both a radical break from the cautious modernizing efforts of their parents' generation and a conscious rejection of the activist attitudes and behavior of their sons and daughters. The intellectual debt of Zhitlowski, Dubnow, and Ahad Ha-Am to the Haskalah was clear. It was the maskilim, after all, who first proposed the ideal of

Jewish self-regeneration based upon a reshaping of traditional values and beliefs. Yet despite their profound respect for learning, transitional thinkers disdained the pained and stilted apologetic arguments of early reformers that had been directed as much to non-Jewish authority as to Jews. Though indebted to the West for many of their perspectives, Zhitlowski, Dubnow, and Ahad Ha-Am did not suffer from what they believed was the Haskalah's inferiority complex toward the societies that had provided them with many of their ideas and programs. Rather than "improving" Jewry to make them worthy of admission to the modern world, as the maskilim insisted, transitional thinkers sought instead to recover the basic truths of Jewish life so that a self-confident Jewish people would once again take its rightful place in the community of nations.[31]

Gone too were the tirades against the Jewish religious establishment that had characterized Haskalah writing and debate. Despite their hostility toward the rabbinate, Zhitlowski, Dubnow, and Ahad Ha-Am were not unaware of the continued power that rabbis held even in the most assimilated Jewish communities. Both Dubnow and Ahad Ha-Am took an active part, for example, in the debate over the appointment of a supporter of the Haskalah, Chaim Tchernowitz, to a rabbinical post in Odessa.[32] By the time Zhitlowski, Dubnow, and Ahad Ha-Am had reached their maturity, however, the struggle between religionists and secularists for control of the Jewish community had long since lost its bitter quality. Traditional leadership with its emphasis on *shtadlanut* (intercession with government officials on the part of religious or economic leaders of the community) seemed to be crumbling under its own weight. Either rabbinical authority would recognize the need for new sources for Jewish survival, Zhitlowski, Dubnow, and Ahad Ha-Am reasoned, or it would simply disappear or become irrelevant. At the same time, Orthodox Jewish leaders saw the three thinkers as a far greater threat than either revolutionary socialists or assimilationists. While the latter two groups were merely following in the footsteps of countless others in the past who had sought to deny Judaism, "secular prophets" like Zhitlowski, Dubnow, and Ahad Ha-Am were attempting something radically new: the remolding of tradition to create a new Jewish consciousness.

While denouncing modernizing tendencies in the West, members of the transitional generation were also angered by the radically modern writings and philosophies of end-of-century Jewish intellectuals within eastern Europe. For Zhitlowski, Dubnow, and Ahad Ha-Am, writers such as Micha Yosef Berdichevsky and Yosef Haim Brenner seemed totally divorced from Jewish tradition, living in an eternal present and oblivious to the thread of continuity that bound contemporary Jewry to both the past and the future. Generally products of gymnasiums and universities rather than traditional Jewish schools, the latter espoused a radically new form of national identity— grounded in biological reality, tied to the objective realities of state and land, and ultimately defined by the daily struggle for existence. The quest of the *tse'irim* or *yingern* ("young ones"), as they were called in Hebrew and Yiddish respectively, was for "normalization." In contrast to their parents' generation, they saw the past uniqueness of the Jewish people as the source of its isolation and retardation.

For all their emphasis on assertion of self and their fiery defense of extreme individualism, however, the writings of rebellious young Russian Jewish intellectuals seemed to Zhitlowski, Dubnow, and Ahad Ha-Am to be little more than pale imitations of western Jewish attitudes. When examined closely, they revealed an uncritical appropriation of contemporaneous European culture and a total rejection of the specific needs and distinctive characteristics of the Jewish nation. In addition, the trumpeting by the *tse'irim* of the virtues of courage and their romantic attachment to physical labor as reflected in the push for the establishment of settlements in Palestine struck Zhitlowski, Dubnow, and Ahad Ha-Am as precipitous and foolhardy adventurism that ignored the central cultural and emotional concerns of a people whose existence was threatened by forces they could not control. Though arguing for the Jewish community's need to incorporate many of the progressive ideals and attitudes that had emerged in nineteenth-century Europe, the transitional thinkers were convinced that Jewish history clearly demonstrated that Jewry could not confront the outside world without first developing a strong and self-confident national consciousness.[33]

In contrast to the *tse'irim*, Zhitlowski, Dubnow, and Ahad Ha-Am proudly traced the intellectual origins of their own ideas and programs to the influence of past Jewish thinkers. In particular, the transitional generation was profoundly influenced by the writings of eighteenth- and early nineteenth-century western Jewish thinkers like Moses Mendelssohn, David Luzzato, and Nachman Krochmal. The struggle of Jewish intellectuals on the threshold of a new era to synthesize the old with the new, their recognition of the power of religious values and symbols in Jewish consciousness, their fascination with the power of reason and rational analysis, the centrality of history in their under- standing of Jewish survival—all found their reflection in the writings of Zhitlowski, Dubnow, and Ahad Ha-Am. All three also shared the early modern Jewish intellectual's sense of personal embattlement in the face of the massive problems facing Jewry. Like these thinkers, members of the transitional generation had to grapple with the chal- lenge of Jewish survival on the eve of modernization.

In many cases, Jewish thinkers in the West also served to intro- duce the distinct generation of Russian Jewish intellectuals to major currents in western philosophical thought. Of special significance were romanticism, which stressed the relationship between language, culture, and collective identity; and liberalism, which emphasized the struggle against oppression and foreign domination. Most im- portant, the nation-building experiences of western Europe provided Zhitlowski, Dubnow, and Ahad Ha-Am with examples of a tolerant nationalism informed by modern ideals and opposed to the domina- tion and persecution of minorities. In a more general sense, Jewish intellectuals in Russia were spurred to action by the vision of western societies in the throes of rapid change and by the fear of being left behind in the general drive toward modernization.[34]

Equally important in shaping the modernizing consciousness of Russian Jewish intellectuals was the overwhelming influence of west- ern science and pseudoscience. Like many Russian intellectuals, Zhitlowski, Dubnow, and Ahad Ha-Am found in science the "genu- ine" and unambiguous truths that they felt they needed to tackle the massive problems confronting society.[35] Science also served as an important counterpoint to Jewish religious tradition, providing ex- planations for cosmic events and offering an "objective" method of analysis. In particular, Jewish intellectuals shared their Russian coun- terparts' fascination with organic and evolutionary theories that were popular among nineteenth-century western biologists and social think- ers. The mingling of constancy and change implied in such theories had a special appeal for the transitional thinkers, who sought to create a national identity that maintained traditional values of Jewish life while responding to the challenges of contemporary life.

One also sees in their writings and theories the impact of post-1848 scientific theories of human behavior and development such as Social Darwinism, Marxism, and Comteism, which stressed the role of conflict as a motor force for change and attempted to combine rigorous analysis with programs for social, economic, and moral improvement. Like the dominant European social thinkers of the nineteenth century, all three individuals were convinced that there was a need to combine theory and praxis. Political action must be preceded by full consciousness and awareness; to act precipitously was to risk disappointment and failure. Yet Zhitlowski, Dubnow, and Ahad Ha-Am were hardly clearheaded social and economic reformers, much less violent revolutionaries. Preeminently intellectuals, they were more interested in the theory than in the practice of social science.

Struggling to describe the condition of Jewry in "scientific" and "objective" terms, Zhitlowski, Dubnow, and Ahad Ha-Am discovered the writings of nineteenth-century French historians and social psychologists. The distinctive melding of innovative social science with traditional emphases upon morality and human happiness that characterized the French perspective seemed especially relevant to the challenge of examining the Jewish plight in Russia and providing a viable solution. In particular, scholars like Ernest Renan and Gabriel Tarde provided the transitional generation with a way of defining the nation as both an objective entity and a reflection of the subjective consciousness of its individual members. Zhitlowski, Dubnow, and Ahad Ha-Am also employed French-inspired psychological theories concerning pathological nervousness, the nature of the human psyche, and anomie to explain the inability of the Jewish assimilationist to adapt to both Jewish and general society.

In their effort to challenge traditional Judaism, Zhitlowski, Dubnow, and Ahad Ha-Am embraced many of the prevailing scientific attitudes in nineteenth-century Europe toward religion and toward Judaism in particular. Thus, for example, they tended to accept the arguments of the German proponents of biblical "higher criticism" such as Julius Wellhausen, who associated the origins of monotheism with the later Prophets. Yet they could hardly accept Wellhausen's view of rabbinic

Judaism as a perversion of the true faith. Far from seeking to eradicate the influence of Jewish tradition, the three thinkers sought instead to reformulate its ideals in a nontheistic form, while at the same time reducing religious belief and practice to one of many expressions of Jewish identity with no vested or coercive power. Their secularized vision of a future Jewish community rested on a commitment to a limited pluralism where religious and nonreligious Jews would respect their differences while sharing a common culture and loyalty to the Jewish people. As "secular prophets" at work in an environment that traditionally made no distinction between the sacred and the profane, Zhitlowski, Dubnow, and Ahad Ha-Am thus sought to rescue traditional Jewish ideals and rituals from the "stranglehold" of religious authority and to reaffirm them as a freely chosen system of values and symbols that had direct relevance to the daily struggle of all Jews for collective survival and self-definition. In this sense, they mirrored the goals of all secularizers of tradition who, as the sociologist Bernard Meland has cogently argued, seek "to lift what has been deemed sacred out of its hallowed setting and [to] thrust [it] into the vital operations of the living present . . . [to disinter] a sacred symbol or image, thereby releasing its potential power into society as a social energy of immediate magnitude."[36]

In general, western philosophers and writers served as models of individual assertiveness for a group of thinkers only beginning to emerge from the tightly knit milieu of the traditional Jewish family and community. The fact that Zhitlowski, Dubnow, and Ahad Ha-Am absorbed western and central European ideas during their impressionable adolescent years only heightened the impact of such ideas on the developing consciousness of the three men. Unlike maskilim of the mid-nineteenth century and youthful fin de siècle Jewish rebels in Russia, however, the transitional generation reflected a more cautious response in which perspectives such as Utopian socialism and linguistic nationalism were filtered through the distinctive optic of the Russian Jewish experience.

In the end, however, it was the East European context that had the greatest impact on Zhitlowski, Dubnow, and Ahad Ha-Am. For all their disdain for Russian culture and their suspicion of Russian radical intellectuals, thinkers of the transitional generation shared the latter's distrust of politics as corrupt and bureaucratic and their veneration of the literary figure as social critic and philosopher. Like many young middle-class Russians who sought to find an appropriate arena that would enable them to engage in both contemplation and activism, transitional thinkers in the Jewish community pursued careers in journalism and teaching. Thus Zhitlowski, Dubnow, and Ahad Ha-Am were all extensively involved in publishing while Dubnow held a number of appointments as an instructor of Jewish history. All three were also frequent contributors to the Jewish journals and newspapers that emerged in Russia in the 1880s and 1890s.

Like their Russian counterparts, Zhitlowski, Dubnow, and Ahad Ha-Am were highly suspicious of communal authority, which they saw as obstructing social, economic, and cultural change. Drawing upon the writings of Russian social thinkers and activists, they viewed their own community as a caste rather than a class society, rooted in legal tradition and ultimately defined by a dominant set of cultural values rather than by socioeconomic or political criteria. In creating their vision of the future society, Zhitlowski, Dubnow, and Ahad Ha-Am understandably rejected the Russian social reformers' call for the assimilation of ethnic minorities into the larger society. At the same time, however, they unconsciously incorporated the Slavophiles' view of the idyllic Russian society of the future with its emphasis upon what one historian has called "the autonomous development of social, economic, and moral life" and "the emergence of organs of 'self-administration.'"[37]

In defining their own role and the role of their supporters in the program of Jewish renewal, Zhitlowski, Dubnow, and Ahad Ha-Am appropriated the Russian social activists' emphasis upon the defining role of the "intelligentsia." Preaching in environments with little opportunity for popularly inspired political activity, both Jewish and Russian modernizers stressed the role of a select group of educated, committed, and independent thinkers who would spur the apathetic masses to demand change. It was to be the role of these intellectuals, who stood above and apart from the existing society, to envision the future society and to provide the moral courage necessary to achieve it.[38]

Though they were averse to admitting it, transitional thinkers were also strongly influenced by nation-building efforts within Russian society. Despite important differences in objective conditions, the

Jews' struggle to formulate a new national self at the end of the nineteenth century mirrored the emerging national consciousness of other minorities in the Russian Empire. Like Poles, Ukrainians, and Rumanians, Jews would have to rediscover and redefine their identity without the objective support of territory and sovereignty and in the face of constant pressure from the larger society to assimilate or at least to deny their distinctiveness. Like other ethnic groups faced with present calamities and reversals, Jewish nationalists would also have to draw upon the past to justify the survival of the nation. Like other East European nationalists including pan-Slavs, Jewish intellectuals would have to construct a coherent and meaningful historical and mythological framework that would explain collective survival and growth.[39] At the same time, they would have to recognize the crucial historical role of religion in establishing communal distinctiveness and ensuring collective pride.

In creating their vision of a modern Jewish identity, Zhitlowski, Dubnow, and Ahad Ha-Am also looked to developments in neighboring European societies. Of special significance were the attempts by national minorities in the Austro-Hungarian Empire to uncover the distinctive origins and character that justified their continued existence as separate communities and defined their unique roles in human development. As formative Jewish nationalists, Zhitlowski, Dubnow, and Ahad Ha-Am were also profoundly impressed by the various theories supporting the concept of a multinational state that developed in the Austro-Hungarian Empire in the late nineteenth century. Particularly influential were the writings of two prominent Austrian socialists, Otto Bauer and Karl Renner, who sought to synthesize their commitment to social equality with a defense of the rights of national minorities. Their vision of a future social democratic state with full cultural and political autonomy for ethnic minorities had special significance for Diasporists, as defenders of Jewish life in the Diaspora such as Zhitlowski and Dubnow were known.[40]

For all their insistence on the need to "secularize" and to "modernize" Jewry, Zhitlowski, Dubnow, and Ahad Ha-Am rarely defined what they meant by these terms. At times, they seemed to have associated secularization with the influence of general European thought upon Jewish consciousness throughout Jewish history. At other times, they contrasted modernity with the power of religious authority and belief. More often than not, they saw the modernization of Jewry in terms of the incorporation of ideals of pragmatism, reasonableness, and aesthetics into Jewish consciousness and behavior.[41]

The failure of Zhitlowski, Dubnow, and Ahad Ha-Am to define their concepts of modernity and secularization was not mere oversight on their part. In reality, all three individuals remained deeply ambivalent toward many aspects of modernization as it developed in the West. In particular, the extreme individualism that underlay much of nineteenth-century western European thought found little appeal among Russian Jewish thinkers seeking to develop strategies for collective survival. For all its vaunted technology and progress, the western model of modernization seemed primarily concerned with the struggle for material well-being. Its hallmarks were seen as selfishness and greed, characteristics that Zhitlowski, Dubnow, and Ahad Ha-Am were convinced explained the western Jew's desperate desire to assimilate.

One gains a clearer insight into their ambivalence by measuring their commitment to progress and change in terms of the sociologist Talcott Parsons' commonly accepted definition of modernization. For Parsons, the transformation is marked by the movement from affectivity to affective neutrality, from particularism to universalism, from ascription to achievement, and from diffuseness to specificity.[42] On the one hand, Zhitlowski, Dubnow, and Ahad Ha-Am professed a belief in rationalism, universalism, and individualism. Yet as deeply passionate nationalists seeking to realize the collective unity of the Jewish people as a precondition for its survival and growth, they stressed the centrality of traditional values of faith, ethnicity, and community. Their goal was not to break the fetters of the past in the name of individual self-actualization but rather to rekindle the innate creative spark that they believed lay deep within all members of the Jewish people.

It is for this reason that, despite their openness to the outside world, Zhitlowski, Dubnow, and Ahad Ha-Am consciously restricted their contacts with the larger society to intellectual and business matters. (It is interesting to note in this context, for example, that Ahad Ha-Am claimed not to know the civil date of his own birthday until he was sixty years old.[43]) As we examine the lives and ideas of the three individuals, we will see many examples of their disdain for and at times even ignorance of the non-Jewish world around them. Such incidents should serve to remind us that the transitional generation lived in an era when even "enlightened" individuals believed that it was possible to function almost totally within the perimeters of the Jewish community.

Struggling to synthesize the Jewish past and the Jewish future, Zhitlowski, Dubnow, and Ahad Ha-Am were often frightened and intimidated by the myriad of programs and proposals for modernization that emerged in Europe at the turn of the century. In time, the transitional thinkers grew to believe that the growing influence of such divergent views on Jewish modernizers and the emergence of new centers of Jewish life were unraveling the intricate weave that had bound Jewry together over the centuries. Faced with competing perspectives in both the larger and Jewish societies, members of the transitional generation increasingly felt themselves adrift. Ahad Ha-Am summarized the ambivalence of his generation when he wrote after returning from a trip to Palestine: "Just as we cannot fully be westerners in the West so we cannot fully be easterners in the East."[44]

In many ways, then, early Jewish nationalists like Zhitlowski, Dubnow, and Ahad Ha-Am can be seen as figures frozen in a historical moment and a geographical environment that did not long survive the onslaught of disruptive and destructive forces both within and outside Jewish society in the twentieth century. But, as I will try to demonstrate in my Conclusion, there is much in their view that commands renewed attention by contemporary Jewry. Zhitlowski, Dubnow, and Ahad Ha-Am were obsessed with three central issues that still define the agenda of the contemporary Jewish community: the lessons of history for Jewish survival; the development of a modern Jewish identity and communal leadership; and the choice of an appropriate language and/or cultural forms to transmit Jewish ideals for future generations. Remarkably, the crisis that produced the transitional generation a century ago has been dramatically replicated in the modern Jewish communities of the Diaspora and Israel. As Jewish leaders grapple with the challenge of assimilation in an environment in which they can no longer easily rely on traditional loyalties such as religion, the Holocaust, and the development of a Jewish state to maintain communal solidarity, the call of an almost forgotten generation of Jewish nationalists for a synthesis of old and new Judaism has unexpectedly gained new relevance.

In summary, a study of the attitudes and behavior of the transitional generation can serve as a useful starting point to examine three larger issues. Open to both new Jewish and general philosophical and cultural trends, the writings of Zhitlowski, Dubnow, and Ahad Ha-Am reflect the variety of influences interacting in the Russian Jewish community at a crucial period in its development. To the extent that they straddle tradition and modernity, members of the transitional generation also provide important insights into the complex process of modernization and distinctive mode of collective identity formation for a small and rooted minority population in eastern Europe. Finally, despite the time-bound nature of many of their ideas and activities, the intellectual and practical concerns of the transitional generation shed light on the challenge facing the Jewish communities of the United States and Israel as they attempt to define a consistent and satisfying Jewish identity beyond its traditional religious base.

CHAPTER 1

The Secularization of Russian Jewry in the Nineteenth Century

THE POSITING OF so-called secular Jewish ideologies in Russia at the end of the nineteenth century took place against a backdrop of social, economic, and political developments that had been evolving over decades. Challenged by pressures from the larger Russian society and dramatic changes within the Jewish community itself, the most articulate elements in the population gradually began to reassess traditional Jewish values and behavioral patterns. By providing clear justifications and explanations for the transformations that the community was undergoing as well as a direction for its future survival and growth, intellectuals like Haim Zhitlowski, Simon Dubnow, and Ahad Ha-Am found a small but eager audience for their message of Jewish national renewal.

Scholars of the history of East European Jewry traditionally have emphasized the impact of anti-Semitic persecution and the role of intellectual developments in the modernization and secularization of the Jewish community. Combining elements of *Leidensgeschichte* ("lachrymose" history) and *Geistesgeschichte* (spiritual history), the standard works of Jewish historiography maintained that the advent of the Haskalah, or Jewish Enlightenment, in midcentury and activist Jewish political movements in the 1890s were responses to the inability of traditional leadership and institutions to react effectively first to political pressures and later to physical attacks upon Jewry from Russian society.[1] More recently, a number of historians have begun to introduce structuralist analyses of Jewish society that place the process of Jewish modernization in a broader context. In minimizing both the distinctiveness of the crisis of Jewish traditionalism and the impact of conscious intellectual and political activity, they have stressed the role of long-term demographic and socioeconomic factors in European society during the eighteenth and nineteenth centuries in reshaping Jewish concerns and behavior.[2] This book attempts to strike a balance between the two approaches by incorporating the study of the shaping of a modern secular Jewish identity in late-nineteenth-century Russia within the context of both Jewish and general developments in the Russian Empire.

Before proceeding any further, however, a few words of explanation about the concepts of secularization and secularism and their relevance to modern Jewish history are in order. The terms themselves have had a checkered career since their introduction into popular and scholarly discourse in the mid-nineteenth century by George Jacob Holyoake, a self-proclaimed "agitator" whose career spanned numerous British movements of social and political reform including Owenism, Chartism, and "free thought." For Holyoake and his protégé Charles Bradlaugh, secularism was synonymous with enlightenment and stood unalterably opposed to all forms of religious belief and practice. In their view, secularization, which they defined as the slow but inexorable spread of unbelief throughout Europe, would provide the necessary preconditions for radical social and economic change.

The glib association of the ideology of secularism and the process of secularization with the destruction or at least disappearance of religious ideals and institutions would be taken up by polemicists of various causes in the nineteenth and early twentieth centuries. For vulgar Marxists and proponents of Scientism among others, secularism became a battle cry against religious obscurantism, which was said to buttress the forces of mystification and oppression and to hinder the appropriate consciousness necessary for effective individual and collective action. As we shall see, such attitudes could even be heard within the East European Jewish community among Bundists and radical Nietzscheans by the end of the nineteenth century.

In recent decades, sociologists and historians such as Owen Chadwick, David Martin, and Susan Budd have succeeded in break-

ing down the simplistic association of secularism with atheism and social progress and thus have helped to broaden the scope and sophisti-
cation of the study.[3] Far from monolithic concepts, the ideology of
secularism and the process of secularization differ from society to society and are ultimately dependent upon the nature of the particular
society's religion and religious institutions. To cite one obvious example, the growing emphasis upon individual faith or responsibility at
the expense of institutionalized religion might be seen as a movement
toward religiosity in a Protestant environment and an antireligious tendency in a Catholic community. Similarly, we have grown to understand that religious belief and practice are not inextricably linked.
Religion cannot be reduced to a simple system of explanation, and
thus religious commitment and practice will not necessarily be reduced
as human beings allegedly become more rational, as many early secularists believed. In turn, we have learned that there are significant
differences between anticlerical and antireligious attitudes. As studies
of nineteenth-century European secular movements have revealed,
for example, much of the rhetoric of so-called freethinkers was highly
moralistic and centered on the failure of established religious leaders
to remain true to the ideals of Christianity and particularly to its commitment to justice and social betterment.

In stressing the multidimensional and often ambiguous nature
of secularism and secularization, such studies have served to correct
the simplistic analyses of the impact of modernization on religious
thought and behavior. By far their most important contribution has
been their emphasis upon viewing the decline in traditional belief
and practice as part of the general process of modernization characterized by the erosion of traditional authority, the development
of social and economic differentiation, and the disappearance of a
commonly held weltanschauung. As a result, the efforts to create a
secular consciousness in the nineteenth century must be understood
as leading not to the rejection of religion but to its relegation as one
of many concerns of daily life or, in some cases, as a desire to reaffirm
religious values and ideas in a nontheological form.

While modern European historiography is awash in provocative
analyses of secularism, Jewish historians seem strangely oblivious to its
relevance to their research. The few references to the phenomenon in
general Jewish historiographical literature are of little value in helping
us understand their role in the modernization of Jewry. Respected

scholars such as Salo Baron, Arthur Hertzberg, Raphael Mahler, Jacob Katz, and Milton Himmelfarb, to cite just a few, use the terms interchangeably with modernization, unbelief, integration, and assimilation, with little clarification or analysis. Those works that have examined specific aspects of Jewish secular thought and activity have been either too narrow in their focus or unnecessarily polemical in their approach. In the case of the former, they have failed to tie the various ideologies and movements to general patterns in modern Jewish and general European history; in the case of the latter, they have viewed secular ideology as a consciousness-raising tool for contemporary Jewish youth alienated from their ethnic roots.[4] Nor have the studies of modern Jewish intellectuals, who are generally viewed as the harbingers of secular ideas, shed much light on the issue. Isaac Deutscher's "non-Jewish Jew," John Murray Cuddihy's "uncivil Jew," Hannah Arendt's "Jew as pariah" — all generally describe individuals whose ties with Jewish culture and community were minimal and whose marginality often led them to become alienated from both the larger society and their fellow Jews.[5] The result, as the examples of Karl Marx, Rosa Luxemburg, and Leon Trotsky clearly demonstrate, was a bold and insightful critique of the evils of modern society in which the Jewish light was glaringly absent, even deliberately ignored.

The issue is far too complicated to be discussed in great detail in this work. Indeed, a study of the general process of secularization among East European Jewry in the nineteenth century is a major lacuna in modern Jewish historiography. This chapter attempts to briefly examine the economic, social, political, and cultural factors that facilitated the creation of secular Jewish ideologies at the end of the nineteenth century. Given the limitations of space, I have chosen to concentrate on the most significant conditions, both objective and subjective, that weakened the religious foundations of the Jewish community. Where possible, I have attempted to incorporate perspectives and approaches from general studies of secularization and secular ideology, while recognizing that conditions of Russian Jewish life differed markedly from those of western society that provide the subject matter for most of the works. It was the subtle interplay between Russian society and its Jewish minority, between the objective conditions of social, economic, and political change in Russia and their resonance in the Jewish community and the intense pressure from both Jews and non-Jews to "reform" Jewry, that explains both the phenomenon of the secularization of Russian Jews during the nineteenth century and the formulation of modernizing ideologies by individuals like Zhitlowski, Dubnow, and Ahad Ha-Am.

By far the most fundamental factor in the transformation of Russian Jewry was the impact of population growth and distribution. Of the nearly 8 million Jews in the world in 1880, more than half lived under tsarist rule.[6] According to the Russian census of 1897, there were over 5 million Jews living in Russia and tsarist Poland, the fourth-largest group of non-Russians after Ukrainians, Poles, and Byelorussians and a little more than 4 percent of the total population of the Russian Empire. During much of the nineteenth century, the Jewish community in Russia was subject to intense socioeconomic pressures stemming from a population explosion that affected world Jewry as a whole. In the nineteenth century, Russian Jewry more than quadrupled in size with over half of its growth occurring after 1850. Anti-Semites were often quick to ascribe the fecundity of Jews to early marriage; statistical analysis, however, suggests that the growth in population was largely a result of a declining mortality rate.[7] Though the significant emigration of Jews westward at the end of the century lessened the socioeconomic pressures on the community caused in part by overpopulation, it could not stem the natural increase of Russian Jewry, which averaged approximately 100,000 to 110,000 annually. By 1914, despite the exodus of 1.4 million people, the Jewish population of Russia stood at 5.7 million.[8]

Much as in underdeveloped countries today, limited economic opportunities for those who refused to emigrate transformed the traditional ideal of the large family into a communal curse. Reports from both contemporaneous Jewish and Russian observers portray scenes of massive malnutrition and poverty in the Russian Jewish community. It was not uncommon for several families to inhabit one ramshackle shack, huddling together to keep warm.[9] According to one source, at the end of the century 23.9 percent of all Russian Jews and between 25 percent and 39.7 percent of those residing in cities lived in poverty.[10] Inadequate food, clothing, and shelter resulted in an increase in family violence and divorce, and exacerbated tensions in the community in general. Malnutrition and overcrowding also led to the spread of disease. The result was that in many areas, Jews had a higher mortality rate than their Russian neighbors.

Already in the 1860s, there was a significant movement of Jews within Russia as thousands of desperate families fled the overpopulated and economically depressed north in search of greater economic opportunities in the developing southern zone. Thus while in 1847 only 2.5 percent of Russian Jews lived in the southern provinces, by 1897 the proportion had increased to 13.8 percent.[11] Lack of food and employment opportunities also contributed to Jewish emigration from Russia that began in the 1820s and reached a peak in the 1870s. In the decade before the outbreak of pogroms, between 15,000 and 20,000 Russian Jews arrived in the United States, largely from the overcrowded areas of Lithuania and the northwest.[12]

The effect of internal population growth was further exacerbated by geographic concentration. Before the partitions of Poland in 1772, 1775, and 1796, there were barely 1,000 Jews in all of the Russian Empire. As a result of the annexation of Polish territory, Russia inherited some 400,000 Jews. In a desperate effort to both prevent unrestricted Jewish settlement and provide fresh blood for new and relatively undeveloped southern territories of New Russia which had been captured from the Ottoman Empire in 1783, Catherine the Great created the so-called Pale of Settlement in 1794. The Pale itself, whose exact dimensions were not firmly established until 1835, stretched from Lithuania in the north to the Black Sea in the south and from Poland and Bessarabia in the west to White Russia and the Ukraine in the east (see map). It included fifteen districts in the Ukraine (including New Russia), White Russia, Lithuania, and ten districts of partitioned Poland.[13] By the end of the nineteenth century some 94 percent of Russian Jewry lived within its borders, a population that constituted 20 percent of European Russia.[14] An ever-present reality for Russian Jews in the nineteenth century, the Pale of Settlement would not be abolished until the Bolshevik overthrow of tsarism in February 1917.

Regional differences among Jewish settlements in Russia were marked, especially between older and more traditional areas of the north (where Jews constituted some 12 percent of the total population) and the more recent urban settlements of the so-called New Russia in the south (where Jews represented approximately 9.5 percent). Government officials generally maintained lax control over the population in the southern provinces in the hope of fostering innovative economic activity. The result was that Jews in the Ukraine and New Russia were more likely to accept integration into the larger

The Jewish Pale of Settlement in Russia, 1835–1917

SWEDEN

Baltic Sea

St. Petersburg

KOVNO

VITEBSK

Moscow

Vilna
VILNA

Vitebsk

GERMANY

MOGILEV

Bialystok
GRODNO

Minsk
MINSK

Warsaw

R U S S I A

Lodz
POLAND

Pinsk

Lublin

VOLHYNIA

CHERNIGOV

Berdichev

Kiev
KIEV

POLTAVA

AUSTRIA-
HUNGARY

PODOLIA

EKATERNOSLAV

BESSARABIA

Kishinev

KHERSON

Odessa

TAURIDA

RUMANIA

Black Sea

BULGARIA

—•—•—•— Pale of Settlement. The boundaries of the Pale of
Settlement were intermittently altered.

Adapted from a map drawn by F. Inoue. Source: From *The Jew in the Modern World, 2/e* by Paul R.
Mendes-Flohr and Jehuda Reinharz. Copyright ©1995 by Oxford University Press, Inc. Reproduced
by permission.

society than their coreligionists in the north, who were subject to clumsy government-inspired pressures to assimilate. Not surprisingly, the strongest proponents of both Russification and communal reform and modernization often came from southern cities such as Kiev, Ekaterinoslav, and Odessa. Contrasting policies in different regions thus served to exacerbate communal tensions and to prevent Russian Jewry from establishing a unified response to external and internal pressures for change.

Jews were further segregated within the Pale itself. In an attempt to ensure that the Jewish population did not exert a baneful influence over a traditional peasant population and did not provide undue economic competition for Russian merchants, tsarist officials systematically denied Jews the right to settle in rural areas. In some cases, Jews were officially expelled from specific villages. In other cases, they were prohibited from living in general areas of peasant settlement.[15] Jews were further induced to migrate to cities from the countryside by the general decline in the rural economy brought about by industrialization and urbanization. According to the 1897 census, while Jews represented more than 11 percent of the entire population of the Pale, they made up one-third of the urban residents and only about 3 percent of the agricultural population. Some 82 percent of Russian Jewry lived in 324 cities and 1,522 towns. One-third resided in communities numbering 10,000 or more. Because of restrictions, in some cities and towns Jews made up as much as 70 to 80 percent of the entire population.[16] The combination of overpopulation and geographic segregation created a situation of alienation from Russian society and internal instability that spurred demands for change within the Jewish community.

Russia's restrictive policies toward Jews reflected its general perceptions of the so-called nationalities question. From the beginnings of the empire until the collapse of tsarism, Russia's leaders demonstrated little sensitivity toward the more than one hundred non-Russian peoples within its borders. By the end of the nineteenth century, ethnic minorities accounted for 56.7 percent of the population.[17] Obsessed with defending traditional cultural values as a buttress to the maintenance of absolutist political control and fearful that concessions to non-Russians would open the door to demands by other groups in society for change, government officials were unwilling to follow the more liberal examples of other multinational empires such as Austria-Hungary. Even modernizing rulers such as Catherine II, who pressed for the reorganization of government and the limited rationalization of society, were convinced, not without justification, that the maintenance of national and ethnic diversity was a major obstacle to Russian social and economic development.

Whatever their personal feelings toward national minorities, most Russian officials realized that the number of Great Russians was in constant decline relative to other ethnic groups and that the differences in social, cultural, and economic level among the various nationalities were too vast to create a coherent and homogeneous political structure that included all residents of the empire.[18]   Like much of its activity in the nineteenth century, tsarist policy toward national minorities reflected a recognition of the need for limited modernization within the narrow perimeters of the empire's traditional social, economic, and political framework. The result was a fundamental contradiction that became increasingly evident as the century progressed. While exploiting the economic skills of the various groups, government officials sought to maintain their relative segregation and isolation from the larger Russian population. The fact that most national minority groups balked at even limited Russification efforts that promised them little in return only served to harden the attitudes of bureaucrats. Such concerns became especially acute during the last two decades of the century in the wake of an intensive effort by tsarist officials to make the Russian language compulsory in all schools. At the same time, efforts to modernize Russian society by improving communications and transportation and centralizing administration only served to reinforce group solidarity among the disparate groups that made up the empire.[19]

Jews presented a particularly troublesome problem because of their distinctive combination of national identity and religion and their lack of territorial concentration. Despite its often obsessive concern with Jews, however, the Russian government never successfully developed a workable and consistent definition of the category "Jew."[20] Officially, Jews were classified as part of the *inorodtsy*, a grouping of indigenous ethnic communities that included most of the nomadic peoples of the empire. *Inorodtsy* generally were subject to special laws promulgated in the territories that they inhabited. Unlike other nomads, however, Jews were prevented from integrating into the areas in which they lived.[21]   Instead, they were segregated through laws preventing them from moving outside the Pale, acquiring Russian citizenship, or settling outside of towns.[22] Furthermore, they could not take Christian or Russian first names or teach Russian in Hebrew schools. Unlike other *inorodtsy*, Jews were denied the opportunity for self-government based on tribal customs, could not transact business on Sundays and Christian holidays, were prohibited from acquiring real estate in rural districts, and were forced to endure long terms of military service.[23]   Even during the brief constitutional period after 1905, when other ethnic minorities benefited from a certain loosening of restrictions, Jews remained outcasts.[24]

On the most basic level, tsarist government attitudes toward Jews reflected the xenophobia of the majority Russian population that arose from daily contact with non-Russians. Yet anti-Jewish sentiment was also fueled by deep-seated religious beliefs that defined Jews as Christ killers and destroyers of fundamental Christian values. Such fears were shared by tsars and their government administrators from the very beginnings of the period of empire building and national consolidation. Thus, for example, as early as the fifteenth century, tsarist officials brutally suppressed "Judaizing" sects that accepted the Old Testament and rejected the New, viewing them as a threat to the unity of the Russian Church, an important cornerstone of the emerging national identity. In triggering fears of Jewish proselytism among the masses, the sects reinforced government and Church insistence on the need to segregate the Jewish community. So strong was anti-Jewish sentiment among both religious traditionalists and government bureaucrats that in 1741 the accession of the devoutly Orthodox tsarina Elizabeth was quickly followed by an edict expelling Jews. Even the protests of merchants, who feared an economic downturn as a result of the loss of Jewish middlemen trading with neighboring Poland, could not dissuade the government. Ironically, one of the results of the decision was that until the late eighteenth century, Russia generally was free of popular anti-Jewish canards such as the charge of ritual murder.[25]

During the nineteenth century, cultural stereotypes borrowed from western anti-Semitic movements and ideologues strengthened traditional anti-Jewish notions that existed deep within Russian society. Increasingly, slavophilic nationalists portrayed Jews not only as murderers of God but as fierce opponents of Russian values and ideals that were said to be grounded in Christian orthodoxy.[26] Anti-Semitism was an important component of the literary and philosophical struggle between the older and younger generation of Russian intellectuals.[27] At the same time, new forms of racial anti-Semitism born of rising nationalist sentiment in the latter half of the century and the general ignorance of the actual political, social, and economic conditions under which Jews lived fed exaggerated notions of Jewish economic prowess and fueled hopes among tsarist officials of exploiting the Jews' much vaunted commercial talents in the development of the modern Russian economy.

The result was that for most of the period under study, the "Jewish question" perplexed tsarist officialdom. As an alien element with few ties to traditional Russian beliefs and values, Jews were at times viewed as a distinctive threat to the larger society and at other times as useful partners in its efforts to modernize. The nature of tsarist political administration and bureaucracy only served to complicate matters further. As with all governmental decisions, Russian policy toward Jews in the nineteenth century generally reflected the views of the autocratic tsar and his advisers currently in power rather than a clearly defined goal and program that was universally understood and accepted throughout the empire. The result was that the interpretation and execution of Jewish policy varied from region to region according to the interests and perceptions of local officials. While some local bureaucrats could be bribed by local Jewish communities in return for lenient treatment, others, especially members of the vast police network, had a vested interest in maintaining close watch over the actions of "deviant" members of the population, including Jews.[28]

The origins of the tsarist treatment of the "Jewish question" in the nineteenth century are to be found in the government's response to the massive influx of Jews resulting from the annexation of western Poland in 1775. Given the relative absence of Jews in prepartition Russia, the incorporation of hundreds of thousands of strangely dressed people speaking an unfamiliar language and professing a despised religion was bound to create confusion and fear. At first, Russian officials chose to simply continue the policies of the Polish government, thereby hoping to maintain order in the annexed territories. It did not take long, however, for the government to formulate the legal precept that the Jews were a separate group for whom everything was forbidden unless specifically allowed.[29]

The reign of Alexander I (1801–1825) signaled the first attempts to develop a comprehensive policy toward the newly incorporated Jewish population. As a result of the Statute Concerning the Organization of the Jews, issued in 1804, Jews were expelled from villages and restrictions were placed upon traditional Jewish livelihoods such as the liquor trade. Yet contradictions were already evident in the statute that reflected the dilemma of a government caught between a desire to isolate Jews and a wish to exploit them economically. While legally defining the Pale, for example, the law also encouraged Jews to settle and organize agricultural settlements in the relatively underdeveloped areas of the Ukraine and the south and allowed them to attend government schools.[30] By 1815, Alexander's renewed interest in European diplomatic relations, spurred by the defeat of Napoleon and the tsar's growing religious mysticism, began to overshadow concerns with internal reform. As a result, many of the stipulations of the statute of 1804 that had never been feasible simply fell into disuse. Despite its rather short-lived existence, the statute's basic formulations — its notions of the "improvement " of the Jews, its concerns with protecting the Christian peasantry from Jewish influence, and its tendency to grant Jews certain benefits while taking away others — would eventually become the cornerstone of later government policies.

Under the conservative Nicholas I (1825–1855), persecution was intensified as the government strove to create a spiritually united nation rooted in the values of religious orthodoxy, autocracy, and nationalism. Fearing the invasion of European ideas and attitudes, Nicholas's regime prohibited Jews from settling near the western borders of Russia. In order to speed up and intensify the complete assimilation of the Jews and to root out what one official called the "worthless beliefs and primitive and harmful ideas that are infected by Talmudic teachings,"[31] in 1827 the government initiated the so-called cantonist system. By requiring that Jewish males between twelve and eighteen receive special preparatory military training before their regular twenty-five year army service, the regime sought to weaken young Jews' attachment to Judaism and to rob the community of its future leaders. To compound the tragedy, in their desperate efforts to fulfill the rigid quotas imposed by the government, Jewish community leaders often hired individuals to kidnap youths for the army. The result was public outcry and bitter division between Jewish leaders and the general population within the community. Combining a carrot with a stick, the cantonist program was accompanied by the promulgation of policies that increased opportunities for "productive" Jews to settle in southern Russia. At the same time, the government established state-sponsored Jewish schools that included general and religious instruction. As in the case of the statute of 1804, the regime naively assumed that it could eliminate Jewish separateness while at the same time exploiting Jewish skills in the Russian effort to modernize.

Nicholas's successor Alexander II (1855–1881) initially appeared to favor a more liberal policy toward Jews. Inspired by the defeat of Russia in the Crimean War to restructure society, he abolished forced conscription for all Russians in 1856. Three years later, he expanded Nicholas I's policies of granting limited rights of permanent residence outside the Pale and opportunities to participate in the civil service to "useful" Jews, a definition that included wealthy merchants, university graduates with advanced degrees, and skilled craftsmen who were seen as contributing to Russia's economic growth.[32] In addition, the government halted all efforts to induce Jews to convert through the granting of special privileges and dispensations. At the same time, it prohibited the baptizing of Jewish minors without the consent of their parents, which had been a common practice under the cantonist system.[33]

Such actions led many Jews to assume that emancipation was imminent. In actuality, Alexander remained steadfastly opposed to any fundamental change in the legal status of Jews. His general goal in instituting changes had not been to liberalize the regime but merely to make it possible for the Russian regime to survive in the face of the pressures of modernization.[34] Alexander's seemingly favorable attitudes toward his Jewish subjects thus reflected economic pragmatism more than a sincere change of heart. Like his predecessors, the tsar remained firmly convinced that the primitive nature of "Jewish morality" would prevent their full assimilation into Russian society.[35] In any event, many local and regional government officials opposed even his limited policies of liberalization. Fearing that they would lead to the granting of civil equality to Jews, they often worked actively to subvert them.

A major setback to Jewish hopes for acceptance into Russian society occurred after the suppression of the Polish uprising in 1863. Alexander had already demonstrated his growing conservative leanings in the beating, arrest, and expulsion of protesting students in the fall of 1861 and in the arrest of several prominent radicals in the wake of a series of fires of suspicious origin that swept through St. Petersburg in 1862.[36] In heightening Russian nationalist sentiment, the suppression of the movement for independence in Russian-occupied Poland led to a hardening of attitudes toward all national minorities, including the Jews.[37] Already in 1859, the government had reimposed a ban on the settlement of Jews on government lands in western regions of the Pale. Five years later, it abandoned all programs of Jewish colonization.[38] Similarly, the execution of a law of 1865 granting opportunities for Jewish artisans to settle beyond the Pale was effectively stymied by a myriad of restrictive regulations and interpretations.[39]

By the 1870s, Alexander's "liberal" policies were on the wane. Urged on by the influential journalist Mikhail Katkov, a former supporter of liberal reform who had been won over to the side of reaction, government officials cracked down on all movements for constitutional reform, attacked "radicalism" in the educational system, and reinforced the power of the Orthodox Church. In implementing its program, the regime singled out Jews for special attention. Thus in 1873, officials decided to close most government-sponsored Jewish schools and yeshivas. Continued unrest among Russian students in cities such as Kiev and Odessa in the 1870s and the creation of terrorist movements such as Narodnaya Volya (People's Will), which counted a number of Jews among its leading activists, led to serious proposals to institute a numerus clausus or quota system for Jewish students in Russian schools.[40]

Given the climate of growing hostility toward Jews, it is not surprising that the assassination of Alexander II in 1881 by elements of Narodnaya Volya was followed immediately by pogroms. In the next two years, there were more than 200 recorded anti-Jewish attacks within the Pale. Blaming the Jewish victims for the outbreak of violence, the newly crowned tsar Alexander III (1881–1894) issued the infamous May Laws of 1882 which saw a return to more restrictive policies. As a result of these so-called Temporary Rules, no Jews were allowed to remain in rural areas of the Pale or to own or manage land outside its cities. Because of the arbitrary interpretation of the May Laws, which affected even those who were gone from their villages for business or religious obligations when the law was promulgated, thousands of Jews suddenly found themselves homeless. In addition, as part of a general attack upon ethnic and religious minorities, the more privileged Jews living in the interior of Russia were now subject to periodic searches in an effort to root out individuals who were living illegally outside the Pale.

Other persecutions and restrictions against Jews soon followed. Decrees were now issued to restrict the number and activity of Jews in the civil service, military, and legal profession. A pronouncement of 1890 reversed an 1870 law that had allowed Jews to vote for and to participate in provincial and town councils (*zemstvos*) but retained the stipulation that Jews should be taxed to pay for their administration. In 1888, the Pahlen Commission, a government-appointed body that had been formed soon after the pogroms to investigate the legal status of Jews in Russia, had recommended the initiation of emancipatory legislation for Jews. Tsar Alexander chose to ignore its findings, however, and instead publicly reaffirmed the continuation of discriminatory policies. In one of the more brutal governmental actions of the period, in March 1891 on the first day of Passover, the 30,000 Jews of Moscow were expelled from their homes. Three years later, a decree prohibited Jews from selling liquor, which was viewed as a major factor in the "corruption" of Russian peasantry. Thousands of people were suddenly thrown out of work. Though some of Alexander's harsher regulations were eventually reversed by the courts, the basic laws were to remain in effect until the triumph of the Bolshevik Revolution in 1917.[41]

The advent of a new century brought little change in tsarist policy. In 1903 the minister of the interior, Vyacheslav von Plehve, had unsuccessfully attempted to bribe community leaders into suppressing radical Jewish activity in return for the promise of an improvement in the condition of Russian Jews. Plehve was personally obsessed with Jewry, regarding them as second only to the agrarian crisis as the most serious problem plaguing the country.[42] Not surprisingly, therefore, his assassination in July 1904 led to renewed hope among

Jews for the end of anti-Semitism and the advent of their much awaited emancipation. Such hopes were buoyed by the accession of the relatively liberal count Sergei Witte to power in the wake of Russia's disastrous war with Japan.

Witte's programs were quickly overshadowed by the outbreak of the Revolution of 1905, however. The months following the January demonstrations by crowds of urban merchants, artisans, and workers appeared to bring the first indications of a more tolerant administration and acted as a catalyst for the growth of political activism and national self-consciousness among Russian Jewry as well as other national minorities in the empire. Jewish leaders were especially pleased by an edict issued in April that granted toleration to all religious communities in Russia. In October, the government published a manifesto that called for a constitution that would include the right of Jews to vote for a reconstituted Duma (Parliament). Though the manifesto made no mention of abolishing the Pale or granting full citizenship to Jews, its publication triggered an intensive drive within the Jewish community for equal rights. The campaign was spearheaded by the so-called Union for the Achievement of Full Rights for Jews in Russia, which was dominated by wealthy and more assimilated Jews. More militant elements within the community like the Bundists, or Jewish Socialists, were skeptical, however, and chose instead to organize self-defense groups to fend off anti-Jewish attacks that broke out during the period.[43] In early 1906, twelve Jewish deputies who were all affiliated with the union took their seats in the newly reestablished Duma. Despite serious ideological differences within the group, the Jewish deputies were united in their support of the principle of Jewish equality within the larger context of Russian social, economic, and political development.[44]

Such efforts would prove stillborn, however, since the Duma continued to function in a largely autocratic political system committed to maintaining the status quo. In any case, neither tsarist officials nor members of the Russian Parliament were willing or eager to deal with the "Jewish problem." An ominous reflection of the Duma's attitude could be found in the preamble to its fundamental laws, which reaffirmed the principle of Russia "one and indivisible," code words for the rejection of national minority rights. In the debates on the "Jewish question," government officials and conservative members of the Duma urged restraint in granting Jews equality and warned of an anti-Semitic backlash if the issue was raised too soon. Even members of the liberal Constitutional Democratic party known as the Kadets, who were fearful of raising an issue that they were certain would bitterly divide the newly created legislative body, dragged their feet.

In June 1906, in response to the outbreak of pogroms in Bialystok, deputies elected a committee to examine the issue of civil equality for Jews. A fierce debate ensued in the Duma in which liberal representatives assailed the government for actively fostering anti-Jewish activity and demanded the granting of rights to Jews. The proposal was still buried in committee when the tsar dissolved the parliamentary body in July 1906. The marked turn to the right among deputies to the Second Duma in 1907 spelled the end of any hopes for Jewish equality through parliamentary legislation. In May 1910, two Jewish deputies would make a last-ditch effort to introduce legislation to abolish the Pale but the proposal would never come up for a vote.

The government's crackdown on reform was accompanied by renewed restrictions upon Jews. In 1910, 1,200 Jewish families were expelled from the Ukrainian city of Kiev. The following year was a particularly difficult one for Russian Jewry. In a move that had a profound impact upon young Jews who had been seeking to gain higher education, tsarist officials extended the numerus clausus to externs, that is, students who were not officially registered but who could take examinations and thus secure degrees from government schools. Two other events in the same year, the assassination of Prime Minister Peter Stolypin and the arrest of Menahem Beilis, a young Russian Jew who was accused of ritual murder, raised fears of further pogroms.[45]

The onset of war in 1914 saw the entrance of hundreds of thousands of Jews into the Russian army and again led to expectations of an improvement in the condition of Russian Jewry. Military reversals quickly dashed such hopes, however. In an effort to avoid blame, military officials accused Jews of siding with the German enemy to bring down the hated tsarist regime. The retreat of the Russian army from western borderlands in August–September 1915 created further havoc as vengeful peasant soldiers destroyed hundreds of Jewish villages and slaughtered tens of thousands of their inhabitants.[46] Two years later, the Revolutions of March and November finally brought an end to the hateful legislation of tsarism and led to the granting of full civil rights to Russian Jewry.[47]

In retrospect, it seems clear that though much of the Russian officialdom in the nineteenth century was viscerally anti-Semitic, its attitudes toward Jews were largely shaped by concerns over the effect of the maintenance of Jewish communal and religious life on nation building and economic development. The twists and turns of the government's treatment of Jews reflected the complex interplay between the pressures to modernize placed upon the regime and the deeply rooted prejudices that informed its leadership, specifically the desire to establish a national polity in a multinational environment and the drive to compete with more developed nations without sacrificing Slavic distinctiveness. In a more general sense, the contradictions of tsarist policy toward Jews pointed up the inability of the government to enact meaningful reforms and engage in economic modernization while maintaining its traditional power base. In their desperate attempt to deal with a hated enemy within their midst, Russian leaders seemed caught between a desire to assimilate the Jewish population as quickly as possible and fears of the consequences of such an action. More than with any other national group in the empire, a radical change in the condition of the Jews in the form of either greater liberality or stricter control represented a leap into the unknown that threatened to undermine the tsarist system itself.

It was the uncertainty as much as the brutality of tsarist regulations that served to alienate most Jews from the government and from Russian society in general. Interspersing policies of relative toleration with brutal acts of violence, the regime forced most of its Jewish inhabitants to choose between forced assimilation or continued persecution. In turn, the inability of the government to deal effectively with the "Jewish problem" only served to confuse the Russian population and to reinforce its hostility toward Jews. Michael Aronson insightfully summarizes the nature and impact of Russian policy toward Jews in the following statement that deserves to be quoted at length:

> On the one hand, Russian officials aimed at Jewish assimilation, either in the distant or relatively near future, to be achieved with great difficulty or relatively painlessly. On the other hand, officials revealed doubts about the possibility or even the desirability of such a development. The result of these crosscurrents was to make the Jewish question insoluble on Russian soil. If the Jew retained his distinctive identity, he

was condemned by all. If he attempted to shed his identity, he did not cease to be looked upon as a Jew; if he did not become suspect of fraud, deception, duplicity, mendacity, he at least continued to be feared as an alien threat to the "native" Russian population. The Jew could not escape his fate of being looked upon as wholly other.[48]

Of the various programs devised to deal with Jews in the nineteenth century, it was the government's economic policies that had the most profound effect on the Jewish population. As noted earlier, tsarist officials often sought to exploit the talents of select Jews who they were convinced would help spearhead Russia's drive to become economically self-sufficient. Benefiting from the support of government officials and economically powerful Russian interests, a small Jewish bourgeoisie had begun to emerge by midcentury. A number of Jewish merchants and tradesmen were granted lucrative government contracts as a result of their willingness to partake in tsarist educational programs created in the 1840s.[49] In some Jewish towns, enterprising Jewish businessmen were able to establish large stores that in time began to draw customers from Russians living in surrounding areas. Increasingly self-confident but limited in their influence in the larger society, businessmen and financiers soon assumed leadership positions in the Jewish community.

The onset of economic modernization also opened up opportunities for enterprising individual Jewish manufacturers and industrialists, especially in the fields of sugar refining, water transport, insurance, and oil production. It is estimated that in 1897, for example, more than one-half of all the match and brush factories in the Pale and most of the textile trades in Lithuania and Poland belonged to Jews. All told, by the end of the century Jews owned close to 3,000 factories in the Pale (excluding Poland).[50] Nevertheless, legal limitations placed upon Jews skewed their representation among the economic elite. The fact that Jews were prohibited from owning land in rural areas where there was often a ready supply of labor and where sanitary restrictions were more lax than those in the cities, for example, meant that there were few Jewish owners in industries such as metallurgy and mining.[51]

Jews also played a significant role in the development of Russian banking and investment. Capital accumulation and formation were fundamental prerequisites for the economic modernization of Russia. Those Jews who had international contacts, liquid capital, and fluency in foreign languages took advantage of the opportunities to earn quick profits, especially in the early stages of Russian capitalist development. In 1859, the Guenzburg family of St. Petersburg opened the first Jewish bank outside the Pale. Branches would soon follow in Odessa and Kiev. Ten years later, members of the Poliakov family established dozens of lending institutions first in, the burgeoning cities of St. Petersburg and Moscow and then eventually throughout all of Russia. Both banking firms were instrumental in the expansion of international trade and the development of national railroads, which were vital for the distribution of Russia's scattered resources. Jewish-owned banks were also involved in financing Russia's war with Turkey in 1878. As with other economically powerful Jews, however, the very success of these individuals rested on their exceptionality, since their acceptance into Russian society often meant their divorce from the Jewish community. Even in cases such as the Guenzburgs, who maintained close ties with Russian Jewry, it was the fact that they were privileged Jews (as well as their dependence on favors and subsidies from the tsarist government) that enabled them to serve as *shtadlanim*, or semiofficial representatives of the Jewish community at the imperial court. In any event, by the end of the century Jewish financiers were beginning to lose their influence and power, largely as a result of the nationalization of privately owned railroads that had been heavily financed and owned by Jews.[52]

The Poliakovs and Guenzburgs were highly visible examples of the ability of at least some Jews to take advantage of the strong desire of the central government to modernize the Russian economy. Yet the number of Jews who benefited from economic modernization remained small. According to one historian who has examined the statistical evidence, only 5 to 10 percent of the Jewish population of the Pale at the turn of the century could be said to have had significant income.[53] The majority of Jewish businessmen were no more than itinerant peddlers and middlemen, forced to eke out a living from day to day. Most were involved in the trade of traditional agricultural products; few sold manufactured consumer goods.[54] According to the 1897 census, nearly 90 percent of the Jews of the northwest could be classified as petty merchants. Even in New Russia, with its more open economic environment, 75 percent of the Jewish population were members of the lower middle class.

Blocked from most economic pursuits in the cities, Jews concentrated in artisan and crafts trades. In part, this reflected a continuation of established trades in prepartition Poland; in part, it represented the limited opportunities available to newly arrived workers
in the cities. According to the 1897 government census, 40 percent
of all employed Jews were artisans and laborers. Artisan production
generally consisted of home labor arrangements in which entire families or individuals subcontracted to produce items for middlemen.
As in the case of Jewish tradesmen, they generally limited their economic activity to local markets. It was a precarious existence marked
by long periods of unemployment and constant bickering with greedy
entrepreneurs over rates for piecework.[55]

The contradictions in tsarist policy meant that as long as financial
inducements were not accompanied by more liberal treatment of
ethnic and religious minorities, the material plight of the majority of
Jews would not appreciably benefit from Russian economic development. Indeed, in many cases Russian modernizing efforts actually
worsened the Jews' economic conditions. Thus, for example, the
abolition of serfdom in 1861, which was hailed as major step in Russia's
entry into the modern world, actually proved disastrous for most Jews.
Among its many harmful effects, the proclamation weakened the ar-
istocracy upon which Jews had relied for support and increased competition in the cities by introducing cheap, unskilled labor. Emancipation also made peasants less dependent upon Jewish merchants as
providers of goods and services and led the government to reduce
opportunities for Jewish agricultural settlement in order to satisfy
the needs of the new class of landless Russians.[56] Similarly, the numerous attempts to "productivize" Jews engaged in petty trade and
commerce by forcing them into occupations deemed useful for Russian economic growth only exacerbated their relations with native
Russians. The imposition of harsh excise and license taxes and the
appearance of non-Jewish distillers and innkeepers, for example, dras-
tically reduced the Jews' share in previous economic strongholds such
as the liquor, salt, and tobacco trades.[57] So too, the development of
permanent markets meant the disappearance of the traditional fair
economy that had been so vital to Jewish peddlers and itinerant merchants. Finally, the advent of the railroads and electric tram lines
hurt Jewish carters and haulers, while at the same time making serious inroads into the trade and business of local Jewish merchants

and small manufacturers. Improvements in transportation also worsened economic conditions in the Jewish community by increasing the general exodus of Jews from rural regions and their concentration in cities.[58]

Nor did Jewish laborers benefit from the growth of factories toward the end of the century. In most cases, new industries grew up in areas that were outside the Pale and thus off-limits to Jewish workers. Within the Pale itself, the few factories that were established in the late nineteenth century were generally run by Russian manufacturers who refused to hire Jews. Newly arrived workers from the countryside refused to have Jews work alongside them.[59] As a result, Jews generally were only hired to work in Jewish-owned factories where harsh physical conditions, severe competition for scarce jobs, and the common ethnic background of employers and workers increased the potential for exploitation. Before the advent of labor legislation, it was not uncommon for Jewish laborers to work eighteen hours a day. In the poorer northwestern region of the Pale, children and women made up more than one-third of the laboring workforce. In many cases, entire families had to work together to earn enough money to survive. Even in the more prosperous southern region, over half of the Jewish artisans and laborers in 1898 were earning less than an annual subsistence wage.[60]

Chronic overpopulation and the intense competition for limited resources only exacerbated the situation. By the 1870s a small but distinctive Jewish proletariat had begun to form in the congested northwestern provinces of the Pale. For the most part, Jewish workers concentrated in factories manufacturing cigarettes, leather goods, brushes, and cloth. Tensions between Christian and Jewish workers and the failure of traditional Jewish institutions and leadership to recognize the latter's distinctive plight increased their social and cultural isolation. With the development of social consciousness in the 1880s, Jewish workers in cities such as Vilna, Bialystok, and Minsk set about organizing their own associations (*kassy*), embryonic trade unions that would play a crucial role in the development of an independent Jewish socialist movement at the turn of the century.[61]

The numerous restrictions imposed upon Russian Jews and their expulsion from rural areas also led to the creation of bands of itinerant paupers who roamed the Pale in search of employment. Government welfare programs proved of little help since they were poorly administered and earmarked primarily for peasants.[62] It is estimated that at the beginning of the twentieth century, nearly 19 percent of Jews in the Pale needed assistance from some 2,300 private charitable organizations. In many communities, up to 40 percent of heads of families were *luftmenschen*, or individuals without steady jobs.[63]

The growing realization that Jewish economic interests and the interests of the majority of the Russian population were often diametrically opposed was an important factor in the development of government programs for Jewish economic renewal in the last three decades of the century. It also influenced many young Jews to join movements such as the Populists, which sought to reinterpret peasant values and institutions as forces for progressive social change. Later, after the decline of such movements in the 1870s, the realization on the part of the general Jewish population that, under existing conditions, Jews could only be harmed by Russian economic development would spur the wave of emigration to the United States.

In attempting to deal with the "Jewish question" in the nineteenth century, Russian government officials placed special emphasis upon state-controlled education as a means of rooting out ethnic solidarity and national sentiment. Here, too, the drive to incorporate Jews into Russian society clashed with fears of the infiltration of the Russian populace by alien elements. The clumsy attempts by officials at the beginning of the century to induce Jewish parents to send their children to government schools occasioned little response, however. Jews were understandably alienated by the emphasis of the curriculum on Christian teachings. As former residents of Polish areas, they had little interest in learning Russian. The result was that with the exception of Jews in New Russia, enrollment in non-Jewish schools in the Pale was almost nonexistent before the 1840s.

Even the establishment in the 1840s of government-sponsored Crown schools which taught both Jewish and secular subjects did not significantly alter Jewish attitudes. Despite the support of such efforts by elements of the Haskalah, most Russian Jews quickly realized that the basic goal of such schools was not to broaden their education but to root out Jewish religious and cultural traditions that stood in the way of their conversion to Christianity.[64] Indeed, a significant percentage of those attending such schools ultimately did convert to Russian Orthodoxy.[65] The fact that the principals of Crown schools generally were local Russian headmasters with no particular sympathy for Jews, and that most of the teachers were unemployed graduates of rabbinical seminaries with little experience in Jewish education, only increased suspicions among the general Jewish population.

Crown schools tended to appeal to poorer Jews hoping to avoid military conscription of their sons rather than to wealthier elements of the community who had originally been the targets of the government's educational program. Rich Jews quickly found that they could just as easily bribe government officials to protect their children from army service.[66] The status of Crown schools declined dramatically after the decision by Alexander II to grant Jews permission to attend general Russian educational institutions. In 1873 they were finally abolished with little fanfare in those areas where general schools were accessible to Jews. The two Crown rabbinical schools established by the government in Vilna and Zhitomir in 1847 were also shut down.[67]

Yet even the opening up of Russian schools did little to attract Jewish parents. By 1870, only 2,045 Jewish children were attending Russian schools, a mere 5.6 percent of the total Jewish student population. The number of enrollees actually increased during the first decade of Alexander II's reign to 7,004 or 12 percent of eligible Jewish students, thanks largely to a government decree exempting Jews who attended such schools from long army service. In areas of greater opportunity such as Odessa, the percentage of Jewish students attending the local high school or gymnasium approached the percentage of Jews in the local population.[68] Yet the numbers of Jews in Russian schools paled in comparison with the more than 350,000 children being taught by *melameds* (traditional Jewish teachers) in more than 25,000 heders (traditional elementary schools) and 500 talmud torahs (communal Jewish schools) in Russia and Poland, according to a study conducted by the Jewish Colonization Association in 1898. In the 1898–99 academic year, 53.8 percent of the Jewish children in the Pale still attended traditional religious schools while only one in seven eligible students attended either Russian or government-run Jewish schools.[69]

Despite the opposition of much of Russian Jewry to government assimilationist policies, dramatic changes in settlement patterns, economic activity, and schooling of important segments of the Jewish population were bound to have a profound effect upon the classic shtetl or small Jewish village in the Pale. The shtetl's origins are to be found in sixteenth-century Poland when Jews from German lands were invited by the king to settle in private towns owned by the Polish nobility. In time, Jews began to inhabit the villages surrounding these towns and to establish their own communal institutions. The Jews' role as middlemen for local landowners increased their significance in the local economy and led to a further influx of Ashkenazic Jews. By the time of the partitions of Poland at the end of the eighteenth century, Jews constituted a significant majority in many of the villages that were annexed to the Russian Empire. In the relatively compact and closed environment of the small Jewish village, traditional institutions and beliefs maintained themselves. By the nineteenth century, the shtetl had become the paradigm of established East European Jewish life for both observant and modernizing Jews — a symbol of the unalterable nature of Judaism for the former and a major obstacle to social, economic, and cultural change for the latter.[70]

The rootedness of Jewish life in prepartition Poland reinforced the power and authority of the Jewish community structure or *kahal*. Established early in the thirteenth century with the first influx of Jews to Poland from western Europe, Jewish communal autonomy in eastern Europe originally reflected a common interest on the part of both Jewish and non-Jewish leadership to keep the community separate from the host society. Government demands for the orderly collection of taxes meshed with Jewish desires to maintain distinctive institutions and values. By the seventeenth century, however, the community's institutional structure was in crisis. The loss of royal protection and the growing involvement of Jewish merchants with local landlords as tax collectors and product leaseholders had led to explosions of anti-Semitic violence culminating in the infamous Chmielnicki Revolt in 1648. Communal leadership proved incapable of responding to the psychological trauma and massive social and economic dislocation that resulted from the death of an estimated 40,000 to 100,000 Jews, more than a quarter of the Jewish population of Poland.[71] Ironically, the community's demographic recovery in the eighteenth century did little to improve the situation. The increase in population in the sharply circumscribed Jewish settlement threatened to create a permanent underclass within the community and taxed the meager resources of communal institutions.[72]

The shtetl's communal structure was weakened still further after the Russian annexation and the onset of the government's contradictory policies toward Jews. The combination of the increasingly restrictive nature of laws concerning Jewish settlement throughout the nineteenth century and growing mobility stemming from increased economic and educational opportunities, especially during the reign of Alexander II, loosened the tightly woven fabric of small-town Jewish life. Despite increased animosity and suspicion on both sides, however, tsarist officials and traditional Jewish leaders continued to maintain an uneasy alliance. Though Russian government leaders constantly sought to restrict the *kahal* as part of a general drive toward developing strong centralized institutions, their inability to make significant changes in bureaucratic administration and their desire to maintain public order in the interim ensured the temporary survival and even revival of the Jewish community structure throughout the first half of the nineteenth century.[73] While tsarist bureaucrats relied upon rabbis and members of the Jewish financial oligarchy to maintain peace and stability within the community, traditional Jewish leaders looked to the government to help preserve their authority and power over the general population.

All too often, the result was that when efforts were made by Russian officials to forcibly assimilate Jews, the rabbinate and Jewish lay leadership became their unwilling accomplices. Thus there were few protests from community leaders in 1844 when the government formally abolished the semiautonomous communal structure of the *kahal*, since rabbis and businessmen were allowed to continue collecting special taxes on kosher meat (the so-called *korobka*) and candles used for ritual purposes. Though the proceeds were used to maintain the hated Crown schools, the religious and economic elite seemed mainly concerned with ensuring that the community continue its control over religious and fiscal affairs. Most contacts between government authorities and communal leadership took place on the local and regional level. The cementing of these relations led to growing opposition from young Jews who denounced the communal leadership for negotiating with individuals who had little understanding of Jewish affairs and little sympathy for the continued survival of Jewish communal life. With hindsight, however, it can be argued that such contacts proved to have some limited benefits for a largely powerless Jewish authority structure. While decentralized control often led to increased tensions between Jews and Russians, it also allowed for greater maneuverability on the part of individual Jewish leaders.[74]

Particularly galling to many Jews was the involvement of community leaders in the cantonist system of forced military conscription. The burden of conscription fell most heavily upon the poor of the community since wealthier elements often bribed community leaders to avoid military service. The cantonist system thus served to heighten class divisions within the community and to weaken the moral and political integrity of the traditional leadership. Relations between the communal elite and the masses were exacerbated by the *kahal*'s decision to hire kidnappers (*poimaniki* in Russian; *khapern* in Yiddish) to search out potential conscripts. During periods of forced conscription, mobs often attacked the homes of community leaders. In some cases, individual Jews formally denounced *kahal* functionaries before the government for violating the law. In a number of communities, protesters disrupted religious services. In some shtetls, attempts were made to break away from the *kahal* rabbinate to form separate congregations.

Government leaders further compromised traditional authority by creating the position of *kazyonny ravvin* ("Crown rabbi") in 1857. Tsarist officials saw these rabbis as more reliable than the established religious leadership for keeping watch on a closed and suspect community. In contrast to "spiritual rabbis," state-authorized rabbis were expected to foster Jewish cultural assimilation and to ensure that laws and decrees were carried out within the community. Unlike traditional religious leaders, they were able to call upon the police to enforce their decisions. In the beginning, many of the appointees were maskilim who sincerely believed in the need for the "improvement" of Jewry. By the 1880s, however, the position of Crown rabbi had become an elected one and had lost whatever little sanctity it once had. Posts were bitterly contested among unemployed intellectuals, Hasidic loyalists, wealthy businessmen, and even representatives of nonreligious and antireligious movements seeking political power within the Jewish community.[75]

The power of traditional religious and lay leadership was also weakened by the activity of charitable and philanthropic institutions established by Jews living outside the Pale and supported by western Jews to meet the growing economic and physical needs of Russian Jewry. Traditional rabbis fought bitterly against their new foreign rivals, yet there was little they could do to counter the influence of organizations that offered services they were unable to provide. Indeed, the rabbis suffered as much as their congregants from the general immiseration of the Russian Jewish community in the late nineteenth century. No longer able to rely on support from a destitute general community, they became increasingly dependent upon rich lay people and more open to bribery and corruption. Already suffering from a loss of status, the traditional rabbi's economic plight only served to reinforce popular hostility toward established Jewish authority.[76]

The significant decline in communal independence and discipline gradually took its toll on the quality of leadership. The loss of the *kahal*'s status as a state-sanctioned corporate body meant that authority in the Jewish community rested increasingly on the personalities of individual religious leaders and wealthy notables in a local setting.[77] As fewer and fewer Jews aspired to positions of leadership, power often became concentrated of the hands of cliques.[78] The traditional Jewish authority's loss of authority and stature also enabled both maskilim and ultra-Orthodox elements to disseminate their ideas in an increasing number of Jewish communities.[79]

Despite the *kahal*'s formal abolition, the maintenance of harsh government policies toward the Jewish community in the latter half of the nineteenth century ensured that it continued to function in fact if not in name. Because Russian courts were often biased against Jewish plaintiffs and defendants, for example, many Jews preferred to seek out the decisions of the local Jewish rabbinical court or *bet din* on matters of dispute. Similarly, Jews still relied on Jewish religious authority to sanctify and validate life-cycle events such as births, marriages, divorces, and funerals. Despite the breakdown of communal structures, the majority of Jews in the Pale remained dependent upon traditional religious leadership to carry on Jewish belief and practice.

Not surprisingly, therefore, it was the perceived failure of Jewish communal leaders to fulfill their religious obligations that led to the first conscious assault from within the community upon traditional Jewish leadership in eastern Europe. The attack came not from modernizers but from disaffected traditionalists who became associated with the movement known as Hasidism. Even before the advent of the Pale and the intervention of government officials in internal Jewish communal affairs, the rise of Hasidism at the end of the eighteenth century introduced a limited form of religious pluralism, or at least denominationalism, into East European Jewish society. Originating in the Polish regions of Podolia and Volhynia, the movement quickly spread to areas of the Pale. Often compared with Protestant pietistic movements that flourished in early modern Europe,[80] Hasidism reflected the desire of the Jewish masses for a more personal religious experience. Though hardly democratic in attitude or practice, the new movement emphasized religious fervor and simple piety, which were said to be available to all Jews regardless of their degree of learning. Its positing of a charismatic leader, the tzaddik or righteous one, whose power rested on his devotion and honesty rather than his formal education, invariably led to the questioning of rabbinic authority and scholarship and contributed to the fragmentation of Jewish leadership. Hasidism's growing appeal among the Jewish masses also stemmed from popular hostility toward the wealthiest elements of the community, who often passed on tax burdens to those least able to afford it. By the beginning of the nineteenth century, the movement had already gained control over a significant number of Russian Jewish communities.[81]

As with other charismatic religious movements, Hasidism's gradual accession to power in the nineteenth century diminished its "populist" character. The ideal of the tzaddik soon gave way to the reality of dynastic houses and courts that mimicked Russian nobility and ensured continuity in a growingly influential movement. More important, Hasidic leaders soon found it necessary to ally with their former rivals, rabbinic Orthodoxy, in the general struggle of traditionalists against both government bureaucrats and maskilim. Nevertheless, in establishing an alternative religious system and institutional framework, the Hasidic movement unwittingly served to undermine the religious and cultural monolith of traditional Judaism in Russia and thus weakened its resolve in the face of ideologies and movements of modernization in the nineteenth century.[82]

Ultimately, the general assault upon traditional authority from both within and outside the Jewish community in the nineteenth century would lead to a breakdown in what the sociologist Peter Berger has called the "plausibility structure" of religious faith.[83] Though it is difficult to gauge the impact of the weakening of traditional Jewish institutions on individual belief, it seems clear that the gradual collapse of both the institutional and social framework and the consensual symbolic universe on which Orthodoxy rested severely affected the general religious commitment of the community. Classical Judaism emphasized the absolute nature of the rabbinate's control over all aspects of society; no boundary existed between religion and daily life and between the sacred and profane. The gradual degeneration in the status of traditional authority and its inability to respond effectively to social, political, and economic crisis thus was bound to foster the creation of alternative perspectives on the Jewish present and future.

By the 1860s "deviant" versions of Jewish identity and behavior already had begun to root themselves in small coteries of young Jewish modernizers, intellectual subgroups of individuals drawn from similar social circumstances who shared their own "plausibility structure." In their activity, they bore the signs of religious sects, providing a coherent community organization, legitimating commonly held norms and values, and sanctioning particular modes of conduct and aspirations.[84] The formation of such groups was spurred by the general questioning of institutions and beliefs within Russian society itself that accompanied the accession of Alexander II to power in 1855. Their beginnings generally can be traced to informal discussion circles in synagogues and yeshivas, the only legally recognized venues for open debate of Jewish issues in midcentury. By the 1860s, clusters of Jewish modernizers could also be found scattered throughout the state-sponsored Jewish schools and seminaries that generally were shunned by more traditional elements in the community. In time, such movements began to expand their influence among the Jewish masses. By providing practical services such as moneylending, vocational education, and mutual aid, they helped to fill the social service vacuum left by a weakened and often discredited community structure. As the groups gained in strength and self-confidence, they soon developed regional and national networks of affiliated associations.[85]

The formation of such subcommunities within the Russian Jewish community enabled those individuals who might have wavered in their decision to break with religious tradition to take the final step. As such, modernizing groups often attracted young Jews who were seeking emotional substitutes for the family ties that they had given up or rejected in their quest for economic, social, and intellectual independence. At the same time, the growing literacy within the Russian Jewish community created a ready market for the cultural products of modernizing groups. The fact that most participants came from the middle class meant that members of these groups could support themselves during periods of unemployment and inactivity, while generally avoiding both persecution by authorities and anti-Semitic attacks.[86]

As forums for intellectual discussion, movements of Jewish renewal drew heavily for their membership upon the hundreds of aspiring professionals, teachers, and writers who were denied entrance to government schools of higher learning. Jewish student enrollment in Russian universities had increased almost fourteenfold in the period between the 1850s and '80s. By 1887, Jews made up nearly 15 percent of the entire student body in the major districts of Warsaw, Kiev, Vilna, and Odessa. The efforts by children of the Jewish middle class to gain admission into Russian society through attendance at universities, however, collapsed in 1887–88 in the wake of the institution of a numerus clausus by Alexander III. Influenced by Constantine Pobedonostsev, Procurator of the Holy Synod, and Ivan Delianov, the new minister of education, tsarist officials increasingly began to view Jewish students as a menace to Russian society. In a significant reversal of previous government policy, Jews were now restricted to 10 percent of the university student body in the Pale of Settlement, 5 percent in other provinces, and 3 percent in St. Petersburg and Moscow. Between 1886 and 1902, the percentage of Jews attending Russian universities decreased from 14.4 percent to 7 percent.[87] Although the quotas frequently were ignored by local officials, they remained officially in force until 1917.

In an attempt to pursue their education, more than 8,000 Jewish students left Russia to study abroad. Angered by government intolerance and removed from their home environment, they quickly were absorbed into the radical student emigré communities that grew up in Germany, England, and Switzerland at the end of the nineteenth century. During the first decade of the twentieth century, for example, Russians made up more than half the number of foreign students at most German universities; in many cases, the majority of them were Jewish.[88] Those who chose to remain in Russia were forced to become externs. Externs faced a life of great uncertainty. They never knew whether they would find room in already overcrowded classrooms. As a result, they could never be assured that they would be adequately prepared to take formal entrance examinations. In 1911, the hopes of externs were cruelly dashed by the institution of a numerus clausus on external admissions. Embittered against a Russian society that prevented them from participating fully in academia, emigrés and externs actively sought out companionship among a growing mass of Jewish "academic proletarians."

Young women played a crucial role in the growing interest in modernization and renewal within the Jewish community. Broader toleration of women learning secular subjects and the incorporation of feminist attitudes borrowed from Russian intellectual circles into public Jewish discourse gave women's views increased credibility, at least within nontraditional circles in the community.[89] Women made up a significant percentage of the Jewish student population in Russian schools. According to the Russian historian Barbara Engel, for example, nearly one-third of the entering classes to the medical school in St. Petersburg in 1878 and 1879 were Jewish women.[90] Women also were instrumental in introducing books on European literature and philosophy to members of the Jewish community (Simon Dubnow's daughters, for example, were active in the dissemination of Russian books in his hometown of Mstislav).[91] Despite such developments, however, women were almost completely absent from leadership positions in the two major Jewish political movements—Bundism and Zionism—that arose at the end of the nineteenth century. Nor did members of the transitional generation demonstrate much interest in the views of their spouses and female associates. In his recollections of Ahad Ha-Am's household in the 1880s, for example, Yehoshua Barzilay, a member of Hibbat Zion, noted that it was not the custom for women to participate in "nationalist activity" and that husbands rarely brought their wives to meetings of activists.[92] A notable exception was Zina Dizengoff, the wife of Meir Dizengoff (later to become the first mayor of Tel Aviv), who ran a salon in the style of Paris and Berlin during her stay in Odessa from 1897 to 1905. Dubnow and Ahad Ha-Am frequently attended her get-togethers along with most of the leading intellectual lights in the Jewish community.[93]

The breakdown of traditional values and the growing strength of movements of Jewish national renewal were aided by the development of a Jewish popular press, which cemented the cohesiveness of the emerging subsocieties. On the most obvious level, newspapers helped disseminate the ideas of modernizers to a growing audience of disaffected Jews. The press could also act as a mediator between the Jewish community and the government, explaining and at times even defending government actions while at the same time presenting the Jewish case to tsarist officials.[94] Jewish newspapers benefited from a government decree in April 1862 that extended to Jews the right to set up printing presses anywhere in the empire within the limitations of the censorship laws of 1817.[95] The efforts of journalists and publicists were also aided by the fact that Russian Jews had a literacy rate almost twice as high as that of Russians as a whole. Nevertheless, as with the Russian press in general, most Jewish newspapers had a restricted circulation and reflected a "journalism of opinion" targeted to an elite rather than a "journalism of information" geared to a mass readership.[96]

The influence of the Jewish press was strengthened by the Crimean War in 1853, which piqued Jewish interest in current events. Jewish writers and publishers were also quick to use the emancipation of peasants in 1861 as a launching point for a drive to press for the granting of civil rights to Jewry.[97] The period of the 1860s and 1870s saw an explosion of Jewish newspapers in Russia. Modeling themselves after German Jewish journals, they expounded conflicting views of cultural change. *Ha-Melits* (The Interpreter), a Hebrew weekly founded in 1860 that was published first in Odessa and then in St. Petersburg and survived until 1905, preached the virtues of the Haskalah while claiming to defend the best of religious tradition. Drawing its readership largely from lower middle-class elements trained in the study of sacred texts, it provided an entree for many young Jews in the Pale to the larger world of European culture. *Kol Mevasser* (The Voice of the Messenger), a Yiddish weekly published between 1862 and 1871, helped to spread both "enlightenment" and practical information to a larger, less-educated audience that could not read Hebrew and was often hostile toward modern ideas. *Rassvet* (Dawn), published under various titles between 1860 and 1871 and then again between 1879 and 1883, provided a forum for the assimilated Russian-speaking Jewish populations of cities such as Odessa and St. Petersburg while at the same time presenting Jewish viewpoints to interested Russian readers.[98]

As Jewish editors and writers gained experience and readers, they soon learned how to work around the numerous censorship restrictions imposed by the government. Those journalists whom the government considered too radical published their papers outside of Russia and smuggled them across the border from Germany. Despite its chronic lack of funds and a fickle readership, the Jewish press was disseminated widely within the Pale and played a crucial role in familiarizing the general Jewish reading public with modern ideas. At the same time, the continual insistence by journalists that their articles merely reflected popular desires helped to create a sense of self-importance and self-consciousness among the Jewish masses, which was a necessary precondition for the development of political movements such as Zionism and Bundism at the turn of the century.[99]

The growth of a Jewish press coincided with the growing availability of non-Jewish literature in the community. As noted earlier, general European and Russian works were often smuggled into homes and schools by radical youth, especially young women. Many young Jews, including both Dubnow and Ahad Ha-Am, learned foreign languages by studying bilingual religious works.[100] In time, translations of foreign books appeared in Hebrew and Yiddish. The establishment of the Society for the Promotion of Enlightenment among Jews in Russia in 1863 and the beginnings of socialist study groups among Jewish workers of the Pale in the 1870s further strengthened efforts to disseminate modern literature and thought within the Jewish community.

The rise of a dynamic new generation of Jews did not go unnoticed by established Jewish authority. In most cases, the questioning of traditional Judaism's "plausibility structure" by modernizing elements of Russian Jewry only reinforced the effort by its defenders to reassert their hegemony over the community. Increased efforts by rabbis to win back lapsed Jews led to a significant revival of Orthodoxy toward the end of the nineteenth century. Traditional Jewish support was also strengthened as a result of the massive emigration westward at the end of the century, which tended to drain off radical and disaffected elements of the community. Within the Orthodox community, efforts at spiritual renewal led to the rise of the so-called Musar (Ethics) movement in Lithuania. Under the leadership of Rabbi Israel Salanter, Musar sought to combine rabbinism and Hasidism by stressing scholarship, ethics, and individual integrity. In so doing, it attempted to unite the forces of tradition against the common enemy while at the same time incorporating many of the criticisms leveled by modernizers against the rabbinical establishment. In many cases, the revival of traditionalism enabled its adherents to renew Orthodoxy from within by replacing the declining central religious leadership with militant local religious associations.

The very emphasis of the new Orthodoxy upon piety and personal faith, however, pointed to the development of a more restrictive religious role for rabbis in the changing society of Russian Jewry. Equally revealing of the shift in rabbinic function was the fact that in the absence of the *herem*, the traditional right of excommunication, militant Orthodox groups were forced to adopt mass media techniques of printed newspapers and flyers pioneered by their enemies in order to counter the inroads of secular ideals and movements.[101] What the rabbis feared was not the rise of new religious movements. The continued control by Orthodoxy of religious symbols and institutions and the refusal of the larger society to consider Jewish emancipation meant that movements of religious reform would have little impact on Russian Jewry. The danger was far greater. Unlike their counterparts in western Europe, Jewish modernizing movements in Russia sought not to transform religion but to transcend it in the name of some new personal and collective Jewish identity. No wonder that rabbis often described the rise of secularizing movements as foreshadowing the imminent approach of the Messianic era.[102]

The rejection of religious belief and leadership did not always manifest itself in conscious rebellion, especially among the general Jewish population. The gradual replacement of arranged marriages by notions of romantic love, the need to work on the Sabbath and religious holidays, the growing availability of European and Russian publications, the eating of nonkosher food in social gatherings with non-Jews—all signaled an unconscious movement away from strict adherence to religious tradition. Modernizers were often quick to emphasize the need to separate oneself from parent and community as the first step toward independence. More often than not, however, self-styled modern attitudes and behavior coexisted with at least the external manifestations of religious observance.

In time, of course, the young Jews' heightened consciousness of the inexorable breakdown of traditional institutions and behavior would lead to a determined effort to create a new foundation for Jewish life. In searching for a redefined collective identity, Jewish innovators were influenced by their interaction with Great Russian culture. On the surface, Russian national and cultural values would appear to have had minimal appeal to Jewry. The vast majority of Russian Jews lived in two areas of the Pale, Lithuania and the Ukraine, which were populated by elements that were largely non-Russian. Thus they found Russification to be of little value in their attempts to make their way in local society. Even in situations where Jews were able to penetrate government and university circles, the fact that the dominant culture was so heavily imbued with traditional Christian concepts and so closely associated with the tsarist state generally made Jewish intellectuals reluctant to adopt the beliefs and mores of the larger society. This was especially true after the onset of anti-Jewish pogroms in the 1880s, and again after the resurgence of anti-Semitism in the first decade of the twentieth century.[103]

Nor were the programs of most Russian nationalists particularly appealing to young Jewish modernizers. While Russian activists often sought to replace European culture with the "primitive" (and thus allegedly more genuine) values of the peasantry, Jewish nationalists saw their role as that of elevating the Jewish masses in order for the Jewish people to play its historical role among the nations of the world.[104] All too often, Russian modernizers ignored the anti-Semitism of the peasant masses. As Jews bitterly learned after the outbreak of pogroms in 1881–82, some nationalists even went so far as to justify the violence as a cathartic liberation for an oppressed population.

Though suspicious of Russian nationalism, Jewish intellectuals in the nineteenth century were drawn to the writings of prominent Russian philosophers. Two social thinkers in particular, Nikolai Chernyshevski (1828–1889) and Dimitri Pisarev (1840–1868), fired the imagination of Jewish activists with their attempts to combine rational philosophy, natural science, and practical programs of social and economic reform. Young Jews were especially attracted to the emphasis that they placed upon the "intelligentsia." This was a select group of educated and committed young men and women drawn from the *raznochintsy*, that amorphous group situated between merchants and peasants, who would rise above the traditional caste divisions within society and spur the apathetic masses to demand change.[105] The relationship between intellectuals and the general population was most clearly defined in the writings of the social philosopher Peter Lavrov (1824–1900). In works such as his *Historical Letters*, Lavrov stressed the debt that intellectuals owed to the downtrodden masses, and sought to provide an alternative to the abstract philosophizing and political conspiratorialism that he believed were so prevalent in Russian revolutionary circles. While Lavrov's ideas often lost out to more primitive notions of mass spontaneity in debates among Russian activists, they found enthusiastic support among advanced elements within the Jewish community, who were convinced that a populace that respected learning would be eager for enlightenment. At the same time, Lavrov's emphasis on intellectuals gave a collective identity to a group of Jews who felt isolated from the Jewish masses while at the same time providing them with an entree back into communal life. His trumpeting of writers and philosophers as agents of social change, denial of impersonal laws and socioeconomic forces, and absolute belief in the correctness of his position would remain cardinal tenets of East European Jewish intellectuals of all political persuasions at the turn of the century.[106]

Many young Jews gained their first awareness of the larger Russian society and of the importance of a worldview in defining both personal and collective identity through their participation in the Narodnik or Populist movement. Emerging from small radical groups in the 1860s, the *narodniki* pledged themselves to lead the masses toward a new society grounded in the distinctive structure and values of Russian peasant and artisan culture. Until the 1870s, the movement's slogan of "Going to the People" found enthusiastic support among Jewish youth, especially those in yeshivas who were attracted by its contrast with their own sheltered and isolated life.[107] In the 1860s, Jews constituted 3 percent of the members of Russian radical movements. Less than a decade later, they accounted for nearly 8 percent of political activists, roughly equaling the proportion of Jews in the Russian population as a whole.[108]

The failure of the Populist campaign to "go to the people" in 1875 was a grave disappointment to many young Jewish members, particularly since peasant reactions to the campaign often intermingled with strong anti-Semitic sentiments. Six years later, the ambivalent attitude of Populist leaders toward the pogroms led to mass Jewish defections from the movement. Despite the decline of support for the *narodniki* among Jewish intellectuals, elements of Populist ideology would continue to have a profound impact on Jewish nationalist and socialist groups, including the belief in mass politics under the tutelage of an intellectual elite, the centrality of cultural revival in the modernization of society, and agrarian socialism. The slavophilic orientation of Populism also helped to shape the largely negative attitude that many Russian Jewish intellectuals felt toward western Jews while bolstering their confidence in the ability of East European Jewry to find its own distinctive path toward modernization.

In addition to influences drawn from the majority culture, Jews searching for a new direction could not but be affected by the nationalist resurgence against Russian domination among ethnic minorities that swept over the Ukraine, the Caucasus, Armenia, the Baltic region, and Lithuania after the crushing of the Polish revolt in 1863. It was in part through the writings of Ukrainian nationalists, for example, that supporters of Jewish autonomy like Zhitlowski and Dubnow were introduced to the concept of federalism, which sought to balance commitments to the central government with the affirmation of distinctive national identities.[109] As noted earlier, in the absence of objective criteria for defining nationality, Jews shared with other ethnic minorities in the empire the need to stress a common past, religion, culture, and language as elements of collective solidarity. Similarly, the self-perception of many non-Russian nationalists that collective identity had been maintained largely by the poorer elements of society would find its reflection in the association by many Jewish nationalists of Jewish survival with the simple beliefs and loyalties of the masses.[110]

Such influences were largely unconscious, however. In general, Russian Jews, who often constituted the majority or plurality in many of the larger towns of Russia,[111] were oblivious and at times even openly disdainful of the specific cultures of their Polish, Lithuanian, and White Russian neighbors. Even in cities where other national minorities dominated, ethnic groups were so deeply divided that they provided no clearly definable model of collective identification for emerging Jewish nationalists. Nor could the cultural level of the various groups compare with the experience of Jews. At the beginning of the twentieth century, only the Poles among the territorial minorities in the empire possessed a school system, a press, and a theater of their own.[112] The fact that the nationalism of non-Russians often included strong dosages of anti-Semitism, chauvinism, and xenophobia also alienated Jewish intellectuals.[113] On the few occasions that Jewish activists referred to the activity of other minorities, they used their national struggle to justify the need for Jews to assert themselves. The general sentiment seemed to be that if "uncultured" peoples such as Ukrainians, Lithuanians, and Serbs could demand rights, why couldn't the more civilized (and by implication more deserving) Jews?[114] In 1905, Jewish leaders attempted to unite with other national groups in a coordinated drive for cultural rights. Deep divisions over the nature of national autonomy for ethnic minorities and the repressive hand of tsarism quickly put an end to these efforts, however. Divorced from the dominant culture and political system and alienated from the surrounding cultures of ethnic minorities, Russian Jews inevitably sought out their own direction and structures to reshape their community.[115]

More significant were the examples of national identity formation in the more "cultured" countries that neighbored the Pale. Jewish nationalists in Russia were clearly attracted to the components of the Polish national mythology that developed in the wake of the abortive revolt of 1863. Here was a collective identity forged by political oppression, charismatic leadership, images of a past golden age, and hope for redemption expressed in messianic terms. Jewish nationalists were also deeply influenced by the efforts of Germans, Ukrainians, Ruthenians, and others to achieve autonomy within the Austro-Hungarian Empire. Of particular importance were the writings of intellectuals like the Czech historian Frantisek Palacky (1798–1876), who pioneered in the rediscovery of his nation's past as a minority in the Austro-Hungarian Empire, and the Polish historian and politician Ignacy Lelewel (1786–1861), who pressed for minority rights within the Russian Empire. In many cases, Russian Jewish activists absorbed nationalist ideas through observing the attitudes and activities of Jewish nationalists in neighboring Galicia and Bukovina, who began to press their demands for cultural autonomy toward the end of the century.[116] As previously noted, the views of the prominent Austro-Marxists Karl Renner and Otto Bauer, which seemed to point to the innate right of nationalities to define their own destiny within a modern socialist state, also had a powerful influence on Russian Jewish nationalist ideologues. Though not all Jewish nationalists were socialists, they could hardly disagree with Bauer's vision of the goals of the future socialist society: "the integration of all peoples into the nation's cultural community, the achievement of complete self-determination for nationalities, [and] the spiritual differentiation of nationalities."[117] In their desperate desire to find intellectual support for their views, most Jewish nationalists chose to ignore the two socialists' refusal to accept Jewish autonomy in their future scheme.

The roots of the movement for Jewish renewal could be found in the 1840s in the efforts of the so-called Haskalah. Drawing extensively upon the experiences of German Jewry in the early nineteenth century, the movement stressed Jewish self-improvement based on education and voiced its hope for the gradual assimilation of Russian Jews into the larger society. Presenting themselves as a new type of Jewish intellectual, Russian maskilim urged the study of both traditional and secular subjects and emphasized vocational as well as scholarly training for young men. Individual Jewish self-betterment, in their view, was bound to lead to formal acceptance as equal citizens within Russia and the end to anti-Semitism.

The Haskalah's major appeal in Russia was among the emerging Jewish bourgeoisie in urban areas such as Vilna, Minsk, and Odessa. Trading with merchants from Galicia, the area of Poland that came under Austrian rule after the partitions of the late eighteenth century and that saw the first inroads of the Jewish Enlightenment in eastern Europe, Russian Jewish businessmen were to become the most important conduits for the infiltration of western ideas into the Pale. Support for Haskalah ideas also came from the small group of young students and professionals who had received their education and training in the West. In time, maskilim were even able to gain adherents among rabbinical students through their use of traditional sources to justify their arguments.

For much of the first half of the nineteenth century, however, the "Berliners" or "Daytchen" (Yiddish for Germans), as Russian maskilim were derogatorily called by their opponents, had little practical success. Struggling against both established Orthodoxy and Hasidism, the young Jewish modernizers faced enormous obstacles in their efforts to make their ideas of productivization and modern education known to the Jewish masses. In particular, they were hindered by the fact that most of their proposals were too abstract and esoteric for the average Russian Jew. The personal writings of maskilim testify to their desperate sense of alienation and loneliness in their quest to force the Jewish masses to be free.[118]

Supporters of the Haskalah thought they could gain a foothold in the Jewish community in the mid-1840s and early '50s by supporting the efforts of government officials to establish state-sponsored Jewish schools that combined Jewish tradition with modern secular subjects. Mimicking the attitudes of the eighteenth-century *philosophes* under enlightened absolutist regimes as well as those of Russian intellectuals in the 1850s who appealed to the tsar to meet their demands, maskilim clearly hoped that cooperation with Russian government officials would break down the stubbornness of traditional leaders and energize the masses within the Jewish community. Accepting the basic supposition of government that anti-Semitism stemmed from Jewish inadequacies, they were convinced that re-education would improve the Jewish condition and silence critics. More radical elements among the maskilim may have also dreamed of personally filling the political and cultural vacuum that they were convinced would result from the inevitable decline of traditional communal authority.[119]

To further its ends, in 1841 the government called upon Max Lilienthal, a German Jewish educator, to direct the establishment of new schools throughout the Pale. Lilienthal's tenure was short-lived, however. Attacked by community religious leaders wherever he went and increasingly suspicious of the true intentions of government officials, the German educator soon left Russia, never to return. Though the schools survived until the collapse of the tsarist regime in 1917, their programs occasioned little response among the Jewish populace as a whole. Ultimately, of course, the relationship between maskilim and government bureaucrats was based on a fundamental misunderstanding. While early Jewish modernizers naively assumed that Russian officials were interested in perpetuating the ideals of western modernization, government leaders wrongly believed that the Haskalah represented a wholesale attack upon Judaism in the name of total assimilation. As soon as the government's true intentions became evident, the Haskalah's program for educational reform was quickly abandoned.[120]

Despite their fascination with emancipation, maskilim made little effort to adopt the ideas and programs of movements of Jewish religious reform that had grown up in western and central Europe in the mid-nineteenth century. With few exceptions, the Russian Haskalah roundly denounced both Reform and Conservative ideologies as the creations of assimilationist Jews. Indeed, religious reform angered East European Jewish modernizers even more than Orthodoxy since it appeared to be mere mimicry of the Christian world in a desperate attempt to gain acceptance rather than a sincere program for the modernization of Jewish religious life. Similarly, the implied notion of religious reformers that there could be Jewish Russians comparable to Russians of the Christian faith seemed preposterous, given the intermingling of religion and nationality in both Great Russian and national minority consciousness in the empire. The fact that there was no Protestant religious alternative to established Russian Orthodoxy not only hindered any attempt to seek a modus vivendi with the established Church but also meant that there would be no example of Christian religious reform within the larger society to emulate. Movements of religious reform also seemed out of place in an environment where Jews did not have religious rights and where individual freedoms in general were severely circumscribed. Finally, the assumption that the sole difference between Russians and Jews was religious flew in the face of the deep-seated economic and cultural divisions that had characterized their relationship since the establishment of the Pale. The result was that any significant attempt at Jewish assimilation in Russia necessarily meant cultural as well as geographical divorce from the Jewish community.

The inapplicability of the western model of emancipation could be clearly seen in the fate of the so-called Jewish Russifiers. The program of Russification, which gained a limited audience within the Jewish community after the accession of Alexander II to power, rested on the belief that the acceptance of Russian values and the Russian language by the Jewish masses would pave the way to their integration into the larger society. As Joachim Tarnopol, one of the founders of the Russian-language Jewish newspaper *Rassvet*, noted in a book written in 1855: "Our social and civil regeneration must be in pure Russian . . . and when a greater Russian element and Russian education will be propagated amongst our masses, then all the sooner will there be a place for the rapprochement between us and the Russian people."[121]   In contrast to the earlier reformers of the Haskalah who preached Jewish national revival through Hebrew language and literature, supporters of Russification rejected the notion of communal reform and adopted the model of western Jewry, which relegated Jewish identity to the home and the synagogue. Such views were reflected in the famous slogan by the Hebrew writer Yehuda Leib Gordon published in 1866: "Be a man in the street and a Jew in one's tent."[122]

The most vocal advocates of Russification could be found among individual Jews who settled in cities outside the Pale in order to pursue business and professional careers. By the 1880s, there were over 17,000 Jews living in St. Petersburg and some 35,000 in Moscow, slightly more than 7 percent of that city's total population.[123] Made up largely of merchants and businessmen, the leadership of these communities was mainly interested in creating an environment that would facilitate their economic and social advancement in Russian society.[124] In 1863, wealthy Jewish elements in the Russian capital founded the Society for the Promotion of Enlightenment among Jews in Russia, which called for the teaching of the Russian language among Jews as the first step in their integration into the larger society. Pledged to eradicating Jewish "peculiarities," the society subsidized the publication of Russian-language volumes on Jewish themes, commissioned Jewish writers to translate books on history and the natural sciences into Hebrew, and helped support Jewish students in universities. It is estimated that close to 20 percent of Jewish students in Russia at the turn of the century were educated in schools sponsored by the society.[125]

In extreme cases, Russification would often lead to conversion to Russian Orthodoxy. According to one contemporary observer, there were 30,000 Jewish converts in St. Petersburg and Moscow in the 1840s, most of whom came from the more cultured Baltic provinces.[126] From 1844 to 1860, at the height of the cantonist experience, Jews were converting at an average rate of more than 1,600 per year.

Despite the urgings of Russian Orthodox leaders and a few ardent Jewish converts, however, tsarist officials generally opposed efforts to establish an official Church mission to Russian Jewry. Most undoubtedly felt that the Jews' fierce attachment to their religion made them unlikely candidates for conversion to Christianity. Others were convinced that entrance into the Russian Orthodox Church would not necessarily transform Jews into loyal Russian citizens. Such sentiments were reinforced with the introduction of western racist writings into Russian clerical and governmental circles. It did not take long for decrees to be promulgated that were predicated on the assumption that religious conversion would not necessarily rid the Jew of his "innate" evil character.[127] Thus, for example, from 1850 on, any Jew who converted to Christianity was permitted to change only his first name. Similarly, the government enacted specific rules

that limited the number of baptized Jewish lawyers and made proposals to bar converted Jewish youth from admission to military
schools.[128]

By the 1860s, despite the growing involvement of individual Jews
in Russian society, the annual average number of Jewish converts to
Russian Orthodoxy had declined to 460. The desperation that many
Jews felt after the outbreak of the pogroms undoubtedly explains the
increase in the annual average number in the mid-1880s to 700. Between 1890 and 1905, as the fear of anti-Semitism subsided and hope
was expressed in the possibility of civil equality for Jews, the number
returned to prepogrom figures of approximately 500 a year. By the
end of the nineteenth century, it is estimated that there were between
30,000 and 80,000 Jewish converts to Christianity in the empire.[129]

By far the most bizarre reflection of the appeal of Christianity to
young Jewish intellectuals was the creation of two syncretistic religious
movements, the Spiritual-Bible Brotherhood, founded by the playwright Jacob Gordin in Elizabethgrad in 1879, and New Israel, established by Jacob Priluker, a teacher in a government Jewish school in
Odessa, early in 1880. Both movements advocated the abolition of
specific Jewish ritual observances and sought to create farming com-
munes to be settled jointly by Jews and Russian dissenters. Priluker,
for example, described his goals as "a reformed synagogue, a mitiga-
tion of the cleavage between Jew and Christian, and recognition of a
common brotherhood in religion."[130] Such movements appear to have
appealed to desperate Jews in the more assimilated southern regions
of the Pale as a means of maintaining some tie to their Jewish heritage
while at the same time avoiding the more stringent demands of Russian Orthodoxy. At first, Jews flocked to services led by Jewish-Christian groups, if only to hear a Yiddish sermon on Jesus. Interest soon
waned, however, as the novelty wore off.[131] The general lack of Jewish
support led to the merger of the two movements in 1884. In 1891,
Priluker left for England, where he converted to Lutheranism. In the
same year, Gordin settled in America, where he would soon begin a
successful career as a Yiddish playwright.[132]

The failure of the efforts of the maskilim at educational reform
and the limited success of the Russifiers forced young Jewish intellectuals to question their assumptions about the viability of Jewish
emancipation in Russian society. The result was a growing realization that whatever the process of integration may have meant to indi-

vidual Jews, it was clearly inapplicable as a solution to the plight of Russian Jewry en masse. In emphasizing the need for a balance between Jewish interests and loyalty to the larger society, assimilationist schemes had little relevance for the vast majority of Jews in Russia, who faced physical oppression and political persecution and whose interests lay in the social, economic, and cultural revival of Jewry as a whole. In the highly charged political atmosphere of eastern Europe, assimilation connoted denationalization, a conscious act of national suicide as opposed to the more gradual and often unconscious act of integration in the West.

In addition, Jewish modernizers soon grew to recognize that Russian society was unwilling to accept integration as a solution to the "Jewish problem." As noted earlier, Russian officials could not afford to grant equality to Jews without upsetting the fundamental institutions and behavioral patterns that characterized Russian society under tsarist rule. The emancipation of Jewry would have required a more liberal interpretation of citizenship and nationality and greater confidence in the government's ability to withstand significant change. It would also have necessitated greater wisdom and humanity on the part of tsarist officials.[133]

Nor was there any significant support for emancipation among the Russian middle class, whose counterparts in western and central Europe had often pressed for a more open society. Despite gradual economic expansion and growth, the Russian bourgeoisie remained relatively weak and highly dependent on the state for support. The fact that Russian Jews were largely merchants and tradesmen who were forced to compete in a limited economic environment not only isolated them from the peasant majority but also made them a distinct threat to groups who in other societies were their natural class allies. Unlike the situation in other countries, Russia's involvement in international trade was not significant enough to necessitate the granting of freedoms to more than a handful of Jews who maintained ties with coreligionists abroad.

Though supporters of classical liberalism could be found among a small group of commercial and industrial bourgeoisie as well as elements of the intelligentsia, their weak position, especially after the suppression of the Polish revolt in 1863, and their concern with Russian economic backwardness led them to emphasize individual freedom within the framework of traditional authority. Thus, for example, Russian liberals supported the abolition of serfdom, not because of its inherent injustice but because of its deleterious social and economic effect upon Russia. Not surprisingly, therefore, even political movements that favored the liberalization of the regime such as the Kadet party were averse to publicly supporting Jewish equality for fear of alienating both the peasant and bourgeois populations.[134] Despite their public professions of belief in the goodness of humanity, many Russian liberals shared the attitude of the Russian masses that Jews were corrupt, subversive of the socioeconomic order, and utterly alien. Though often opposed to segregation in the Pale, which they felt was largely responsible for the allegedly malevolent behavior of Jews, they generally agreed with their conservative opponents that only total Russification could solve the "Jewish problem."[135]

Nor would Jews find ready support among Russian radicals and revolutionaries. Despite the significant involvement of young Jews in the emerging revolutionary movements of the 1860s and '70s, Russian militants displayed little interest in the plight of Jews per se. Most Russian radicals were ardent assimilationists and assumed that problems of ethnic and national minorities would disappear in the general restructuring of a unified society that would follow a revolution. Such attitudes were often reinforced by young Jewish militants who saw participation in revolutionary activity as a means of demonstrating their unwavering commitment to general Russian society and culture. In addition, Russian radicals at the turn of the century generally shared the general opinion that Jews were an exploitative element in society, an attitude that became painfully evident in their support of pogroms in the 1880s as an expression of growing consciousness on the part of the Russian masses.[136] Even those Russian radicals who were seen by Jewish youth as spiritual leaders of their generation, such as Lavrov and the Marxist Georgy Plekhanov, generally remained silent in the face of anti-Semitic outrages in Russia for fear of alienating the peasant masses. As Lavrov stated in response to the Jewish activist Leib Deitsch who had denounced the refusal of Russian radicals to protest the outbreak of pogroms: "I must thank you [for your comments] . . . [nevertheless] I see the Jewish question as more complicated and from a practical standpoint—as extremely problematic for a party whose intention is to win over the masses and prepare it for the struggle against the regime; to solve the problem accordingly on paper may be simple. But in recognizing [that] the origins [of the problem] have become rooted among the masses and thus must be taken into account by socialists [who wish] to strengthen as much as possible the attachment of the nation to their cause—[that] is another matter entirely.[137]

Such developments clearly challenged the fundamental assumption of both maskilim and Russifiers that hostility toward Jews would decline as a result of the spread of "enlightenment." Even before the advent of the pogroms in the 1880s, the growing realization by Jewish intellectuals that assimilation was impossible for the mass of Jewry had already led to profound resentment over the attempts to mimic Russian intellectual thought and social behavior and to a re-evaluation of the distinctiveness of Jewish values and traditions. In particular, the famine of 1868–69, which devastated the northwestern section of the Pale, turned attention away from Russian-inspired spiritual renewal and government-sponsored educational reform and toward mustering strength within the community to meet the pressing needs for food, clothing, and shelter.[138] The new generation of the 1870s and '80s would find little in the early Haskalah that answered their profound psychological and social needs.

The outbreak of pogroms in 1881–82 would deal the final blow to most dreams of a Russian-Jewish symbiosis. Scattered pogroms had occurred throughout the reign of Alexander II, most notably in Odessa in 1871. For the most part, they reflected the continuing socioeconomic tensions between Jewish merchants and peasants. Anti-Jewish sentiments were also fueled by the publication of a number of pseudoscientific works in the 1860s and '70s that purported to demonstrate Jewish desires to dominate Russian society. Of particular importance was Jacob Brafman's *Kniga kagala* (The Book of the Kahal), published in 1869, which had a wide following not only among Russian intellectuals but also within official tsarist circles. A Jewish convert to Russian Orthodoxy and later an adviser to the government on Jewish affairs, Brafman meticulously chronicled the alleged conspiracy by leaders of the Jewish community to control the Russian economy and to weaken the Russian state. Brafman's work was quickly followed by a spate of other anti-Semitic treatises which attempted to prove that Jewish law condoned ritual murder and preached unremitting hostility toward Christianity. Largely under the influence of such writings, government leaders increasingly began to call for severe restrictions upon Jewish communal activity and religious practice.[139]

Anti-Semitic sentiments were given a further boost by the Russo-Turkish War of 1873–74. In a climate of intense pan-Slavism, fantastic stories concerning alleged Jewish corruption, embezzlement, and cowardice spread throughout the Russian political and economic elite. According to one rumor, Russian Jews were allied with the British prime minister Benjamin Disraeli in a conspiracy to rob the empire of a clear-cut victory through artful diplomatic maneuvering at the Congress of Berlin. The 1870s also saw the emergence of anti-Semitic sentiments in Russian bourgeois circles. Many members of the emerging middle class openly expressed fears that the potential emancipation of Jewry would lead to their swamping of the liberal professions and industry and would increase revolutionary activity.[140]

The pogroms of 1881–82 thus broke out in a climate of economic and political crisis and xenophobic fear. The timing of the pogroms mirrored previous anti-Jewish riots that generally occurred shortly before Easter, when celebrations of the Resurrection stirred up images of Jews as Christ killers. The immediate cause was the general confusion and chaos that followed the assassination of Alexander II in March 1881 by members of the Russian terrorist organization Narodnaya Volya. Rumors soon spread that Jews had masterminded the assassination and that government leaders had authorized attacks on them. The first pogroms occurred in the town of Elizabethgrad in the Ukraine in April and quickly spread to about thirty other villages in the southern and southwestern regions of the Pale. Though hostility toward Jews was stronger in the more concentrated and traditional Jewish areas of the northern Pale, it appears that specific conditions in the more developed and "freer" south helped to trigger the violence. These conditions included the local population's general attitude toward authority, which one historian has described as "active frontier rebelliousness"; the chaotic nature of local administration; the difficulties of controlling disturbances in towns as opposed to rural areas; and the effect of new economic opportunities, which created expectations of quick financial gain and heightened tensions between Jewish and non-Jewish parvenus.[141] For the most part, the riots seemed to be restricted to destruction of property and limited beatings and were generally instigated by local mobs. Modern scholarship has concluded that tsarist officials had little involvement in the initiation of the riots. Nevertheless, local officials were often implicated in the violence and government troops often stood idly by during the riots. By the summer of 1882 the pogroms had subsided, though there were occasional outbursts throughout Russia in 1883 and again in 1884.[142]

Tsarist officials responded to the anti-Jewish riots by hardening their attitudes and policies toward Jews. A subtle but clear shift could be discerned in government discussions of the "Jewish question" from an emphasis upon the difficulties involved in changing Jewish attitudes and behavior to a view of Jews as permanent aliens. The issuance of the May Laws of 1882, mentioned earlier, signaled a triumph for conservative forces concerned about protecting Russian peasants from "Jewish exploitation" and marked the end of attempts to assimilate Jews into society. As the deliberations of the Pahlen Commission charged with reviewing existing laws concerning Jews revealed, government officials increasingly viewed the "Jewish problem" as a biological issue. The decree of 1891, which expelled most Jews from Moscow, and the City Statute of 1892, which barred Jews from participation in local government, seemed to point to a new and more ominous policy in formation. Whether intentional or not, the escalation in government hostility toward Jews after the accession of Alexander III to power played an important role in the resumption of pogroms in the last four years of the century.[143]

The outbreak of pogroms also marked the beginnings of significant migration of Russian Jews. Though, as we have seen, emigration was a constant factor in Russian Jewish life from the 1820s, the new wave triggered by the pogroms was significant for its size—some 2 million in less than twenty years—and the underlying desperation that fueled the exodus. In contrast to previous migrations, which were largely motivated by economic deprivation and primarily affected the northwest sections of the Pale, most immigrants after 1880 came from southern Russia, fleeing political and religious persecution. In forcing many Russian Jews to seek a freer and more open society, the pogroms unintentionally accelerated the process of Jewish modernization, thus partially accomplishing what the government's carrot-and-stick policy had failed to do in the preceding three-quarters of a century.

The relationship between emigration and Jewish renewal was first given organized expression in Am Olam, a movement dedicated to the establishment of agricultural settlements in the United States. Founded in Odessa in 1881 before the outbreak of the pogroms, the movement quickly spread to other cities throughout the Pale. Several hundred young idealists helped establish colonies in Louisiana, South Dakota, and Oregon. As with most utopian communities, however, the lack of practical experience and internal quarrels ultimately led to the collapse of the colonies. By 1890, Am Olam had ceased to exist.[144]

Most Jewish modernizers rejected mass emigration to the West as a long-range solution, since they were convinced that it would only lead to the replication of conditions in Russia. Activists were also concerned that the wave of emigration would trigger panic in the Russian Jewish community, hindering efforts at a rational analysis of and solution to the "Jewish problem" within the Pale. Even before the outbreak of pogroms, they had concluded that the solution to the Jewish plight would have to be found within an existing Jewish community, either in a restructured Russia or in a new Jewish society in Palestine. Such approaches implied a recognition that the fate of Jewry lay in the hands of Jewry themselves. In contrast to the West, Jewish modernization in Russia would take the form of "autoemancipation," an inner-directed movement for Jewish revival which recognized that individual self-betterment could never be achieved without advancement of the community as a whole.

The onset of the pogroms accelerated processes for change within the Jewish community that were already visible during the late 1870s and early '80s. Among them was the return of a significant number of Jewish intellectuals to the Jewish fold. The development of embryonic movements of national revival within the community, the need to find an arena for emerging programs for social and economic change, and a growing awareness of the existence of the Jewish intelligentsia as a distinct social and cultural group, all played a role in the intellectuals' return. Disappointment with the response of Russian revolutionaries to the pogroms led to the emergence of a new slogan among young Jews: *Para domoi* ("It is time to go home").[145] Intellectuals such as Haim Zhitlowski, Simon Dubnow, and Ahad Ha-Am now found a ready audience for their ideas. The concerns expressed by such thinkers were not only for the physical safety of the community but also for its spiritual and cultural survival. They would now help direct an intellectual elite which, drawing upon Jewry's long and rich history, could develop the appropriate institutions and beliefs that would guide it boldly into the twentieth century.

Even Jewish Russifiers now began to turn inward, as the many articles and essays in the Russian-language publication *Voskhod*

(Dawn), founded in 1881, clearly demonstrate.[146] For many of the relatively assimilated and well-to-do Jews who inhabited cities outside the Pale, the "Jewish question" had been seen as primarily a legal and economic issue that would be solved as soon as anti-Semitic legislation restricting Jewish occupations was abolished. Now, in the period after the outbreak of pogroms, Russified Jews assumed a more active role by countering anti-Jewish sentiment voiced by Russian opinion and policy makers in the general press and in literary and government circles. More significantly, prominent Jews in St. Petersburg and Moscow began to become more involved in communal affairs. Through the activities of the Society for the Promotion of Enlightenment among Jews in Russia, they attempted to create new schools and curricula for the Jewish settlements of the Pale. Others supported the efforts of the Society for Spreading [Artisan and Agricultural] Work [Among Jews] (known as ORT, an abbreviation of its Russian name), which was established in 1880 to develop vocational training programs in Russia. Still others aided Baron de Hirsch's Jewish Colonization Association (ICA) in its various colonization efforts in Argentina. It was in this milieu that Simon Dubnow would first present his proposals for the development of a modern Jewish community in the Diaspora.

A far different approach was taken by so-called Palestinophiles, proto-Zionists who began to call for the settlement of Russian Jews in Palestine in the 1870s. Of special significance were the activities of Hibbat Zion (Love of Zion), a group founded in Odessa in 1883 which was committed to the establishment of pioneering Jewish colonies in the Holy Land. Born less of economic and political reversal than of a sense of moral decay within the Russian Jewish community, Hibbat Zion gained a small but dedicated following among middle-class Jewish intellectuals in less traditional communities such as Odessa and Kharkov.

The ideology of the movement was largely derived from the works of two men, Peretz Smolenskin (c. 1840–85) and Leon Pinsker (1821–91). Writing from self-imposed exile in Vienna in the early 1870s, Smolenskin rejected both religious traditionalism and the Haskalah as solutions to the problems of Russian Jewry. Instead, he called for a recognition of the existence of a Jewish nation that necessitated in turn a new set of ideals grounded in the spiritual values of Jewish history. A decade later, Pinsker, a prominent doctor in Odessa, took up Smolenskin's challenge. In his famous work, *Autoemancipation*, published in 1882 after the outbreak of pogroms, he renounced his previous support of Russification and now applied his medical background to a pathological study of anti-Semitism. The continued existence of a Jewish minority in any society, he posited, was unhealthy for both Jews and non-Jews. The cure to Jewry's plight, Pinsker concluded, was a systematic effort to revitalize itself in its own land.

Coincident with the publication of Pinsker's work, precursors of Hibbat Zion began to experiment with settlement in Palestine. The first settlers arrived in Palestine in July 1882. Members of the so-called Bilu, a small group that drew its name from the Hebrew phrase in Isaiah, *Bet yaakov, likhu vi-nelkha* (House of Jacob, let us go), they had originally hoped to establish independent colonies that would serve as models for a new Jewish society. Unfortunately, they quickly found themselves forced to seek financial support from the French Jewish philanthropist, Baron Edmond de Rothschild, who cared little for notions of Jewish national revival and was primarily interested in ensuring the economic profitability of Jewish settlements in Palestine. Only a few scattered settlements established by Hibbat Zion were still functioning when Herzl founded the first Zionist Congress in 1897. Though early pioneering movements in Palestine were largely unsuccessful, the idealism and self-sacrifice of their leadership and followers would have an important influence on the development of Russian Zionism in the Herzlian era and East European Jewish nationalism in general during the late nineteenth century. As we shall see, it was in meetings of Hibbat Zion that Ahad Ha-Am first emerged as a leading spokesman for Jewish cultural renewal.

The 1880s would also see the first important developments in the creation of a specifically Jewish working-class movement. Like Zionism, Jewish socialism was rooted in general concerns that preceded the panic of the early 1880s. The development of a Jewish labor movement stemmed in large part from the social, economic, and cultural distinctiveness that marked Jewish working-class life in the Pale. The concentration of Jewish artisans in the cities of the Pale and the resultant immiseration, the general unwillingness of Jewish as well as non-Jewish employers to hire individuals whom they considered to be contentious and physically weak, the high level of literacy among Jewish artisans, the common bonds of religion and language, the growing experience in mounting strikes—all helped to solidify Jewish labor militancy in late-nineteenth-century Russia. The very same factors, however, also served to distance Jewish workers from the emerging Russian proletariat and led inevitably to the development of a separate Jewish trade union movement. As time went on, growing activism and self-confidence would lead early Jewish militants, including Haim Zhitlowski, to demand autonomous political and cultural institutions for the Jewish masses within a new revolutionary society to be established in Russia.[147]

Such attitudes would reach their culmination in the 1890s with the development of sophisticated organizations and programs of radical social and political change. In 1897, activists created both the modern Zionist movement and the Jewish Socialist Bund. The two movements would gain even further support and significance as a result of the militant response to the anti-Jewish riots in Kishinev, the capital of Bessarabia, in April 1903 and in Gomel in White Russia the following September. On the eve of World War I, Russian Jewish activists were deeply split ideologically between those who sought to integrate Jewry into an emerging Russian revolutionary movement and those who were convinced that the only salvation for Jews lay in the establishment of a separate homeland in Palestine. What united the two movements and defined them as "modern" was a shared vision of the need for an aggressive response to persecution, a reaction that signaled an important departure from previous Jewish responses to catastrophe.[148] Between them lay the vast majority of Jewry, uncertain of the present and concerned about the future.

Yet even before the rise of mass politics in the Russian Jewish community, there were already a prescient few at the end of the nineteenth century who had seen the need for a new Jewish perspective that resulted from the weakening of traditional institutions and beliefs. Of this modernizing generation whose ideas would provide the foundation for later activism, three stand out: Haim Zhitlowski, the advocate of Yiddishism and Jewish socialism; Simon Dubnow, the proponent of Jewish autonomism; and Ahad Ha-Am, the supporter of Jewish cultural renewal. Their goal was to channel the energy and enthusiasm engendered by the crisis facing the Russian Jewish community into the development of what they hoped would be a new "secular" foundation for Jewish life. The thoughts and activities of these three individuals illustrate the distinctive challenge and opportunities facing Russian Jewry on the eve of its entrance into the modern world.

Haim Zhitlowski

CHAPTER 2

HAIM ZHITLOWSKI

Language, Political Radicalism, and Modern Jewish Identity

THE EMPHASIS that many East European intellectuals placed upon Yiddish as the central element of a modern Jewish national identity demonstrates in a particularly striking manner the synthesis of tradition and modernity so typical of late-nineteenth-century Russian Jewish thought. Here was a centuries-old language, long associated with deeply rooted patterns of popular culture, that was to serve as the vehicle for the rejuvenation of a Jewish people. For Yiddishists, the linkage between old and new offered distinct advantages in their struggle for domination of the Jewish community. The fact that Yiddish was generally perceived as a language of the Jewish masses meant that it could serve as a bridge both to alienated Jewish workers and artisans within the community and to young intellectuals seeking to reintegrate themselves back into Jewish life. Most important, as opposed to other manifestations of secular Jewish identity in late-nineteenth-century Russia, a Yiddishist program seemed to allow for the creation of a collective Jewish consciousness with little or no effort. Because it drew upon the daily experiences and perceptions of the Russian Jewish masses, its proponents argued, Yiddishism did not necessitate the acceptance of a particular ideology to bind Jewry together.

Though claiming to be tolerant of all views, Yiddishism at the end of the nineteenth century found its most ardent defenders within Russian Jewish socialist circles. In general, left-wing militants viewed Yiddish as an authentic expression of the values and ideals of the

Jewish "proletariat" and a useful tool in their struggle against ideological enemies within the community. When Russifiers and Zionists derided Yiddish as a jargon that lacked formal rules and grammatical forms, Jewish socialists responded that the language's "primitive" nature only demonstrated its democratic roots. In attempting to ward off the attacks of rabbis and traditionalists who denounced them as "pagan rebels in Jewish garb," left-wing Yiddishists boldly proclaimed Yiddish culture as an alternative to a dying and irrelevant religion.[1] At the same time, they argued, since its most adept speakers—the poor, children, and women—were furthest removed from the political and religious elite, Yiddish could easily aid in reconnecting alienated radical intellectuals to the Jewish masses while at the same time serving as the basis for a modern progressive Jewish culture.[2]

As supporters of the struggle for Jewish rights in Russia and opponents of Zionist efforts to establish a Jewish homeland, most socialist militants linked Yiddishism with the cause of Diaspora nationalism. Jewish socialists portrayed Yiddish as the preeminent language of the Diaspora, a creative amalgam of the many cultures in which Jews had rooted themselves over the centuries. The close association of Yiddish with German, they maintained, made it particularly useful in bridging the gap between eastern and western Jews. In contrast to the esoteric nature of Hebrew and Zionist ideology, Yiddish was the language of pragmatism and realism. Unlike Hebrew and Zionist visions of the future, Yiddish language and culture already existed and did not have to be willed into being.

Ultimately, of course, the very strengths of Yiddish so championed by its supporters also proved to be debilitating weaknesses. Thus the reliance upon language as the basis of national identity proved difficult to maintain when juxtaposed against the "objective" territorial claims of Zionism. In turn, the romanticized image of Yiddish as a folk language often hindered the formulation of concrete programs and plans for defining the Jewish future. Finally, the Yiddishists' lack of a clearly defined and specifically "Jewish" perception and solution of the plight of Russian Jewry, which was trumpeted as proof of their tolerance of opposing points of view, in fact severely hampered their efforts to develop a distinctive program for Jewish renewal.[3]

The figure of Haim Zhitlowski points up both the opportunities and challenges that a Yiddishist/Diasporist position offered left-wing Jewish thinkers in late nineteenth-century Russia. An eclectic thinker whose views defy simple categorization, Zhitlowski was a proponent of almost every major progressive Russian and Jewish ideology at the end of the century, from Populism to autonomism, from radical socialism to left-wing Zionism. As such, he reflected both the confusion and the enthusiasm of his generation in its search for an appropriate response to the challenge of modernization.

Like his contemporary Nahman Syrkin, Zhitlowski's most noteworthy contribution to the development of a modern Jewish identity at the end of the nineteenth century was the melding of Jewish nationalist aspirations with classical socialist yearnings.[4] Despite his radical commitments, however, Zhitlowski was constantly in search of an ideological construct that would synthesize traditional Jewish concerns with modern European culture. Like other transitional thinkers, he was strongly attracted to modern ideas but could not break with the Jewish past. In his attempt to steer a path between what he regarded as the extremes of Zionist nationalist exclusivism and Russian socialist cosmopolitanism, Zhitlowski stressed the role of Yiddish as a portable national treasure that was easily accessible to the Russian Jewish masses and that reflected the best of Jewish collective existence in the Diaspora.

Ironically, Zhitlowski spent very little of his most productive years in his native land, preferring instead to preach his distinctive brand of Jewish nationalism to young Russian Jewish emigrés in western and central Europe. His writings became widely known in Russia only during World War I and again in 1917 as the result of the publication of his collected works in New York.[5] Similarly, his decision to go and work in the American Jewish community after the failure of the Revolution of 1905 may have been motivated in part by his desperate desire to seek out a virginal Jewish environment for the realization of his diverse programs. In this sense, his espousal of Yiddish may be seen as an attempt to find a common thread that would weave together the patchwork quilt of ideological perspectives he espoused during more than sixty years of tireless activity on two continents and in five countries.

Zhitlowski's geographical and ideological wanderings meant that he had a mixed influence upon the members of the young generation of activists who read his works and heard his speeches. On the one hand, Zhitlowski's failure to establish himself in any one organization or movement clearly limited his effectiveness. On the other, his multivaried ideology gave Zhitlowski a unique status among transitional thinkers as an individual who was able to transcend the petty squabbling of narrow party interests to speak to what he believed were the interests of the Jewish people as a whole.[6]

Despite his efforts to secure a new foundation for Jewish identity in the freer atmospheres of central Europe and the United States, Zhitlowski remained wedded to the East European Jewish experience of the late nineteenth century. His ideological crusade and tireless journeys throughout the Jewish world would carry him through a momentous period of modern Jewish history that included two world wars, the foundation of the *yishuv*, the massive immigration of East European Jews to America, the Bolshevik Revolution and Stalinism, and the rise of Nazism. Yet Zhitlowski remained a figure of the transitional generation throughout his life. For all his social, economic, and political radicalism that seemed to separate him from the more cautious perspectives of individuals like Dubnow and Ahad Ha-Am, Zhitlowski was more a "rebel of the word" than a revolutionary of the deed, an individual who was far more comfortable with idealizing than with actualizing the Jewish future.[7] Like Dubnow and Ahad Ha-Am, he remained convinced that only a firm sense of Jewish self-consciousness grounded in the values and ideals of the Jewish past as developed in eastern Europe could ensure Jewish survival and growth in the future.

Haim Zhitlowski was born in 1865 in the rural backwater town of Ushatz (Ushatsi) in the Vitebsk region of White Russia. In his memoirs published in the 1930s, Zhitlowski notes that for most of his youth he believed that he lived in a self-contained and all-inclusive "Jewish Land."[8] In many ways, it was an accurate perception that undoubtedly influenced his later espousal of Diaspora nationalism. At the end of the nineteenth century, 35,000 of the residents of Ushatz were Jewish, nearly 78 percent of the total population of almost 45,000.[9] Nevertheless, during Zhitlowski's youth the area was in the throes of economic modernization as the result of the completion of a railroad linking the Baltic Sea with Germany. Jewish merchants and tradesmen (including Zhitlowski's own father) clearly benefited from economic expansion. Zhitlowski thus experienced at an early age the impact of rapid social and economic change upon traditional institutions and values.

As was the case with many of his contemporaries, Zhitlowski's family reflected the mingling of traditional Judaism with the forces sweeping through the East European Jewish community in the latter half of the nineteenth century. His mother came from a strict Hasidic home. Her father, who seemed to be in continual conflict with Haim, had studied in the famous Volozhin yeshiva and had served as a rabbi in a congregation for a short time. In contrast, Zhitlowski's father, Yosef, embodied the ideological syncretism that would later characterize his son's intellectual development. Though he came from a religious anti-Hasidic, or misnagdic, background, he soon became affiliated with the Lubavitcher movement that dominated the region and that had undoubtedly penetrated his father-in-law's home. At the same time, the elder Zhitlowski delighted in attending operas on his business travels to Riga, Danzig, and Königsberg as a buyer of flax for an English firm. He also prided himself on reading the literature of the Haskalah and writing Hebrew poetry. A strong Polonophile and Germanophile despite his insistence upon speaking Yiddish at home, he impressed the young Haim with an appreciation of national difference. He also provided Zhitlowski with an early example of the synthesis between communal loyalty and cosmopolitanism that the latter would later develop as a central component of his new Jewish identity.[10]

A major factor in Zhitlowski's early alienation from traditional Judaism appears to have been the decision by his family to move to Ushatz's city center in the 1870s. Within a short period of time, his mother stopped wearing a *sheytl* (the traditional wig worn by married Jewish women) and his father began to wear stylish short coats instead of the typical *kapote* (long coat) of the Hasidic community. In distancing himself from the Lubavitcher movement, Yosef Zhitlowski no longer engaged in religious study. Though these changes were typical of many Jews in the Pale, the idealistic adolescent decried his parents' decision as a betrayal of Jewish ethical values. Their religious worship, Zhitlowski would later write, had now been replaced by the "worship of money."[11]

It was during this period as well that the young man came into contact with non-Jews. As a result of his father's mistreatment of the peasants who worked in his home, Zhitlowski would state in his memoirs, he became increasing aware of how Jewish merchants exploited non-Jews through the sale of liquor and cheap industrial goods and the charging of exorbitant rent for land. He soon concluded that all Jews in the Russian capitalist system, both rich and poor, were "economic parasites . . . [who] fed upon the sucked-out juice" of Russian peasantry. Wherever he looked, he saw only one thing—the deleterious effect of Jewish trade and commerce on the Russian peasantry.[12]

As with many of Zhitlowski's retrospective writings, it is difficult to know how many of these recollections were filtered through his later ideology. Nevertheless, there seems little doubt that these early experiences deeply disturbed the young idealist and profoundly affected his more mature attitudes. Thus, for example, despite his later overtures to the Jewish petite bourgeoisie after his settlement in the United States, Zhitlowski would never lose both his visceral hatred of capitalism and his idealization of the peasant. Even in his more sophisticated analytical writings in the 1920s and '30s, he continued to frame his critique of capitalist activity almost exclusively in moralistic terms and to press the case for agrarian socialism.[13] Similarly, Zhitlowski continued to express throughout his life a contempt for rabbinic Judaism; in his mind, religious behavior was little more than mechanical observance. Yet he could never fully escape his family's religious heritage. For all his hostility toward Orthodox belief and practice, he maintained a deep admiration for what he believed were the underlying ethical ideals of traditional Judaism. Like others of his generation, Zhitlowski would spend his life attempting to reaffirm them in a modern "secular" form.

The decreasing interest in religious life at home alienated Zhitlowski from Jewish belief and practice. So too did his bitter experiences in heder, or religious school. Steeped in a romantic Hasidic tradition that he treasured throughout his life, Zhitlowski recalled in his memoirs his longing in childhood for a poetic and spiritual religious experience. Instead, he found an educational system characterized by rote memorization and strict discipline. The fact that Zhitlowski took private lessons in both Hebrew and Russian while attending heder may have also influenced his negative view of his religious training.

Zhitlowski's hostility toward Judaism was reinforced in the late 1870s when his parents allowed him to enroll at the gymnasium, or high school, in Vitebsk. It was here that he had his first contact with revolutionary youth, most of whom were not Jewish. It was during this period, as well, that Zhitlowski engaged in impassioned debate over the fate of Jewry and socialism with his childhood friend Shlomo Anski. Anski, a fiery speaker and writer who would later have an active career as a radical Populist before becoming a prominent Yiddish playwright, constantly impressed upon the young Haim the need to abandon the corrupt and limiting confines of the Jewish community and to seek out the invigorating atmosphere of Russian society. By 1879, Zhitlowski claims, he had become an atheist and a revolutionary socialist.[14]

In 1881, Zhitlowski left the gymnasium. A year later, after a bitter quarrel with his father over his newfound radical beliefs, he decided to enter a new school in the neighboring city of Tula, which lay just outside the boundaries of the Pale. Zhitlowski described his year there as the low point in his attachment to Judaism. In the highly assimilationist environment of the small Tula Jewish community, which was comprised largely of "cantonists," he seemed to have been almost totally oblivious to the growing Jewish panic over the outbreak of pogroms. Struggling to become fully assimilated, Zhitlowski appears to have spent much of his time reading Russian literature and poetry. Already an avid autodidact, he was especially enamored with N.G. Chernyshevski's *What Is To Be Done?*, which he claimed was instrumental in deepening his knowledge of economics and of socialism in particular. It was in honor of the great Russian writer and social critic that Zhitlowski decided to adopt a Russian name— Yefim Ossipovich (Haim son of Joseph).[15] In addition to reading, Zhitlowski took an active part in the local student group of Narodnaya Volya, the movement of radical Populism that preached a form of agrarian socialism based on a romanticized image of peasant and artisan society and production. Unlike his friend Anski, however, he did not spend much time with local peasants. He much preferred the idealized vision of rural life that he found in Populist tracts.

It is not exactly clear what brought Zhitlowski back to the Jewish community, if indeed he ever clearly left it. One must remember that he was only in his early teens when he departed for Tula. Much of his negative response to Jewish life represented little more than an adolescent's rebellion against his father. Yet Zhitlowski seems to have idolized his father; hence his choice of a Russian name. The frequent bitter criticisms of the older Zhitlowski in the early part of his memoirs suggest more disappointment than disdain. Zhitlowski would later claim, for example, that a major turning point in his attitude toward religious Orthodoxy occurred when his father became drunk in front of a religious friend. Morally outraged, the young Haim was troubled not so much by the act itself as by the failure of a believer to adhere to the tenets of his faith. For Zhitlowski, the incident signaled the end of his association with Hasidism. "A torch was extinguished," he would note in his recollection of the event a half century later, "and none was lit in its place."[16] A poignant story, to be sure, yet the truth is that however much the event may have disturbed Zhitlowski, it did not lead him to break with family and tradition. Despite his seemingly uncompromising attitude, he continued to live at home for another decade in a situation of relative harmony and peace. His parents tolerated his revolutionary ideas as long as the young Haim agreed to participate in religious ceremonies at home.[17]

In his own retrospective account of his sudden and dramatic "return," Zhitlowski assumed the epiphanic style of other Jewish writers of the period who chronicled their alienation and renewal. A visit to his home in Ushatz at the insistence of his mother rekindled pleasant memories of his youth and pointed up the visceral differences that he felt existed between Jews and non-Jews in Tula. Walking through the Jewish cemetery, he heard a young woman weeping beside the grave of her husband. "To whom have you abandoned me?" she cried. Zhitlowski, moved by the scene, vowed never again to desert the Jewish people. Whatever the factors that led to Zhitlowski's change of heart, his flirtation with radical assimilationism did not last long. By the spring of 1884, he began to use his original Hebrew name, Haim, as a sign of his return to the Jewish fold.[18]

It seems likely that Zhitlowski's romanticized account of his "change of heart" reflected his attempt to personally symbolize the general soul-searching that affected young Jewish intellectuals in the 1880s. Yet unlike many other young Jewish modernizers, his return to the community did not diminish his ardor for socialism. One of the first authors Zhitlowski read upon his return to Jewish life was Moshe Leib Lilienblum. Though Lilienblum would later become one of the ideological founders of Hibbat Zion, in his early works written in the 1860s and '70s he had trumpeted the virtues of socialism and had called for the normalization of Jewish life through agricultural labor. Lilienblum's autobiography, *Hataot neurim* (Sins of Youth), published in the mid-1870s, was widely ready by many of Zhitlowski's fellow Jewish intellectuals.[19] At the same time, Zhitlowski continued to spread the message of Populism among his fellow students in the Tula gymnasium. Though he was disturbed by the failure of Russian radicals to condemn the pogroms, it did little to discredit the ideology of agrarian socialism in his eyes.

Not surprisingly, therefore, at times Zhitlowski seemed almost apologetic about his renewed loyalty to Jewry. Defending his active commitment to Jews in the 1880s, he would later maintain that he would have accepted assimilation as the ideal solution if he had been able to approach the "Jewish" problem logically and analytically.[20] At the same time, Zhitlowski was insistent that he was not a "klal-yisrueldike" isolationist, that is, an individual who was only concerned about the fate of Jewry. In attempting to synthesize his early experiences of Judaism and socialism, Zhitlowski would claim that his decision to fulfill his responsibility toward the Jewish people was predicated on a belief that only through a commitment to one's own nationality could the ideals of universal brotherhood and equality be fulfilled. More than any other factor, it was the antipodal pull of Russian and Jewish loyalties formulated in Zhitlowski's youth that explains the idiosyncrasies that emerged after his "return," including his eclectic views, his fascination with dialectics, and his continual jockeying between Jewish and general Russian movements. Shlomo Anski correctly characterized his childhood friend's own views when in 1912 he characterized Zhitlowski's ideological peripatetics as "only a restless search for the right path."[21]

For the remainder of his life, Zhitlowski would search for an appropriate ideological formulation that would incorporate his opposing views. At first, he attempted to find a spiritual home among the movements of national renewal that were developing within the Jewish community in the wake of the pogroms. In 1883, he returned from Tula to Vitebsk and became involved in the local branch of Hibbat Zion. Zhitlowski initially voiced optimism that the Palestinophilic movement would offer him a way to synthesize his growing Jewish nationalist sentiments with his agrarian socialist views. As he noted in his memoirs, he was convinced that the "communist students" of Hibbat Zion were establishing a new covenant, a "socialist Torah."[22] Yet Zhitlowski soon found himself repelled by the movement's "religious-reactionary" nature and especially by what he believed was its kowtowing to rabbinic leadership and corrupt businessmen. The Palestinophiles could not pass the simple test that was demanded of every movement: "A pure cause demands clean hands."[23] True to his dual commitments, Zhitlowski argued that there was a need for a solution to the Jewish problem that was compatible with social and economic equality for all of humanity. Jews must not live in the Palestinian past but instead must help to build a new future as part of a general revolution in Russia led by Narodnaya Volya.

Alienated by the "narrow-mindedness" of nationalists within the Jewish community, Zhitlowski now attempted to approach the problem of Jewish collective identity through participation in the Russian revolutionary movement. In late 1883, he joined the local Narodnik group as a "nationalist Jew" and began to espouse the ideals of Yiddishism and Jewish Diaspora nationalism. Yet his synthesis of universalist and Jewish concerns found little favor among Populist militants in Vitebsk. His application to create a separate Jewish branch and newspaper, which he called *Tshues Yisroel* (Salvation of Israel), was rejected by the Executive Committee of Narodnaya Volya, the majority of whom were Jewish.[24] Nor did he have much success in countering the growing appeal of Palestinophilism among young Vitebsker Jews. In 1886, he decided to go to St. Petersburg, in part to join up with what he hoped to be a more tolerant and responsive Populist movement, in part to use the state library to deepen his understanding of Jewish history.

Attending classes at the University of St. Petersburg, Zhitlowski came under the influence of a professor of law who stressed the role of deeply rooted national sentiments in shaping a country's legal tradition. The young Jewish intellectual now became increasingly convinced of the need to offer a "scientific" explanation for Jewish national survival over the centuries. In an attempt both to satisfy his socialist critics and to counter what he believed to be the romanticized views of Palestinophiles, Zhitlowski was moved in 1887 to publish his first essay, "Thoughts on the Historical Destiny of Judaism." A synopsis of his research and thought since his arrival in the Russian capital, the essay traced the history of the Jewish people with particular emphasis upon the distinctive contribution that Zhitlowski was convinced Jewry was fated to make to humanity as a whole.

Rejecting traditional religious explanations of chosenness, Zhitlowski argued that the true source of Jewish distinctiveness lay in its social and moral ideal as embodied in the writings of the biblical Prophets and in the communal life of the Essenes, the obscure sect of millenarians who were active during the period of the Second Temple and whose ideas were said to have had an important influence on the teachings of Jesus. Defeat at the hands of Rome and the onset of the Diaspora, Zhitlowski claimed, forced Jewry to redirect its concerns from social justice to national survival and to transform the basis of its existence from ethical idealism to religion. It was the ossification of religious belief and practice and the attendant deterioration of the Jewish moral individual through the centuries that explained the decadence of contemporary Jewish life and had raised concern among committed intellectuals over the fate of the Jewish people. In choosing a path to personal and national growth, Zhitlowski argued, modern Jews were caught between the extremes of assimilationism in the West and Zionist isolationism in the East. Zhitlowski concluded his work by suggesting the possibility of a third way: the revival of ancient ethical ideals that would serve both to preserve Jewry and to reintegrate the Jewish people into the mainstream of progressive human history.

Written in Russian and thus inaccessible to many Jews, "Thoughts on the Historical Destiny of Judaism" nevertheless was banned by government censors who overestimated Zhitlowski's influence within the Jewish community. The government action forced the young intellectual to publish the tract abroad. As a result, it did not become known to the Russian Jewish public until decades later when it was included in Zhitlowski's collected works. Outside Russia, the essay appears to have been warmly received among the small radical emigré communities of Germany and Switzerland. Within Russia itself, its publication received a mixed response from the few who did manage to read it. The radical Russian press generally applauded the essay's appearance. Understandably, it downplayed Zhitlowski's preachments of Jewish nationalism while emphasizing his effort to link Jewish values with socialism. Russian reactionaries quoted the work to prove that Jews were parasites and exploiters of the peasantry. Jewish intellectuals and community leaders in Russia, on the other hand, were appalled by many of its basic arguments. Having recently "returned" himself to the Jewish people, Simon Dubnow denounced it in the pages of the Russian Jewish journal *Voskhod* as a confused and dangerous tract. Specifically, he attacked Zhitlowski's positive view of early Christianity as reflected in the teachings of the Essenes, which he claimed would lead to mass conversion while creating the impression among Russian readers that the acceptance of Christianity by masses of Jews would obviate the need for the granting of civil rights.

The work was also condemned by Palestinophiles and Orthodox Jewish leaders, both of whom regarded Zhitlowski as betraying the interests of the Jewish people.[25] For his part, Zhitlowski saw the negative response to his work by the Jewish "establishment" as a confirmation of the correctness of his views concerning the dangers of rabbinism, assimilationism, and Palestinophilism. He now proudly proclaimed himself the enfant terrible of the Jewish people.[26]

Frustrated by the attitude and behavior of socialist militants and Jewish intellectuals within Russia and frightened by the actions taken against his essay by government officials, Zhitlowski was eager to discover the radical and Jewish world beyond the borders of Russia. In the summer of 1888 he decided to leave for Berlin, whose small but active Russian Jewish emigré community had responded enthusiastically to his essay.[27] When government antisocialist laws forced Zhitlowski out of the German capital at the end of August, he chose to settle in Zurich. There he began to work with a fledgling Jewish socialist organization that had begun to publish works on socialism in Yiddish.[28] In 1891, Zhitlowski was on the move again. This time, he settled in Bern. Within a short time he had assumed the leadership of a Populist student movement opposed to the Marxist ideology of George Plekhanov that had begun to gain dominance in the Russian emigré community. In 1892, he and a group of local Hibbat Zion students in the Swiss capital founded the Yiddish-speaking Farayn far vissenshaft un lebn dem yidishn folkes (Association for the Study and Life of the Jewish People), an informal study group that served largely as a forum for various Jewish socialist and nationalist emigré thinkers. Yet Zhitlowski's first love remained philosophical speculation. In 1892, despite his intensive political and cultural activity, he managed to earn a doctorate for a work on the influence of Aristotelianism on Jewish religious thought.[29]

The 1890s would see a significant influx of bright and motivated Jewish students into Switzerland, largely as a result of the imposition of a numerus clausus on Jewish enrollment at Russian universities. They soon became a majority of the Swiss emigré colony. Many eagerly responded to Zhitlowski's fiery appeals for a synthesis of socialist and nationalist ideals and he soon became a frequent speaker at student meetings. His handsome looks, poise, and academic bearing gave him a significant advantage over his ideological rivals within the emigré community. Zhitlowski would remain in Switzerland until

1903, when the combination of his wife's affair with a young student and events in the Pale of Settlement would lead him first to journey to the United States and then home again to Russia.

In an effort to unite the disparate groups of Populists and Palestinophiles that made up the Jewish emigré community, Zhitlowski decided to publish a revised statement of his perspectives on socialism and the "Jewish question." The result was the Yiddish tract *A Id tsu idn* (A Jew Speaks to Jews), which appeared in 1892. More sophisticated than his first effort five years earlier and more directly targeted to a Jewish audience, the work was meant to map out an activist position for Zhitlowski that was distinct from both proto-Zionism and Russian social activism.[30] Mixing elements of Jewish nationalism and Populist socialism, Zhitlowski argued for a radical change in the Jewish social structure. In casting off its capitalist past and embracing manual labor, a revitalized Jewry could make a major contribution to social and economic change. Denouncing western emancipationism, Russian assimilationism, and Palestinophilism, Zhitlowski called for a return of Jewish intellectuals to help in the community's effort at national renewal within the boundaries of a revitalized Russia.[31]

Despite its naiveté and glibness, *A Id tsu idn* is a remarkable document. For the first time in eastern Europe, a Jewish activist was criticizing the regnant socialist solution to the Jewish problem—assimilationism. By offering a significant alternative to Palestinophilism, Zhitlowski's perspective enabled many intellectuals who wished to remain in Russia to reestablish their ties with the Jewish community. In linking Jewish national revival with socialist revolutionism, Zhitlowski offered Jewish activists a way of maintaining their allegiance to the Russian socialist movement. It would take another five years for his ideas to find political and practical expression in the Jewish Socialist Bund. During the early 1890s, Zhitlowski had yet to find a significant audience within the Jewish community in Russia for his ideas.

Much of Zhitlowski's activity over the next decade reflected his continuing attempt to meld general socialist and Jewish concerns. As his ideas began to become known among young Jewish intellectuals, his focus shifted from an evaluation of Jewish history and thought along with criticism of alternative ideologies of Jewish modernization to what the Russian Jewish historian Jonathan Frankel has called "the theory and strategy of mass mobilization."[32] Yet, like most of his contemporaries, Zhitlowski was unable to effectively respond to the challenge. The rapidly shifting political and economic climate within both Russia and the Jewish community thwarted his effort to establish a firm position and led him to espouse a variety of stances over the next twenty years, from agrarian socialism to territorialism and finally to Yiddishism.

Throughout his ideological peripatetics and despite disagreements with the Populist leadership over the role of the Jewish people in a future society, Zhitlowski's loyalties remained with the agrarian socialist movement. In 1893, he was one of seven founders of a student group in Bern that would serve as the basis of the Socialist Revolutionary Party. The SRs, as they were popularly known, were pledged to change within Russian society based on the model of a peasant community. Between 1900 and 1903, Zhitlowski continued his work within Russian revolutionary circles as an active member of the SRs and the so-called Young Narodniks. His proposals for an agrarian socialist solution to the Jewish problem, originally mapped out in *A Id tsu idn*, now became closely linked to the SRs' vision of the future Russian society. Jews must return en masse to the land and to agricultural labor, Zhitlowski had insisted in the tract. In this way, they would demonstrate their loyalty to Russia and gain the respect of the peasantry who historically looked upon Jews as exploiters and parasites. Once they became true "proletarians," he now argued, the Jewish masses would earn the right to become full participants in the SRs' plan for a federation of nations that would serve as the basis of the future Russian society.[33]

In attempting to mobilize the Jewish masses and to counter the influence of alternative programs of national revival within the Jewish community, Zhitlowski increasingly stressed the role of the Yiddish language. As he noted in an article entitled "Farvus davke yidish?" (Why Necessarily Yiddish?), written in 1897 and published in the New York Yiddish daily *Der Forvertz* (The Jewish Daily Forward) in 1900, Yiddish was a bridge between the Jewish and socialist worlds and an invaluable weapon against both religious traditionalists and Zionists within the Jewish community.[34] Speaking at a Yiddishist meeting held immediately following the First Zionist Congress in 1897, Zhitlowski championed a distinctive Jewish language as an alternative to utopian visions of land and pleaded with intellectuals to learn Yiddish in order to reassume their leadership of the Jewish masses.

During the same period, Zhitlowski's hostility toward Zionism continued to grow. Shortly after the convening of the First Zionist Congress in 1897, he published an article entitled "Tsionizmus oder sotsializmus" (Zionism or Socialism). Originally appearing in the Bundist newspaper *Der Yidisher arbeter* (The Jewish Worker) in 1898, the article boldly proclaimed the demise of Theodor Herzl's movement. Despite its infancy, Zhitlowski argued, Zionism had already proved to be a great disappointment to young Jewish intellectuals because of its middle-class and clerical leadership. The simple truth that Zionists refused to admit was that Jews did not need a land to survive. At the same time, however, Zhitlowski shocked many Jewish socialists by demanding that they recognize the importance of Jewish nationalism. Indeed, activists should work to create a distinctive, unified, and developed Jewish culture under the guidance of secular intellectuals. Only then would the Jewish proletariat be able to take its rightful place in the struggle for socialism and freedom.[35]

In searching for a home for his ideas and a vehicle to realize his programs, Zhitlowski was naturally drawn to the Bund. Established in 1897, the Bund had already achieved significant success in a number of domains that were central to Zhitlowski's political agenda — the organization of the Jewish masses in defense of their collective rights in Russia, the reintegration of young militants within the Jewish community, and the involvement of the Jewish "proletariat" in the general struggle for a socialist Russia. In 1896, Zhitlowski had established a Yiddish group in Bern that published socialist works on Jewish and general themes. He was clearly pleased when he was called upon to contribute to *Der Yidisher arbeter*, the newspaper founded by the Bund in 1898. In joining the Bund a year later, Zhitlowski hoped to further his activity on behalf of Jewish socialism while at the same time lobbying for the inclusion of support for Yiddish into the platform of the organization.

Zhitlowski's association with the Bund would prove to be short-lived, however. In many ways, his rocky relationship with the Jewish socialist movement reflected the ideological and programmatic differences between the transitional generation and turn-of-the-century Jewish activists. Caught up in a vision of agrarian socialism, Zhitlowski could never fully accommodate himself to the Bund's exclusive emphasis upon the urban proletariat. In addition, his pen-

chant for freewheeling philosophical debate and his highly idiosyn-
cratic views placed him at odds with the ideological and administrative centralism of the Jewish socialist group and of Russian revolutionary movements of the period in general. According to his friend
Anski, Zhitlowski always voiced his disapproval of decisions made by
fiat and had "absolutely no understanding for politicking."[36]
Zhitlowski's willingness to voice his many concerns publicly only further angered many Bundist militants who were convinced of the need
for absolute loyalty to the dictates of the movement on the part of
the rank and file. Most important, the Bund's Marxist treatment of
the "Jewish question," especially its position of "neutralism" on the
question of Jewish national autonomy after the revolution and its alleged hostility toward intellectuals and their cultural activity among
the masses, raised serious questions in Zhitlowski's mind about the
movement's ability and willingness to develop and carry out an effective program of national regeneration.[37] In 1904, after bitter debate
with the Bundist leadership, he resigned from the Jewish socialist
group.[38]

One of the major reasons for Zhitlowski's break with the Bund was
his disagreement over the movement's meek response to the pogroms
in Kishinev in April 1903. While the Bund continued to speak in vague
terms of collective national rights within the general context of a future socialist society, Zhitlowski was clearly shaken by the brutal outbreak of anti-Semitism. Why, he wondered, didn't Russian socialists
speak out against this unspeakable horror? Proclaiming that hatred of
Jews was a fundamental reality in modern life, Zhitlowski now joined
with the Zionists in calling openly for a national homeland as a safe
haven for the oppressed Russian Jewish masses.

As a reflection of his growing interest in a territorial solution to
the "Jewish problem," in 1904 Zhitlowski agreed to meet with Theodor
Herzl during the Sixth Zionist Congress held in Basel, Switzerland.
Herzl, for his part, appears to have mistakenly assumed that Zhitlowski
was an active and leading member of the Bund. According to
Zhitlowski, the Zionist leader hoped to convince him to intercede
with his fellow militants to stop their revolutionary activity in exchange
for Russian government recognition of a charter with the Turkish
government for Palestine.[39] In the end, nothing much came of the
meeting. Zhitlowski emerged convinced that Herzl's dreams of establishing a Jewish homeland held little hope for the Jewish people.

Nevertheless, rapidly changing events that followed the meeting, including the hostile reaction of East European Zionists to Herzl's plan to settle Jews in Uganda and the inability of the Zionist leader to convince Russian Foreign Minister Vyacheslav von Plehve of the need to support his cause, convinced Zhitlowski of the need to look elsewhere for a concrete solution to the "Jewish problem." Herzl's death in 1904 only confirmed Zhitlowski's belief that Zionism was bankrupt. Undaunted, he now began to turn his attention to forging a territorialist solution for Jews within Russia itself.[40]

Already in 1903, Zhitlowski had helped create Vozrozhdenie (Rebirth), a splinter group of left-wing Jewish nationalists and "Zhitlowski-style" Socialist Revolutionaries who felt betrayed by Herzl's leadership of the Jewish nationalist movement. In particular, they were angered by the Zionist leader's accommodation with the tsarist government, his seeming unconcern with events in Russia, and his disdain for those among the Jewish masses who did not accept his views. At the same time, members of Vozrozhdenie were frustrated by the activities of the established Zionist Left. Many of the group's supporters had originally been members of Poale Zion (Workers of Zion), the leading socialist Zionist movement in Russia, which had been organized in 1903. They chose to break away from the Zionist movement, however, because of what they felt was its overemphasis on the distant goal of a Jewish homeland and its ignoring of the immediate needs of Russian Jewry.[41] In contrast to the passivity of Zionists of all stripes, Vozrozhdenie emphasized the need for an active response to anti-Semitism in Russia. Despite its hostility toward Zionism, however, the movement continued to stress the importance of a territorial solution to the "Jewish problem." Vozrozhdenie thus distanced itself from the Bund and Jewish civil rights activists in Russia who it claimed ignored the central ideal of a Jewish nation in its own land. Only the return of the Jewish people to the Land of Israel, leaders of the movement maintained, would ultimately rescue Jewry from economic, social, and political degradation.

While positing territorial concentration as a long-term objective, Vozrozhdenie argued that in the meantime it was possible to effect significant change in the Diaspora. Specifically, the movement called for ethnic minorities in Russia to have autonomous jurisdiction over all of their national affairs, advocated the formation of regional unions of communities, and demanded the convocation of a Jewish national assembly

(Sejm in Polish) to be elected by a universal, equal, direct, and secret ballot.[42] The movement was officially established at a meeting held at the congress of the Second International in Amsterdam in the summer of 1904. Vozrozhdenie's eclectic program, which included contrasting elements of Jewish self-defense, revolutionism, and territorialism all united under the banner of the call for national unity, encapsuled Zhitlowski's distinctive approach to the "Jewish problem." The socialist activist who had guided the movement from its infancy now had a platform and a political base which he could use to formulate a Diasporist program for Jewish renewal.

Despite his developing plans for Jewish life in a future Russian society, Zhitlowski had remained abroad since his departure for Berlin in 1888. In concentrating his attention on organizing and leading the young emigré communities in the freer environments of Germany and Switzerland, he was able to avoid the bitter struggles between Marxists and Bundists that characterized the activity of Jewish militants in the Pale. At the same time, Zhitlowski's experiences in central Europe deeply impressed him. It seems highly likely, for example, that his inclusion of autonomism in the platform of Vozrozhdenie stemmed in large part from his exposure to the Swiss cantonist system.[43] In addition, Zhitlowski was increasingly beginning to think in terms of an international Jewish organization that would coordinate the scattered efforts of East European settlements on the continent and in America on behalf of both Russian revolutionism and Jewish national revival. In 1904, for example, Zhitlowski had journeyed to the United States under the aegis of the Social Revolutionaries (and informally on behalf of members of the Vozrozhdenie group) to investigate and to establish links with the newly emerging Russian immigrant community. His visit appears to have been highly successful, highlighted by a clear "victory" over Abraham Cahan, the editor of the *Jewish Daily Forward*, in a debate on Marxism.[44] Though the visit was cut short by the outbreak of the Revolution of 1905 in Russia, Zhitlowski's positive initial encounter with America would have fateful consequences for his future political activity.

The 1905 Revolution brought Zhitlowski back hurriedly to Russia for the first time in nearly twenty years. In many ways, the events of 1905 reinforced Zhitlowski's Diasporist commitment by creating a groundswell of enthusiasm for change within the Jewish community while at the same time appearing to demonstrate the irrelevancy of a

Zionist solution. In 1906, Zhitlowski ran for the Vitebsk seat in the Duma on the newly created ticket of SERP or the Jewish Socialist Workers' Party. Party membership quickly grew to 13,000 within the space of a few months as elements of the Vozrozhdenie group who were convinced that the Revolution of 1905 offered Jews the possibility of significant political change and socialist Zionists who were disappointed with the pronouncements of the Zionist congresses flocked to its banner.[45] The platform of SERP was a statement of Zhitlowski's own political program: national personal autonomy for every Jew no matter where he or she lived in Russia, the realization of Jewish communal autonomy, and the development of agrarian socialism within a liberated Russia. Supporters of SERP were also known as "Sejmists," a name that had first been applied to supporters of Vozrozhdenie in 1904 because of their insistence that a Jewish national assembly, be convoked to treat major issues affecting the Jewish community. To further his cause, Zhitlowski strove to establish an organizational link between the leaders of SERP and the SRs.

Under Zhitlowski's guidance, SERP mounted an aggressive preelection campaign against its rivals in the Jewish community. The party was especially critical of supporters of both mass migration and Zionism for their insistence that the only solution for Jewry was to leave Russia en masse. At the same time, it denounced the Bundist movement and the newly emerging Folkist movement led by Simon Dubnow, both of which preached forms of cultural autonomism that denied the need for a separate territory.[46] Sejmists also took pains to distance themselves from supporters of the Zionist Socialist Workers Party or SS, their principal rival on the Jewish Left. Unlike the Sejmists (and despite its Zionist appellation), the SS opposed both national autonomy and settlement in Palestine and instead preached emigration, territorialism, and support of the revolutionary struggle in Russia.[47]

Zhitlowski approached the campaign with great enthusiasm. He was convinced that he had finally succeeded in synthesizing his Jewish and socialist goals into a coherent and popularly accepted form. Despite important differences among its various proponents, the ideal of Diaspora nationalism seemed to be gaining acceptance within the Jewish community. Its doctrine could be heard across the entire Jewish political spectrum from "illegal" radical groups like the Bund to established moderate figures like Dubnow. Zhitlowski pointed to the statements by Ahad Ha-Am that Palestine could never hold more than a minority of Jews as evidence that even Zionists were slowly and grudgingly accepting the importance of the Diaspora in Jewish life.[48]

Zhitlowski's venture into Russian national and Jewish communal politics did not last long. Only a few months into the campaign, the government voided Zhitlowski's candidacy because of his past revolutionary activity. The Russian senate reversed the government's decision in 1906, but by that time the first Duma had already been dissolved. In a last-ditch effort to salvage the Diasporist ideal, the Sejmists participated in a special meeting of national parties organized by the Social Revolutionaries in Tampere, Finland, in 1907. At the meeting, Zhitlowski pressed for approval of the Sejmist demands for Jewish communal autonomy. Divisions among the various groups were too great to forge a political alliance, however, and Zhitlowski returned to Russia in great despair. He now proclaimed that the opportunity for the triumph of Diaspora nationalism in Russia had come and gone. By 1908, with the movement for social reform slowly fading in Russia and attempts to link the SERP with the SRs stillborn, Zhitlowski gladly accepted an offer to come to the United States to serve as an emissary of both the SRs and SERP to the Russian immigrant population of New York.[49]

The possibility of observing firsthand a young Russian immigrant community removed from the petty ideological squabbles of the Old World gave Zhitlowski a tremendous psychological boost. Here was an opportunity for the Jewish socialist and Yiddishist to assume a dominant role in a fledgling activist community that lacked leadership and direction. The fact that many of Zhitlowski's most ardent supporters in Europe had settled in America seemed to give him an advantage over other militants vying for control of the community. Most important, he could now participate directly in the establishment of a totally new Jewish society resting upon the principles of progress and brotherhood. In Russia, Zhitlowski would note in an essay written in America in 1911, he had worked "for" the Jews. Now he was working "with" the Jews.[50]

From his very first trip to the United States in 1904, Zhitlowski had become convinced that America could enable him to finally realize the Populist ideal of "going to the people" within the framework of the emerging immigrant Jewish community. Impressed with America's diversity of population, federal system, and political and economic freedoms, he joined with members of the New York-based Jewish Socialist

Labor Party in proclaiming the ideal of a "United Peoples of the United States," a society of autonomous cultural groups based on a shared vision of brotherhood and justice.[51] Zhitlowski also believed that America would look favorably upon efforts to create cooperative villages that would bring about an economic revolution in the Jewish community. In contrast to the "assimilationist" schemes of Jewish philanthropists who wished only to see immigrants disappear into anonymous crowds of America's urban centers, Zhitlowski proposed the model of Jewish agricultural settlements led by nationalist intellectuals who would devote all of their energies to the realization of the ideals of Populism and Utopian socialism.[52] He worked tirelessly to support the training of Jewish farmers in the United States that in his view would enable the Jewish people to "live directly from nature's full and free hand." At the same time, Zhitlowski remained true to the ideals of the SERP movement. The development of agricultural colonies would not only strengthen Jewish life in the United States, he claimed, but would also provide the necessary experience and personnel for the future colonization of a Jewish homeland.[53]

Despite his distrust of urban life, Zhitlowski could not avoid the reality of immigrant Jewish settlement in cities like New York and Chicago. True to his autonomist ideals, he proposed the establishment of a *kehillah*, or independent Jewish communal structure, modeled on the institutional pattern of the East European Jewish shtetl. Zhitlowski was an active supporter of the New York Kehillah that existed between 1908 and 1922, though he was sharply critical of its failure to include nonreligious elements in its ranks.[54] Momentary reversals did little to cloud his belief in a bright future for the American Jewish community. Even in the midst of World War I, Zhitlowski could enthusiastically proclaim that America would soon see a momentous event in modern Jewish history: "[t]he birth of a free proud Jewish tribe that will soon assume hegemony over the broad web of the Jewish historical fabric, which will in any case be a part of the vanguard in the struggle for existence that our people have been forced to wage for a significant and secure existence and for a progressive national development."[55]

Whether because of unbounded optimism or his desperate desire to finally realize his goals, Zhitlowski erred badly in his evaluation of the possibilities for Jewish cultural and communal development in the United States. In particular, he seemed oblivious to the distinctive nature of immigrant assimilation in American society that made the development of communal autonomy impossible. In concentrating all of his attention on immigrant Jewry, he ignored contextual issues such as the sheer size of immigration to the United States, the nature of American urban settlement, and the lack of any historical precedent for the support of an autonomous ethnic community. In his naive enthusiasm, Zhitlowski swallowed whole the myth of a limitless American frontier. Misreading the future of both general and Jewish settlement patterns in America, he assumed that the majority of East European immigrants who dwelled in cities at the turn of the century would soon find their way to the countryside and adopt his programs of agrarian socialism. In part, Zhitlowski's expectations concerning the future of the immigrant Jewish community in the United States were based upon a misapplication of his experiences with emigré settlements in Germany and Switzerland. In so doing, he failed to recognize that while young radicals in Europe often saw their residence abroad as an opportunity to develop their progressive ideas and programs in a more tolerant and liberal environment, immigrants to America were mainly concerned with their economic livelihood. Struggling to survive in the face of adverse economic and social conditions, they had little interest in serving as a training ground for some future society, whether in Russia, Palestine, or the United States.

Like many others of the transitional generation, Zhitlowski did not grasp the nature of mass politics in an industrializing democratic society. Immersed in an emigré environment for much of his formative years, he continued to view the concerns of the Jews as radically different from the interests of the larger society. Schooled in Russian political philosophy and praxis, he remained convinced of the need for an intellectual vanguard to provide the ideological foundation and direction for political activity. As more pragmatic socialist activists in America such as Abraham Cahan recognized, however, the future of immigrant Jewish life in the United States lay with mass propaganda and the organization of Jewish trade unions integrated into the American labor movement, rather than with cultural activity led by intellectual elites or isolated agrarian settlements.[56]

Zhitlowski also badly misperceived the role of immigrants in American society. Though growing in numbers, newly arrived East European Jews could not overcome the hostility of the majority population as well as the more established Jewish community to even limited programs of cultural and political autonomy. It was not that Zhitlowski was unaware of the opposition of American Jews and non-Jews to many of his ideas. It was simply that in his romanticized defense of cultural pluralism and his unwavering commitment to the ideals of Populism, the socialist activist blithely ignored the reality of radical assimilationism on the one hand and nativism on the other.[57]

In an attempt to counter what he believed to be the limited assimilationist vision of Jewish socialists in America like Cahan, in 1909 Zhitlowski founded the Yiddish monthly *Das Naye Lebn* (The New Life). In its first editorial, Zhitlowski staunchly defended his program for Jewish revival in the United States. The variegated immigrant Jewish population in America, the editorial boldly proclaimed, provided Jews with a historic opportunity to synthesize the antithetical ideals of religion and atheism on the one hand and the goals of a Jewish homeland and efforts to build a new life in the Diaspora on the other.[58] A series of articles published in 1911–12 reiterated Zhitlowski's other major concerns: the rejuvenation of the Jewish people in the Diaspora through the principle of agricultural labor, and the involvement of the Jewish intelligentsia in the life of the Jewish people. Reiterating his belief in the broad opportunities that the American immigrant community seemed to offer, Zhitlowski urged the Jewish masses and intelligentsia to unite in order to revitalize Jewish culture through the spread of the Yiddish language. Despite Zhitlowski's tireless efforts to keep it afloat, *Das Naye Lebn* never found a significant audience among immigrant readers in America. Unable to compete with the simple, straightforward, and often sensationalistic articles of the popular Yiddish press, the journal died a quiet death in 1920. A short-lived effort to revive the paper in the early 1920s met with similar failure.

Zhitlowski's effort to develop a Yiddish newspaper in America pledged to progressive culture and national renewal demonstrated his continuing commitment to Yiddishism. In 1909, Zhitlowski had helped to spearhead the convocation of a conference of Yiddishists which was held in Czernowitz in the Ukraine. Though much of its program was philosophical and abstract, the conference was clearly seen by Zhitlowski as the first salvo in the battle against Zionists in the American Jewish community. In a more general sense, he hoped that it would mark the beginning of a campaign to unite those left-wing elements interested in forming a mass movement for Jewish cultural and political revival in the Diaspora. At the conference, Zhitlowski gave an impassioned speech in which he called for the translation of religious texts into Yiddish so as to make "national treasures" readily available to the Jewish masses throughout the world. According to at least one participant, Zhitlowski made the greatest impression of all the speakers.[59] Heartened by the response, he returned triumphantly to the United States and proceeded to establish the first Yiddishist school in America. For the remainder of his life, Zhitlowski would work tirelessly to develop a network of Yiddish cultural and educational institutions to serve as a basis for the development of what he believed would be a new Jewish culture grounded in democracy and humanistic values.[60]

In preparation for the dramatic changes in the American Jewish community that he was convinced were imminent, Zhitlowski vainly attempted to seek an accommodation with the major Jewish socialist parties in the United States—the Bund, the Sejmists, the Socialist Territorialists, and the Poale Zion movement. Yet the Jewish socialist and Yiddishist's dogged adherence to Populist ideas and unflagging belief in distinctiveness of the American Jewish experience placed him at odds with all of the movements. Despite his overtures, he continued to attack the Bund for its narrow Marxist view and for limiting its demands for national autonomy to Russia. Similarly, while praising his one-time allies in SERP for defending the ideal of political autonomy, he berated them for ignoring the fate of immigrants in the United States.[61]

Zhitlowski faced similar problems in his attempt to seek a modus vivendi with the Zionists. He had actually moved closer to Zionism in 1908 as a result of the Young Turk revolution in the Ottoman Empire, which he was convinced would facilitate the establishment of a Jewish state. He had always believed in the ultimate goal of a Jewish homeland. Now that the goal seemed realizable, he embraced it wholeheartedly.[62]

In a burst of excitement, Zhitlowski made his first (and last) visit to Palestine in the summer of 1914. The experience proved to be a bitter one. He searched in vain for an audience that would respond to his eclectic blend of Jewish nationalism and socialism. When Zhitlowski attempted to lecture on Jewish cultural revival in Yiddish, he was shouted down by the largely Hebrew-speaking crowds, who were mainly interested in concrete proposals for economic growth. The socialist activist was also shocked by what he perceived as the harsh attitudes and brutal behavior of the Jews in Palestine toward the resident Arab population. The *yishuv*'s failure to extend its hand to its "Semitic brethren" only seemed to substantiate his deep-seated suspicions concerning the reactionary nature of the Zionist ideal. At the same time, rumors of impending Arab violence against the *yishuv* created doubts in Zhitlowski's mind that the new Turkish regime would provide physical and economic security for the fledgling Jewish settlement. After a two-month stay in Palestine, he returned to the United States just as World War I broke out.[63]

Like others of the transitional generation, Zhitlowski was profoundly shocked by the violence and devastation of the war. He pleaded for Jews to remain neutral, often citing prophetic writings to denounce the conflict as a brutal struggle for power among capitalist powers. The progress of the war and the patriotic response of American-born Jewish rabbis and community leaders only confirmed Zhitlowski's belief in the bankruptcy of both traditional Judaism and western assimilationism and spurred him on in his efforts to ensure Jewish national revival and growth through the development of an autonomous socialist society.[64] Reaffirming his Sejmist ideals, in 1915 Zhitlowski successfully lobbied for the creation of the American Jewish Congress as a way of both expressing collective Jewish concerns during World War I and its aftermath and increasing the voice of the burgeoning immigrant community in American Jewish life. His efforts in the postwar era to develop organizations that reflected his own ideals of Jewish socialism and Diasporism in America, however, were stillborn. By the end of the decade, Zhitlowski's early dream of a unified Jewish socialist movement in the United States had collapsed in the wake of bitter quarrels among Zionists, SERPists, and Territorialists.[65] Nor was Zhitlowski able to secure recognition for a Jewish section in the socialist Second International.[66]

Disenchantment with the Jewish socialist movement and the proclamation of the Balfour Declaration in 1917 led Zhitlowski once again to look more favorably upon Zionism. He now argued that a massive Jewish settlement in Palestine would enable the Jewish proletariat to serve as a socialist vanguard in Asia. An active supporter of the establishment of the Jewish Legion to fight with the Allies to liberate Palestine from the Turks, Zhitlowski also pressed for the development of additional agricultural projects by the *yishuv*. Despite his renewed interest in Palestine, however, the socialist activist continued to voice doubts about the Zionist enterprise that were rooted in his first confrontation with Hibbat Zion in the 1880s and were reinforced by his recent visit to the Holy Land. In deciding to join Poale Zion in 1917, for example, he made sure to distance himself from the movement's insistence on a rigid Marxist definition of the Jewish "proletariat" and from its emphasis on Hebrew to the exclusion of Yiddish.[67] Zhitlowski also cautioned Zionists against assuming that the granting of the mandate in Palestine necessarily signaled the triumph of their ideas. If anything, it only reconfirmed his own beliefs in Diaspora nationalism and in the need for a progressive Jewish culture. What was significant in the League of Nation's acceptance of the Balfour Declaration, Zhitlowski wrote in an article published in *Das Naye Lebn* in 1922, was not that it that it recognized a Jewish homeland but that it conferred the rights of nations upon nonterritorial peoples. The major goal of a Jewish homeland, he reminded the Zionists, was to help create a modern progressive Jewish literature and Yiddish language to replace the crumbling and decaying religious pillars of Judaism.[68]

The year 1917 also saw the victory of the Bolsheviks in Russia. Zhitlowski's response to the Russian Revolution was ambivalent. On the one hand, he praised the Bolsheviks' commitment to the triumph of equality and justice in his homeland. He was especially impressed with Lenin's support of autonomism for ethnic minorities. In contrast to the French Revolution, Zhitlowski argued in an article written shortly after the victory of the Bolsheviks, the new regime seemed to reject centralized authority and forced assimilation and to recognize the need for a federal political structure in which the rights of all nationalities would be respected and fostered. Reversing his previous support of Palestine as a Jewish homeland, he now proclaimed that the Russian Revolution signaled the triumph both of Diaspora nationalism over Zionism and of the Yiddish language over Hebrew.

For all his enthusiasm with the events of 1917, however, Zhitlowski instinctively distrusted the Bolsheviks and their followers within the Jewish community. Lingering doubts born of his early quarrels with Marxist "dogmatists" in the Russian emigré community remained. Zhitlowski also voiced concerns that the Bolsheviks' penchant for autocratic rule and ideological narrowness might threaten the realization of his goals of agrarian socialism and national political autonomy for the Jewish people.[69] For the time being, he stated, he would take a "wait and see attitude" toward the Soviet experiment. Summing up his ambivalence toward the Revolution, he proclaimed himself "an anti-Bolshevik Bolshevik."[70]

Zhitlowski's contradictory writings on the nature of the Bolshevik Revolution reflected his growing desperation and confusion over the future direction of Jewry in the immediate postwar period. As with other members of the transitional generation, events seemed to be outstripping Zhitlowski's ability to comprehend their significance and meaning. His frantic attempts to respond to separate developments in the three distinctive Jewish communities of America, Russia, and Palestine blinded him to the increasing globalization of Jewish life, which necessitated long-range concrete solutions. Instead, he fell back on convenient and secure ideological constructs from the past. At the same time, new ideas and trends were emerging within both the radical and Jewish communities with which Zhitlowski was affiliated that demonstrated the datedness of his ideas and proposals for Jewish renewal. In attempting to incorporate them into his worldview, the socialist activist seemed like a will-o'-the-wisp, flitting from one movement to another.

Not surprisingly, therefore, the 1920s found Zhitlowski without a solid organizational base. Never fully comfortable with Zionism, he now attacked the movement in its postwar "practical" phase for being too accommodationist and for lacking ideological fervor. He had never really liked Herzl. Looking back, however, he had grown to respect the idealistic nature of classical Zionism. From Herzl's lofty notion of the "ingathering of the exiles," Zhitlowski argued, the movement under Chaim Weizmann had been reduced to "small colony Zionism" pledged to realizing Ahad Ha-Am's limited goal of establishing a spiritual center in Palestine.[71] Zhitlowski's fears that violence would result from decades of Jewish insensitivity and cruelty toward the Arab population seemed to have been corroborated by the riots of 1929 in Palestine. Shocked by the murder of dozens of Jewish colonists, he was more firmly convinced than ever that Palestine could never serve as a settlement for the vast majority of Jews.

After an extended stay in Poland, Lithuania, and Latvia in the early 1920s where he had an opportunity to observe the attempts by their Jewish communities to develop cultural autonomism, Zhitlowski re-

turned to the United States in 1925. The celebration of his sixtieth
birthday that year attracted thousands of supporters to a party in New
York and resulted in the publication of the first edition of his collected
works. After another short trip abroad, Zhitlowski returned in 1930 to
settle permanently in America. His inability to gain a foothold among
the immigrant Jewish masses, however, led him to question many of
his basic tenets. In an article written in 1923, for example, Zhitlowski
admitted that the only remaining hope for the realization of autonomism
in America lay in the unlikely unity of Jewish working-class and religious elements to further Jewish education.[72] By the late twenties, the
socialist activist was suggesting that Yiddishism might be an inadequate
foundation for the revival of Jewish life. After all, Zhitlowski mused,
only one-third of the Jewish people spoke Yiddish. More important,
he was troubled that Jewish history seemed to demonstrate that language was not sufficient to ensure Jewish survival.[73]

Disappointed by developments in America and Palestine,
Zhitlowski now began to look more favorably upon the Soviet Union.
Despite his reservations about Bolshevism, he clung to the hope that
his ideals could be realized in his homeland. In the early 1920s,
Zhitlowski had decried the Soviet regime as "a suffocating and crip-
pling all-powerful bureaucracy."[74] By the end of the decade,
Zhitlowski seemed genuinely impressed with the noticeable decline
of anti-Semitism in the Soviet Union, especially in light of the increasing anti-Jewish sentiment on the European continent that he
had observed firsthand during his stay in the Baltics and Poland. He
was also enthusiastic about the establishment of Birobidjan, the Russian Jewish self-governing territory near the Pacific Ocean, which
seemed to represent the realization of his own autonomist and Populist ideals. Zhitlowski's growing identification with Stalinist Russia
was reinforced by the overtures that the American Communist Party
had begun to make to Jews, particularly its frequent use of Yiddish in
party propaganda addressed to immigrants. On the international level,
he praised the convocation of the World Jewish Culture Congress in
Paris in 1937, which had been organized under the auspices of YKUF,
the communist cultural organization.

Zhitlowski's attraction to the Soviet Union grew stronger with the
onset of Nazism. By the 1930s, his public statements supporting
Stalin verged on hagiography. In various articles published in the
left-wing Yiddish press, Zhitlowski praised the Soviet leader as a sup-

porter of ethnic nationalism (in contrast to Lenin's assimilationist policies), a heroic fighter against Nazism and anti-Semitism, a proponent of agrarian socialism, and an advocate of true internationalism (in contrast to the cosmopolitan ideals of rigid Marxists). Impressed by the Birobidjan project, Zhitlowski even deluded himself into believing that Stalin probably had read his works and had been influenced by the Diaspora nationalist.[75] Though occasionally critical of aspects of the Bolshevik program, he was careful to differentiate between specific policies, which he claimed were a result of misguided leadership, and the general goal of the realization of democracy and socialism in Russia that he believed he shared with Soviet leaders.[76] Zhitlowski's loyalty to Stalinism led him not only to defend the Moscow Trials of 1936 but also to parrot the communist argument—which recalled his youthful criticisms of the Russian Jewish petite bourgeoisie—that Nazi persecution of Jewry resulted from the latter's exploitative role in the capitalist system. He undoubtedly was shocked by the signing of the Nazi-Soviet NonAggression Pact in 1939, yet he made sure not to express his reservations publicly. In 1941, Zhitlowski greeted the German invasion of Russia with mixed feelings. Though he expressed deep concern over the impact of the German occupation on Russian Jewry, he was deeply thankful that the Soviet regime could now return to its true role as a bulwark against Nazism. For the next two years, Zhitlowski would devote himself tirelessly to pro-Soviet causes in the United States.

Zhitlowski's adulation for the Soviet Union cannot simply be dismissed as the naiveté of an aging radical. True, there was much in the Soviet regime that appealed to him—its reliance upon a *minorité agissante*, its call for the revitalization of agriculture, its opposition to both "reactionary" Zionism and socialism. Yet Zhitlowski's trust in the power and authority of the Russian government to ameliorate the condition of Jewry flew in the face of the most cherished ideal of the transitional generation—the ability of Jews to create a modern consciousness through a self-directed movement of cultural renewal. In retrospect, Zhitlowski's sycophantic support of Stalin must be seen less as a belief in the ability of the Soviet regime to realize his hoped-for programs of Jewish regeneration than as a bitter realization that a threatened Jewish people risked annihilation without the aid of a powerful ally. Zhitlowski would not live long enough to learn of the true horrors of both Nazism and Stalinism, however. He died on May 6, 1943, in Calgary, Alberta, while on a speaking tour for the communist-led International Workers Order.

In attempting to assess Zhitlowski's thought, one is confronted by a bewildering array of positions that seem to defy easy categorization and understanding. His voluminous and didactic writings on a wide range of topics and his fiery and impassioned oratory occasioned bitter debates among his contemporaries. Yet no one could ignore Zhitlowski. While some lauded him as a prophet, others denounced him as a self-hating Jew. In his search to find a niche for himself in the ideological spectrum of the Jewish communities in which he lived and worked, Zhitlowski doggedly refused to associate himself with one ideology or political movement. One historian has aptly described Zhitlowski as "a kind of ideological nomad, forever on the move."[77]

Zhitlowski's intellectual wanderings were reflected in his leaps from one Jewish political organization to another in search of a resting place for his ideas. When he could not find an appropriate movement, he simply created a new one. Like many others of the transitional generation, he seemed to prefer the small and informal grouping of like-minded intellectuals to the more disciplined mass political organizations that had begun to emerge in both general and Jewish society in the first decade of the twentieth century in Europe and America. In this sense, he reflected in a remarkable way the fluid, unformed, and even erratic nature of Jewish activism among East European intellectuals at the end of the nineteenth century.

In his own mind, Zhitlowski saw himself as a proponent of a novel solution to the Jewish problem that would transcend both the isolationism of Zionism and the assimilationism of dogmatic socialism, by synthesizing Jewish nationalist longings with humanitarian aspirations. For most of his contemporaries, the task seemed an impossible one, given the broad chasm that existed between the two movements. Other transitional thinkers often despaired of their ability to overcome the stark contradictions of nationalism and universalism, religion and reason, and isolation and assimilation that framed the debate between traditionalists and modernizers within the Jewish community. Zhitlowski, on the other hand, seemed to revel in the paradoxes of Jewish life and voiced confidence that he could overcome them in a bold new synthesis. And while others were quickly overwhelmed by the new and dangerous challenges that threatened world

Jewry in the twentieth century, he steadfastly maintained, at least publicly, his belief in the realization of ideas and programs that he had first formulated in his youth.

Central to Zhitlowski's concern was the reintegration of Jewish intellectuals into the community fold. In this sense, his peculiar blend of socialism, nationalism, and Yiddishism can be seen as an attempt to find an appropriate language of discourse and strategy that would unite the progressivist concerns of alienated young Jews with the basic values and ideals of traditional Jewish culture. It was Zhitlowski's contention that only a secular Jewish consciousness geared to the ideological concerns of the most articulate members of the Jewish community and grounded in the culture and language of its most genuine elements, that is, the Jewish masses, could rescue the Jewish people from its decadent and corrupting existence. In turn, only a socially conscious Jewish identity could enable the Jewish nation to once again play a vital role in the progress of humanity as a whole. The central vehicle for the transmission of Zhitlowski's new ideas was to be Yiddish—at once a repository of the best of traditional Jewish culture and a vital tool for the inculcation of new values and ideals among the Jewish masses. Ideally, the creation of a progressive Jewish culture should take place among the nations of the world; hence Zhitlowski's trumpeting of Diaspora nationalism and his condemnation of Zionist "isolationism."

Like Dubnow and Ahad Ha-Am, Zhitlowski's assessment of the needs of the Jewish people in a rapidly changing world began with a critique of the traditional basis of Jewish survival, the Jewish religion itself. An ardent socialist, his ideas about religion reflected the strongly secularist orientation of left-wing philosophical thought. Far more than any other member of his generation, Zhitlowski's program of national revival was challenged by the power of religious tradition in Jewish life. The only way to overcome the weight of Orthodoxy upon Jewish communal life was to place Judaism in a well-defined historical context that would clearly demonstrate the irrelevance of rabbinism to modern-day thought and activity.

Influenced by late-nineteenth-century anthropological research and theories of evolution, Zhitlowski viewed Judaism as the outgrowth of the need of a tribal people to maintain its identity in a hostile world. During its initial stages of national development, he maintained, Jewry had woven a "steel web of laws and customs" in its "heart" so that it was impossible to differentiate between the people and its religion. To help soothe the pain and anguish of a powerless and oppressed people scattered throughout the globe, Jewish leaders had reinforced the community's faith system by developing a belief in the Messiah and in the "chosen people." In an age of suspicion and superstition, Zhitlowski maintained, such forms of collective identity were not only natural but necessary to maintain Jewish survival.[78]

It was Zhitlowski's contention that the rise of universalism and the onset of the Enlightenment in the eighteenth century broke the ties that had cemented the nation to its faith. Religion now became a private matter while the concept of the nation became linked with land and political sovereignty. To insist that Jews remain bound to their ancient faith in the modern world, as religionists demanded, thus not only denied individuals the right of freedom of conscience but also endangered the future of the nation. In limiting the capability of Jews to develop new ideals and attitudes, Zhitlowski argued, those who obstinately sought to maintain Orthodoxy also separated the Jewish people from important developments affecting humanity as a whole.[79]

Beyond Zhitlowski's seemingly dispassionate assessment of Judaism lay a deep-seated resentment of religious tradition that remained with him throughout his life. Zhitlowski's obsession with religion resulted from a number of factors, including his own critical response to his parents' religious observance, his personal fascination with philosophy and with the role of ideas in shaping human behavior, and his desperate desire to rouse a passive and traditional Jewish population to action. In most of his writings, Zhitlowski portrayed Judaism as a major obstacle to normal national development. Denouncing the Jewish masses' "slavish" reliance upon the religious past, he openly called for the destruction of the system of halakhah (Jewish Law), which he claimed prevented interaction with the outside world.[80] As he noted in an especially virulent article, "Tsvay farlezungn vegn id un mensh, ershter artikl" (Two Lectures Concerning the Jew and Humanity, First Article) written in 1911–12: "The entire unnatural belief in angels, devils, spirits, and saints; the stupid nonsense that by differentiating between good deeds and sins, between man and God, man can find grace in the Lord's eyes or even worse [khalilah] appease his anger; the entire Code of Laws [Shulchan Arukh] with 613 laws and customs—all of them or almost all . . . cannot stand up to the criticism of modern thought."[81] At times, Zhitlowski associated proponents of religious Orthodoxy with his Marxist enemies in the Russian revolutionary movement. Defenders of rigid ideologies, both were seeped in authoritarianism and hero worship. In adhering to a faith system grounded in dogmatism, both denied reality and weakened the will and ability of simple and honest believers to confront their enemies.[82]

Like many of his contemporaries, however, Zhitlowski's hostility ultimately was directed more toward the attitudes and behavior of religionists than toward religious belief per se. Even in later years, when the desire to cement unity in the fledgling immigrant community in America eventually led Zhitlowski to temper his ideological critique of Judaism, he never lost his strong animosity toward what he regarded as the immorality and corruption of the upholders of traditional Jewish observance. Throughout his life, he viewed religious Orthodoxy as synonymous with closed-mindedness and disregard for humanity as a whole. The emphasis upon the minutiae of religious law, the concept of Jews as a chosen people (which Zhitlowski cynically referring to a daily prayer called the "ata bachartanu," or "chosenness" mentality), the unwillingness of Orthodox tradition to borrow ideas from the outside world—all led to a social and economic parasitism that threatened both Jew and non-Jew. Given their hostility toward the outside world, he maintained, Jews should not be surprised that they aroused suspicion and hatred within the larger society. In a situation in which Jewish survival depended on the exploitation of individuals who were considered by religious tradition to be primitive and unworthy of respect and sympathy, Zhitlowski argued, there was bound to be anti-Semitism.[83]

It was Zhitlowski's negative attitude toward Orthodoxy and his search for the true essence of Judaism that explained his fascination with Christianity and with the figure of Jesus in particular. Yet the reasons for Zhitlowski's attraction to Christian thought went well beyond mere disenchantment with traditional Judaism. Like many of his contemporaries, Zhitlowski was drawn to the period of the Second Temple, in which Christianity made its first appearance. Jewish nationalists in late-nineteenth-century Russia were convinced that the cataclysmic events in Palestine during the first century C.E., characterized by dramatic ideological conflicts over the fate of the Jewish people and by bitter social and economic divisions, paralleled the crisis of Jewish life in their own era.

In studying the Second Temple period, Zhitlowski focused his attention upon the Essenes, the ascetic group of Jewish millenarians whom biblical scholars of the late nineteenth century had viewed as proto-Christians. Having originally dismissed them as antisocial fanatics who thought little about the fate of the larger Jewish community, Zhitlowski claimed to have discovered their commitment to communism and activism shortly after his return to his Jewish roots. He was now convinced that the Essenes' distinctive synthesis of moral ideals and commitment to community could serve as a valuable historical model for the task of national regeneration that had to be carried out in the modern era. Equally important were the social dynamics of the sect. The Essenes' unbending loyalty to their cause, strong sense of purpose and direction, and elaborate supportive structure all seemed to mirror Zhitlowski's own experiences as a member of various social activist groups within the Russian emigré communities in Switzerland and Germany. The sect's reliance upon a small group of committed activists mirrored Zhitlowski's own beliefs in the central role of a *minorité agissante*, while their decision to segregate themselves from the corruption of urban life appealed to his Populist sentiments.

Zhitlowski was convinced that the clearest embodiment of the ideals of the Essenes could be found in the figure of Jesus. The roots of Zhitlowski's fascination with Jesus are unclear. In his memoirs, he claims to have been influenced by the work of Yisroel Pik, a Hungarian Orthodox rabbi who had converted to Christianity and engaged in missionary activity within the Jewish community. He also appears to have been profoundly affected by the christological writings of Leo Tolstoy, and even considered visiting the Russian writer and philosopher at his estate at Yasnaya Polyana, a village not far from Tula.[84] Whatever the origins of Zhitlowski's interest in Jesus, it seems clear from the frequent allusions to concepts about death and resurrection and sinfulness and salvation in his writings that the Jewish socialist strongly identified with many of the fundamental teachings associated with the central figure of Christianity. Throughout his life, Zhitlowski continually stressed the similarities in their thought and activity. Like Jesus, he saw himself as rejected by both rabbinic Judaism and assimilationists because of his attempt to synthesize Jewish national and universal social ideals. Like the founder of Christianity, he stressed the eternal longings of the human soul for goodness rather than a "bargain" with God for redemption or the egotistical drive for personal success and social acceptance. Zhitlowski also looked to Jesus as a powerful historical and personal symbol of the embattled Jewish nationalist during a period of rupture in established Jewish life. Though denied and rejected in his own time, Zhitlowski believed that his message, like that of the historical Jesus, would eventually gain respectability and acclaim within his own group of Jewish "disciples" and among progressive men and women everywhere.[85]

Despite his admiration for Jesus, Zhitlowski never considered converting and rejected any notion of mass conversion as a solution to the Jewish plight. Significantly, his discussions of Jesus generally emphasized the latter's "prophetic" rather than "miraculous" character, a depiction that closely linked the religious figure with the concerns of contemporary Jews while at the same time distancing him from the formal tenets of Christianity. Though often professing a personal belief in the holiness of the teacher of the New Testament and fully accepting of individual Jews who chose to convert, Zhitlowski rejected the demand of Christianity for a dogmatic and ritualistic avowal of faith on the part of its believers. For Zhitlowski, Jesus' major importance was as a symbolic figure whose life, like those of other metahistorical figures, embodied significant truths about the human condition. As he remarked in an article honoring the sixtieth birthday of Max Nordau, the famed Zionist leader, in 1909: "I believe in Jesus Christ as much as [I believe] in the Jewish Messiah and both no more than in the Graeco-Roman Venus-Aphrodite. None is superior to the other. All three are more or less Divine manifestations that have undergone periods of holiness, impurity, purgatory, and resurrection and paradise [as reflected] in human poetry."[86]

Zhitlowski was also troubled by the efforts of Christians to impose their beliefs on others, policies that seemed to him to parallel the obscurantism and authoritarianism of Jewish Orthodoxy. More important, like many others of his generation Zhitlowski could not ignore the tortured history of Jewish-Christian relations over the centuries. In his general writings, he was always careful to differentiate between "primitive" Christianity with its lofty ideals and the "corrupt" nature of Christian churches. Zhitlowski's contemporaneous frame of reference, of course, was the Russian Orthodox Church, which he believed betrayed Christian universalism in the name of a virulent and narrow-minded religious nationalism that incorporated strong anti-Semitic sentiments.

In a more profound sense, Zhitlowski's commitment to Jewish national revival led him to conclude that Jewry could not partake of an
ideal that did not in some way emphasize its own distinctiveness and
national purpose. Given his belief that the association of religion with
group identity reflected a primitive stage of national development,
Zhitlowski could not accept the notion of replacing one religious faith
with another as a solution to the problem of national degeneration.
Once Jews had regained their national integrity, he maintained, religion would lose its central significance and individuals would be free
to adopt whatever faith they preferred. At that time, they could decide whether they should wait for the Messiah or accept Jesus. In the
meantime, Jews could profess whatever religion they wished as long as
they remained committed to the national cause.[87]

Such arguments clearly demonstrate that for all his hostility toward
traditional Judaism, Zhitlowski could never accept assimilation as an
alternative to the maintenance of religious faith. In much of his writing, Zhitlowski attempted to connect the drive to assimilate with the
Jewish bourgeoisie's desire for economic and social advancement in
western Europe. The efforts by middle-class Jewish intellectuals in
eastern Europe to deny the existence of the Jews as a people and to
reduce Judaism to a personal belief led them to parrot empty and irrelevant phrases used originally by German and French Jews to facilitate their embourgeoisement. For Zhitlowski, assimilation thus was
not only a denial of one's Jewish identity but also an assault upon one's
individual integrity and humanity. In a clear reference to his father,
Zhitlowski argued that the rejection of religious belief in the struggle
for acceptance invariably resulted in the triumph of petite bourgeois
values over spirituality and the loss of an "inner moral balance." In
placing economic self-interest as the paramount concern of the tal-
ented Jew, assimilationism atomized the Jewish middle class and led to
a denial of the basic role of the Jewish intellectual—the formulation
and dissemination of the ideals and values of his people. Even among
"progressive" assimilationists within the contemporary socialist movement, Zhitlowski argued, the striving for the betterment of humanity
as a whole, which in the past had given birth to the ideas of Karl Marx
and Ferdinand Lassalle, had long since been replaced by the egotistical struggle for political power and social respectability.[88]

Ultimately, Zhitlowski maintained, assimilation had failed to ad-
dress two main challenges facing the Jewish people: anti-Semitism

and survival. In terms strongly reminiscent of his enemies the political Zionists, Zhitlowski argued that the larger society would never allow individual Jews to forget their past. At the same time, the assimilationists' desperate efforts to integrate into the host society threatened the Jewish community with extinction. In his view, Jewry at the turn of the century seemed caught between two undesirable alternatives. If Jews continued to hold to their outmoded religion, they risked alienating their own youth and cutting themselves off from the larger world around them. Without a binding identity such as religious belief, however, the Jewish people would lose its raison d'être and would be absorbed into the host society.

Yet like most of his contemporaries, Zhitlowski could never accept the notion that Jewry would simply disappear, whether by religious ossification or by assimilation. Somehow he had to find a new way of defining Jewish identity that would transcend individual will and at the same time protect the freedom of any Jew to differ from the majority. While rejecting the religious notions of a covenantal and "chosen" people, Zhitlowski nevertheless had to formulate a Jewish consciousness that bound one generation to the next and linked the individual Jew, no matter what his or her beliefs, to the Jewish people.

But how to unite objective and subjective definitions of Jewish identity? Zhitlowski was convinced that he had found the answer in the combination of organic and biological concepts of social organization made popular by the sociologist Herbert Spencer and perspectives borrowed from cultural nationalism. Though there could never be a unity of views or one specific national form imposed by a central authority upon the Jewish masses, he argued, Jewry was nevertheless "a culturally creative organism" and each of its members "the biological carrier of these specific culturally creative forces." Like any autonomous living creature, each people instinctively struggled to survive. Yet only those nations whose members had attained full and clear self-consciousness would succeed. In turn, nations could only disappear by an act of human will, either through annihilation from external forces or by suicide from within.[89]

As a synthesis of notions of biological determinism and élan vital, Zhitlowski's attempt to define Jewry was riddled with contradictions and ambiguities. At times, he seemed to suggest that Jews were a distinctive race and that their national identity was largely instinctual in nature. In most cases, however, his use of anatomical and genetic terminology in his discussions of Jewish peoplehood generally was meant to be understood in a figurative rather than a literal sense.[90] More typically, Zhitlowski referred to culture as the distinguishing characteristic of collective identity. Ultimately, he argued, the individual's commitment to the future of his people was a question of sensitivity and sentiment rather than logic or moral obligation. Zhitlowski summarized his attitudes concerning the objective and subjective nature of Jewish identity and the relationship between the individual and the Jewish people in the following terms: "A Jew therefore is anyone who is born into the world with Jewish creative forces, and a national Jew is one who wishes his people to survive in a world as an independent, culturally creative organism, regardless of what he believes or does not believe."[91]

It was Zhitlowski's fear of assimilation and his emphasis upon Jewry as a "culturally creative organism" that would eventually lead him to reevaluate his unremittingly hostile attitude toward Judaism. After his "return" to Jewish life, Zhitlowski began to reject the vulgar anti-religious attitudes of his youth. Though his animosity toward traditional religious leadership was unabated, he was now forced to admit the importance of religious belief and practice as a means of maintaining communal solidarity. In time, Zhitlowski's search for a purified embodiment of his socialist ideals that had originally led him to flirt with Christianity combined with his awakening nationalism to bring him back to the ethical teachings of the biblical Prophets. After his arrival in the United States, Zhitlowski also grew to recognize the role that religion played as a vital link to the past for deracinated immigrants, which could not simply be wished away. At the same time, his experiences in a pluralistic and open society undoubtedly contributed to his growing toleration of Judaism. Reflecting popular attitudes toward religion in his newly adopted homeland, Zhitlowski now maintained that individual religious faith could continue to exist alongside rational understanding as "twin" truths as long as the former did not interfere with the needs of the collectivity as a whole.[92]

More important, Zhitlowski began to realize that in emphasizing the centrality of culture in defining collective identity, he could not avoid the fact that Jewish culture was religiously based. Already in 1892, Zhitlowski had been confronted by the issue in daily discussions with his boyhood friend Shlomo Anski. Anski had insisted that without religious belief, Jewry was little more than a voluntaristic community that one could join or leave at will. Such arguments echoed the sentiments of many young Russian Jewish intellectuals who, having rejected Judaism, now found no reason to continue to identify with the Jewish community and sought out acceptance in the larger society. At the time of their discussions, Zhitlowski was clearly troubled by the implications of Anski's argument. To deny Judaism as a core belief was to endanger Jewish survival in the future; yet to reaffirm it blindly would alienate the very individuals who would be responsible for leading the Jewish people into the modern era.[93]

The issue of the relationship of intellectuals to religious tradition continued to haunt Zhitlowski throughout his life. A partial answer to the question of the role of religion in a reemerging Jewish nation and its relationship to the intellectual elite can be found in a series of articles, meant to summarize his thinking during the previous two decades, which Zhitlowski wrote in the United States between 1911 and 1912. The titles—"Religie un natsie" (Religion and Nation), "Tsvay farlezungn vegn id un mensh" (Two Lectures Concerning the Jew and Humanity), "Toyt un vidergeburt fun der idisher religie" (Death and Resurrection of the Jewish Religion), and "Di natsional-poetishe vidergeburt fun der idisher religie" (The National-Poetic Renaissance of the Jewish Religion) — suggest just how removed Zhitlowski had become from normative Jewish socialist and nationalist thought.[94] Though they found only a faint echo among the immigrant Jewish community in the United States, the articles provide an important insight into Zhitlowski's continual effort to synthesize tradition with modernity.

In the first article, Zhitlowski reiterated his longstanding belief that faith in God could no longer serve as a definition of a modern collective identity. At best, its survival reflected the inability of some individuals to absorb modern philosophical ideas. Nevertheless, under certain circumstances, the personal quest for spirituality could serve the interests of the nation. In his discussion, Zhitlowski stood Voltaire's famous statement concerning the role of religion on its head. While for the masses religion was "nothing but a false science, a poor morality, and a clumsy philosophy" whose disappearance was to be welcomed, for poets, artists, and other intellectuals who yearned for holiness and eternal truths it provided the language for the expression of deep-felt individual and collective yearnings. Zhitlowski now understood that the contradiction between his fervent denial of religious faith as the foundation of collective Jewish unity in the modern era, on the one hand, and his affirmation of its central place in the perspective of the future "spiritual" leaders of the Jewish community, on the other, could only be resolved through a creative restructuring of traditional Jewish symbols and rituals. While accepting the right of the freethinker to attack Judaism for its superstitions and "stupidities," Zhitlowski maintained, the modern Jew had to look beyond the rigid framework of Orthodoxy to find the inner spirit of religious belief.[95]

In recognizing the interplay between changing external religious forms and the unchanging spiritual core of what he called the Jewish "ethos," Zhitlowski could maintain a respectful attitude toward religious tradition while rejecting what he regarded as its coercive and absolutist nature. It was a view that he was convinced would find favor among East European immigrants in America who continued to exhibit strong emotional and spiritual ties with the Old World. The Jewish people desperately needed a rebirth of Judaism, Zhitlowski wrote in "Di natsional-poetishe vidergeburt fun der idishe religie" (published in 1912), not because it contained some absolute truth but because it was imbued with feelings and thoughts that were central to national survival and growth.[96] Thus, he commented ironically, the intellectual's complete dismissal of religion was actually a form of religious fanaticism. Undoubtedly recalling many of his own youthful diatribes against Judaism, Zhitlowski described the *apikores* or radical freethinker as an individual who was merely attempting to transform his own psychological obsessions into a solution to the problems facing the Jewish people as a whole. In denigrating Judaism, he had joined the camp of the assimilationists who uncritically accepted the judgments of the larger society and who ignored the distinctiveness of the Jewish people. At the same time, Zhitlowski attacked those who clung to ancient religious beliefs and practices because of their inability to find alternative forms of national expression. Such an attitude, which Zhitlowski disparagingly labeled "Judaeomania," was a sign of a spiritual sickness and signified a rejection of modern life.[97]

In arguing for a restructuring of religious rituals and practices rather than the creation of new ones within the context of an emerging new sense of Jewish peoplehood, Zhitlowski seemed to be paralleling the view of Conservative Judaism that was gradually gaining a foothold in the East European Jewish immigrant community of New

York. In his public statements, however, he rejected all forms of religious reform. Jewish religious reformers were mere imitators of Christianity, Zhitlowski noted. As bourgeois assimilationists who denied any sense of Jewish peoplehood, they were often no better versed in Jewish lore than their parishioners. Anyone examining their pitiful behavior, Zhitlowski cynically commented, could only conclude that "one would have to be a failure in all other scientific and liberal professions in order to make Jewish theology a profession."[98]

Despite his bitter critique of religious reformers, Zhitlowski eagerly adopted their emphasis upon *Geistesgeschichte* to explain Jewish development. Until the advent of Emancipation, he maintained, Jewish national existence could only be defined in a religious context. Any attack on religious beliefs and practices thus was seen as endangering national survival. In the nineteenth century, the growing participation of individual Jews in the larger society had disentangled Orthodoxy from national loyalties. Without an alternative to traditional religion, however, the basis of Jewish survival was threatened. Lacking the "normal" attributes of a modern national consciousness such as territory and sovereignty and with little hope of ever attaining them, Zhitlowski argued, Jewish nationalist intellectuals had no alternative but to revive the ideals of eternal Israel embedded in Judaism through the creation of new cultural forms and patterns. Only then could Jewry rediscover its raison d'être and at the same time earn the right to participate in the progress of humanity as a whole.[99] Borrowing from an essay written by Heinrich Heine, Zhitlowski argued that Judaism had progressed through four stages: it was born in holiness, grew old in impurity, died forgotten, and was now to be resurrected in poetry.[100]

The result of Zhitlowski's analysis of Jewish religious development was a significant reevaluation of Judaism that stressed the universalist implications of biblical and prophetic ideals. In the past, he had denounced the Tanakh (Pentateuch, Prophets, and Writings) as a compendium of fairy tales and archaisms. Zhitlowski now described the sacred text as "a colossal cultural document" embodying ideals of brotherhood, social justice, and the unity of God, man, and nature, which the Jewish people had transmitted to humanity.[101] Similarly, he now viewed the Talmud as contributing to modern conceptualization and problem solving, its legal codes containing laws to protect the oppressed against exploitation. Were Jewish radicals who called for the total disappearance of the Jewish people aware that the Talmud's view of employee-employer relations actually underlay the Marxist labor theory of value? Zhitlowski wondered.[102] Even later religious works that he had previously ignored or had ridiculed as gibberish were now said to reflect the underlying ethical and aesthetic nature of Jewish national culture. Thus, for example, Zhitlowski described the works of medieval Jewish poets as embodying in religious form the hopes and dreams of the Jewish people which modern Jews now had the opportunity to realize. Similarly, Kabbalah, the classic expression of Jewish mysticism, should be seen not as mere superstition but as "a fantasy world full of mystical beauty."[103]

Zhitlowski's search for spiritual and cultural alternatives to traditional Judaism as well as his own self-styled rebellious nature also led him to reexamine heretical religious movements in Jewish history. He was particularly fascinated by messianic movements, such as that of Shabbatai Zvi, which he viewed as expressions of the popular struggle for national survival that arose in response to the ossification of rabbinical Judaism in the early modern period.[104] Similarly, he now interpreted the ideals of Hasidism, from which he had fled in his youth, as "transcendent poetry" reflecting an inner beauty, sense of justice, and a yearning for redemption.[105] Such lofty notions were not restricted to past heresies alone. The social ethical core of Jewish ideals, Zhitlowski maintained, could be found not only in the writings of the prophet Isaiah but also in the theories of the "atheist" Jew Karl Marx.[106]

Zhitlowski was convinced that the poetic revival of Judaism would not only reconnect modern Jews with their past but would also link them to the ideals of Jewish socialism.[107] As "poetic embodiments of feelings and thoughts [that reflect] . . . human holiness," Jewish myths and rituals could serve as models for the progress of all of humanity.[108] Thus, for example, Zhitlowski described the recounting of the Exodus story at Passover as a celebration of national freedom and defined Shavuot (the Feast of Weeks), which commemorates the giving of the Torah at Mount Sinai, as the celebration of a social code embodying social justice and humanity. Similarly, he emphasized the role of the High Holy Days of Rosh Hashanah and Yom Kippur in encouraging self-examination and soul-searching among the Jewish people that would lead to effective social and political action. Zhitlowski placed special emphasis upon Sukkot (the Feast of Tabernacles), which he argued expressed the sanctification of agriculture and the manual la-

borer. Even minor holidays now took on spiritual and "socialist" significance. Purim was a national catharsis; the fasts a reminder of the
Jews' loss of freedom and independence. Zhitlowski placed the Sabbath apart from all the others. The loveliest of all holidays, he argued,
it embodied the essence of socialism. The biblical commandment to
cease from work attested to the Jewish people's commitment to a belief in the right of each individual to control his or her labor.[109]

The association of the spiritual ideals of Judaism with socialism
marked Zhitlowski's attempt to unite his two central concerns: the
future of the Jewish people and the fate of humanity as a whole. His
efforts to synthesize nationalism and universalism clearly placed him
at odds with the prevailing Marxist view that dominated both the
Jewish and Russian radical communities by the 1890s. As a Jewish
nationalist, Zhitlowski remained steadfastly convinced that a commitment to socialism did not preclude loyalty to the Jewish people.
The triumph of socialism would not only end class divisions, he argued, but would also end the dominance of one nationality by another. Rejecting both Marxist internationalism, which denied
peoplehood, and Zionist "chauvinism," which placed such differences
above the interests of humanity, Zhitlowski called for the defense of
"cosmopolitanism," the recognition that only through the development of distinctive national identities and cultures could the interests of humanity be advanced.[110]

Zhitlowski's defense of national culture also placed him at odds with
what he regarded as the determinism and falsely prophetic nature of
Marxist dogma. In defining society purely in terms of class divisions,
Marxist materialism ignored the complex reality of late-nineteenth-
century relations within and among nations in the name of a theoretical abstraction. In denying the validity of national distinctiveness and
in denigrating national identity, Zhitlowski claimed, Marxist dogma led
not to a firm sense of the truth but to skepticism and philosophical
agnosticism.[111] Zhitlowski also rejected what he regarded as Marxism's
narrowly materialist interpretation of society, which he argued ignored
the power of the individual will and denied the role of ideas in shaping
society in the name of economic determinism. Like many of his contemporaries, he employed a dialectical argument to justify his position. Neither an idealist nor a materialist, Zhitlowski claimed to preach
"monism," a synthesis of the two views that rested on the principle of
harmony arising out of seeming chaos and that rejected the notion of

an "absolute truth" in the name of the ability of each individual to understand his or her existential situation.[112]

In denouncing Marxist theory and praxis, Zhitlowski attempted to remain true to the early socialist ideals of Populism. His perspective was that of the First rather than the Second International—a defense of socialist ideals that rested upon the distinctiveness and independence of individual nations and movements and that reflected the first stages of the systematic struggle against capitalism.[113] More than anything else, however, Zhitlowski's elaborate defense of an open-ended socialist vision resulted from a desperate desire to create a theoretical framework that would incorporate his eclectic views as well as the diverse elements of the "progressive" Jewish community in a common struggle for national renewal. As Victor Tchernov, a fellow Jewish SR activist, noted apologetically in an essay written in honor of Zhitlowski's fiftieth birthday: "He believed that the philosophical-socialist credo of every revolutionary Jew . . . was a private matter and that the unity of abstract principles with narrow revolutionary practice is so broad and ill-defined that no one had any reason to fight a life-and-death struggle over it."[114]

If there was one constant in Zhitlowski's socialist vision, it was the ideal of agrarianism. In the 1880s and '90s, his vision of the Jewish worker was based less on the reality of factory life in the Pale (which he knew little about) than upon the Populist myth of the Russian peasant. In Zhitlowski's mind, the plight of peasantry was a microcosm of the mass of humanity. Unschooled, the peasant was nonetheless deeply aware of his loyalties to the collectivity; committed to bettering his condition, he generally was resigned to his fate.[115] As an activist among East European immigrants in New York City, Zhitlowski romanticized about Jewish settlements in the small towns of the American prairie. Similarly, his support of territorialism in the first two decades of the twentieth century rested in large part upon his conviction that in contrast to agricultural communities in Palestine that were built allegedly on the backs of Arab workers, settlements in Russia, the United States, and Argentina reflected the highest ideals of Jewish manual labor.[116] Like the early Populists and their intellectual heirs the SRs, Zhitlowski remained convinced throughout his life that the future socialist society could avoid the excesses of industrial capitalism entirely by adhering to the ideals of agricultural communalism. There seems little doubt that it was in part Lenin's promise to skip the stage of western industrial development that first attracted Zhitlowski to the Bolshevik Revolution. If anything, his fascination with rural life deepened in his later years, largely as a result of his interest in Soviet agricultural projects directed toward its Jewish population in the 1920s and early '30s. As late as 1937, Zhitlowski was still bemoaning the fact that "with the exception of the Soviet Union, Jews live everywhere as an urban merchant people."[117]

Zhitlowski's espousal of socialism and of agrarianism in particular as a solution to the plight of Jewry in the modern world rested upon both his analysis of anti-Semitism and his prognosis for the future of the Jewish people. As noted earlier, Zhitlowski had long believed that Jewish life in the Diaspora was characterized by economic parasitism. The factory, whether run by capitalists or Marxist revolutionaries, promised the Jew only physical debilitation and psychological alienation.[118] Manual labor, on the other hand, was both antithetical to the character and the interests of the parasitical Jewish bourgeoisie and more closely attuned to the daily life of the masses. The return to the land therefore would lead to the end of anti-Semitism by demonstrating the honesty and industriousness of the Jewish people. Intimately tied to personal and collective spiritual development, it could also serve to accelerate the development of a "progressive Jewish culture."[119] For Zhitlowski, agricultural production thus was a panacea for the internal ills besetting the Jewish community. Not only would it rescue Jewry from the pollution and decay of factory and urban life, it would also end class divisions. In so doing, manual labor would serve to reconnect both the Jewish masses and alienated young intellectuals with their true selves.[120]

Given his association of agrarian socialism with the national revival and moral regeneration of the Jewish people, it is not surprising that Zhitlowski never specifically outlined the nature of his agricultural utopia in any of his collected writings. Like the early colonizers in Palestine, his vision of Jewish economic life did not extend much beyond the transformation of the manual laborer and tradesman from an urban to a rural setting.[121] The few references one finds to the future society in Zhitlowski's articles emphasize the achievement of cultural goals such as the triumph of the Yiddish language and the relegation of religion to a private concern rather than socioeconomic issues.[122] His ringing endorsement of the SRs' program calling for the collective ownership of land, for example, ultimately rested on the party's willingness to support the right of linguistic and cultural self-determination for non-Russians, including Jews. It is true that in his debates with Marxists he stressed his belief that it was possible to skip the stage of industrial capitalism and advance directly to socialism through the establishment of cooperative farms. Yet Zhitlowski's ideological quarrel with Marxism had less to do with specific socioeconomic concerns than with his general suspicion of rigid theoretical constructs and his moral revulsion for urban industrial life. Even his sycophantic praise of Stalin's program for agricultural collectivization in the 1920s and '30s can be partially explained in terms of his mistaken belief that the son of Georgian peasants would support Jewish national revival through hard work. Nowhere did he attempt to examine the dictator's policies in depth. In the end, Zhitlowski's vision of a Jewish agrarian socialist society stemmed from his concern with issues of national regeneration rather than from any real understanding of the specifics of farming or agriculture.

Implicit in Zhitlowski's arguments concerning both the redefinition of Jewish identity and the reshaping of Jewish society was the need to develop autonomous institutions in a separate territory. Zhitlowski had first proposed territorial autonomism as a solution to the "Jewish problem" in his earliest works that he wrote for emigré Jewish students in 1887 and 1892. He elaborated further on the idea during his campaign to found Vorozhdenie and later the SERP party. Despite Zhitlowski's fascination with autonomism, however, he could hardly be credited as the originator of the concept. The idea of cultural autonomy for national minorities had been the subject of intense discussion in central and East European political and intellectual circles at the turn of the century. Within Russia, much of the impetus came from the general popularity of Populist, Utopian socialist, and romantic notions of a future society based on the model of the local peasant or agricultural community. Such ideas were easily translated by nationalist leaders of ethnic minorities into a vision of the replacement of the nation-state with a decentralized "state of nationalities." In their view, the future Russian society had to return not only to nature but also to the deeply rooted cultural and linguistic ties that bound individuals together.

The movement for national minority rights was bolstered by the writings of two prominent Austrian socialists, Otto Bauer and Karl Renner, who had proposed the granting of national rights in the future Austro-Hungarian socialist state. Bauer and Renner envisioned a decentralized republic in which members of each nationality, whatever their residence, would form a single association that would deal with "national-cultural" affairs, including control over the educational system and the right of taxation. Each national assembly would have the right to choose a minister as head of state who would also represent his group in a central state organization. Despite their support of national minority rights, however, both Bauer and Renner rejected the notion of Jewish autonomy. Repeating Marx's argument that the advent of capitalism marked the end of the Jews as a nation, the two socialists called upon Jews to cease demanding national cultural rights.[123] Not surprisingly, therefore, the Austrian Socialist Party's resolution supporting autonomous rights for minority groups within the Austro-Hungarian Empire, which was passed at its conference held in Brünn in 1899, made no mention of Jews.

In their search for institutional models for the new Jewish society, many supporters of autonomism were attracted to the experience of the *kahal*, if only because it promised change in Jewish life without significant social, economic, and cultural dislocation. Others were fascinated with the *mir*, the peasant community, and the *artel*, the artisan workshop, that had been proposed by Russian intellectuals as models of social and economic life superior to western forms of modernization.[124] Still other "autonomists" sought to replicate in the Diaspora the Zionists' colonization schemes and programs for building a Jewish homeland. Already in 1882, the proto-Zionist Leon Pinsker had proposed the need for a Jewish land (though not specifically Palestine) in his seminal work *Autoemancipation*. Other prominent Jewish nationalist thinkers, most notably Simon Dubnow, would soon surpass Zhitlowski in developing highly complex analyses of Jewish autonomism. By the first decade of the twentieth century, a fullfledged territorialist movement had developed to counter both Zionism and assimilationism.

What was distinctive in Zhitlowski's program for autonomy was his synthesis of socialism with Jewish minority rights. Such a view was not easy to maintain, given the Marxist socialists' commitment to internationalism and later the Bolsheviks' insistence upon centralized control as a necessary precondition for the establishment of a socialist state. As noted earlier, Zhitlowski chose to emphasize the attitudes of early socialists of the First International who showed a more tolerant attitude toward the question of nationalism and national minorities. For early socialists, he commented, true internationalism meant the brotherhood, not the elimination of nations. At the same time, Zhitlowski never actually envisioned a Jewish homeland as an immediate need or an imminent reality. In his constant emphasis on the need to wait for the establishment of a socialist society before creating a Jewish land, he undoubtedly hoped to reduce territorialism to an abstract ideal that would only indirectly affect his day-to-day political activity.[125]

The truth, however, was that Zhitlowski was constantly forced to respond to attacks upon his ideas from within the socialist community. The result was that his concept of autonomy underwent many changes over the course of his intellectual and political career. The classical formation of Zhitlowski's ideas could be found in such early works as *A Id tsu idn* and "Tsionismus oder sotsialismus," which stressed the importance of Jewish cultural autonomy within a socialist Russia. In the immediate postrevolutionary period, Zhitlowski believed that Jews would gain personal autonomy, that is, the right to be considered as part of Jewish people no matter where they lived in the world. In the Russia of the future, he envisioned the creation of an elaborate network of schools and cultural organizations that would serve as the necessary precondition for the concentration of Jewry in a homeland of their own. By the first decade of the twentieth century, Zhitlowski had helped create a political party that pressed for political autonomy and the establishment of a Jewish territory in the distant future. As we have seen, however, the failure of the Revolution of 1905 led him to look to Palestine as an increasingly realistic possibility. By the 1930s, Zhitlowski had returned to his original view. Denouncing the Zionist experiment as reactionary, he stressed the need for Jewry to find a safe refuge from anti-Semitic persecution in a territory within the friendly confines of the Soviet Union.[126]

Despite his on again, off again relationship with Zionism, Zhitlowski steadfastly opposed any attempt to associate Jewish national identity with political sovereignty. Too often, he would argue in 1915 in a clear allusion to both tsarist Russia and what he feared would occur in Palestine, political nationalism degenerated into patriotism and led to the domination by the ruling nation over ethnic minorities within its midst.[127] Zionists, he maintained, had the same imperialist worldview as Pan-Slavists and Pan-Germanists. For autonomists, on the other hand, the Land of Israel was a territory just like any other territory. Unlike Zionism, autonomism established an objective definition for Jewish nationhood without the taint of governmental control and the potential danger of economic exploitation.[128]

Though he clearly influenced the formation of both socialist Zionism and the territorialist movement, Zhitlowski took greatest pride in the development of his theory of Diaspora nationalism. Despite his ever-changing perspective, he never lost his firm conviction that a national culture could only effectively develop within a self-contained national unit. In this, he differed markedly from both the Bundists and the Folkists (under the leadership of Simon Dubnow), who were content to defend the limited notion of cultural autonomy, as well as the Zionists, who argued for the creation of a separate sovereign state. Instead, Zhitlowski envisioned a decentralized polity where each national minority would have its own communal structure and autonomy but which would remain united with other citizens of the state in the commitment to building a socialist society. Such attitudes explain both his championing of a "United States of Nations" in America and his obstinate defense of the Birodbidjan experiment in the Soviet Union during the late 1920s and early '30s.

By far the most significant challenge to Zhitlowski's defense of Diaspora nationalism came from another thinker of the transitional generation, the historian Simon Dubnow. In his *Letters on Old and New Judaism*, published in 1907, Dubnow had posited the notion of Jews as a spiritual nation that sustained itself in history through the maintenance of distinctive and autonomous communal institutions.[129] In a review of the work written a year later, Zhitlowski criticized Dubnow in terms that could well have been leveled against his own views of the autonomy question.[130] Zhitlowski's main attack centered on Dubnow's disregard of the socioeconomic needs of the Jewish masses in the name of the development of the "national spirit." Though he himself had never clearly confronted the politically sensitive issue of economic divisions within the Jewish community, Zhitlowski claimed that it was absurd for the Jewish historian to argue that an emphasis on issues such as the class struggle would weaken the Jews' struggle for survival. An ardent supporter of minority national rights in the period after the Revolution of 1905, he nevertheless denounced Dubnow's program of full civil equality for the Jewish people as nothing more than a thinly disguised imitation of the assimilationist goals of the party of the Russian bourgeoisie—"a national-Jewish Kadetism" with an "evolutionary

Jewish lining," as he called it. Finally, Zhitlowski attacked the Jewish historian's emphasis upon Jewry as a distinct "spiritual" people whose roots were in the ancient past, while ignoring the fact that he himself had constantly argued for the need to recognize the centrality of biblical ideals in Jewish historical development.

Zhitlowski was equally insistent that Dubnow's program of autonomism was derivative. Aside from his own writings, he noted that the idea of cultural autonomy had been adopted by the Bund in 1897, a full decade before Dubnow. (In so doing, Zhitlowski ignored the fact that the Jewish historian's first discussion of autonomism in the first of his *Letters on Old and New Judaism* actually preceded the foundation of the Bund.) Unlike Dubnow, however, the Bund did not chain Jewry to outworn traditions. Instead, it insisted that Jews should remain open to the influence of other cultures. The fact that the Jewish socialists' lukewarm response to his own views on autonomy was one of the reasons that Zhitlowski broke with the Bund went unmentioned. Further, Zhitlowski attacked Dubnow's unwillingness to accept a Jew who converted to Christianity. To refuse to accept a committed Jew who believed in Jesus, he argued, would most certainly alienate radical intellectuals seeking to reintegrate themselves into the Jewish community. In the same breath, however, Zhitlowski criticized the historian's defense of cultural autonomy within Russia as ignoring the centrality of the yearning for Zion in Jewish religious tradition! It was only in his concluding remarks that Zhitlowski clearly enunciated his differences with Dubnow. Only a people with its own territory, he proclaimed, would be able to develop a full and satisfying cultural life of its own.

In his diatribe against Dubnow, Zhitlowski had championed the virtues of Yiddish, which he claimed would incorporate the divergent views of Jewry in a new, progressive cultural form. Yiddish had been a central component in Zhitlowski's writings throughout his intellectual meanderings, if only because it provided a stable anchor for his ever-changing perspective. The concern with language also reflected the limited tools available to the Jewish activist in his attempt to revitalize a powerless, stateless, and economically impoverished Russian Jewish community under tsarism and later in the United States. Yet Zhitlowski's growing fascination with Yiddish had deep roots in both the European and Jewish communities in which he lived and worked.

The emphasis on language as the basis of national identity was common fare among national minorities in the Austro-Hungarian and Russian empires in the late nineteenth century. With the notable exception of the Jewish nationalist Nathan Birnbaum, Yiddishists rarely admitted their debt to other ethnic groups, however. To do so would not only have been to deny the distinctiveness of their own ideas but would have associated Jewish nationalism with "culturally inferior" populations.[131] Instead, supporters of Yiddish drew from the writings of German romantics in the eighteenth century and specifically from the works of Johann Gottfried von Herder.

In one of his most famous works, *Über den Ursprung der Sprache* (On the Origins of Language), published in 1772, Herder had argued that language was the preeminent medium through which human beings became conscious of both their inner selves and the nature of their relationships with others. Through language, human beings linked themselves vertically with the past and horizontally with members of the same *Volk,* or people. As the core of group identity, Herder argued, language was the most important means by which national ideals and values were passed on from generation to generation. It was also a vital force in modernizing a national culture since it was equally accessible to all and could easily replace traditional ritual as an outward manifestation of national identity. In forsaking its language, Herder concluded, a *Volk* thus destroyed its most distinctive and sacred possession at the same time that it endangered its future.[132]

Herder was especially fascinated with the Jews, whom he looked upon as an excellent example of an ancient people that had managed to preserve its own distinctive character over the generations through language and culture. In a romantic evocation of ancient Israel, the German philosopher described the Jewish people as a natural community bound by common beliefs, values, and laws and imbued with a clear sense of national purpose and destiny. For Herder, Hebrew literature from Genesis to rabbinic times was a philosophical continuum of unique quality and power. Similarly, he viewed Hebrew as a primitive language reflecting the most basic aspects of human life. Herder was also attracted to Jews as a nonterritorial nationality that depended upon language as a primary vehicle for group survival. Convinced that European civilization needed to be rejuvenated, he looked to "unspoiled" nations such as the Slavs and the Jews to inject new life into a degenerating humanity.[133]

Many East European Jewish intellectuals, concerned with the Jewish future in an atmosphere of impending crisis, were quick to appropriate elements of Herder's linguistic nationalism. The German romantic's concerns with cultural imperialism as practiced by the dominant society seemed to be corroborated by the crucial role that Russian-language schools played in tsarist government efforts to assimilate Jews. In contrast to their coreligionists in western Europe, both assimilationists and antiassimilationists in the Russian Jewish community understood that the choice to participate in the larger society centered primarily on the adoption of the dominant language rather than its religion.[134] Similarly, Herder's emphasis on the need to maintain a distinctive language in order to ensure national survival spoke to the limited opportunities for national expression available to ethnic minorities in the Russian Empire. Jewish nationalists quickly recognized that in the absence of political sovereignty, geographical unity, economic power, and social mobility, Jews would have to turn to their spiritual and cultural sources to preserve their distinctiveness. Many shared Herder's perspective that a distinct Jewish language could serve as a replacement for religious tradition as an outward and portable manifestation of national identity. Finally, Herder's emphasis on the unity of mankind through the multiplicity of nations convinced many radical Jewish intellectuals that the maintenance of a distinctive language would help rather than hinder Jews in their effort to make their own distinctive contribution to the betterment of humanity.

Though generally agreeing on the importance of language for the revitalization of East European Jewry, supporters of Jewish modernization were often bitterly divided along ideological lines over which language to choose. Despite their obvious political differences, both revolutionaries active in radical social movements in Russian society and abroad and assimilationists seeking to integrate into the larger society insisted that Jews concentrate upon learning and speaking Russian. Some internationalists even argued for the adoption of a universal language as a precondition for the creation of a progressive world culture in which Jews could participate as equal members. The creator of Esperanto, Ludwik Zamenhof, for example, was a Polish Jew who had originally begun his career as a Yiddish grammarian and philologist and had been one of the founders of Hibbat Zion.[135]

By far the most bitter debates occurred between supporters of Hebrew and Yiddish. Hebrew was the preferred language of Jewish nationalists in the Zionist movement at the end of the century. Even among non-Zionists, its association with the biblical chronicle of the birth of the Jewish people, and with the treasures of sacred Jewish literature that were written and carefully preserved over the centuries, assured it a distinguished place in Jewish national consciousness. Proponents of Yiddish countered that their linguistic heritage faithfully reflected the daily experiences of the Ashkenazic Jewish masses throughout the generations. Born of the intermingling of Hebrew and the languages of the surrounding societies in which Jews found themselves, Yiddish was described as the preeminent language of the Diaspora Jew, symbolizing his desire to participate in the larger society while at the same time preserving his cultural and ethnic heritage.

There was little doubt that Yiddish played a far more important role than either Russian or Hebrew in the daily life of Jews in late-nineteenth-century Russia and Poland. According to the Russian census of 1897, 96.9 percent of the Jewish population in the empire spoke Yiddish as their primary language.[136] With the exception of a small number of assimilated Jewish intellectuals, most Jews viewed Russian as little more than a language of commerce and trade with no significance for Jewish communal concerns. Similarly, although many Russian Jews continued to use Hebrew in daily prayers and religious rituals, only a small number—no more than a few hundred thousand—were accustomed to reading secular Hebrew books. By the turn of the century, Hebrew readership had actually declined as a new generation emerged that no longer knew how to read traditional texts. Even those Jewish intellectuals who championed the revival of Hebrew were often frustrated by the inability of Hebrew writers to escape the literary excesses and sentimentalism of the Haskalah and to focus on contemporary issues facing the Jewish community.[137]

Yiddish, on the other hand, stood midway between the Russian language of the larger society and the sacred tongue of Hebrew. As such, it served as both a spiritual and "profane" language for Jews in the Pale. While religious leaders used Yiddish for the moralistic and popular education of children, women, and others untrained in Hebrew, Jewish merchants and tradesmen spoke it in their business dealings with each other and with consumers in the community. As the language of both the marketplace and the home, Yiddish bridged the gap between the public and private lives of Russian Jewry.

Nevertheless, for much of the nineteenth century modernizing intellectuals generally ignored Yiddish, regarding it as a primitive jargon with little literary merit. Educated Jews who continued to use the language generally found that they had to justify their position to other members of the intelligentsia.[138] Early efforts to demonstrate that Yiddish could be something more than a utilitarian language for popular education and commerce were unsuccessful. The first Yiddish newspaper in Russia, *Kol Mevasser* (The Voice of the Messenger), published in Odessa in 1862 (first as a supplement to the Hebrew weekly *Ha-Melits* (The Interpreter) and then from 1869 to 1872 as an independent paper), quickly ran into trouble with critics both within and outside the community. While traditionalists and Russifiers denounced the paper for being too secular or too parochial, government officials opposed it because they could not find anyone knowledgeable in the language who was willing to serve as an official censor![139]

The movement to promote Yiddish as a vehicle for cultural and national revival was given new impetus in the 1880s with the return of young intellectuals to the community. Of particular significance was the activity of Jewish socialists. At first, political activists saw Yiddish merely as a useful tool to radicalize Jewish workers and artisans. The choice of Yiddish also allowed Jewish militants to avoid making choices among competing nationalities within the Russian working-class movement. In time, however, Jewish socialists began to portray the language as a crucial element in the class struggle within the Jewish community. Yiddish was a genuine and natural reflection of the daily life of the Jewish masses, they argued, and stood in stark contrast to the Russification of the assimilationist Jewish bourgeoisie.[140] Political activists readily adopted the name "jargon" instead of Yiddish, thereby transforming a derisive term originally used by maskilim, assimilationists, and Zionists to describe an insignificant folk tongue into a badge of pride.

The goals of Yiddishists were also influenced by the activities of other national groups in the Russian Empire who saw the maintenance of their distinctive language as a bulwark against government attempts to forcefully assimilate them. Both Ukrainian and Lithuanian nationalists, for example, juxtaposed the masses' use of the national language against the desperate drive by assimilating elements of the upper classes to become Germanized and Polonized respectively.[141] East European nationalists also promoted their languages in the struggle for political rights and freedoms. In 1905, in the wake of the revolution, for example, Jewish owners of newspapers joined with other editors of non-Russian language papers published in St. Petersburg to press for rights for all national minorities in the empire.[142] At the same time, supporters of Yiddishism were not averse to using techniques borrowed from slavophilic intellectuals in the larger Russian society who pointed to folk culture and language as reflections of the distinctive nature of Russian life.

Such notions of the use of language and literature as a tool for enlightenment and progress (which ironically could be found among the early maskilim, whom Yiddishists often ridiculed) quickly took root among a small circle of Yiddish writers that began to emerge in the last three decades of the century. In contrast to the pragmatic and politicized Yiddishism of Jewish socialists and then later Bundists, the trenchant depictions of shtetl life by individuals like Mendele Moykher Sforim and Isaac Leyb Peretz fostered cultural innovation among East European Jews while at the same time reframing traditional values and themes in modern form.[143] In 1903, in response to growing interest, a group of young writers in St. Petersburg managed to issue the first daily Yiddish newspaper in Russia, *Der Fraynd* (The Friend). The paper was moved to Warsaw in 1908 and maintained a readership of nearly 100,000 until its demise in 1913.[144] As we have seen, by 1908 supporters of Yiddish in central and eastern Europe felt confident enough to organize an international conference in the city of Czernowitz to define the future of the language in Jewish life.

Developments at the Czernowitz Conference clearly pointed up the fundamental divisions within the Yiddishist movement. Organizers claimed to have chosen the site of the conference—a major Jewish settlement in Bukovina which was then under Austro-Hungarian control—because of the Hapsburg Empire's recognition of Jews as a nationality. In actuality, however, the competing elements only agreed on the site after bitter debate and only because it stood midway between central and eastern Europe. The discussions among the seventy participants centered on a number of issues. On the most fundamental question, the nature and role of the Yiddish language, there was little agreement. While some participants defended Yiddish as a folk tongue and thus reflective of the daily life of the Jewish masses, others emphasized the need to formalize the language in preparation for its future role as a vehicle for cultural revitalization. Even more divisive were the participants' ideological views over the future of the Jewish people, which defined their approach to Yiddish. Representatives of religious Orthodoxy, fearing that any changes in the language would have repercussions within the community, argued for the need to maintain the status quo. In contrast, Bundists demanded that Yiddish be proclaimed as the distinctive language of the Jewish people, thereby hoping to fend off efforts by Zionists who championed Hebrew. In the end, the conference had to settle for a compromise resolution that declared Yiddish as merely a, rather than the, national language of the Jewish people.[145]

Haim Zhitlowski was one of the central organizers of the Czernowitz Conference, and his speeches at the meetings were long remembered for their fervent defense of the Yiddish language against the inroads of both Hebrew and European culture. For Zhitlowski, Yiddish language and literature seemed a clear alternative to both Orthodox Judaism and Zionism as the basis for Jewish national identity. While the latter two represented a retreat from modern society and ideas, he argued, Yiddish was a progressive tool that could incorporate both ancient Jewish traditions and new values in contemporary life. Whereas religion and homeland created division and separation from the outside world, language united antagonistic elements within each nation while embodying universal ideals and goals that could be understood by all of humanity. Zhitlowski also maintained that only the Yiddish language held out the possibility of reintegrating elements of the Jewish people, especially intellectuals, who had strayed from the "communal hearth." Available to all and tolerant of all beliefs, Yiddish potentially could serve as the motor force for the development of an autonomous Jewish existence in all of the emerging modern Jewish communities, including the United States, independent Poland, the Palestinian *yishuv*, and the Soviet Union.[146]

Zhitlowski's support of Yiddish was grounded in his view of the nature of humanity, a view that borrowed liberally from the writings of Herder and his disciples. In an early essay entitled "Id un mensh" (Jew and Man), Zhitlowski had echoed the German thinker's argument that language was the most basic means of attaining self-knowledge since it was inculcated from birth and provided the most direct means of connecting with the external world.[147] Language also served to differentiate nations from one another. The fact that no language was superior to any other, however, was irrefutable proof of the equality and interconnectedness of nations. Finally, since actions were grounded in thought and thought must be expressed in language, a people's language best expressed the distinctive conditions under which each nation lived and developed.[148]

Using Herder's criteria, Zhitlowski argued that Yiddish was the most solid cornerstone of Jewish national existence because it provided a portable identity for a people who lacked the objective and external characteristics of territory and sovereignty.[149] Yiddish thus reflected the popular will of the Jewish people in the Diaspora. It existed because the masses willed it so, not because of some externally imposed condition. Because it required no prior ideological commitment, Zhitlowski maintained, a Jewish identity grounded in Yiddish was more malleable and more democratic than either traditional Judaism or Zionism. A Jew who immersed himself in Yiddish culture did not have to believe in Judaism. Even a convert to Christianity could still be viewed as Jewish as long as he spoke Yiddish. His mere use of the language, Zhitlowski claimed, qualified him as "part of the Jewish spiritual national home."[150]

Zhitlowski's defense of Yiddish was based on a fervent belief, common among linguistic nationalists, that language was indistinguishable from culture. Traditions and national memories that embodied the deepest sentiments of a people had little meaning unless they could be communicated and transmitted from one generation to another. For Zhitlowski, the fate of a people's language was thus the most sensitive barometer of its inner strength and its will to survive. For Jews, the disappearance of Yiddish would not only represent a cultural loss; it would also signal their inevitable destruction through assimilation.[151] In turn, only the revival of Yiddish would rejuvenate an ossified Jewish culture and weakened Jewish people.[152]

Much of Zhitlowski's defense of Yiddish was shaped by his response to attacks made by supporters of Hebrew within the Jewish community. Zionist critics had claimed that since Yiddishism was linked to the fate of Jewry in the Diaspora, it was bound to disappear within a few generations as Jews were absorbed into the larger society. Turning the Hebraist argument on its head, Zhitlowski claimed that it was actually Hebrew and not Yiddish that was assimilationist. In ancient times, he argued with little historical support, biblical Hebrew had been the language of all of the peoples in Canaan. As the policies of biblical kings clearly demonstrated, the goal of ancient Hebraists was to forcibly assimilate nations rather than to assert a distinctive national identity. Though Jews no longer had political power, Zhitlowski claimed, contemporary Hebraists continued to be obsessed with assimilation. In mimicking the literature of other nations, however, they only demonstrated their alienation from the Jewish masses.[153]

Zhitlowski was particularly incensed by the Hebraists' claim that Yiddish was no more than a jargon, a derivative tongue of no intrinsic worth. All languages began as jargons, he claimed, yet Yiddish was one of the few folk languages that was able not only to survive but to thrive. The fact that Jews took a medieval non-Jewish tongue and forged a new language was not a sign of weakness, as opponents of Yiddish often argued, but rather an indication of the strength of the Jewish people. Indeed, Zhitlowski insisted that the closeness of Yiddish to German benefited Jews by enabling them to become acquainted with the Roman alphabet and thus more broadly with European culture. Nevertheless, the value and strength of a Jewish national language could not be determined by the attitudes of non-Jews. Even "if we threw in a couple of Hebrew words in our language and attempted to 'Yiddishize' each German word," Zhitlowski cynically noted in an article written in 1923, "would the 'beasts,' i.e. the people of the world, show more respect for Yiddish?"[154] Instead, one had to examine the manner in which a language helped to further the interests of its people. Here too, Zhitlowski maintained, Yiddish had a clear advantage over Hebrew. In contrast to Hebrew's "Orientalist" and "anti-Europeanist" nature, Yiddish's association with German would help to bridge the gap between western and East European Jewry. As the language of the majority of Jewry, it would serve as a powerful barrier against assimilationism.[155]

Indeed, if any Jewish language could be deemed inauthentic, Zhitlowski argued, it was Hebrew. To an outside observer, it "sounded like an arcane artistic language known only by the 'inner circle' who alone know the secrets of its art."[156] As long as the majority of Jews did not speak Hebrew, Zhitlowski concluded, Hebraism was an unrealizable ideal, "an aristocratic oasis" that could not meet the needs of the Jewish people who were wandering in the spiritual "desert sands." It had as much chance of successfully winning over the masses of Jewry as a message "written in coal in a chimney stack."[157]

In his defense of Yiddish, Zhitlowski was fond of drawing parallels between the backwardness of the Yiddish language and the desperate fate of Jewry. In suggesting that the similarity between the two demonstrated their natural compatibility, the Jewish socialist undoubtedly hoped to link his defense of Yiddishism with the plight of the Jewish masses. The result, however, was more fanciful than factual. Like the Jewish people itself, Zhitlowski mused, Yiddish was in constant danger of disappearing. Like its most adept practitioners, Yiddish lacked a solid infrastructure and had to occasionally steal from other languages in order to survive. The "poverty" of Yiddish also resulted from its functional nature. As a language of everyday life for a downcast people, Zhitlowski claimed, it was too busy struggling to survive and had little time to develop a formal grammar or an aesthetic sense. No wonder Jewish intellectuals refused to write in it.

Yet like "a wild unplowed field," the potential of Yiddish and its people had yet to be fully cultivated.[158] Here Zhitlowski interwove a number of his central concerns. As preeminently a folk language, he maintained, Yiddish could help realize the socialist vision within the Jewish community by introducing universal ideals into Jewish popular consciousness. In this sense, he argued, an emphasis upon the Yiddish language as the source of national identity would enable the Jewish people to link their fate with the general struggle for human progress. The result would be a "progressive" culture that would synthesize the best of Jewish tradition and modern life.[159]

Aside from his insistence on infusing traditional religious ideals with contemporary social and ethical relevance and his discursive essays on philosophy (which were meant in part to demonstrate how Yiddish could be used in scholarly research and writing), however, Zhitlowski did not elaborate on exactly what he meant by a "progressive" Yiddish culture. His definition of progress rested on four major principles: the absolute autonomy of the individual, free cultural development, social justice and equality, and international brotherhood.[160] Yet apart from his discussion of religious holidays and rituals, Zhitlowski never demonstrated how these principles could be reflected and realized in the daily life of the Jew. Nor did he explain how individual and collective goals would coexist. In the end, he seemed trapped in a tautology that argued that a "progressive" culture rested upon the blending of "progressive" aspects of Jewish tradition with modern "progressive" ideals. The few specific indications in Zhitlowski's writings concerning the creation of new cultural forms merely reemphasize the need for a linkage between nationalist concerns and universalist ideals and seem more directed at his Zionist opponents than at his supporters. Thus, for example, he suggested that the heroes of the new culture should be philosophers and playwrights whose goal was to affirm humanistic and universalistic values, rather than diplomats whose victories resulted from the defeat of others.[161] No wonder that Zhitlowski's critics often accused him of placing the needs of "progressivism" above the interests of the Jewish people.[162]

In his writings, Zhitlowski sought to link Yiddish with yet another of his central ideals, the return of the intellectuals to the Jewish community. Reflecting upon his own "return," he argued that thoughtful young Jews would never participate in the Jewish community if it continued to ground itself in traditional Judaism. Only a reemphasis upon a national language—the sole method by which collectivities expressed their humanity, esthetics, and morality—could convince young Jews to return to their people. Zhitlowski claimed that in the past intellectuals had been ashamed to speak their native tongue. Instead, they had sought out the language of other, "culturally superior" nations to express their thoughts. The result, however, was a deep sense of alienation. Though intellectuals might materially benefit from their participation in the larger culture, they could not clearly express their own thoughts in a foreign tongue.[163] Only by resuming their use of Yiddish, Zhitlowski argued, could Jewish intellectuals hope to express the ideals of their own people while remaining true to their own values and beliefs. At the same time, only the use of the language of the masses could inspire elements of the lower classes to assert their creativity in the name of the nation as a whole. The development of a democratic and progressive Yiddish culture at the hands of young "proletarian" writers, poets, and dramatists, Zhitlowski concluded, would be the clearest and most obvious expression of the Jewish people's independence and inner strength.[164]

Despite his fervent belief in Yiddishism, Zhitlowski readily admitted that linguistic nationalism could not solve all of Jewry's pressing problems. In particular, he recognized that Yiddish had little to offer in the way of concrete economic proposals. Given his belief in territorialism, Zhitlowski was forced to admit that, ultimately, the fate of the Yiddish language rose and fell with the fate of the Diaspora. Should Jews achieve their own homeland, he argued, they would have the right to speak whatever language they chose, since their national survival would no longer be an issue.[165] In one of his writings, he even suggested that once the Jews had attained cultural autonomy or had gained political sovereignty, the Yiddishist campaign would end. In the meantime, however, the struggle for collective national rights in the Diaspora necessarily implied the defense of the Jews' distinctive language. While awaiting the realization of their physical homeland, Jews had to continue to struggle for their spiritual homeland—Yiddish.[166]

Such comments suggest that for all the contradictions and ambiguities in his thought, Zhitlowski firmly believed that his major concerns—the development of a progressive Jewish culture and modern Jewish identity, the implementation of agrarian socialism within the Jewish community, the return of the intellectuals to the Jewish fold, the need for communal autonomy, and the centrality of Yiddish—were inextricably intertwined. The constant leaps in his thought, however, point to the constant struggle he faced in attempting to integrate these concerns into a meaningful and consistent conceptual framework. Part of the problem lay in Zhitlowski's own eccentric personality, especially his inability to fully and clearly develop his ideas. Part of the problem lay with the rapidly changing conditions that forced Zhitlowski, along with other members of his generation, to respond quickly and dramatically to events that at times seemed to overtake them. Most important of all, the fact that Zhitlowski's ideas and proposals had arisen within the specific context of Russian Jewish society in the late nineteenth century meant that they would not easily survive the transfer of Jewish life from the Pale to new centers of settlement in Palestine and America.

Unlike Dubnow and Ahad Ha-Am, Zhitlowski boldly proclaimed his commitment to a radically new Jewish collective identity and purpose. Yet despite his seemingly progressive view of Jewish and general European life, the socialist activist remained unwilling to break with the past. Zhitlowski's intellectual peregrinations and his fascination with intellectuals struck many of his contemporaries as indicative of his commitment to change. To the modern historian, however, they seem motivated largely by the scholar's love of ideas over action and the traditional leader's discomfort with mass movements. Similarly, Zhitlowski's socialist vision, for all its fervor and commitment, was rooted in preindustrial agrarian perspectives and reflected a distrust for modern urban life and the class struggle. In turn, Zhitlowski's elaborate defense of Yiddish as a vehicle of "progressive" Jewish culture ultimately rested upon the emotional power of folkways rather than the rigors of defining and structuring a modern language and culture.

In the end, the specifics of Zhitlowski's definition of a modern Jewish identity proved to be little more than a creative reworking of traditional religious ideals and structures. Such notions enabled him to play a crucial role in the early formation of modernizing ideas and movements within the Jewish community but proved an obstacle in his desperate effort to respond to the ever-changing conditions of the twentieth century. Like other members of the transitional generation, Zhitlowski seemed caught between a past he could not recapture and a future he could not clearly comprehend.

CHAPTER 3

SIMON DUBNOW

History and
Modern Jewish Identity

THE TWENTIETH CENTURY has seen a growing divergence between popular and scholarly perceptions of Jewish history. While contemporary Jews selectively adopt elements of the Jewish past in an attempt to discern the mysteries of their collective survival, Jewish historians have struggled to transcend pietism and apologetics by incorporating their study into the general framework of current historical methodology and analysis. Yet barely a century ago, Jewish scholars saw little contradiction between the creation of collective memory and historical analysis.[1] Indeed, as reflected in the writings and ideas of Simon Dubnow, the rigorous study of history often served both to explain the continued survival of Jewry and to demonstrate the need for the creation of new forms of Jewish identity in the face of internal and external challenges.

For Dubnow, the key to developing a modern Jewish identity lay in understanding the constants of daily Jewish thought and behavior that often went unnoticed among the rapidly changing events of Jewish history. He believed that these transcendent and central ideas and institutions not only explained Jewish survival in the past but would also enable Jews to confront the challenges of modern life that threatened their physical and spiritual well-being in the present. By tracing the evolution of the Jewish people from its primitive roots to its maturing in the modern era, Dubnow also hoped to integrate the

Simon Dubnow

history of Jewry into the general development of humanity. Armed with a solid institutional and ideational base, the Jewish people would finally find an honored place in the future community of nations.

Rejecting both the maskil's romanticizing of the past and the turn-of-the-century activist's disdain for Jewish tradition, Dubnow clearly saw himself as a member of a distinct generation. Through the study of history, he hoped to demonstrate how one could immerse oneself in the Jewish past without becoming enslaved by it. At the same time, Dubnow was keenly aware of the need for self-styled "modern" Jews to find an appropriate balance between the events and ideas of the Jewish community and of the larger society in which they lived. Dismissing both religious Orthodoxy and Zionist statism as isolationist responses to the challenge of modernization, Dubnow was convinced that the answer lay in the Jews' historical memory. It was a search that would consume his professional activity and that frequently intruded upon his personal life. The immensity of the task was aptly summed up by Dubnow's thoughts upon hearing his young daughter read aloud from Ivan Turgenev's novel *Rudin*. "Two worlds, two generations, and between them a man of both worlds," Dubnow commented in his memoirs in a clear allusion to his own work; "[h]ow are these worlds going to come together?"[2]

A self-described "missionary for history," Dubnow would spend his life preaching the lessons learned from the Jewish past to a population confused about its present and anxious about its future. More than ever before, he had noted in his philosophical treatise on Jewish history written in 1893, Jewry was "in need of the teachings of the past, of the moral support and the prudent counsels of its history, its four thousand years of life crowded with checkered experiences."[3] For Dubnow, history thus took the place of midrash, or rabbinic gloss on a sacred text, as a didactic tool for a people that he was convinced no longer believed in the existence of a God of Israel but still wished to maintain their "holy" treasures.[4] Like biblical texts, the events of Jewish history cried out for an interpreter to explain the *drash*, or deep truth, which often lay hidden beneath their *p'shat*, or surface phenomena. Dubnow was undoubtedly thinking of himself when he commented upon the view of the traditional redactors of the Bible: "[The] historian himself here emerged as a kind of prophet in reverse: instead of predicting the future, with prophetic fervor he explained the past and justified through it the implacable power of moral law."[5]

Simon Dubnow was born in September 1860 in Mstislav, a small provincial town in White Russia, not far from the city of Smolensk. At the time of his birth, Mstislav had approximately 4,000 Jews. By the end of the century, the Jewish population had increased to over 5,000 out of a total population of 8,500.[6] Dubnow's father was a lumber merchant employed by his father-in-law; his mother worked in a notions store in Mstislav's central square. In his memoirs, Dubnow recalls that his father was away half of the year, returning only for the High Holidays. During his short stays at home, the lumber merchant seems to have kept to himself, nursing a chronic illness that would bring on an early death in 1887 at the age of fifty-four.[7] Not surprisingly, therefore, Dubnow reveals very little about his father in his memoirs and barely mentions his death. The fact that Simon had few ties with his father suggests that for all his emphasis upon his adolescent rebelliousness as an important turning point in his intellectual development, the young man's search for an appropriate identity would not be marked by a wrenching break from his family. At the same time, the lack of paternal involvement and support in his youth may help to explain Dubnow's later intellectualism, social aloofness, and general lack of emotional expressiveness.

In the absence of his father, Dubnow focused much of his attention on his paternal grandfather, Ben-Tsiyon, a Torah scholar descended from the eighteenth-century kabbalist Yosef of Dubnow.[8] Despite his heritage, Ben-Tsiyon Dubnow was an ardent opponent of Hasidism and mystical thought. There seems little doubt that his grandson inherited his love of learning and rigorous approach to scholarship. At times, Simon Dubnow likened his own scholarly interests to those of his grandfather, the Talmudic sage who stood above the rabble and who remained steadfast in his beliefs.[9] Unlike Ben-Tsiyon, however, the young Dubnow was fascinated with his Hasidic roots and maintained a strong personal and scholarly interest in Hasidism throughout his life.

Like many of his generation, Dubnow's experience with traditional religious training was largely negative. Though educated in Talmud and Hebrew, Dubnow hated his early education in the heder, which typically was characterized by long hours, rote memorization, and corporal punishment for those whose attention lagged. For the young Dubnow, it was akin to the enslavement of the Jews in Egypt.[10] Already at an early age, his real love was traditional "histories," and he soon immersed himself in Bible stories, prophetic descriptions of national tragedies such as Megilat Ekha (Book of Lamentations), *aggadot* (fanciful tales created to embellish and elucidate biblical accounts), and depictions in Jewish liturgy of medieval religious martyrs. A voracious reader throughout his life, Dubnow claimed that at the age of ten he was already secretly reading works of modern Hebrew literature by Abraham Mapu and Micha Yosef Levinson, as well as Hebrew translations of European literature. Like others of his generation, he was especially fascinated with Kalman Shulman's abridged translation of Eugène Sue's *Mystères de Paris*, published between 1857 and 1860, which represented one of the first efforts to translate a popular European novel into Hebrew.[11] By age thirteen, Dubnow was being labeled an *apikores* (freethinker) by his friends and teachers as a result of his passionate defense of the Haskalah and his refusal to observe many religious rituals. Among other public acts of defiance, the young Simon wrote an essay in Hebrew against religious fanaticism and refused to deliver the traditional speech at his bar mitzvah on tefillin (phylacteries) for left-handed persons.[12]

Dubnow's interest in modern Jewish and general European culture was undoubtedly fostered by his father's and mother's business contacts with the larger society. Like many of his contemporaries, Dubnow grew up in a Jewish household that was beginning to experience the effects of economic and cultural modernization. At home, Dubnow spoke Russian and he continued to use the language throughout his early writing career and in his public declarations.[13] The young man's education seems to have been a point of contention in the Dubnow household. Dubnow's grandfather desperately wanted Simon to continue his religious training at his own yeshiva. Nevertheless, in 1874 Dubnow's parents, with the grudging consent of Ben-Tsiyon, enrolled Simon and his brother Zev in a Jewish Crown school. Undaunted by the government's decision to close the school before the two boys could finish their studies, the parents transferred them to a Russian high school frequented by the children of bureaucrats and notables.

What followed was a bewildering series of futile efforts by Dubnow's parents to secure a general education for their son. Between 1877 and 1890, Dubnow drifted from school to school in a desperate attempt to complete the requirements for a degree that would enable him to matriculate at a university. At first he thought of enrolling at a Jewish teachers' institute in Vilna. He quickly discovered, however, that school officials generally refused admission to young men born before 1861, for fear that they would be unable to complete their coursework before being drafted into the army. In 1878 he entered a high school (*Realschule*) in Duenaburg (later Dvinsk) in Latvia. He was soon forced to return home, however, in part because of the anti-Semitic sentiments of one of the teachers, in part because of lack of money. The young Simon then tried to enroll in a school in nearby Mogilev. This time he was rejected because he did not know classical languages and was thought to be a political troublemaker. Dubnow next chose to become an extern at a school in Smolensk, a city that lay outside the Pale of Settlement. Within a short time, however, the school administrator began to voice suspicions about the young man's unorthodox political views. His father's concerns about the police response to an attempt by his son to help some "radical" women flee their home brought an abrupt end to yet another effort by Dubnow to obtain a high school degree.[14]

Dubnow's bitter experiences with formal education undoubtedly fueled his desire to succeed as a self-taught scholar. Throughout the period in which he unsuccessfully attempted to enroll in high school, he continued to read avidly and widely. Upon returning to Mstislav from Smolensk, Dubnow sought to create what he called a "university at home" by studying on his own the works assigned in courses.[15] The Jewish historian would later look back at his failure to receive a diploma with a certain philosophical detachment. Perhaps it was destiny that a Jewish writer concerned about the future of his people should share the pain of the overwhelming majority of his brothers who were denied educational opportunities and privileges. As Dubnow noted in his memoirs, Fate had determined that he would not succeed. In that way, his fellow Jews could take comfort in knowing "that a Jewish writer would not make use of the superfluous privileges of a diploma, that instead he would suffer with all of his brothers en masse, so that he would be able to describe from his own experience their suffering in works . . . [that expressed] the 'great rage' of the publicist and the controlled pathos of the historian."[16]

In actual fact, Dubnow devoted little attention to Jewish thinkers and Jewish thought during this period. Instead, he immersed himself in radical Russian social thought, including the works of the social thinker Dimitri Pisarev, the writer Nikolai Chernyshevsky, the revolutionary

Nikolai Dobrolyubov, and the poet and political activist Nikolai Nekrasov. What Simon did read in Hebrew and Yiddish generally reflected his growing alienation from traditional Jewish life. Like Zhitlowski, Dubnow delighted in reading Moshe Leib Lilienblum's *Hataot neurim*, which chronicled the author's rejection of Orthodoxy and his passion for the world outside the Pale.[17] The young man's goal at this stage of his life was to become an "Encyclopedist," a worldly autodidact unfettered by professional obligations and religious loyalties who would use his knowledge and his bitter experiences of persecution and rejection to reflect upon the human condition.

Despite his rebelliousness, however, Dubnow expressed little interest in political activism. Unlike Zhitlowski, his youthful radicalism remained deeply personal and did not manifest itself in a commitment to radical social and economic change.[18] Though he studied Karl Marx's writings intensively, for example, Dubnow remained unmoved by the German thinker's arguments and was deeply disturbed by the revolutionary implications of his thought.[19] Instead, he was drawn to the writings of European rationalists who stressed the importance of understanding as a prerequisite for action. French *philosophes* like Diderot and Voltaire would provide him with what he would later describe as a "new religion," a belief in the absolute power of human reason that would triumph over superstition and baseless hatred. At the same time, Dubnow also began to absorb the ideas of proponents of the "science of society." Particularly influential was the English historian Thomas Buckle, who provided Dubnow with the basic tools of sociological investigation as well as a model for the writing of a universal history with a central theme that explained historical development. Buckle also served as an exemplar of the self-taught scholar who could attain international prominence despite his lack of formal education.[20]

It was in this period as well that Dubnow was introduced to two central ideas that would remain with him for the remainder of his life: the theory of the evolution of society as developed in the writings of Herbert Spencer and Auguste Comte, and the tenets of liberalism as espoused by John Stuart Mill. Like others of his generation, evolutionism would provide Dubnow with a methodology to explain historical development within the context of rooted Jewish institutions and beliefs. On a practical level, Spencer's ideas would offer Dubnow a way to balance his commitment to the past with his belief in the need for change in the Jewish condition.

But it was John Stuart Mill more than any other thinker who would frame Dubnow's view of society and history. In his memoirs, Dubnow describes Mill's books as "kitve kodesh" (holy writings) and claims that reading Mill's work transformed him into a lifelong "apostle for individualism."[21] It is a doubtful contention, given Dubnow's constant emphasis on the need for Jews to sacrifice their personal desires to ensure the collective survival of the Jewish people. Nevertheless, in his later proposals to modernize Jewish life as well as his views of the relationships between Jews and non-Jews, Dubnow would remain true to Mill's liberal vision of a just society that was committed to civil liberty, social justice, the welfare of the masses, and the spiritual evolution of the nation. The influence of liberalism on Dubnow would also be found in his openness to religious and linguistic pluralism within the Jewish community.[22] In a more personal sense, during Dubnow's period of adolescence, the struggle of the young British genius against his father's tyrannical control clearly appealed to the young Russian Jew who saw himself, with some exaggeration, as rebelling against his own upbringing in his search for self-understanding. Like Mill's rebellion, Dubnow's quest for truth was tempered by a commitment to rationalism and order that would later prevent him from joining forces with the more radical Jewish thinkers in the Nietzschean mold. His new faith was to be a scientific religion, Dubnow would later write about his views during this period, "a belief based upon rational thought rather than thought based upon belief."[23]

Like Zhitlowski, Dubnow was drawn to St. Petersburg as an ideal environment in which to pursue his scholarship. In 1880, he joined his brother and the small colony of Jews recently arrived from the Pale of Settlement who lived illegally on the outskirts of the Russian capital. For the budding young scholar, St. Petersburg was a magical city. Immersed in history and culture, breathtaking in its vistas, and fiercely cosmopolitan, the Russian capital seemed to fulfill Dubnow's most secret hopes and dreams.[24] Here he spent many hours at the national library in the company of other autodidacts. Here too, he would make yet another attempt to secure a high school equivalency diploma. This time, the combination of the assassination of Alexander II, a chronic eye problem, and Dubnow's lack of preparation would spell an end to his efforts.[25]

While his brother Zev responded to his failure to matriculate by immigrating to Palestine in the summer of 1882,[26] Simon chose to remain in St. Petersburg to pursue his education privately. In order to survive, he now began writing articles for two new Russian-language Jewish journals, *Russkii evrei* (The Russian Jew) and *Rassvet*, which sought to raise the cultural consciousness of Jewish youth. Shortly thereafter, he joined the staff of *Voskhod*, which served as a major forum for Jewish intellectuals. Though he desperately needed money, Dubnow seems to have viewed his work as a journalist primarily as an opportunity to put down in writing some of his ideas concerning Russian and Jewish culture. As an up-and-coming *kulturkritiker*, he also was eager to absorb the insights and observations of veteran writers on the staff.

Between 1883 and 1895, Dubnow published nearly 300 book reviews in *Voskhod* under the pseudonym "Kriticus." Safely guarding his anonymity, he was able to comment on many of the major political and cultural issues confronting the Jewish community without fear of personal reprisal. Most of the articles were predictable and preached a "modernizing" assimilationist view. In his first published essays, for example, Dubnow examined the economic plight of the Jews of the Pale and the woeful state of Jewish education in traditional schools. His solution was to establish a new educational system with special emphasis on vocational training. Such a system would not only "enlighten" Jews but would also enable them to more easily find an economic niche in Russian society. As a defender of assimilationism, Dubnow also attacked the Hibbat Zion movement as utopian. Similarly, though he defended Yiddish against the attacks by Hebraists, he was quick to praise Russian as the language of Jewish renewal. In the future, Dubnow proudly proclaimed, the Jewish masses would dispense with Yiddish and would embrace the language of the larger society in which they lived.[27] Dubnow's experience as a literary critic also prepared him for his future work as a historian by sensitizing him to the importance of literary documents.[28] Indeed, it was in this period that Dubnow began to compose his first historical essay—"an insignificant historical study," he would later recall—that reflected his youthful protest against Jewish tradition.[29]

The outbreak of pogroms in 1881 led to police crackdowns on Jews living illegally outside the Pale. Dubnow was expelled from St. Petersburg and returned to Mstislav. (He had planned to return to his hometown anyway in order to present himself for military service. After only a few weeks, he was released from the army due to his poor eyesight.) Despite his expulsion from St. Petersburg, Dubnow's written response to the pogroms was one of guarded optimism. Disassociating himself from what he regarded as the frenetic writings of other Jewish intellectuals, he described the riots as a passing phenomenon in Russia, mere "echoes" resulting from the assassination of the tsar. The power of historical law, Dubnow proclaimed, ensured that "egoism" would soon give way "to love even in international relations, much like relations between man and his neighbor." The civil and legal status of Jews was bound to change for the better in the near future. In the meantime, he concluded, the Jewish community must rid itself of its internal religious "baggage" to be prepared for the new world that lay on the horizon.[30]

Dubnow also felt obligated to respond to the wave of migration that swept over the panicked Jewish community. In an article written soon after the pogroms, he welcomed emigration to the United States while condemning the efforts to settle Palestine as doomed to failure. Sharing in the general romanticism that many Russian Jewish intellectuals expressed in their writings about conditions in America, he pronounced the United States a "new world" where Jews could establish a separate communal existence. Settlement in Palestine, on the other hand, would only attract the "leeches" and wastrels of the community who would swell the ranks of the ultra-Orthodox in the Holy Land.[31]

It was in these early writings that Dubnow perfected an analytical technique that he would employ throughout his life—the use of historical precedents to evaluate contemporary issues. Thus, for example, he invoked the Chmielnitski massacres of 1648 in his discussion of the anti-Jewish riots of 1881.[32] Similarly, his criticism of both the rabbinic establishment and the Zionists was laced with allusions to past false messiahs such as Shabbatai Zvi and Jacob Frank, whose movements in the seventeenth century swept across Europe and the Middle East before collapsing in disarray. Dubnow may have originally adopted the strategy of using past events to analyze contemporary events in order to avoid the long arm of government censorship. In an article on the French Revolution and the Jews published in *Voskhod*, for example, he was able to use the statements of Girondins and Jacobins to criticize the tsarist government's treatment of Jews in the 1880s.[33] In time, it would become more than a clever technique to escape prosecution, however. As he matured, Dubnow came to see the relationship between past and present events as demonstrating the fundamental continuity of Jewish history. Increasingly, he would become convinced that the study of Jewish history revealed important insights into both the challenges and opportunities facing Russian Jews at the end of the nineteenth century. Despite his rejection of his early views, many of the parallels between the Jewish past and present that Dubnow first enunciated in his polemical writings in the 1880s would be repeated in his mature historical works.[34]

Dubnow would later describe the early 1880s as "the antithetical years of my youth," characterized by bitter opposition to Orthodox Judaism and an unwavering commitment to assimilationism.[35] Between 1881 and 1884, he wrote five long essays in which he attacked traditional Jewish belief and practices, railed against rabbinic leadership, defended heretics of the past such as Elisha ben Abuya and Baruch Spinoza, and called for Jewish emancipation.[36] Much of the criticism was imitative of the anticlericalism of the Enlightenment and of nineteenth-century western Jewish reformers as reflected in the writings of the Haskalah. Denouncing religion as an obstacle to free thought, Dubnow looked forward to the day when all religions would die away. As for religious reform, it was at best a temporary palliative to satisfy the demands of the ignorant masses.[37] In more extreme moments, Dubnow would argue that traditional Judaism was not a religion at all but only "a compendium of laws that approach the absurd."[38] Echoing the sentiments of early maskilim, Dubnow proposed the imposition of a tax on parents who sent their children to heder, the receipts to go toward the development of government schools and a modern rabbinical seminary.[39] At the same time, he adopted the Reform Jewish leader Abraham Geiger's view that the mere observance of mitzvot (commandments) reduced religion to a "mechanical act" and ignored the underlying ethical concerns of Judaism. He also shared the Reform movement's insistence upon the need to eliminate all references to the Messiah and to the return to Zion.

Dubnow had similarly harsh words for the embryonic Jewish nationalist movement. In opposition to Russian Jewish thinkers like Leon Pinsker who called for the "autoemancipation" of Jewry, the young Dubnow championed the western ideal of social and economic integration. For Dubnow, Pinsker's ideas were nothing short of "a menace to all our hopes of civic equality and cultural revival in a European spirit." Jewish nationalism was an "ephemeral theory," a perverse reflection of anti-Semitism that would inevitably disappear.[40] The program of Hibbat Zion, Dubnow argued, was at best a partial solution to the larger question of Jewish equality. Its insistence on the need to return to Zion smacked of religious Orthodoxy and political reaction. The Palestinophilic movement wanted nothing less than "to turn history back by reverting . . . to the period of the ancient Near East." The only hope for the Jew, he concluded, was to link himself like a small boat "to the great ship that is bringing progress to humanity."[41]

True to his antireligious sentiments, in 1883 Dubnow adamantly refused to marry his fiancée in a Jewish ceremony. In the absence of civil marriages in Russia, the couple chose to live together. Returning to Mstislav in 1884, Dubnow was forced to undergo a traditional marriage. He insisted that it held be held in private, however, because, as he self-mockingly remarked in his autobiography, he did not want his friends to be "witness to my treason."[42] Despite his acquiescence to communal and familial pressure, Dubnow purposely chose to live apart from the Jewish community. In order to prevent anyone spying on him to see if he was working on the Sabbath, he rented rooms connected to a church. Following in the footsteps of one of his Jewish heroes of the past, Elisha ben Abuya, Dubnow was determined to be an "acher"—a radical "other" estranged from his fellow Jews.[43]

Yet much like Zhitlowski, his divorcement from the Jewish community was more imagined than real. While insisting on the need to separate himself from traditional Jewish life, he yearned to find a place for himself among the Jewish intelligentsia. In 1885, Dubnow decided to return to St. Petersburg to rejoin the Jewish literary circles of the Russian capital. What he found was a disheartened Jewish population, hounded by tsarist officials, culturally stagnant, and economically oppressed. It was the fear of the disintegration of the Jewish community combined with his intensive reading and writing about the Jewish past that appear to have revived Dubnow's interest in collective Jewish life. Much of Dubnow's original interest in Jewish history had been motivated by an intense desire to strengthen his arguments against traditional Jewish leadership and belief. He gradually began to realize the complex interplay between Jewish survival and the undying national ideals and structures that defined the Jewish people.[44] He now understood that religion was not merely a philosophical doctrine but a dynamic ideal that had served to ensure the survival of Jewry in the past. The degeneration of Judaism thus was a tragedy rather than a welcome event. Far from liberating Jews, its collapse had only resulted in wholesale assimilation and the continued isolation of the Jewish people from rapidly changing events in the world community at large. In this period Dubnow also seems to have developed a new appreciation of the role of the Land of Israel and of the Hebrew language in maintaining Jewish ideals and values.[45]

Dubnow's reassessment of the role of traditional Jewish values and ideals also led him to reevaluate the role of the Jewish intellectual. Once he had urged thoughtful young Jews to denounce their religious past; he now called upon them to guide the Jewish people in its quest for self-actualization. Like Dubnow himself, Jewish intellectuals had to begin to examine the manner in which Judaism had strengthened Jewish life in the past in order to create a new collective identity that would reconcile Jewry to the demands of modern life. Only in remaining true to their own selves could they fulfill their historical role as liberators of humanity as a whole. As he explained in the Russian edition of his memoirs: "I now understood that my path to the universal lay precisely through the field of the nation in which I was already working. You could serve humanity only by serving one of its parts, all the more so if that [part] was a nation [bearing] . . . the most ancient culture."[46]

At the same time that Dubnow was undergoing an intellectual transformation, he seems to have been experiencing a personal crisis of faith. In the style of the writings of fin de siècle rebels whom Russian Jewish intellectuals read avidly, Dubnow described his transformation in romantic terms. For all its superficial excitement, his life in St. Petersburg suddenly seemed barren and empty. For the first time, he began to experience gnawing doubts about the ability of rationalism to explain the underlying questions of human existence and increased skepticism concerning the moral progress of humanity. He longed to find an ultimate truth that would give meaning to existence and provide direction to his own life. In his desperate effort to "know the unknowable," Dubnow even dabbled in extrasensory perception and hypnotism.[47]

Much like Zhitlowski's discussion of his "return" to the Jewish people, Dubnow's epiphany was highlighted by a dramatic event that signaled his transformation from adolescence to adulthood. In the midst of his inner turmoil, Dubnow met with his grandfather. During their conversations, he was struck by a prophetic passage from Hosea—"I will go and return to my original nature because it was good for me then"—that his grandfather had recited to him years earlier upon hearing that the young Dubnow had publicly renounced his ties to Judaism. He now realized that the solution to his emotional angst lay not in escaping his past but in confronting it honestly and creatively. Only then could he find meaning in his personal life and the values that would enable him to believe in the possibility of human progress. Dubnow was now reconciled with his grandfather (and thus with his heritage), an event that symbolized for the "prodigal son" his dramatic return to the Jewish fold.[48]

In response to his newly rediscovered loyalties, Dubnow now began to distance himself from his previous radical views. His change of heart could be seen in an article he wrote in *Voskhod* in 1887 denouncing Zhitlowski for his dismissal of Jewish tradition and for his naive belief in the ability of socialism to solve the "Jewish problem" in Russia. Judaism was more than a simple compendium of beliefs that were interchangeable with other ideas, Dubnow argued. It must be understood as an integral part of the spiritual development of Jewry and as a distinctive creation of the Jewish creative mind over the centuries. Though he would continue to remain a religious skeptic, Dubnow had become a devout believer in the saving power of history and of Jewish history in particular. As he noted in his retrospective autobiography: "I reasoned thus: I am an agnostic in religion and philosophy to the extent to which they solve the riddles of the world, but I can know how mankind lived in the course of the millennia, by means of what paths it searched out truth and justice. I have lost faith in personal immortality, but history teaches me that there is collective immortality."[49]

In 1886, Dubnow decided to return to Mstislav to begin writing a "Spencerian" study of the evolution of Jewish thought. His model was to be the work of the French historian Ernest Renan, who had expressed ambivalence about the ability of science to explain all of reality and who had argued for the need for an intuitive and empathetic view of the religious past.[50] Dubnow's first efforts centered on the mystical writings of Hasidism, which he was convinced reflected in a remarkable manner the process by which Jews reinterpreted and restructured ancient ideals and values to ensure the survival of the Jewish collectivity. He believed that his study would rescue the Hasidic movement and its ideas from obscurity and would restore them to their rightful place in the development of Jewish thought.[51]   On a personal level, Dubnow was attracted to Hasidism because it mirrored his own rejection of rigid religious tradition and his search for spiritual meaning. As he would later state in his introduction to his massive work on Hasidism, the major concern of the movement was to reaffirm the "internal personal basis" of Judaism that had been all but "swallowed up" by the collective and external nature of Jewish life in the Diaspora.[52] Dubnow's interest in Jewish mysticism and spiritualism may have also arisen out of a fascination with nature and natural phenomena that had its origins in his childhood. His memoirs reveal a deeply rooted love of the forests and mountains of Poland and Lithuania, where he often went to contemplate and occasionally to write.[53]

Yet if Dubnow was to pursue his study seriously, he could not remain in a small provincial town like Mstislav.[54] In 1890, after a number of unsuccessful efforts to gain permission to settle in St. Petersburg and following an extended stay in Warsaw to research his book on Hasidism, he decided to go to Odessa. Dubnow chose Odessa because of its warmer climate, liberal Jewish community, and cultural and intellectual openness. His move away from the centers of Russian intellectual life also coincided with his growing disillusionment with the possibility of substantial progress in Russian society, brought on in large part by the brutal expulsion of Jews from Moscow in the summer of 1891.[55] For the next thirteen years he would immerse himself in the intellectual currents sweeping through the port city on the Black Sea and its Jewish community of 40,000.

Dubnow arrived in a city that had already become a mecca for young Jewish intellectuals fleeing from the Pale. Situated in New Russia, Odessa provided an escape from both the traditional Jewish community and tsarist restrictions upon Jewish life. Here Dubnow would meet and share his ideas with the major figures of three generations of Jewish intellectuals, including Ahad Ha-Am, Haim Nahman Bialik, Mendele Moykher Sforim, and Sholem Aleichem.[56] Here too he would find a captive audience for his theories of national renewal among the growing numbers of young Jewish men and women who had come to the city to share in its cultural life.[57] Like his colleague Ahad Ha-Am, Dubnow would later describe his years in Odessa as the period of his spiritual maturation.

It was in Odessa that Dubnow would begin the arduous and daunting task of writing a general history of Russian Jewry. Nineteenth-century German Jewish historians had generally ignored the development of the Russian Jewish community, choosing instead to concentrate upon what they regarded as the more "sophisticated" and "spiritually minded" communities of western Europe. As an East European Jew, Dubnow was convinced that a serious study of the self-contained traditional community of the Jews in Russia and Poland would reveal important general truths about the nature of Jewish survival. To foster research, in October 1891 he founded the Jewish Historical Ethnographical Commission. Organized under the auspices of the Society for the Promotion of Enlightenment Among Jews in Russia, its major task was to collect and classify documents on Russian Jews that were scattered throughout the Pale. His distant hope, which was shared by colleagues like Mendele and Ahad Ha-Am, was to establish a rabbinical seminary modeled after those in western Europe. Unlike traditional yeshivas, the modern school for the training of Jewish leaders in Russia would be committed to Wissenschaft, that is, the "scientific study" of East European Jewry.[58]

It was in Odessa as well that Dubnow would write his first major theoretical work on Jewish history. First published in *Voskhod* in 1893, "What Is Jewish History?" outlined his fundamental views concerning the role of culture as a creative force in ensuring collective survival among both western and East European Jewry.[59] The work also marked Dubnow's first public statement concerning the role of Jewish nationalism as a spiritual force. Dubnow would later claim that the work's philosophical emphasis reflected an early stage of his historical understanding in which he was largely under the sway of the German Jewish historian Heinrich Graetz and the *Geistesgeschichte* school. It is true that in his later writings, Dubnow constantly sought to disassociate himself from what he called "subjectivist" views of Jewish life and history. Yet his indebtedness to Graetz remained strong throughout his life. In 1892, Dubnow spearheaded the publication of a Russian edition of Graetz's first volume. A modern reader of Dubnow's works finds numerous reflections of the German Jewish scholar's "spiritual" and "lachrymose" approach to Jewish history in the Russian scholar's continual emphasis on Jewish values as the source of collective survival and on the central role of Jewish persecution in shaping Jewish responses to the larger society.[60]

The positive response to his essay encouraged Dubnow to continue his investigation of Jewish history. In 1897, the first of his "Letters on Old and New Judaism," which outlined his views concerning the nature of Jewish autonomy in a multinational State, appeared in the pages of *Voskhod*. A year later, Dubnow published a children's textbook of Jewish history in Russian that would eventually go through numerous editions. In 1901, he completed the first volume of his *World History of the Jewish People* (translated as *History of the Jews*) with subsequent volumes appearing annually between 1902 and 1905. It was with renewed confidence that Dubnow could write in his diary in 1902 that the "dissemination of historical knowledge about Judaism" was now the central goal of his life.[61]

Dubnow's growing interest in Jewish history as a tool to understanding the nature of Jewish survival was spurred by the general unrest within the community at the turn of the century.[62] He was especially troubled by the dramatic appearance of two mass movements on the Russian Jewish scene, Bundism and Zionism. As radical departures from the evolutionary development of Jewish life over the centuries that he had begun to trace in his histories, they threatened to bring about deep collective disappointment and even national tragedy. Dubnow had previously expressed his opposition to Marxism as a theoretical construct. He now lashed out against its proponents within the Jewish community for denying the unity of the Jewish people in the name of class conflict. For the Jewish historian, Bundists were wrong to apply a materialist perspective devoid of any ethical concern to a people who were the bearers of a prophetic weltanschauung in history.[63]

Dubnow's response to Zionism was more complex. His writings had increasingly emphasized the centrality of peoplehood in Jewish history and the young nationalist movement was eager to win him over to its cause. In early 1897, Zvi Belkowsky, a Russian Zionist leader and a close confidant of Theodor Herzl, visited Dubnow in Zurich to try to convince him to be a delegate at the First Zionist Congress in Basel. Though vacationing in Switzerland at the time, Dubnow refused to attend even as a visitor.[64] His excuse was his fear of being shunned (or worse, ignored) as a "Diasporist." The Jewish historian had more serious reservations about the congress, however. As a movement that thrived on the enthusiasm of a small segment of the community, political Zionism bore all the signs of a Jewish messianic movement of early modern Europe. Herzl's insistence that "if you will it, it is no dream" may have lifted the hearts of many Jews. For Dubnow, however, it smacked of the worst form of "subjectivism" that ignored the lessons of Jewish history in the name of blind faith and individual will.

Nor was Dubnow pleased with the political tenets of Zionism. He could never forgive Herzl for making Jewish nationhood contingent upon the acquisition of territory. Dubnow's writings on the role of the Diaspora in Jewish history had led him to emphasize time rather than space as the defining characteristic of Jewry. Like many Diasporists (as well as traditional Jews), he stressed the spiritual dimension rather than the concrete reality of Jewish life as the source of the community's collective strength. Though praising Herzl for supporting the idea of a democratic Jewish society in its own homeland, Dubnow was disappointed that the Zionist leader's vision was devoid "of the individual imprint of a Jewish national culture" that had been so carefully developed over the millennia.[65]

In response to Bundist and Zionist agitation, Dubnow made his first foray into Jewish political life. In a series of colloquia attended by students in Kharkov in 1894 and in Odessa in 1896, he called for the development of a concrete program for Jewish renewal grounded in what he defined as the essential continuities of Jewish life. The central focus of the colloquia was Jewish history with particular emphasis on the insights that the Jewish past could shed on the viability of movements and programs of national renewal in the modern era. These discussions would later form the basis of *Letters on Old and New Judaism*, Dubnow's major theoretical work on Jewish identity and survival.

Increasingly, Dubnow also began to side with cultural nationalists against his former allies within the Jewish community, the Jewish Russifiers. In 1901, the Jewish historian found himself embroiled in a struggle between nationalists and assimilationists within the Society for the Promotion of Enlightenment among Jews in Russia. Dubnow would later describe it as a veritable *Kulturkampf* to determine the fate of Russian Jewish life in the future.[66] While the majority of the society's members insisted on the need to retain a curriculum based on general Russian studies in schools subsidized by the organization, a group of intellectuals led by Ahad Ha-Am and Yehuda Leib Katznelson demanded the teaching of Hebrew and Jewish culture. In the debate Dubnow championed the cause of Hebrew, insisting on the need to educate young Jews in both Jewish national values and modern European culture.[67] Not for the first time, he found himself arguing for a synthesis of old and new forms of Jewish identity.

In 1903, Dubnow again was forced to respond to dramatic events within the community. The outbreak of brutal pogroms, most notably in the city of Kishinev northwest of Odessa, led the Jewish historian to demand civil and national rights for Jews within Russia. Together with Haim Nahman Bialik and Ahad Ha-Am, he issued a proclamation calling for the establishment of a bureau of information to gather and disseminate information on the history of pogroms, the creation of permanent self-defense units in all threatened Jewish communities, and the convocation of a general assembly of Jewish representatives from all over Russia.[68] In an effort to create a unified communal stand, Dubnow now spoke positively about Zionism and announced that he no longer opposed the involvement of Jews in the socialist movement as long as the interests of Jewry remained primary.[69] In response to panic in the community, he also publicly expressed his support for an organized and orderly migration to America.[70]

Yet Dubnow was distinctly uncomfortable with the political turmoil surrounding him. He also feared for his family's welfare. In 1903, thirteen years after his arrival in Odessa, the Jewish historian left to settle in the more peaceful environs of Vilna. In moving to the Lithuanian city, Dubnow also hoped to resume his scholarly studies and to pursue the publication of his historical works. He could not have picked a more appropriate city in which to continue his work. At the turn of the century, Vilna was the most cultured Jewish city in the Pale of Settlement. Its 60,000 Jewish residents, more than 40 percent of the total population, proudly referred to their community as "the Jerusalem of Lithuania." Though suffering from unemployment and overcrowding, the Vilna Jewish community remained the intellectual and administrative center of religious Orthodoxy, Zionism, and Jewish socialism. It also boasted a flourishing Hebrew and Yiddish literary and popular press.[71]

For a while Dubnow was able to work in almost scholarly isolation.[72] It did not take long, however, for Vilna to become caught up in the political turmoil sweeping across the Pale. Dubnow now sadly realized that it was simply impossible "to write history in a period when you have to make it."[73] Even his research into ancient Jewish civilization seemed to resonate with implications for contemporary issues.

The brutal suppression of Jewish riots in first- and second-century Alexandria, for example, reminded him of the Kishinev pogrom. Similarly, the anti-Semitic rantings of minister of the interior von Plehve seemed to mimic the paranoiac tirades of the first century Roman ruler Caligula against the Jewish inhabitants of his empire.[74] Dubnow became more convinced than ever that the study of the Jewish past held the key to understanding Jewish survival in the present.

Unexpectedly, Dubnow found himself deeply moved by the excitement surrounding the Revolution of 1905. According to his daughter, on at least one occasion he tore himself away from the tranquility of his study in order to participate in a funeral procession for Vilna residents who were killed by police gunfire during a demonstration.[75] In the aftermath of the events, he began to push for a petition for Jewish rights and communal autonomy within a revitalized Russia. Despite his distaste for political activism, Dubnow became active in the Union for the Attainment of Full Rights for the Jewish People in Russia. Organized in March 1905, the movement attempted to develop a united front of Poles, Jews, White Russians, and Lithuanians to demand national autonomy. As a first step, the newly created group joined the Union of Unions, a loose constellation of workers, professionals, and intellectuals that had been organized in May to press for political and economic reform.

At first, Dubnow voiced great confidence in the Union for the Attainment of Full Rights. He believed that its establishment would mark a novum in modern Jewish history—the first Jewish movement to demand not only civil and political emancipation but also the national liberation of the Jewish people.[76] The reality proved to be somewhat less than he had hoped, however. Dubnow's proposal to transform the organization into a permanent representative body of Russian Jewry that would lobby for full autonomy was accepted only after bitter debate at the union's Second Congress in 1905 and found little support within the Jewish community as a whole. Most damaging was the failure of the union to gain the support of the Bund, which opposed its effort to unite all Jews under one political banner and which rejected any attempt to gain political rights through "constitutional" means. At the same time, the refusal of Polish nationalist leaders to recognize the rights of other ethnic groups doomed hopes for an alliance of all ethnic minorities and led the union to support Jewish candidates exclusively for the national elections to the First Duma.

Dubnow had anticipated great changes after the convening of the the First Duma in April/May 1906. While sympathetic to the idea of a Jewish political bloc in the reconstituted Parliament, he urged Jews to vote for the Kadets in constituencies where a Jewish representative could not be elected.[77] Yet Russian liberals had remained relatively silent in October 1905 during the bloody pogroms in Odessa and again in the spring of 1906 after riots in the northwestern city of Bialystok. A proposed law granting equal rights and ending discriminatory legislation on the basis of religion had been introduced by the Kadets in the Duma in May. The efforts of the working committee established to study it, however, were never presented to the parliamentary body as a whole. On July 8, Tsar Nicholas II dismissed the Duma after a series of bitter debates in which delegates supported the expropriation of property and leveled accusations against government officials of complicity in the Kishinev pogroms of 1903.

Even before the dissolution of the Duma, there were serious problems within the Jewish parliamentary bloc. Of the twelve Jewish deputies elected to the First Duma, nine were affiliated with the liberal constitutionalist party, the Kadets, and three with a labor faction, the so-called Trudoviki. Bitterly divided on fundamental issues concerning the future of Russia and its Jewish population, members of the bloc generally failed to coordinate their votes. In disgust, in 1906 the Zionists withdrew from the Union for the Attainment of Full Rights. For Dubnow, it meant the end of his dream of a unified Jewish political force and a serious weakening of the goals of the union.[78]

The dissolution of the First Duma in July 1906 and the challenge of upcoming elections to the Second Duma convinced Dubnow of the need to take a new approach. Instead of relying upon the Kadets or on the existing fractious Jewish political bloc, it now was necessary to establish a broadly based and independent Jewish political party that would press for autonomy. In December 1906, the Jewish historian helped organize the Folkspartei or People's Party. In contrast to the electoral strategies of other Jewish movements, which generally insisted on the need to work with established Russian parties, the Folkspartei sought to establish a solidly united Jewish parliamentary bloc that would ally with other national minorities. As outlined in the Fourteenth Letter of his *Letters on Old and New Judaism*, the party's platform reiterated the proposals that Dubnow had first presented to the union two years earlier. Its major goals were the granting of individual autonomy for each Russian citizen on the basis of nationality, no matter where he or she lived, and recognition of the right of each national group to administer its own local cultural institutions, cooperatives, and philanthropic agencies. The platform also called for the establishment of a Union of Jewish Communities in the Russian Empire, a central coordinating council that would defend the interests of Russian Jewry as a whole in its dealings with the tsarist regime.[79] In order to disseminate the party's ideas among the Jewish masses, Dubnow now began to write essays in Yiddish in *Der Fraynd*, the most widely distributed Jewish newspaper in Russia. Urged on by political necessity, he set about transforming the scattered ideas concerning communal autonomism in his earlier writings into a comprehensive program for political, economic, and social change.

Dubnow's determination to press for cultural autonomy had no doubt been influenced by the decision of the Russian Zionist movement at their Third Congress held in Helsingfors (Helsinki) in December 1906 to support efforts to advance Jewish rights in a democratic Russia. In the past, Dubnow had been suspicious of Herzl's negotiations with tsarist officials. He feared that the Zionist leader was trying to seek a modus vivendi with the government that would allow him to press for Jewish emigration to Palestine in Russia in return for opposing efforts to organize Jews in the Pale. Whether admitting it openly or not, the Zionists' support of *Gegenwartsarbeit*, that is, "practical" work within the Diaspora, strongly suggested to Dubnow that they had finally recognized the validity of his call for communal autonomy.[80]

Political events in Russia in 1907 would destroy Dubnow's belief in the possibility of meaningful political change under the tsarist regime. A second Duma had been elected in February but the four elected Jewish deputies, whose names were virtually unknown to the Jewish public, had little political clout. As a result, proposals for communal and personal autonomy fell on deaf ears. At the same time, the government reinstituted restrictions against Jews that had been suspended in 1905, including the notorious numerus clausus. As the tsarist regime reasserted its hold on Russian society, it gradually withdrew its previous concessions to national minorities, including Jews, originally made under the pressure of the revolutionary movement in 1905. In June 1907, the tsar's decision to dismiss the Duma met with little opposition.[81]

Within the Jewish community, disappointment with political developments led to the reassertion of party factionalism and resumption of the search for radical solutions to the Jewish plight. While Zionists again began to look to Palestine, the Bund stepped up its illegal activities. Dubnow's program for cultural autonomy within Russia also came under fire from territorialists within the newly founded Zionist Socialist Workers movement (SS) led by Nahman Syrkin, Wolf Latzky-Bertholdi, and Jacob Lestschinsky, who argued that only an organized emigration to a new territory could ease the Jewish plight. In addition, Dubnow was attacked by the Sejmist party led by Haim Zhitlowski, Ben-Adir, and Israel Jefroykin who, though sharing his belief in the need for Jewish representation in the Duma, nevertheless saw autonomy as a distant possibility that could only be realized after the advent of revolution in Russia.[82] To make matters worse, wealthy Russian Jews such as the noted attorney Maxim Vinaver, who had originally expressed limited support for Dubnow's campaign for Jewish cultural rights, now began to have second thoughts.

By 1908, Dubnow had decided to cease all political activity and return to his first love, teaching and scholarship. In September, he happily accepted an offer to lecture on Jewish history at a school of natural sciences in St. Petersburg. The school had recently been organized by a physician to accommodate Jews who were denied admission to Russian universities as a result of the imposition of the numerus clausus. After so many failures, Dubnow had at last found a place in academe. As a member of the new faculty for social sciences, he was eager to assume the role of a mentor to the young Jews who had read his works and who had come to the Russian capital to study with him.[83] It was not only Dubnow's erudition that impressed these Jewish students. The historian also served as a living example of how a determined Jewish intellectual could triumph over discrimination in his quest for learning.[84] Unfortunately, Dubnow's direct influence upon the St. Petersburg Jewish student community proved to be of short duration. The uncertain political climate led the police to close the school within a few months after the Jewish historian joined the faculty. Dubnow was now forced to fall back on free-lance writing to survive.[85]

In deciding to withdraw from communal activity in 1908, Dubnow had also been motivated by shock over the marriage of his daughter Olga to a Russian nationalist activist. He now sought to bury his sadness in research and writing. Appointed vice-president of the newly established Society for History and Ethnography (the successor to the Jewish Historical Ethnographical Commission), Dubnow eagerly accepted the editorship of *Evreiskaya starina* (The Jewish Past), a journal published by the society devoted to the history of Russian and Polish Jewry. With the aid of a small group of young disciples, he helped prepare the last two volumes of a three-volume edition of primary documents on Russian Jewry, which was published in 1910 and completed in 1913.[86] Two years later, a second and definitive edition of the first volume of Dubnow's *World History of the Jewish People* appeared in Russian.

As much as he tried, however, as a leading Russian Jewish intellectual Dubnow could not avoid becoming embroiled in communal debates. Frightened by the growing politicization of cultural issues, he desperately tried to emphasize shared communal goals for Jewish revival. In 1909, for example, in response to the convening of the Czernowitz Conference on Yiddish, Dubnow reaffirmed his principle of trilingualism—the defense of Yiddish alongside Hebrew and Russian as an appropriate vehicle for the development of Jewish culture.[87] In 1911, he attempted to calm the fears of the Jewish public about the notorious Beilis case by placing it within the general context of blood-libel accusations throughout Jewish history. According to Dubnow's daughter, Sophie Dubnow-Erlich, her father's articles were successfully used by Beilis' lawyers during his trial, which was held in 1913.[88]

The outbreak of World War I was a crushing blow to Dubnow, conjuring up in his mind apocalyptic images of mass death and destruction. He was especially disturbed by the threat that the war posed for the unity of world Jewry and for the physical survival of communities like Russian Jewry that were caught in the crossfire. Unlike many Jews in both eastern and western Europe who were eager to demonstrate their patriotic loyalty in battle, Dubnow found it difficult to accept the notion of Jews fighting against their coreligionists on the battlefield. In his survey of Jewish history published after the war, he would recall a harrowing tale that symbolized the tragedy of 1914. A Jewish soldier in the Russian army bayoneted an Austrian soldier. When he heard the dying man utter the Jewish prayer "Shma Yisrael" (Hear O Israel), he went berserk.[89]

Within what he called "the darkness of Egypt" that characterized wartime Russia, Dubnow was convinced that Jews were undergoing a profound spiritual crisis marked by deep despair and emotional paralysis.[90] Nevertheless, as the fighting dragged on, he supported the Russian cause against Germany in the hope that a free and democratic society would emerge from the struggle. Much to his dismay, the war did not bring the lifting of tsarist restrictions on Jews. Dubnow's pessimism was deepened by the collapse of his intellectual circle in Russia as many of his friends scattered throughout the globe in in search of refuge from the hostilities.[91] For a while, Dubnow tried to lose himself in what he called the "sanitorium of history,"[92] but he soon found that anxiety and frequent bouts of depression disturbed his thought and concentration. It was not without exaggeration that he entitled the sixteenth chapter of his memoirs, written during the war, "The Darkest Chapter of My Memoirs."[93]

Dubnow thought he saw a significant turning point in the March Revolution of 1917. For the Jewish historian, the accession of the provisional government to power seemed to signal the fulfillment of the liberal and democratic ideals that he had championed in 1905. Brimming with optimism, Dubnow again pressed for the creation of a national Jewish congress. The Bolsheviks' accession to power eight months later, however, brought a bitter response from the Jewish historian. He blamed the Communists not only for the collapse of his plans for a congress but also for the bitter cold and hunger that his family endured in the winter of 1917. He could never forgive the Leninist regime for forcing him to stop his work in order to stand on a breadline or to break up floorboards to stoke the oven to heat his apartment.[94] On a more profound level, Dubnow's opposition to the November Revolution reflected his longstanding hostility toward Marxism and revolutionism. The triumph of Bolshevism was nothing short of the desecration of "the holy trinity of the French Revolution," he would later write in his *History of the Jews*: "Instead of liberty and authority of the people, there emerged dictatorship of a party, the revocation of the free press, the substitution of a bullet for a free word, and jail or exile to Siberia for expressing a free thought; instead of equality there emerged 'class-justice' and a class-rationed morsel of bread; instead of fraternity there emerged class hatred and fratricidal war."[95]

Nor could Dubnow take much consolation in the actions of counterrevolutionary forces. He was shocked by the outbreak of pogroms in the Ukraine that were launched by White army in 1919. The bloody murder of tens of thousands of Jews not only seemed to signal a return to the evils of tsarism but also marked the end of an experiment in Jewish autonomy that had begun with the declaration of Ukrainian independence in July 1917. Jews seemed caught in the middle between two vicious and ruthless forces that would stop at nothing to achieve their goals. Looking back at the transformation from tsarism to Bolshevism, Dubnow realized that little had changed. As he bitterly remarked in an article written in 1919-20, the murderers of Jews were like a beast that periodically emerged within the peasantry "to spill Jewish blood, destroy hundreds of communities, and then, having finished its work, returns to its pit, until it [once again emerges to] explode in the same form."[96]

Unlike Zhitlowski, Dubnow never believed that the Bolshevik regime was favorable toward ethnic distinctiveness and religious belief. Increasingly, he also doubted that it would carry out on its pledge to end anti-Semitism. The Jewish historian was especially upset when the Department of National Minorities decided to abolish a commission that he had spearheaded to investigate past blood libels. Nevertheless, in order to save the project, Dubnow grudgingly agreed to join a new government-controlled coordinating committee for research on Jewish topics.[97] Though his plans for the establishment of a national Jewish body had actually resulted in the holding of elections in January 1918, the dissolution of the Constituent Assembly in the same month doomed all hopes of convening the congress.[98]

Dubnow would remain fiercely opposed to the Soviet regime throughout his life. By 1922, he was convinced that Lenin's government was an even greater evil than tsarism. Two years later, he would write a letter to Ahad Ha-Am in which he denounced Bolshevism as the greatest obstacle to the redemption of humanity.[99] Despite the Jews' economic and social integration into Soviet society in the 1930s, which Zhitlowski had trumpeted as the fulfillment of emancipation, Dubnow steadfastly held to his belief that Russian Jews were fundamentally debased and enslaved as human beings under Bolshevik rule.[100] The Jewish historian no longer believed in his original dream that Russian Jewry would become the source of Jewish revival. By the late 1930s, he was publicly voicing his fear that the community might disappear completely as a result of Soviet efforts to deny ethnic distinctiveness. As he wrote prophetically in an Epilogue to the Russian edition of his *History of the Jews* published in 1938: "If the present regime continues [to exist] for a long time then the future generations will have no national link with world Jewry. . . . The two million Jews— completely assimilated, without any contact with their own people— will be submerged in a uniform mixture of nationalities: The Union of Soviet Socialist Republics."[101]

Whenever Dubnow lapsed into deep despair, he could always find a measure of consolation in Jewish history. Increasingly he searched for reasons for optimism in the experiences of an eternal people that had survived all manner of misfortune in its determination to shape its own destiny. The pronouncement of the Balfour Declaration in 1917 buoyed Dubnow's hopes, for it seemed to corroborate his historical theories concerning the continual revitalization of Jewish life through the development of new "national centers." For a while, he even considered immigrating to Palestine. His deep-seated doubts concerning the viability of the Zionist experiment and his close ties to Russia, however, prevented him from taking the step. According to Ahad Ha-Am, Dubnow had planned to meet the Zionist leader at the Western Wall in Jerusalem at Passover in 1909. Because of his own poor health, Ahad Ha-Am suggested that they put off their meeting until the following year. Dubnow never responded to Ahad Ha-Am's suggestion, however. Dubnow would again consider visiting the cultural Zionist in the spring of 1924. Once again he begged off, citing publishing responsibilities that prevented him from leaving his home.[102]

The fact that Dubnow never traveled to Palestine cannot be explained simply by his failing health and professional obligations. The Jewish historian refused to visit the *yishuv* because, like many of his contemporaries, he feared rejection from a new generation of Palestinian Jewish intellectuals and activists. Similarly, his insistence on the importance of Jewish life in the Diaspora stemmed at least in part from the realization that his most loyal readers were men and women of his own generation who had remained in eastern Europe. Typical of his attitude was his response to the publication of the first volume of Ahad Ha-Am's correspondence in 1924. It was good to recall the generation of Odessa whose memory should never be forgotten, Dubnow noted in a laudatory letter to his friend. Yet the pessimistic mood of Ahad Ha-Am's letters struck a familiar chord in Dubnow and reminded him of the words of Lord Byron,which he quoted in the original English: "Oh, talk not to me of a name great in story:/The days of our youth are the days of our glory."[103]

Though Dubnow refused to abandon eastern Europe in the aftermath of the Russian Revolution, he was now determined to leave the Soviet Union. While awaiting the issuance of an exit visa, the Jewish historian had begun his autobiography. It was a work characterized by emotional longings and a prevailing pessimism that reflected his troubled state of mind during the period. Burdened by growing financial debt and concerned about the fate of his ten-volume history of the Jews, he lived in a constant state of anxiety. Finally, after a short stay in Riga, Latvia, in 1922 Dubnow accepted a position in Jewish history at the University of Kaunas (Kovno) in Lithuania. It was as if he had emerged from the darkness into light. As he stated in a letter written to his student and fellow historian Mark Wischnitzer: "Coming from a land of destruction, I am in quest of lost friends, and am happy to hear that some are still alive and continue to spin the cut thread [of Jewish life]."[104]

Dubnow's stay in the Lithuanian capital lasted only a few months. The combination of the hostility of Dubnow's colleagues toward his appointment, an impoverished Jewish environment, and his inability to secure a publisher for his general history led Dubnow to Berlin. He would remain there until the accession of Adolf Hitler to power in 1933. Dubnow's arrival in the German capital coincided with the flowering of Weimar culture. Nevertheless, he quickly gravitated toward the small Russian Jewish emigré community, which was largely composed of fellow refugees from the Bolshevik Revolution. Surrounded by such luminaries as Haim Nahman Bialik and Shmaryahu Levin, the Jewish historian was able to at least partially recreate the intellectual circle that he had left behind years before in Odessa.

Fortunately, Dubnow had been able to take his library and archive with him when he left the Soviet Union and his research continued unabated. In 1925 the first volume of his massive general history of the Jews was published in German, with the tenth and last volume appearing in 1929. During his stay in Berlin, Dubnow helped found the Vilna-based Yiddish Scientific Research Institute (YIVO), which he believed would serve to unite eastern and western Jewish scholars. It was also in the German capital that he published the definitive version in Hebrew of his *History of Hasidism* along with a series of important articles devoted to Yiddish. In 1930, Dubnow's seventieth birthday and fiftieth year of literary activity were celebrated with the publication of a Festschrift in his honor. To commemorate his reaching the milestone of "three score and ten," Dubnow's friends established an institute in his name that was pledged to publish a Jewish encyclopedia.

Despite his scholarly activity, Dubnow could not avoid noticing the danger signs in Weimar that threatened Jewish security during the 1920s and early '30s. He was only too well aware of the impact of inflation, the failure of middle-class political parties, and the increase in street violence upon the rise of Nazism. Though he was not personally confronted with anti-Semitism in Berlin, Dubnow found the daily onslaught of anti-Jewish propaganda and activity emotionally intolerable.[105] The rise of anti-Semitism only added to Dubnow's sense of being doubly in exile, from the Land of Israel and from Russia. The departure of Bialik for Palestine in 1924 was an especially cruel blow, marking Dubnow's last direct link in Berlin with his Odessa past. Though he tried to establish ties with German Jewish intellectuals, the Jewish historian could not bridge the gap between his own perceptions and those of western Jews.[106] Having completed his major work, Dubnow was also wracked by fears of old age and by self-doubts about the relevance of his writings to contemporary Jews faced with immediate and pressing problems of survival and escape.

Increasingly convinced that Nazism was no passing phenomenon, in August 1933 Dubnow left Berlin to settle in Kaiserwald, a quiet suburb of Riga. (Ironically, a decade later the area would become a concentration camp for the survivors of the Nazi liquidation of the Riga ghetto.) Dubnow now would be closer to his children in Poland and in Russia. He also hoped that his spirits would be revived by settling in a dynamic city with a seashore nearby. Fortunately, he had managed to escape Germany with all of his research material. Once again, Dubnow would try to escape the present evils of Jewish life by immersing himself in the Jewish past.[107]

In the 1930s, Dubnow continued to work on his memoirs, producing the third and last volume in 1940 only months before his death. He also completed his *History of the Jews*, which was published in Hebrew in the same year. Calling for courage in the face of the Nazi danger, Dubnow lobbied world Jewish groups in vain to form organizations of self-defense. His proposal to establish an International League to Combat Aggression against the Jewish People was debated in the World Jewish Congress.[108] In one of his last letters, he pressed for an economic boycott against Germany and insisted that Jews join the Allied armies in the struggle against Nazism.[109] Despite his physical and emotional weariness, Dubnow continued to defend the values and ideals of liberalism and emancipation and to voice hope in a shared future for Jews and Christians in Europe after the clouds of Nazism had dissipated. Once again, he sought consolation in the lessons of history. What, after all, were the dangers of the present, he argued, when compared with the 4,000-year history of the Jewish people? As Dubnow noted in 1938 in a statement that aptly summarized the conclusions of his decades of historical research: "[I]n times past there were similar anti-Jewish fronts in Europe, and nevertheless we survived—through tenacity, passive resistance or active struggle."[110]

Throughout the 1930s, friends pleaded with Dubnow to flee the European continent and to find refuge in various countries including Palestine, Sweden, England, and the United States. He kept putting off the decision with an almost fatalistic consistency, however. In his responses, Dubnow repeated the by-now familiar litany of reasons for his refusal to leave eastern Europe, including his failing health, the difficulties he would face in learning to speak a new language, and the fact that he would not be able to find a teaching appointment in a new land. Most important, he insisted, to abandon Europe was to turn his back on his commitment to the Diaspora and to the roots of what he believed would be an emerging contemporary Jewish consciousness after the impending war.[111]

As hostilities loomed ever closer, however, Dubnow even despaired of the power of historical research to provide meaning and hope for the future. Shortly before the outbreak of war, he would describe a scholarly study on Jewish history as little more than "a gravestone on the ruins of Europe." Dubnow could not even find solace in the imminent publication of the last volume of his memoirs. It might be published in 1940, he commented in passing to Wischnitzer, "if by that time a universal flood will not descend upon us."[112] Yet the Jewish historian stubbornly refused to abandon completely his faith in a better world. Months before the outbreak of war, he was still reaffirming his belief in the need for Jewry to struggle for a better future.[113] As long as he was not directly affected by the war, Dubnow seemed to believe that there was still hope. As late as February 1940 he could still write that "it is more peaceful in America, but we have no right to abandon the old home so long as the danger is still remote and may be averted altogether."[114]

Dubnow's commitment to remain in eastern Europe would ultimately cost him his life. In September 1939 the Nazis invaded Poland but stopped short of the Baltic countries. In response, in June 1940 the Soviet Union established Lithuania and Latvia as Soviet republics and closed their borders. Dubnow refused to participate in the Communist-controlled Jewish community established by the occupying forces. When the Jews of Riga celebrated his eightieth birthday in September 1940, he chose to isolate himself in his study.[115] For the first time in his life, Dubnow felt himself effectively cut off from European Jewry and from Nazi-occupied Europe in particular.[116] His only contact with the outside world were the daily broadcasts of the BBC.[117]

His hopes for European Jewry collapsing around him, Dubnow wrote a series of articles that were never published in which he argued that the Jewish people would suffer their tragedy alone. Those who expected help from any of the other forces fighting against Nazism, he commented cynically, were fools.[118] Nevertheless, Dubnow continued to insist on the need to remain in eastern Europe. In the winter of 1940, he turned down yet another invitation to leave Lithuania, this time to settle in Stockholm in neutral Sweden. He still had research to do, he weakly argued. In June 1941, Dubnow wrote his last letter to his daughter in the United States. In it the Jewish historian bitterly complained of his sense of helplessness and lack of creativity.[119]

On June 11, the German army crossed into Soviet territory. Less than three weeks later, Nazi troops occupied the Latvian capital. Dubnow's friends tried to find him a temporary place of refuge outside the city but he was discovered by the Gestapo. With the help of the Judenrat, the Jewish Council, the eighty-year-old Jewish historian was placed in an old-age home. The onset of mass shootings of Jews in November 1941, however, led community leaders to transfer Dubnow to what they hoped would be a "safe" building inhabited by the family of a Jewish policeman. Their efforts were to no avail. On December 8, 1941, Dubnow was driven into the streets with other aged and sick Jews in a roundup that marked the beginning of the liquidation of the Riga ghetto. Feeble and unable to keep up, Dubnow was shot and killed by a Latvian soldier. According to survivors' reports, his last words were: "Good people, never forget, good people, tell the story, good people, write."[120]

In defining his contribution to the transformation of Jewish life, Simon Dubnow stressed his role as the first modern historian of the Diaspora. Rejecting the tendency of classical Jewish historians to reduce the study of the Jewish people since the destruction of the Second Temple to the polarities of religious persecution and spiritual response, Dubnow claimed to emphasize the importance of political, social, and economic development. Like the Russian positivists whom he read with great interest, he proposed to replace metaphysical analysis of Jewish collective identity and survival with a rigorous empirical approach that stressed the importance of social conditions in shaping human consciousness. In contrast to those who presented a "lachrymose" view of Jewish history, Dubnow was convinced that a study of the past revealed sources of strength and vigor for continued Jewish life in the future.[121] Dubnow was also insistent upon the need to understand the Jewish historical experience in exile on its own terms. In contrast to other historians who felt the need to justify Jewish distinctiveness, he accepted Jewish separateness in the modern era as a given and sought to understand its roots.[122] Unlike Heinrich Graetz and other nineteenth-century Jewish scholars whom he saw as engaging in apologetics and generally unconcerned with the needs of the community, he claimed to feel no embarrassment in addressing his writings exclusively to Jews and to specific Jewish concerns.[123]

Dubnow was convinced that the obsessions of previous historians with the relationship of Jewish thought to general European intellectual history had drawn them to the study of western European Jews and had led them to ignore other "less sophisticated" self-contained communities. The result was that they tended to define Jewish identity and explain Jewish continuity primarily in terms of subjectivist and externally imposed criteria. For Dubnow, on the other hand, the key to modern Jewish survival was to be found not in the religious and intellectual development of western European Jews but in the autonomously developed communal structure of the Jews of Russia and Poland. In contrast to other contemporaneous Jewish communities, the history of East European Jewry embodied underlying truths about Jewish life in the millennial history of the Diaspora. In a larger sense, Dubnow was convinced that despite the diverse paths of Jewish communities, the history of Diaspora Jewry needed to be understood as a unified whole. Challenging the assumptions of both religious traditionalists and classical historians, he figured that a serious study of the complex weave of Jewish history since the end of the Second Jewish Commonwealth would reveal a unique human tapestry.

Dubnow was also insistent upon the need to view Jewish history as a continuum. The ebbs and flows of the nation's development, from traditionalism to reform and from isolation to integration, were not inexplicable and isolated events. Instead, like nature itself, they were manifestations of the development of a living organism alive to both internal needs and the influences of the changing environment in which it rooted itself and grew. Amid the bewildering variety of Jewish experiences over the centuries, the sensitive historian could discern an underlying constancy: the desire of Jewry as a whole to maintain its basic unity and identity through the internalization of ideals in daily collective life and institutional behavior.[124] Despite its dispersion throughout the globe and its minority status everywhere in the world, the Jewish people's continual struggle for survival had steeled it for the future. Responding to contradictory stimuli with renewed strength and self-confidence, the nation would always remain the determinant of its own fate rather than the subject of other peoples' histories. The dialectical development of Jewish history, then, was a positive occurrence—"a witness, a manifestation, that the organism is essentially healthy, and spiritually receptive."[125]

In insisting on an "organic" approach to Jewish history, Dubnow maintained that previous Jewish historians had been wrong to stress the role of individual Jewish thinkers and activists. They were mere reflections of the collective heritage of the Jewish people. Even those individuals who were convinced that they were changing or destroying Jewish life, he argued, were nothing more than actors in the unfolding of the destiny of the Jewish people. In denying the role of God in Jewish history, Dubnow substituted the "cunning of History," which imposed the collective will of a people upon even its most rebellious members. As he commented in an article published in the Hebrew paper *He-Atid* (The Future) in 1912: "Every individual member of a generation, who is not like a dry branch or a leaf fallen from the tree, carries the 'burden of the heritage' of the chain of generations; and he carries it willingly or unwillingly, knowingly or unknowingly. He is nursed and fed by the national forces accumulated in the past even when he rebels against the very means through which the forces were accumulated and even when he strives to destroy them, or to alter their form, or 'reform' them."[126]

The result of Dubnow's insights into the Jewish past was a thoroughgoing revision of Jewish historical understanding. In works such as his *History of Hasidism*, Dubnow turned traditional *Geistesgeschichte* on its head, replacing the abstract examination of disembodied ideas that placed Jews outside of history with a study of the Jewish people which evaluated ideas and movements in terms of their historical impact on collective identity and national unity. Such an approach necessitated a complete rewriting of Jewish history. What the modern scholar had to do, Dubnow commented in an article on Russian Jewish historiography published in 1891, was to go beyond the superficial examination of Jewish life to create a comprehensive history of the Jews, that is, a "detailed description of their social conditions, of their economic existence, of their domestic life, of their spiritual and religious life, in short—of their entire past."[127]

In pursuing his new approach, Dubnow created a new periodization of Jewish history. Instead of emphasizing literary and cultural divisions, such as the age of the Bible or of the Talmud, as classical Jewish scholars had done, he chose to divide Jewish history according to stages of communal development.[128] In his analysis of Jewish communal history, Dubnow also argued for the need to wrest the study of local communities from the hands of both traditional leadership, who had exploited such studies to legitimate their own authority and control, and anti-Semites, who had used the history of Jewish communal autonomy to demonstrate the existence of Jews as a "state within a state."[129] The only way to ensure true objectivity, he maintained, was to rely extensively on archival research.

In developing his new view of Jewish history, Dubnow drew upon various intellectual currents of the nineteenth century. His understanding of the phenomenon of nationalism and national identity owed much to the writings of Ernest Renan, who previously had provided the young Jewish intellectual with an innovative way of looking at religion and religious belief. In his essay *Qu'est-ce qu'une nation?* (What Is a Nation?), the French historian had stressed the ability of nations to survive through their collective memory of the past. For Dubnow, who had placed historical understanding at the center of both Jewish communal development and modern Jewish identity, it was a profoundly important revelation. As noted earlier, Dubnow also borrowed heavily from the sociological writings of individuals such as Auguste Comte and Herbert Spencer, who emphasized the evolutionary development of social structures and their relationship to collective survival. Though he never visited England, Dubnow was deeply impressed by the model of British social development, which he was convinced combined a strong sense of tradition with an openness to gradual change. It was a model that he would apply not only to his analysis of the Jewish past but also to his vision of the future of Jewish communal life.[130] Dubnow may have also been influenced by the the pan-Slavic movement. His discussion of communal institutions and "hegemonic centers," for example, bears strong similarities to the ideas of Nikolai Yakovlevich Danilewski, a Russian social theorists of the 1840s, who defined history in terms of a succession of "cultural-historical" typologies.[131]

Yet another important influence on Dubnow's historiographical approach was John Stuart Mill. As noted earlier, Mill provided the young historian with both an understanding of the methodology of empiricism and a liberal's sensitivity toward the power of religious tradition and majority rule within both the larger society and the Jewish community.[132] In addition, Dubnow's central notions of communal and personal national autonomy in a multinational state were in part extrapolated from Mill's discussions of the autonomous rights of the individual within society.[133] Finally, Mill's emphasis on the importance of individual freedom and commitment, though hardly supportive of Dubnow's concern with Jewish collective survival, undoubtedly gave the Jewish historian the courage he needed to pursue his efforts to develop a new Jewish consciousness in the face of public opposition and/or apathy.

Despite his insistence on the uniqueness of Jewish historical development, Dubnow was strongly influenced by other nationalist historians of central and eastern Europe such as Frantisek Palacky and Ignacy Lelewel. As Dubnow struggled to discover the relationship between historical understanding and national survival, he could not but be attracted to their emphasis on historical consciousness as a means of reviving national identity among peoples lacking objective definitions of nationhood.[134] At the same time, however, the Jewish historian seemed to have had little regard for Palacky's and Lelewel's mingling of intellectual and political activity. Distrustful of mass politics, he was convinced that their insistence upon the need to descend into the political arena to realize their ideals destroyed their credibility as scholars and tarnished their image as true intellectuals. Unlike Jews, Dubnow argued, the Czechs and the Poles were spiritually impoverished peoples who were forced to rely on a small group of individuals for both the conceptualization and actualization of their national agendas. Such statements, which not only contradicted each other but also challenged Dubnow's frequently expressed views on the role of Jewish intellectuals in communal life, point up the overwhelming revulsion he felt toward political activism in the aftermath of 1905. They also suggest that, like many others of his generation, the Jewish historian was never able to clearly define the relationship between the Jewish intelligentsia and the general Jewish population in the struggle to create a new basis for national identity.

Though Dubnow was immensely gratified by the contributions he made to Jewish historiography, his interest in the Jewish past was not purely academic. For Dubnow, history was more than the "objective past." It was, as Robert Seltzer has insightfully written, "the creator, revelation, and redeemer."[135] Profoundly influenced by events affecting the Jewish community at the turn of the century, Dubnow was convinced that the times called for a transformation in the bases for Jewish survival and growth. The first step in defining the Jewish future was to probe the Jewish past. Sharing in his generation's suspicion of the political activism of Jewish youth, he regarded the radical proposals of Jewish socialism and Zionism as antihistorical and therefore unworthy of serious consideration. A study of Jewish history clearly revealed that Jewry had developed through evolutionary means rather than through dramatic leaps in consciousness, communal structure, and collective action. Similarly, Dubnow rejected linguistic nationalism, which he believed rested on a limited analysis of the Jewish past that failed to incorporate all elements of the Jewish people. For Dubnow, the answer to the Jewish national problem lay in the uncovering of the unchanging patterns of daily life that sustained the Jewish people and that underlay the changing economic, social, and political reality imposed from without. As he noted in a speech delivered before the Jewish Historical Ethnographical Society in 1910: "Reform of historical methodology is closely linked with the national movement that has swept Jewry in recent times. . . . We need only point out the interaction *between the awakening of the national spirit and the new understanding of Jewish history . . . .* We shall be the creators of both the new history and the new historiography."[136]

For Dubnow, the central theme of Jewish history and the key to understanding the remarkable survival of the Jewish people was the distinctive nature of Jewish values. Armed with an understanding of the individuality of the Jewish people, the modern Diaspora Jew could develop a new form of identity and communal structure that would incorporate the recurrent ideals of Jewish life in the past with the precepts of modern European thought. Rooted in historical awareness yet alive to the possibilities of evolutionary change, a historically based Jewish identity would ensure national distinctiveness while at the same time allowing for individual thought and expression. The task of the historian thus was absolutely vital to the survival of the Jewish people. No mere intellectual gadfly content to critically analyze the community in the name of scientific objectivity, he would play a central role in enabling the nation to find its true inner strength. More than a researcher, Dubnow was, in the words of the editors of a volume published in honor of the historian's seventy-fifth birthday, "the passionate seeker of a new ideology that would replace traditional religion and philosophical dogmatism and would shed light on the mystery of the Jews' existence over thousands of years."[137]

Though Dubnow saw no necessary conflict between his scholarly and practical concerns, in reality his insistence on using the past to define the future led to numerous contradictions in his methodology. Though claiming to present a sociological survey of Jewish history, he invariably stressed political factors that enabled the community to maintain its authority over its members in response to the pressures of the dominant society. Given his interest in stressing collective unity, Dubnow also ignored social and economic tensions within past and present Jewish communities and concentrated almost exclusively on the attitudes and actions of the dominant elite.[138] In this sense, he used the principles of sociology primarily as a justification for the study of the Jewish people as a distinct collectivity rather than as a tool to examine its inner structure and dynamics. As Dubnow himself explained in the introduction to his *History of the Jews*: "Underlying this [sociological] method is the idea, originating out of the whole range of the phenomena of our history, that the Jewish people at all times and in all countries has had a history of its own, not only spiritually but socially as well. . . . This continuously living nation has always and everywhere defended the autonomous existence not only of its social life but also of all the areas of its culture."[139]

Dubnow prided himself on having transcended the "spiritual" concerns of early historians. Yet his insistence on the continuum of Jewish life led him to emphasize ideas and ideals. As a result, for all his talk of the importance of social and economic factors in Jewish history, Dubnow's historiographical approach remained at base largely spiritual and intellectual. For him to have argued otherwise would have made Jewish life contingent on external factors, an interpretation that a Jewish nationalist like Dubnow could never accept. Not surprisingly, therefore, Dubnow never clearly defined the interaction between external and internal developments in Jewish history, between the pressures imposed by the larger society in which Jews found themselves and the development of distinctive Jewish spiritual ideals and communal structures.

Similarly, despite Dubnow's commitment to the uniformities of "scientific" history, he chose to ignore parallels between Jewish experiences and the responses of neighboring cultures and peoples. In discussing the creation stories of ancient peoples including Jews, for example, Dubnow blithely ignored the similarities among them that reflected their common need to explain the mysteries of the cosmos. The Israelite ideal was, in Dubnow's terms, "entirely alien to the ancient peoples of the East . . . [and] was the exclusive property of the Israelite-Judean nation."[140] Nor was he particularly sensitive to the plight of other oppressed minorities thoughout history. The result was a massive outpouring of historical scholarship that only rarely demonstrated familiarity with or at least interest in general historical development. Though Dubnow was adamant in his rejection of other historical approaches as time-bound and monolithic, he saw no contradiction in defending his own Judaeo-centered historiographical approach as "the one scientifically objective approach . . . independent of the influences of time and place."[141] In the end, despite his insistence upon rigorous scientific scholarship, Dubnow's own perspective often resulted in a unilinear and insular analysis of Jewish history.

Most important, Dubnow's concern with tracing the benign influence of "historical forces" in ensuring Jewish collective development led him to assume a historicist approach that weakened his analysis and betrayed his true didactic intentions. As we have seen, such an approach often led him to go beyond historical analogy in order to anachronistically read back contemporaneous events and ideas into history or to telescope ancient trends into the future. Thus, for example, he approvingly described the two kingdoms of ancient Israel as exhibiting "a certain democratic trend" while labeling the followers of the false messiah Samuel Molcho as members of "the distinctive 'Zionist' movement of the sixteenth century."[142] Similarly, Dubnow's strong emphasis in the early chapters of *History of the Jews* on the tribal divisions within biblical Israel was undoubtedly motivated by his attempt to demonstrate how ideological factionalism within the contemporaneous Jewish community weakened its efforts to maintain itself against the assault by the larger society.[143]

Even the most casual reader can discern the limitations and contradictions in Dubnow's attempt to use historical analysis to justify his attempt to replace religion with a modern "objective" rationale for Jewish survival and growth. Like others of his generation, he desperately sought to find an alternative to traditional Judaism. Yet he could not dismiss its powerful role in the past as the source of Jewish distinctiveness and the key to the Jewish people's tenacity. The reliance upon history enabled Dubnow to maintain a respectful view of traditional Jewish values without necessarily accepting their relevance in the present. The Jewish historian was insistent that there was a difference between the religious fanaticism of Orthodoxy and the "true" religious sentiment, which was inherent in biblical monotheism and which arose from "the depths of the human soul." All too often, however, the latter had been sacrificed in Jewish history in the name of the collective struggle for survival against external forces. The assertion of a modern Jewish identity in a democratic world would restore the personal or psychological dimension of religious belief by lifting the oppressive hand of authority and removing the burden of collective responsibility. In attempting to replace religion with history as the explanation for Jewish survival, however, Dubnow only succeeded in investing historical forces with religious significance. Once the ancient God of Israel had punished and rewarded His people with the aid of divinely inspired messengers. Now "History" as interpreted by its modern-day prophet would determine the fate of Jewry. As Dubnow wrote in a paraphrase of a traditional prayer offered to God by Jews embarking on new ventures: "We must recognize our creator, the forces of the past that created us and our national soul, which have kept us alive and sustained us up to this time."[144]

Ultimately, Dubnow's commitment to justify Jewish survival through historical inference led him to mistake form for content. In retrospect, it seems clear that his attempt to distinguish between his own "objective" analysis of Jewish history and past "subjective" historiography was artificial. In imposing a deterministic framework on Jewish history, Dubnow ended up engaging in metahistorical speculation. Could not Jewish survival simply be explained by contingent social, political, and economic factors and long-range trends rather than the Jews' evolutionary will to survive or the unfolding of some kindly historical purpose? Was the Babylonian Exile that created the Jewish Diaspora the "transition from youth to maturity in the life of the people," as Dubnow insisted,[145] or merely a tragic circumstance that the Jewish people were able to overcome through conscious will and determination? Equally important, even if one rejected the notion that the survival of the Jewish people was divinely ordained, could not one argue that it was precisely the belief in their chosenness that sustained the Jewish people throughout the centuries?[146]

Dubnow's views of the relationship of Jewish history to national consciousness and survival were most clearly expressed in his *Letters on Old and New Judaism*, which were written between 1897 and 1906.[147] The first five essays in particular, which appeared between 1897 and 1902, were intended as an elaboration of many of the theories he had first espoused in his essay "What Is Jewish History?" published in 1893. In examining the present-day fate of Jewry in the light of its history, Dubnow hoped both to provide direction to young Jewish intellectuals searching for a historical perspective on which to base their renewed affiliation with the Jewish people and to enlighten non-Jews whose only image of the Jew was derived from their association with assimilationists.[148] The title of the work reflected Dubnow's ongoing fascination with the philosophical concepts of dualism and dialectics. His goal was to unify the two polar opposites of tradition and modernity to develop a distinctively new Jewish identity and agenda. More specifically, it demonstrated the Jewish historian's oft-stated belief that the future of the Jewish people lay in an understanding of the structure and values of the Jewish past. As Dubnow stated in the Preface to the collected volume of the *Letters*: "My thought functioned simultaneously on two levels—the old and the new Judaism, history and the contemporary world, [both of] which I have always considered organically interconnected through a living link, as moments in a great evolutionary process."[149]

In the *Letters*, Dubnow expanded upon the two central notions that would inform all of his historical analysis: spiritual nationalism and autonomism. (The fact that the two definitions of Jewish life— one philosophical, the other political—appeared to be mutually exclusive was something that he did not seriously consider.) The concept of the Jews as a spiritual nation, which Dubnow had first enunciated in "What Is Jewish History?", was an amalgam drawn from the vision of the biblical Prophets and the approach to human development in the nineteenth century made popular by the German philosopher Johann Gottfried von Herder and the French sociologist Auguste Comte. For Dubnow, the evolution of "national types" proceeded from the material to the spiritual and from "external simplicity to inner complexity." At "lower" cultural levels, differences among nations were largely natural in character, reflecting the influence of the external environment on the collectivity's physical and intellectual character. The most primitive forms of collective life were to be found among "unhistorical peoples," ethnic groups that lacked a "distinctive spiritual individuality and . . . failed to display normal independent capacity for culture."

As human beings gained mastery over nature, Dubnow argued, the impact of material culture became more evident. Nations now began to differentiate among themselves according to their distinctive historical development and cultural creativity. The development of culture weakened the direct influence of natural forces and attenuated the "racial" particularities of the group. Control over the environment also allowed for the development of social organization and collective memory. The result was the emergence of both an authentic culture and historical consciousness.[150] More developed peoples had a conscious and "purposeful" history. Such groups, Dubnow had argued in his essay "What Is Jewish History?", had demonstrated "mental productivity of some sort" and had developed rational principles of social and economic life. In short, they represented "not only zoologic, but also spiritual types."[151]

In most national histories, Dubnow maintained, growing social cohesion eventually led to the development of the most familiar attributes of the modern nation—the sovereign state and political authority.[152] The most important test for a nation, however, occurred when it lost its political independence and territory. Lacking objective definition of nationhood and scattered among the nations, it must "think and suffer," that is, struggle to find within itself the spiritual and ethical ideals to sustain its existence.[153] As the only nation to have survived after defeat and dispersion, Dubnow argued, the Jewish people had reached the highest stage and noblest form of collective identity—"cultural-historical individuality." It was the Jews' embodiment of ethical humanism and not their external or material condition that had transformed them into an exemplary model to be followed by all of the societies in which they lived in the Diaspora.

The result, Dubnow argued, was that Jews were "the historical nation of all times," while Jewish history was nothing but "history sublimated" through a distinctive people.[154] Dubnow was convinced that the lessons of Jewish history had to be understood by Jew and non-Jew alike. Jews had to remind both their friends and foes that they were an eternal people whose ideals resonated with the human spirit and who could never be destroyed.[155] It was not coincidental that Dubnow would eventually choose to entitle his magnum opus a "world" or "universal" history of the Jewish people. The term itself was meant to suggest not only the global dispersion of Jews but the significance of their history for all of humanity. As Dubnow himself commented in the Introduction to the work: "The term 'universal' is applicable to the history of civilization throughout the world, as distinguished from the histories of individual peoples and countries. But the destiny of the Jewish people has manifested itself—through almost the entire extent of the civilized world (with the exception of India and China) and throughout the entire duration of the recorded history of mankind—in such a way as to have its own universal history in the literal sense."[156]

In examining the historical development of the Jewish people, Dubnow argued that the racial or biological element of national life dominated Jewish history from its beginnings in the wanderings of the Hebrews until the period of the kings when the nation became politically united. Even in their earliest history, however, when the Jews' nomadic nature brought them under the influence of many different peoples, they were able to maintain a distinctive worldview based upon the belief in monotheism. In so doing, they resisted what Dubnow described as "the natural phenomena, which, as a rule, entrap primitive man, and make him the bond-slave of the visible and material."[157] The beginnings of true Jewish national consciousness, however, could be said to begin with the period of Egyptian slavery. It took the figure of Moses to nationalize the "God-idea" and to create a synthesis of ideals and practical behavior—"propaganda by the deed," as Dubnow called it in a cynical jibe at the Jewish revolutionaries of his own time.[158]

Beginning with the biblical Prophets, Dubnow maintained, the "center of gravity" of Jewish national survival gradually shifted from the political realm to the social and spiritual spheres. Under the banner of "universal monotheism," Prophets like Jeremiah and Isaiah sought to instill a strong internal spiritual cohesiveness within the Jewish people as a whole. The "spiritual nation" itself, however, emerged only during the First Exile under Persian and Greek rule. In the midst of oppression and despair, the Jewish people now began to fashion the tools for its survival and growth in the Diaspora. "From the heavy chastisement" of exile from their homeland, " Dubnow proclaimed, "the Jewish nation emerged purified, re-born for a new life."[159]

Despite the restoration of political sovereignty in the sixth century B.C.E., forward-looking elements among the Jewish elite led by the Pharisees continued to champion the ideal of spiritual culture. As a result, the destruction of the Second Temple did not result in the disappearance of the nation as was the case with other peoples that lost their political power. On the contrary, the instinct for national survival and the sense of national destiny gained momentum in exile as the Diaspora communities slowly began to establish their communal institutions. The Jewish people now assumed their historically determined role as a light unto the nations. As Dubnow stated in his essay on Jewish history: "The nation is the kernel and the land is but the shell; the shell may be broken but the kernel remains intact, and if the seed is a healthy one the nation will always be able to preserve its autonomy against the heteronomy of the alien surroundings, and will be able to serve as a standard for all the nations as a model of spiritual steadfastness."[160]

Throughout the history of the Diaspora, Dubnow claimed, Jewry passed through a variety of stages in which its economic, political, and social status ebbed and flowed, largely as a result of external influences and forces. In each age, however, one Jewish community served as a "hegemonic center" to ensure that the central ideals of Jewish thought and culture would survive and continue to develop. Hegemonic centers were characterized by a significant concentration of Jews and a situation of relative security that allowed the particular Jewish community to develop undisturbed by outside interference.[161]   Such a view led Dubnow to present a highly selective chronology of the Jewish past.   Only those events and places in history that reflected the unfolding of Jewish consciousness were of historical significance.   From the fifth through the eleventh centuries, it was Babylonia that dominated Jewish life.   From the eleventh century until the expulsion of Jews at the end of the fourteenth century, it was Spain.   Finally, from the sixteenth through the eighteenth centuries, Jewish life was split between a western center in Germany and an eastern center in Poland.

The existence of hegemonic centers meant that despite differences in Jewish communities that were generally reflective of external (and thus inconsequential) influences, Jewish life throughout the ages remained essentially the same.   Here was the key to the survival of the Jewish people.   Amid the vagaries of coincidence and contingent events affecting general history,   Dubnow argued, "[t]he [Jewish] nation as a whole . . . lived and developed as one, as a definite national personality, in all parts of the Diaspora."[162]   Every generation carried within itself "the remnants of worlds created and destroyed" during the course of the previous history of the Jewish people.   Though each individual Jewish community in history might believe that it is actually reshaping Jewish life, in the long run it "continues to weave the thread that binds all the links of the nation into the chain of generations."   Ultimately, Dubnow claimed, the forces of Jewish history would ensure that Jewry will always return to "the point of the nation's existence."[163]

In summarizing the lessons learned from his analysis of Jewish history, Dubnow threw away the guise of scholarly objectivity and assumed the mantle of the ancient Prophets and rabbinic scholars of old.   Having persevered despite all odds to the present day, he boldly proclaimed, the Jews "may be said to be indestructible."[164]   Indeed, in mastering their own history in a situation of dispersion, Jewry had actually transcended the boundaries of human history itself.   As Dubnow proclaimed in his massive study of the Jews of Russia and Poland, the history of the Jewish people clearly demonstrated the ability of a nation to conquer "the two cosmic forces: Time and Space."[165]

In these and other hyperbolic statements, Dubnow clearly reflected the messianic notion of an "end of days." For all his commitment to objective scholarship, the Jewish nationalist historian was convinced that ultimately history would end with the triumph of Jewish values and ideals. In some future time as yet undisclosed, the world would seek out the Jews to learn of the ultimate truths of human existence. As Dubnow commented on Jewish self-consciousness during the Hellenistic period: "[T]he time will come when the world . . . will come to me in confusion and longing to ask: What is truth?"[166]

In emphasizing the eternal nature of the Jewish people, Dubnow seemed to be arguing for a biological definition of Jewish nationhood that survived despite the attempt by individual Jews to assimilate into the dominant culture. Like many nationalists of the late nineteenth century, Dubnow accepted the view made popular by the French naturalist Jean Baptiste Lamarck that traits and characteristics acquired in one generation could be transmitted to succeeding generations. In defining Jewry as a biological organism, he was able to trace the evolution of the Jewish people while at the same time emphasizing its unchanging nature and distinctiveness. Yet fearing that his views might provide ammunition for anti-Semites and cognizant of the powerful pull of assimilationism in western Europe, Dubnow was equally insistent that "the law of historical heredity" and the "national instinct" could be countermanded by exposure to a foreign culture.[167]

Dubnow attempted to clarify the seeming confusion between Jewish biological and cultural identity by differentiating between "nationality," or peoplehood, and "nation." One could only be part of a people through birth, he insisted; membership in any "artificial legal or sociopolitical" collectivity such as a civil society, a state, or a guild, however, was a matter of individual choice.[168] Though maintaining that "spiritual affinity is a more important factor than blood relationship in families" and that religion was not the sole determinant of national affiliation,[169] Dubnow was unwilling to fully accept converts to Judaism. At most, they could be citizens of a Jewish nation in a formal sense, but they could never share in the spiritual heritage of the people.[170] Not surprisingly, therefore, he disdainfully dismissed Jewish converts to Christianity as traitors to collective solidarity and argued that their actions effectively removed them from the community.[171]

In attempting to synthesize the subjective and objective factors that comprised his definition of nationhood, Dubnow concluded that only a thorough grounding in Jewish spiritual values through intensive modern education would end the division between "nationality" and "nation." Only then could an individual be certain that he was Jewish both racially and culturally. But what was the nature of the "spiritual affinity" that Dubnow claimed explained Jewish survival and would ensure the continued existence of the Jewish people in the future? It clearly could no longer to be found in the principles of Orthodox Judaism, which he dismissed as a "fossilized tradition." After all, the essence of Judaism was to stimulate the Jewish people to seek new methods of national self-preservation, not to lull them to sleep.[172] Though religious tradition had been correct to identify the Jewish people as an eternal people, Dubnow maintained, it had erred by assigning responsibility for its survival to divine providence instead of to the day-to-day reality of communal existence. In actuality, Dubnow argued in imitation of the German materialist philosopher Ludwig Feuerbach, the Jewish people had created God in their own image—"a historical God, the ruler of their destiny, who was at the same time a product of that destiny."[173] In foolishly believing that religious observance was practically efficacious rather than a mere symbolic manifestation of the nation's will, he maintained, religious Orthodoxy had denied the psychological role that Jewish tradition played in linking the Jew with his or her past.

Unlike Haim Zhitlowski, however, Dubnow's rejection of Orthodox Judaism as the source of Jewish national revival did not lead him to praise early Christianity. True, he had been attracted to aspects of Christian thought in his youth. In addition, the challenge of Christianity to Judaism remained an important element in his analysis of Jewish national development. Thus, for example, Dubnow clearly shared Zhitlowski's notion that the beliefs of the Essenes and the teachings of the Gospels represented pristine "spiritualized" forms of Judaism that arose in an era in which Jewish religious leaders were forced to concentrate their attention on guarding the community's spiritual unity in the face of the political assault by the Roman Empire.[174] In his historical writings, Dubnow often glorified the heroic martyrdom of Jews throughout the ages in terms that mirrored the apocalyptic visions of early Christians.[175] Similarly, he claimed to see important parallels between reforming Jewish movements such as Hasidism and Christian belief and practice, especially in their emphasis on inward faith and the role of the religious teacher.[176]

Yet Dubnow could not accept what he believed to be an offshoot of classical Judaism as the basis of national survival. To adopt the universalist tenets of Christianity would also deny the distinctiveness of the Jewish people. Most important, the Jewish historian could not ignore the bitter heritage of Christian anti-Semitism, which he blamed not only for the tragic deaths of hundreds of thousands of Jews over the ages but also for the belligerent defensiveness and subsequent ossification of Jewish religious belief that began in the Middle Ages.[177] If he commented extensively on Christianity in his historical writings, it was largely to counter the appeal of the new faith to Russian Jewish youth. Dubnow's attitudes toward Christianity were aptly summed up in his comment that as a result of the Crusades, "Judaism suffered the tragic fate of King Lear," betrayal by its child.[178]

Nor was Dubnow impressed by the attempts of modern Jewish philosophers and religious reformers to define Judaism as a system of abstract thought. In contrast to his friend Ahad Ha-Am, he believed that the efforts by individuals like Maimonides and Moses Mendelssohn to develop a "modern" rationalistic Jewish worldview that denied historical development were as self-destructive as the legalistic framework of rabbinic Judaism.[179] As for religious reformers of the nineteenth century, Dubnow turned their arguments on their head. They too had ignored the lessons of Jewish history, he wrote, particularly the understanding that religious ritual and belief were merely the husk that helped preserve the kernel, the autonomous nation.[180] The key to the survival of Jewish ideals and values, Dubnow stated, was their grounding in a national historical event— collective revelation—and not in the abstruse theology of monotheism. A national ideal that was inaccessible and incomprehensible to the majority of the people and that ignored their spiritual and emotional needs could not long survive.

Dubnow was equally insistent that Jewish spiritual ideals could not be found in the universalist sentiments of assimilationists. The Jewish historian had bitter words for western Jews and Russifiers, equating their attitude and behavior with selfishness and even national betrayal. Like King Herod, whose reign Dubnow regarded as "one of the saddest epochs of Jewish history," they could "only imitate whatever was in vogue in the 'higher circles' at any given time."[181] In their foolish quest for acceptance, assimilationists had debased themselves far more than Jews living under the yoke of past oppression. Even worse, by their actions assimilationists were actually supporting the subjugation of the Jewish people by other nations. For Dubnow, it was a betrayal not only of Jewish independence but of the very concept of equal rights as embodied in the ideals of the French Revolution.[182] The quest for the liberation of humanity so championed by Jewish universalists, Dubnow stated in his Second Letter, was nothing but a mask for the enslavement of the Jewish people by the dominant nation. Ultimately, as the expulsion of Jews from Spain in the fifteenth century demonstrated, "History" would punish Jewish leaders and thinkers who ignored the needs of the community in the name of their own self-advancement. In the meantime, one could only hope that "true" intellectuals would eventually realize the error of their ways and return to the Jewish people.[183]

Dubnow saw the rise of assimilationism in nineteenth-century Europe as reflective of a constant theme in Jewish history—the conflict between the desire of the individual for self-fulfillment and the needs of the community for survival and growth. In the end, much as Dubnow claimed he himself had done, individual members of the Jewish community would have to submit to the dictates of social law and convention in order to preserve the collectivity. The Jewish people was involved in a struggle for its very own existence. In a time of war against internal and external enemies, no nation could tolerate social division and intellectual confusion. As Dubnow wrote in the *History of the Jews* : "Deep tragedy of centuries of Jewish history is inherent in the clash between the freedom of the individual and the uniqueness of the nation. Members of a nation that found itself in a condition of lasting self-defense, must submit to all the severe restrictions of wartime. True, the spiritual rulers of the people often encroached on the bounds of the regulations, aggravating the 'yoke of the law,' but the general trend of their activity was dictated through the imperious needs of life, through the sense of national self-preservation."[184]

Indeed, Dubnow remained burdened throughout his life by a strong sense of guilt about his own youthful rejection of Jewish identity and community. At the same time, he needed to respond to communal fears over the growing strength of Russifiers and radicals. Thus, like the proto-Zionist Leon Pinsker before him, Dubnow constantly associated assimilationism with pathological illness in his writings. The alienation of "progressive" Jews from the Jewish community, he wrote in Darwinian terms in the First Letter, only demonstrated the "process of natural selection, the exclusion of those weak elements of the nation that are unable to bear the pressure of the surrounding environment."[185] One should not mourn the loss of these "renegades." They were nothing but "withered and dead leaves" from the "centuries-old tree of Jewry," socially prejudiced and morally deficient individuals more deserving of pity than scorn.[186] Whatever the power of his personal convictions, Dubnow concluded, no individual Jew could logically demand respect from others if he himself refused to recognize his own biologically defined and culturally rooted national "personality."[187]

In place of religious Orthodoxy and assimilationism, Dubnow argued for what he called "evolutionary Judaism," an approach to Jewish life that rested on the recognition of the need to continually adapt to new cultural conditions.[188] Judaism, he stated in an article written in 1924, was a "national culture" whose roots were eternal but whose branches were renewed from generation to generation. A chain of development rather than a set of ideological constructs, it periodically transformed itself to ensure the continued existence of the nation. As such, the validity of Judaism in the modern world was to be determined not by objective standards of philosophical truth but by its ability to continue to serve the collective interests of the nation in its struggle to survive.[189]

Dubnow's emphasis on evolutionism masked his own inability to define exactly what form the Jews' "cultural-historical individuality" would take in the modern era. Dubnow seemed to have shared both Zhitlowski's and Ahad Ha-Am's vision of the development of a "purified religion" as reflected in the ideals of the biblical Prophets that would serve as a powerful ethical force in the modern age.[190] At the same time, he characterized the new Jewish identity as a form of "spiritual nationalism" in the manner of Herder that sought only to defend itself and rejected any attempt to subjugate other peoples.[191] At some point in the future, Dubnow argued, Jewry would achieve the "secularization of the national idea," which would not eliminate religion but would effectively separate the spiritual ideals of the Jewish people from formal religious belief and ritual. Faced with numerous contradictions in his own thought, Dubnow was ultimately forced to conclude that the nature of Jewish identity could not be defined beforehand but would only emerge from the daily struggle for Jewish survival.[192]

In defining the ideal of Judaism as process rather than as substance, Dubnow undoubtedly sought to avoid the debate between religionists and secularists. Stressing the link with the religious past, he could also emphasize the radically different nature of the present. In a more personal sense, the emphasis on evolution allowed Dubnow to study Judaism without having to commit himself to its beliefs. As Robert Seltzer has remarked, Dubnow learned from historians of religion like Renan that "one could have a relationship with traditional faiths that did not contravene one's firm rejection of their literal truth."[193] Dubnow's own religious observance reflected his perception of the symbolic and historical role of tradition. Before Passover, for example, he would make sure to buy matzot (unleavened bread), not out of a religious obligation but as a statement in his view that during a time of enslavement every Jew had "to make at least a historical-symbolical protest by a conspicuous allusion to our ancient way of life, the ritual supper glorifying liberty."[194]

Dubnow argued that spiritually and culturally strong nations preserved their identity under conditions of political subordination and dispersion through the development of independent communal institutions. He dubbed this phenomenon "autonomism," which he defined as "the aspiration of every dynamic nation to maintain the maximum internal independence . . . as a function of given political conditions."[195] As a reflection of Dubnow's understanding of national history in general, the study of autonomism would demonstrate the way in which concrete and objective reality reflected the inner spiritual nature of the nation. At the same time, an examination of the establishment and maintenance of communal institutions in the past would help to shape the direction of national life in the future.

As noted in the discussion of Haim Zhitlowski's philosophy in Chapter 2, autonomist ideas were common currency in both Jewish and general circles in central and eastern Europe at the turn of the century. Autonomism was given special impetus within the Jewish community by the general struggle for a democratic Russia in the first decade of the twentieth century. Members of the Vozrozhdenie group and later the SERP party, both under the tutelage of Zhitlowski, forcefully defended proposals for cultural and territorial rights in the 1890s.

The idea of Jewish autonomy was also taken up by the Bund after 1901 and was ultimately adopted by nearly all Jewish parties in Russia after the Revolution of 1905. During the same period, the eccentric Galician Jewish nationalist and former Zionist Nathan Birnbaum provided a philosophical underpinning to autonomism. Labeling his ideal *All-judentum*, or non-Zionist nationalism, and proclaiming that *Israel geht vor Zion* (Israel precedes Zion), Birnbaum argued forcefully for the need to gain governmental recognition of a Jewish nationality in Europe.[196]

It was Simon Dubnow, however, who would present the most consistent and most widely heard exposition of the ideal of Jewish autonomism at the turn of the century. Unlike Zhitlowski, who spent most of his life outside of Russia, or Birnbaum, whose ideas were limited to a small group of intellectuals, Dubnow could claim a growing number of sympathetic readers and listeners among his many students in St. Petersburg, Odessa, and Riga. The Jewish historian outlined his ideas of cultural autonomy in the Fourth Letter of his *Letters on Old and New Judaism*. The letter was originally published in *Voskhod* in 1901 and then revised in 1907 in response to both the rise of political Zionism and the drive for political rights in the aftermath of the Revolution of 1905. Typically, Dubnow described the future development of communal independence within a democratic society as the culmination of a dialectical development within Jewish history. The period up to the nineteenth century was the "thesis," characterized by religious Orthodoxy and communal isolation. During this period, Jews had control over their internal life but lacked civil rights in the larger society. Executive power was vested in the rabbinate, who strove to protect the community from both internal dissent and outside intervention. The nineteenth century was the antithesis—the emergence of the "winter sleep," Dubnow called it—and was characterized by the Hasidic spirit of "forgetfulness of self through faith" in eastern Europe, on the one hand, and by assimilation and a rejection of tradition in western Europe, on the other. While Russian and Polish Jewry remained mired in spiritual and social isolation, the "enlightened" Jews of England, France, and Germany retained the ritualistic and literary symbols of their former autonomy but relinquished everything else to the state. As a result, western Jews gained civil rights but were alienated from their true selves.

Dubnow believed that a new era of autonomism was dawning in the twentieth century that would bring a synthesis of East and West. While the nineteenth century had witnessed the freedom of the individual in the West, the twentieth century would see the freedom or autonomy of the "national individual" as reflected in the emergence of a revitalized Russian Jewish community. Autonomy meant that after centuries of division and stunted growth, Jewry would finally achieve both civil and political rights and social and cultural independence.[197] By transforming communal Jewish life from a religiously based structure (a *Synagogengemeinden* or *Kultusgemeinden*) to a truly democratic representation of the Jewish national will (a *Volksgemeinden*), Dubnow maintained, the advent of communal autonomy would demonstrate yet again the synthesis of "old" and "new" Judaism that was the hallmark of Jewish survival and growth through the centuries.

Dubnow claimed to find the origins of the autonomist idea in Jewish history in the teachings of the Prophets, particularly their emphasis on the primacy of the spirit over earthly power. By recognizing the need to capitulate to stronger regimes in the wake of military defeat, religious leaders like Amos, Jeremiah, and Isaiah were able to preserve internal autonomy, which Dubnow defined in the biblical context as "the freedom of spiritual development without the intrusion of a foreign culture into domestic life."[198] By the time of the First Exile in 586 B.C.E., he argued, the exiled Jewish community in Babylon was strong enough to develop new forms of spiritual and religious activity such as prayers and synagogues to compensate for the destruction of the Temple. The return of Jews to the Land of Israel in the fourth century B.C.E. seemed to bring little change since it took place under continuing political subjugation. Yet once again the genius of Israel and the cunning of history reasserted themselves. The establishment of a rigid code of laws under the leadership of Ezra and Nehemiah actually served to reinforce national independence by establishing a policy of strict isolation from the surrounding pagan societies.[199]

After the collapse of the Jewish state and the destruction of the Second Temple in 70 C.E.—an event that Dubnow maintained was a reflection of "punitive historical destiny" that took away the external characteristics of nationhood from the Jewish people[200]—the community leadership in the Diaspora was again forced to turn in upon itself. Unlike the First Exile which lasted only fifty years, however, this was to be a state of permanent exile and dispersion. Yet this time the Jewish people would be prepared for the challenge of survival under difficult conditions. Dubnow argued that the power and discipline of rabbinic law and leadership now replaced military arms and discipline as the ensurer of national survival. Through the creation of an elaborate communal structure that was defined by religious law, the Jewish people was able to maintain its identity and independence despite dispersion and political dependence on others.

For Dubnow, the culmination of the development of communal autonomy in the Diaspora occurred in eastern Europe. The East European Jewish community emerged as the new "hegemonic center" after the dispersal of Spanish Jewry in the fifteenth and sixteenth centuries. By the early 1600s, Polish and Lithuanian Jewry has become a significant economic and social force in eastern Europe. Though economic prosperity was primarily responsible for the intense nature of Polish Jewish culture, Dubnow argued, it was communal autonomy that ultimately ensured the growth of intellectualism in East European Jewish life. The Jewish historian pointed specifically to the creation of the so-called Council of the Four Lands (Vaad arbaah haaratsot), which dominated Polish and Lithuanian religious, social, and economic life from the sixteenth through the eighteenth century, as a major factor in the flowering of East European Jewish literature and thought. On a local level, the *kahal*, or Jewish communal structure, provided the stateless nation with a substitute for national and political self-expression while helping to ensure public loyalty and civic virtue.[201] In creating institutions of communal autonomy, East European Jews not only assured their continued development but also effectively shielded themselves from the deleterious forces that assaulted the larger society in which they lived. How else, Dubnow asked, could one explain the seeming paradox that Lithuanian and Polish Jewry in the seventeenth and early eighteenth centuries was able to transform itself "from a colony into a metropolis of Judaism" in the midst of a disintegrating Polish society?[202]

For Dubnow, the beginning of the decline of East European Jewry as a hegemonic center could be traced to the abolition of the Vaad by the Polish Diet in 1764. Like other declining hegemonic centers in the past, Polish Jewry now could only survive at the behest of local political and religious authority. Yet the community's most glaring weakness was not external oppression but internal division, marked by socioeconomic and religious strife, administrative corruption, and the splintering of communal loyalties that resulted from geographical divisions after the three partitions at the end of the eighteenth century.[203] During the 1800s, it was the same combination of structural and spiritual factors—in this case, the disintegration of Jewish communal authority and internal spiritual decay—that would pave the way for the development of "heretical" movements such as Hasidism, Russification, and the Haskalah. Burdened by "the weight of family chains" and "the pressure of want or material dependence," Dubnow argued, young Jews attempted to deny the pain of state-imposed oppression by retreating into religious mysticism, escaping from the community, or naively seeking the government's support for internal change. Weakened by both the brutality of tsarism and the reactionary nature of Jewish communal leadership, most communities in eastern Europe at the end of the nineteenth century were in a state of ossification, impervious to European culture and incapable of renewing themselves from within.[204]

Dubnow maintained that a radical transformation had also occurred in the West. There, emancipation destroyed communal autonomy for Jewry at the same time that it increased the freedom of the individual Jew. The result paradoxically was that the era had "simultaneously *humanized* and *denationalized* the Jew." [205] At best, western Jewry had experienced a "semi-emancipation," a civic rather than a national equality that liberated individual Jews but not the Jewish people as a whole.[206] As in the East, the weakening of communal structures and loyalties that ensued could be traced to both external and internal forces. The development of the concept of the nation-state in western and central Europe brought with it the desire to oppress national minorities through their forcible assimilation into the larger society. Of greater significance for Dubnow, however, was the willful acceptance of assimilation by individuals within western Jewish communities. Many wealthy Jews rushed to accept individual equality while debasing their collective spirit. In their desperate desire to gain the approval of the larger society, Dubnow bitterly noted, they failed to realize that even a nation without a government and a territory was entitled to demand equal rights. Only the "common people," the true bearers of the national ideal, refused to make humiliating concessions in order to achieve equality. In so doing, however, they were denied the benefits of modern ideas. Though Dubnow saw hopeful signs in the development of international Jewish relief organizations such as the Alliance israélite universelle and the response of western Jewish leadership to anti-Semitic outrages in the Middle East and eastern Europe, his general perception of western Jewry at the turn of the century was that of a weakened community bereft of leadership, reactive rather than proactive, and intellectually stagnant.[207]

In assessing the future of Jewry, Dubnow stressed that those who sought to defend the continued existence of the Diaspora needed to restore independent Jewish communal authority. At the same time, he cautioned, no one could deny the value and importance of emancipation in introducing the Jew to modern ideas. Thus, there could be no simple return to the closed and inflexible structure of traditional Jewish life. The only solution, the Jewish historian maintained, was a "synthesis" of the western Jews' desire for freedom with the East European Jews' recognition of the importance of maintaining communal independence. Modern forms of communal autonomy thus necessitated the development of multinational democracies which defended and encouraged the independence of individual nationalities while at the same time allowing for full participation by members of minority groups in the larger polity. Like Zhitlowski, Dubnow often pointed to the federal system of Switzerland as a model of the relationship between citizenship and minority-group identification. He also expressed enthusiasm for a parliamentary system based on proportional representation, which would ensure that the majority did not run roughshod over minority groups.

In defending his ideal of autonomy in a modern nation-state, Dubnow was forced to respond to those who maintained that the demand for Jewish communal independence would exacerbate anti-Semitism. His argument drew directly from the writings of Herder and other cultural nationalists of the nineteenth century. In order for communal autonomy to succeed, Dubnow claimed, both modern Jews and statesmen had to recognize that there was a difference between the state and the nation. As he wrote in the Second Letter: "[T]he state is a social and legal *formal* union whose objective is to protect the interests of its members, while the nation is an *internal* psychic existential union."[208] As an eternal people, Jews thus constituted "not a state within a state but a nation among the nations."[209] Dubnow did not deny the emotional power of patriotism. Loyalty to the state could be found among all inhabitants with deep historical roots in a particular land, no matter whether their experiences were happy or sad. But true patriotism in the sense of "the mutual solidarity among members of a given socio-political organization" could only occur in situations in which ethnic minorities were granted full cultural and historical rights as distinct nationalities within the larger society. The development of a general policy of cultural autonomy thus would actually lead to the decline of anti-Semitism, since no group could possibly argue that Jews were meddling in their own affairs.[210] Ultimately, the development of communal autonomy not only served the interests of the minority group but would also benefit the majority population. By eliminating interethnic tensions, Dubnow concluded, a multinational state would bolster the confidence and security of its constituent cultural and linguistic groups, thereby ensuring their loyalty and commitment.

Dubnow spelled out his vision of Jewish autonomism in a future Russian democratic state in a series of tracts that he wrote in 1910 to define the platform of the Folkspartei.[211] Unlike geographically concentrated minorities that would receive regional political autonomy, Jews were to be regarded as a nonterritorial nationality with communal and cultural autonomy. Opposing the demands of the SERPists and other territorialists for the geographical concentration of Jews in Russia, Dubnow maintained that individual Jews could be granted personal autonomy as legally recognized members of the Jewish nation wherever they lived. Jewish emancipation thus could be proclaimed almost immediately after the creation of a democratic society without the need for any significant political, social, or economic dislocation. The positing of personal rather than territorial autonomy also enabled Dubnow to balance defense of individual rights with communal responsibilities.

Dubnow envisioned a minimal role for the future state in the internal affairs of the Jewish community. Its main responsibilities would be to ensure that individuals were allowed to celebrate religious holidays without legal impediment and to formally recognize the integrity of Jewish languages. Decision making in the Jewish community would be invested in a national council, or *vaad* (modeled on the Vaad arbaah ha-aratsot), elected through secret ballot and universal suffrage. It would also act as a liaison between the Jews and the government. In addition, Dubnow envisioned the creation of a permanent executive that would be charged with carrying out the decisions of the *vaad*. Subsidized by the state and authorized to collect taxes, the executive body would be responsible for coordinating cultural and social activity including education, charity, and mutual aid, as well as details of internal economic administration. In contrast to the traditional *kahal*, the new community structure envisioned by Dubnow would be decidedly secular. Questions of religious practice would be a matter of private concern. The nature of communal observance would be decided by majority rule in each locality.

Despite the urgings of his supporters, Dubnow refused to develop a general model for communal governance. He was insistent that the structure of the community, form of administration, official language, and relationship to the larger society would differ from country to country and should be left to negotiations between local Jewish inhabitants and government leaders. The result was that many questions concerning the day-to-day functioning of communal institutions within the larger society remained unanswered. Critics also wondered how Dubnow's vision of Jewish communal life could be applied to western societies where membership in the Jewish community was voluntary and where Jewish communal institutions had little or no independent authority and power. Nor did Dubnow clearly explain how his vision of autonomy would apply to other national minorities within a multinational state. In part, the vagueness of his program reflected his general lack of interest in practical details and his belief in the primacy of spiritual ideals in defining communal identity. Like many of his contemporaries, Dubnow disdained politics and diplomacy, regarding them as unworthy of serious concern by individuals and nations with lofty goals.[212] In part, Dubnow's refusal to detail the nature of communal autonomy stemmed from his fear that a discussion of specifics would only divide the community in a period of internal crisis.

In his defense of autonomism, Dubnow was again forced to confront the two most formidable rivals vying for support and power within the East European Jewish community: Zionists and political revolutionaries. In his Sixth and Seventh Letters written in 1898 and 1899 respectively and revised in 1907, the Jewish historian emphasized what he believed was a fundamental inner contradiction in Zionist ideology. On the one hand, Zionists insisted that Jewry had never ceased to be a nation despite centuries of dispersion. On the other, they were convinced that Jewish national identity could never survive in the Diaspora. In Dubnow's view, Zionists thus were "conditional" nationalists who could accept the existence of an established Jewish nation only when it had achieved political sovereignty and territory. In arguing that only the creation of a Jewish state would allow Jews to resume control of their destiny, they denied the lessons of Jewish history. In delaying the fulfillment of Jewish collective existence until the future, they threatened to destroy the nation's commitment to the immediate struggle for collective survival.[213]

In his critique of Zionism, Dubnow was especially fond of drawing parallels with "nationalist-minded" movements in the Jewish past which, in their zeal for political independence, had threatened the physical safety of Jews while ignoring their long-range spiritual needs. Like the Sadducees and Zealots of the Second Temple period, Dubnow wrote in his Seventh Letter, modern-day political Zionists championed the ideal of brute force without any regard for its repercussions on a largely defenseless Jewish population who would bear the brunt of the inevitable backlash. Political Zionists also claimed to be struggling against the evils of assimilation. Yet, as the history of the Zealots clearly demonstrated, their failure to create a Jewish state could only result in a profound "moral distress" for Jewry that would make the evils of assimilation seem benign in comparison.[214]

In their own propaganda, political Zionists had consistently condemned autonomism as utopian. In a brochure published in 1899, for example, the veteran Zionist activist Moshe Leib Lilienblum had spoken of Dubnow as "a far greater dreamer than the founder of the new form of Zionism [Herzl] ever was" and had cynically observed that the idea that Diaspora Jews could develop internal national autonomy was deserving only of a "condescending and contemptuous smile."[215] Dubnow responded with uncharacteristic sarcasm. What could be more utopian, he noted, than a movement that saw the present oppressed condition of Jews as eternal, placed all of its hope in the dream of settling all Jews in a distant and forbidding land, and ignored the indomitable spirit of Diaspora Jewry as reflected in its glorious history?[216] At the same time, in denigrating Jewish life in the Diaspora as corrupt and in blindly championing mass emigration as the solution to the "Jewish problem," Zionists not only demonstrated their underlying cynicism but also unwittingly gave credence to anti-Semitic arguments that Jews were aliens on the European continent.[217]

Dubnow was especially critical of political Zionism for its ignoring of the lessons of the Jewish past and its uncritical appropriation of external ideologies and movements. While autonomism rested upon the millennial communal history of the Jewish people, he argued, the Zionist enterprise was a creation solely of the nineteenth century. Any clearheaded individual would recognize that the movement to build a Jewish state was merely a reflexive response to growing assimilation and anti-Semitism. At best, Zionists accepted a small part of the Jewish past—the period of the Bible—while rejecting the history that followed it as irrelevant to their effort to reestablish political sovereignty. Dubnow insisted that a serious evaluation of Jewish history revealed that the challenges of assimilationism and anti-Semitism were not new. Over the course of centuries, Jews had devised many different strategies to counter them, including most notably autonomism. Zionist activists ignored the positive lessons of the past, however. In their desperate effort to solve the "Jewish question," Dubnow argued, they reflected the most negative and extreme Jewish response to past crises— messianism.

Nowhere was Zionism's underlying irrationalism more clearly evident to Dubnow than in Herzl's clarion call for action: "If you will it, it is not a dream." For the Jewish historian, such romantic rhetoric only demonstrated that Zionism was not a cogent system of thought grounded in an objective analysis of the past, as its supporters claimed, but rather an evanescent social movement arising from the frustration and hopelessness of the moment. Instead of responding to the needs of the Jewry as a whole, Dubnow concluded, the movement for a Jewish homeland in Palestine ultimately appealed to fringe elements of the population. For the Jewish historian, Zionist supporters were a motley group of misfits that included "weak" Jews who were unable to think and act rationally about Jewish matters, individuals who viewed nations only in terms of material wealth and power, schemers who wanted to "play politics" as leaders of the future state, and unthinking enthusiasts who indiscriminately supported any type of Jewish nationalism.[218]

Despite his reservations about Zionism, Dubnow recognized the strong affinities between Palestinophiles and Diaspora autonomists, most notably their united struggle against assimilation and their support of Jewish education and cultural development. In the wake of the rise of Nazism, he began to express public support for Zionist endeavors in Palestine, going so far as to argue in the 1930s that the *yishuv* might well become a future "hegemonic center" for the Jewish people.[219] As a result of his changing views concerning the Jewish settlement in Palestine as well as his recognition of the growing attraction of Zionism within the Jewish community, Dubnow eliminated from the Hebrew and English versions of *Letters on Old and New Judaism* published in the 1930s many of the negative comments that he had written about the movement and its leaders in the original essays. Yet he could never accept the Zionist's Palestinocentric view of the Jewish future. For Dubnow, the struggle to create a Jewish homeland could not rest upon the negation of the Diaspora. Whatever its seeming successes in the short run, Zionism as an ideology and a movement could only serve as a transition "to a higher world view, to spiritual nationalism."[220]

In evaluating Zionist ideology, Dubnow had to take special note of the writings of Ahad Ha-Am. The cultural Zionist's condemnation of political Zionism, his belief in the need for gradual development rather than revolutionary change in Jewish life, and his recognition that the majority of Jews would remain in the Diaspora for the foreseeable future—all mirrored Dubnow's own perceptions of the Jewish present and future. Throughout their lives, the two men maintained a warm relationship. They had first met during Dubnow's stay in Odessa and carried on an active correspondence from the 1890s through the 1920s. Beginning in August 1900, Dubnow and Ahad Ha-Am spent a series of summer vacations together at the home of their mutual friend Mordechai Ben Hillel Hakohen near the Byelorussian village of Reshitsa.[221]   Dubnow joined with Ahad Ha-Am in the struggle to increase the Jewish content in the schools subsidized by the Odessa Society for the Promotion of Enlightenment among Jews in Russia and signed his public statement written after the Kishinev pogrom. Both men had also tried unsuccessfully to establish a Teacher's Seminary in Odessa modeled after the rabbinical training schools of western and central Europe. Despite his criticism of Ahad Ha-Am's positions, Dubnow maintained a deep respect for the cultural Zionist's intellect.[222] In an essay written shortly after Ahad Ha-Am's death in 1927, Dubnow described him as "one of the prophets of truth and righteousness."[223] Four years later, Dubnow dedicated his work *History of Hasidism* to the memory of his friend who had urged him to publish in Hebrew and who had frequently discussed Hasidic thought during their first meetings in Odessa in the 1890s.[224]

Ahad Ha-Am had been one of the first public figures in the Jewish community to criticize Dubnow's autonomist views. In a review of the first two Letters published in 1898, the cultural Zionist described Dubnow's idea of a nation living within another nation and having full cultural and civil rights as a foolish dream. The Jewish historian had to recognize that it was in the nature of majorities to oppress minorities. Reversing Dubnow's arguments concerning the role of Zionism in the shaping of the Jewish future, Ahad Ha-Am claimed that, at best, autonomy in the Diaspora could serve as an intermediary step leading to the development of a Jewish majority in the Land of Israel. Only a Jewish cultural center in Palestine would enable Diaspora Jewry to survive, even in situations where it was denied national rights.[225]

In 1909, in a short essay titled "Shlilat ha-galut"(Negation of the Diaspora), Ahad Ha-Am again took up his pen to denounce Dubnow's proposals.[226] Since no truly committed Jew could possibly support the continued existence of the Diaspora, he wondered, how could anyone develop a program of Jewish national renewal based on its survival and growth? Ahad Ha-Am thought it significant that Dubnow had never fully explained whether national autonomy was an ideal or merely the "best possible" form of communal life under the circumstances. If they did not believe that Diaspora autonomism was the ideal existence for the Jewish people, he concluded, then Dubnow and the autonomists needed to work for the more radical solution of cultural Zionism—the creation of a spiritual center in Palestine that nevertheless recognized the continued existence of the Diaspora.

Dubnow's response to Ahad Ha-Am rested on what he believed to be irrefutable historical evidence. Though it was true that dominant nations often suppressed the rights of national minorities, he wrote in his Seventh Letter originally published in 1899, the example of the Austrian treatment of Galicia demonstrated that majority-minority relations in the modern world were not inevitably oppressive.[227] Indeed, modern history clearly pointed to a movement away from governments dominated by "ruling nationalities" toward the establishment of multinational states. Dubnow was also disturbed by what he regarded as Ahad Ha-Am's acceptance of minority oppression as normal and even "just" in all societies. In a true constitutional system, government policies would be decided by representatives of all nationalities and not by the dominant nationality alone. Such matters were not only determined by "the logic of events," Dubnow argued, but would also arise naturally from the struggle of all ethnic minorities (including the Jews) for self-determination within a multinational state. In contrast to Ahad Ha-Am's conviction that life in the Diaspora was merely a form of "slavery in the midst of freedom," Dubnow concluded that history clearly demonstrated Jews could maintain an active and vital communal life even under oppressive conditions.

Dubnow was especially troubled by what he regarded as major inconsistencies in Ahad Ha-Am's attitude toward the Diaspora. If the cultural Zionist rejected the continued existence of Jewish communities scattered throughout the globe, why did he insist on the establishment of a spiritual rather than a political center in Palestine? If he recognized that the majority of Jews would refuse to immigrate to Palestine, why didn't he offer concrete proposals for the revitalization of Jewish life outside its borders? Ultimately, Dubnow feared that, like all Zionists, Ahad Ha-Am and his followers wished to pronounce a death sentence on the mass of world Jewry. Their dismissal of autonomism reflected an apocalyptic view of the Jewish future in which "Palestine will become Noah's Ark where at least a portion of the Jewish people will be saved from the world cultural deluge while the others will perish!" Diaspora nationalists, on the other hand, were far more optimistic about the Jewish future. In contrast to Ahad Ha-Am's followers who preached the renaissance of the Jewish people by turning toward the ancient East, Dubnow argued, spiritual nationalists looked to the modern West for the revival of Jewry.[228]

And what of Ahad Ha-Am's defense of a Jewish spiritual center in Palestine? Dubnow agreed that it was a lofty goal, but the fact that only a minority of Jews would immigrate to the Land of Israel raised serious doubts about the effective influence of the *yishuv* on Diaspora Jewry. Wasn't Ahad Ha-Am aware, Dubnow wondered, that in one hundred years the Jewish population of Palestine would be only slightly larger than that of Kiev? In the end, Dubnow argued, Ahad Ha-Am remained a "stern centralist" whose insistence that Palestine was the only true national center, with Hebrew the only national language, flew in the face of Jewish history.[229] The continued survival of the Diaspora in the future would demonstrate the folly of the Zionist belief that there was a predetermined "end" to Jewish history and only one path to achieve it. Though written several years after Ahad Ha-Am's death, Dubnow's bitterly ironic comments about the Arab riots of 1929 in his *History of the Jews* encapsuled his concerns about the implications of what he believed was the Zionists' denial of Jewish history: "It turned out that the tragedy of wandering Israel did not come to an end at the threshold of this historic land and that there was still another 'Diaspora'—Israel among the hostile sons of Ishmael. The dream of a Jewish majority in Palestine, and of a Jewish state, had moved away into the distant future."[230]

In 1909, Dubnow specifically responded to Ahad Ha-Am's essay "Negation of the Diaspora" with an article in *Evreîski Mir*. Titled "Affirmation of the Diaspora," it was filled with strong words in support of autonomism.[231] Despite the essay's bold claims and forceful language, however, it was clear that Dubnow recognized that his defense of the Diaspora had been severely weakened by his friend's attacks. Deeply disappointed by the failure of the drive for Jewish civil rights in Russia, he now shared Ahad Ha-Am's belief that the creation of a Jewish state was clearly preferable to the continued existence of the Diaspora. In defending the Diaspora, Dubnow was only recognizing "historical necessity" by making the best of a difficult situation. Given this telling admission, the Jewish historian could only conclude with a plea that the two men reach an accommodation. Just as the autonomist was obligated to help in the development of the Jewish settlement in Palestine despite his doubts about its success, so too the Zionist who did not negate the Diaspora was obligated to help in its revival even though he did not believe that the goal could be fully achieved. If Ahad Ha-Am nevertheless continued to insist on denigrating life in the Diaspora, Dubnow concluded somewhat halfheartedly, his view had to be dismissed as a fantasy—a distant dream—and nothing more.

In his debates with Dubnow, Ahad Ha-Am had revealed the underlying flaws in the historian's autonomist program. Unlike Herzl and his supporters, the cultural Zionist shared Dubnow's conviction that the Diaspora would continue to exist for the foreseeable future. It was one thing to suggest that there was a need to bow to necessity; it was quite another to transform the Diaspora into a creative environment for Jewish development and growth that was justified by history and national destiny. In attempting to counter Ahad Ha-Am, Dubnow found himself caught up in a paradox. The Jewish historian was insistent that Ahad Ha-Am's expectations and hopes concerning a permanent spiritual center in Palestine were unrealistic. Yet what nationalist interested in synthesizing "old and new Judaism" could regard Zion as merely a temporary center of Jewish life that must inevitably give way to others in the future?

Dubnow had fewer difficulties countering Jewish revolutionaries. As far as he was concerned, they were nothing more than modern-day assimilationists. As he argued in his Tenth Letter written in November 1902 in opposition to Bundism, such individuals displayed exaggerated confidence in existing national and political parties and squandered the energies of the Jewish people in pursuing "alien causes."[232] Though claiming to be fiercely independent, Jewish revolutionaries were "only carrying out the bidding of their masters, the bidding of the ruling nationality." In addition, Dubnow claimed, like their enemies the Zionists, Jewish socialists trafficked in unrealizable dreams of radical change in both Jewish and general attitudes and behavior that would allegedly solve the "Jewish question" overnight.

Dubnow was convinced that despite their nationalist aura, Bundists and other Jewish radicals were only working for the good of a small segment of the Jewish people, the working class. In his own historical analysis, Dubnow had deliberately downplayed the role of class in Jewish society, arguing that the divisions within Jewish communities generally reflected distinctions in learning rather than in socioeconomic status. In his zeal to demonstrate the survival of collective Jewish identity throughout the ages, the Jewish historian insisted that the theory of class conflict was an alien import which if believed and acted upon, would severely weaken the Jews' struggle to survive. Those who supported such views thus were no better than the external enemies of the Jewish people who could not understand or tolerate the Jewish people's insistence upon maintaining its national distinctiveness and unity.[233]

As late as 1938, Dubnow was still arguing with the Bund over whether notions of class conflict could be constructively applied to national minorities struggling to survive. He was amazed that Bundists continued to cling to ideas that had been rejected by non-Jewish socialists years earlier. By stressing socioeconomic divisions within the Jewish community, Russian Jewish socialists distanced themselves from other social-democratic movements in Europe that had long since recognized the importance of nationalism in developing a mass movement. In clinging to such outmoded views, Dubnow claimed, the Bund seemed more akin to schismatic movements on the Jewish right such as the Agudah (an Orthodox political party), which weakened the solidarity of the Jewish people and threatened its integrity in the name of rigid dogma, than to left-wing organizations that were increasingly tolerant of ethnic and linguistic differences among peoples.[234]

Nor was Dubnow impressed with the Bundists' commitment to "progressive" Jewish culture. When examined closely, such attitudes proved to be of doubtful practical application. Ultimately, they represented little more than the revival of quaint folkways and of the Yiddish language that had little relevance to the fundamental needs of the Jewish people. How could Bundists claim to be defending Jewish interests, Dubnow asked, when as "good" Marxists they considered assimilation a natural and inevitable phenomenon? Even their support of communal autonomy was subject to question since their major concern was the development of a socialist society rather than Jewish collective survival.[235] If the Bund was ever to gain acceptance within the Jewish community, the Jewish historian concluded, it would have to renounce its opposition to Jewish unity and agree to become an integral part of the Jewish people.

Ultimately, Dubnow's critique of both Zionists and socialists rested upon his firm belief in the evolutionary nature of Jewish life. In his view, the two movements were foolhearty and adventurous. Driven by an obsession with the *Endziel*, or final goal, they promoted a preordained view of the Jewish future that was uncritically appropriated from contemporaneous movements within the larger society. The failure of Zionists and socialists to understand the Jewish past and the religious fervor with which they championed their beliefs also led them to take dogmatic positions. In so doing, the Jewish historian argued, they denied the richness, distinctiveness, and variety of Jewish life and ignored the interests of the Jewish people as a whole. Dubnow also maintained that by their overemphasis on political power, Zionist and socialist activists ignored the centrality of spiritual and ethical ideals as the determinants of the national will and the ultimate source of a nation's strength. As the history of the Maccabees clearly demonstrated, it was "spiritual power, the force of moral indignation, and the thirst for freedom" that ultimately overcame an enemy "who possessed only brutal physical power but without any ethical stimulus."[236]

Though boldly proclaiming that they had transcended Jewish history, Dubnow maintained, Zionists and socialists were actually trapped by the past. Their clamoring for radical solutions revealed a myopic and cataclysmic view of Jewish life. Unable to understand the forces shaping Jewish historical development, the two movements could offer only desperate responses to immediate problems that were geared to a limited audience. In contrast, Dubnow stressed the historical *longue durée*. By emphasizing the role of ideals and institutions in maintaining Jewish life over time, he claimed to have transformed the powerlessness of the Diaspora into a virtue. Grounded as they were in a thorough understanding of the recurrent themes of world Jewish history, spiritual nationalism and communal autonomism in Dubnow's view provided a reasonable and realizable program for survival and growth that would incorporate all Jews, no matter what their ideological or political affiliation.

In defending the ideal of autonomism, Dubnow was also forced to respond to the wave of Jewish emigration that resulted from the onset of pogroms in 1903–4. Typically, he searched the Jewish past for an understanding of the phenomenon. In his Eleventh Letter written shortly after the Kishinev pogrom in 1903, Dubnow attempted to counter the panic spreading through the Russian Jewish community by placing the movement of Jews westward within the context of the history of Jewish migration over the centuries. Though he readily admitted that the mass exodus of Jews from Russia would result in a dramatic shift in Jewish population from East to West, he stressed that the movement of populations was a common theme in Jewish history. Jewish emigration thus was a natural response to catastrophe and should not be feared. Indeed, Dubnow argued, in many ways the East European settlement in the United States might be seen as a new beginning for Russian Jews that could well lead to the formation of a new "hegemonic center" in Jewish history. As he wrote in the Fifteenth Letter published in 1907, America was the "daughter of the Russian settlement, and when the old mother is sick, she directs her hope towards the young daughter in the land of liberty."[237]

In order to ensure that America became a national Jewish center and to counter what he regarded as the utopian emigration schemes of Zionists, Dubnow concluded that it was necessary to ensure that the exodus from Russia was orderly and organized. His solution was the establishment of an international Jewish congress made up of representatives of major European Jewish communities that would coordinate Jewish immigration to the United States. By ensuring that nationalistic Jewish intellectuals would serve as a vanguard for the new settlements, the congress would prevent wholesale assimilation and sow the seeds of communal autonomy in the New World. What many Jews viewed as a terrible tragedy thus could well become a defining moment in Jewish history.[238]

In the end, of course, Dubnow's plans for Jewish autonomy bore little fruit. Despite his fervent belief in the viability of his proposals, events in Europe and America during his lifetime only served to demonstrate their impracticability in the major Jewish settlements of the Diaspora. As we have seen, much of Dubnow's political activity during the first two decades of the twentieth century had centered on the futile effort to achieve communal autonomy for Russian Jewry. Thus he was an active participant in the Union for the Attainment of Full Rights for Jews that arose in the wake of the Revolution of 1905 and that lobbied for Jewish cultural rights. Similarly, his support of the short-lived March Revolution of 1917 was largely predicated on the belief that it would realize cultural autonomy for national minorities. In the period immediately after World War I, Dubnow also pressed for the incorporation of clauses in peace treaties that would ensure the protection of the rights of ethnic, linguistic, and cultural minorities in the newly emerging nations of eastern and central Europe.[239]

During the 1920s and '30s, Dubnow continued to cling to his dream of Jewish autonomy in the Diaspora. Efforts to create independent Jewish educational institutions in Estonia and Latvia in the interwar period seemed to point to the continued viability of his programs.[240] Dubnow was also buoyed by the limited forms of autonomy for Jews that were briefly adopted by a number of the republics under Russian rule in the aftermath of the Bolshevik Revolution. The consolidation of Communist rule in Russia in 1920–21 was quickly followed by the dismantling of Jewish communal institutions, however. In their drive to achieve social and political conformity, the Bolsheviks abolished Jewish political parties, including Dubnow's Folkspartei. In the newly independent nations of eastern Europe, government leaders desperately seeking to maintain national unity in a period of political and economic unrest ignored or reversed the formal guarantees of Jewish cultural autonomy that had been inscribed in postwar peace treaties. The Jewish historian's ideas survived in the Warsaw-based Folkspartei branch, which made significant efforts to develop autonomous institutions in independent Poland in the 1920s. Here too, however, Jewish cultural and linguistic rights came under attack by a growingly chauvinistic and autocratic government intent on Polonization. By the 1930s, Dubnow's political agenda found few supporters in Europe. In most East European countries, the Jewish community gradually fell into the hands of Zionists and Bundists whose aggressive policies seemed a more appropriate response to the rising tide of anti-Semitism. Ironically, autonomism would have a brief albeit perverse last reflection in the activity of the so-called Jewish Councils established by the Nazis in occupied Europe during World War II.

Nor would Dubnow's programs take root in the fledgling East European Jewish immigrant communities of America. Like Zhitlowski's program for a "United Peoples of the United States," Dubnow's vision of America reflected more wish fulfillment than reality. Having never actually visited the United States, his views of the New World were largely shaped by popular books and theoretical treatises on American government and society. Dubnow sincerely believed that the United States would gladly welcome proposals for communal autonomy. After all, he stated, Americans had clearly demonstrated in their revolution their opposition to government interference in the private lives of citizens and their insistence on the decentralization of power. The Jewish historian also pointed to America's enshrinement of freedom of assembly as a basic constitutional right, which he believed provided a legal foundation for the development and expansion of communal rights.

It was not that Dubnow was blind to the challenges facing the new immigrants. He recognized that at first, immigrant settlements in the West and in America in particular would replicate the tight communal structure and isolation from the larger society of Russian cities within the Pale.[241] He was firmly convinced, however, that in the more tolerant atmosphere of a democratic society, Jews would eventually take advantage of the opportunity to dispense with the outdated notion of Jewry as merely a religious community. For the first time since the sixteenth century, Dubnow proudly proclaimed, Jews would be able to maintain their own legal system, convoke national congresses, and open schools at all levels.[242]

In his desire to revitalize Jewish life in the Diaspora, Dubnow seriously misread the nature of nation building in the modern era. His belief that programs for national autonomy would develop among Russian, Austro-Hungarian, and Ottoman Jews were dashed by the collapse of all three empires after World War I. In continually referring to the demands of other national minorities for communal rights to support his argument for Jewish autonomy, Dubnow blithely ignored the fact that the demand for Jewish national autonomy was to be measured not by the society's attitudes toward Czechs and Poles but by its attitudes toward Jews. Equally tragic was the fact that once having achieved independence and sovereignty, ethnic minorities would display little interest in sharing their political freedom with other nationalities in their midst. The future seemed to lie not with multinationalism but with monolithic states that would not tolerate ethnic diversity, much less autonomy. Even democratic societies such as the United States refused to accept the division that Dubnow insisted on between nationality and state. With war looming on the horizon, the future for Jewry in the interwar period seemed to lie either in their integration into democratic society or in the establishment of a separate homeland.

Dubnow's defense of an all-embracing community also led him to reject any efforts to impose a distinctive language upon the Jewish people. He was convinced that the choice of an appropriate language for Jews ultimately would be determined not by external factors such as the numbers of speakers or the ease of use, as both Yiddishists and Hebraists maintained, but by its ability to further the interests of Jewry as a whole. Dubnow's own intellectual biography reveals an individual who was comfortable in a multilingual environment in which Russian, Yiddish, and Hebrew were spoken interchangeably. As we have seen, Dubnow had lauded Russian as a vehicle by which Jews could gain acceptance into the larger society. Though his view changed radically in the 1890s, he retained a love for the language throughout his life. It was not coincidental that Dubnow published his autobiography as well as most of his major theoretical and historical works in Russian and continued to use the Russian language in public forums. As late as 1939, despite the imminent threat to East European Jewry, he could still speak about Russian sharing a role with other host languages as vehicles for the expression of "the universal potentialities" of the Jewish people.[243] Nevertheless, Dubnow remained convinced that the inability and unwillingness of Jewry to adopt the spiritual aspirations, manners, and customs of the larger society meant that the Russian language could never become a major force in the internal life of the community.[244]

Dubnow's attitude toward Hebrew reflected his functionalist approach to the role of language in Jewish national revival. Because its origins lay with the beginnings of the Jewish people itself, he maintained, the Hebrew language embodied many of the deepest sentiments of Jewry. It was for this reason that in the early 1900s Dubnow argued for the need to teach Hebrew to bolster the Jewish studies component of the curriculum of the schools established by the Society for the Promotion of Enlightenment Among Jews in Russia. The proclamation of the Balfour Declaration and the beginnings of serious immigration to Palestine after World War I moved him closer to a Hebraist position. Part of his renewed interest in the language may have also resulted from his desperate desire to appeal to a new readership of young Zionist intellectuals. In the 1920s, he often emphasized his own ability to write and edit scholarly works in Hebrew and voiced mild regret for not having published his earlier works in that language.[245] A decade later, Dubnow was openly supporting Hebrew as a crucial educational and cultural tool in the Zionist effort to resettle Palestine.

Despite his renewed interest in the role of Hebrew in the development of the *yishuv*, however, Dubnow remained skeptical of its viability as a national language. Having lost its status as the lingua franca of Jewry after the onset of the Diaspora, Hebrew could not express the concerns and desires of contemporary Jewry as a whole. Though steadfast in his support of limited Jewish settlement in Palestine, Dubnow refused to believe that the *yishuv* was capable of reviving a language of the past.

Dubnow's linguistic pragmatism also explains his changing attitudes toward Yiddish over the course of his life. In 1881, Dubnow published an anonymous article in *Voskhod* supporting the establishment of a Yiddish newspaper, *Dos Yidishe Folksblatt* (The Yiddish People's Paper). In this early period, however, he shared the belief of most Russian Jewish intellectuals (including the publisher of the new newspaper, Alexander Zederbaum) that it was not appropriate for cultured Jews to speak Yiddish among themselves. Yiddish was little more than a "jargon" that could serve as an intermediary step for the Jewish masses until they could learn Russian. By the time of the Czernowitz Conference, however, Dubnow had become convinced that Yiddish could play an important role in inculcating modern Jewish values and ideals among the masses. Impressed with the blossoming of Yiddish literature, he now proclaimed that Yiddish had emerged from the "secluded corner" of Jewish literature and would soon become the dominant language of Jews in the Diaspora. In the period directly before his death, however, Dubnow's views changed from optimism to wistful nostalgia. In the face of the Nazi invasion of Russia, he could only bemoan the destruction of Yiddish culture in eastern Europe.[246]

In attempting to formulate an approach to the "language debate" that raged through the Jewish community, Dubnow eventually settled on the concept of "trilingualism." It was a term he had coined early in his career in an article written in *Voskhod* in 1888 and again in public statements after the Czernowitz Conference.[247] Dubnow re-affirmed his position over forty years later in a work entitled *Fun "zhargon" tsu yidish* (From "Jargon" to Yiddish). Throughout their recent history, he argued, Jews had expressed their national concerns in the two traditional Jewish languages—Hebrew and Yiddish—as well as in the language of the larger society in which they found themselves. All had their role to play in ensuring survival; none could be seen as superior to the other. Condemning the views of his Yiddishist, Bundist, and Zionist opponents, Dubnow claimed that the fate of the language of the Jews would be determined not by ideological predilection but by the natural flowering of culture in the modern Jewish society that was in the process of formation. Though he was roundly denounced for his refusal to commit himself, Dubnow sought to exemplify his approach by deliberately writing at least one of each of his works in Hebrew, Yiddish, Russian, and German. The first two were the central languages of the Jewish people; the latter represented the dominant languages of the two countries in which Dubnow lived during his lifetime.

In many ways, Dubnow's open-ended treatment of the language question points up a major weakness that informed much of his thought. As we have seen in his discussion of autonomism, the Jewish historian was hesitant to offer specific solutions to Jewish problems, preferring instead to defer all questions to the future. In part, Dubnow's refusal to provide specifics reflected the difficulty that all Jewish modernizers of his era faced in creating appropriate strategies for the transmission of ideals that would replace discarded religious rituals and beliefs. Yet there was more involved in Dubnow's seeming vagueness than the mere inability to communicate his ideas to future generations. For all his deep commitment to the study of the Jewish past, Dubnow's heart and mind remained focused on the issue of survival. The result was often a metahistorical analysis that reflected more his hopes for the future than the lessons of the past. True, Dubnow's central ideal, spiritual nationalism, seemed to rest upon the events of Jewish history. In actuality, however, its value for the Jewish historian was that it enabled him to describe the Jews as an eternal people in the Diaspora, thereby transcending not only geographical space but time itself.

Given his emphasis on Jewish survival, at times Dubnow even had to ignore those "lessons" of Jewish history that threatened the Jewish future. Thus he seriously overestimated the viability of multinational states in the interwar period and misread (or denied) the impact on Jewry of anti-Semitism until it was too late. Indeed, Dubnow remained doggedly insistent throughout his life that history would inevitably favor Jewish hopes and dreams. Without a belief in the future and an unflagging idealism, Dubnow wrote in one of his last published comments, "we would be an ephemeral, and not an eternal, people."[248] In the end, Dubnow's indomitable belief in the power of history to ensure collective survival proved unable to withstand the destructive force of Nazism. It would perish, along with Dubnow and millions of his fellow Jews, in the brutal onslaught of the Holocaust.

CHAPTER 4

AHAD HA-AM

Culture and
Modern Jewish Identity

IN EXAMINING the legacy of Asher Ginsberg—Ahad Ha-Am, as he is more popularly known—one is immediately struck by a strange irony. Few Jews living in the Diaspora have read the cultural Zionist's works or are even familiar with his name. Israeli Jews, for their part, generally know him only as a harsh critic of Theodor Herzl and see little positive value in his writings.[1] Yet the notion of a Jewish spiritual center that Ahad Ha-Am espoused defines the attitude of most contemporary Jews in the Diaspora toward Israel, while his concern with the "Jewishness" of a Jewish state reflects the central problem confronting modern-day Israelis as they seek to define their future. As a figure whose career spanned the entire history of the early Zionist movement from its inception in Hibbat Zion to the onset of the British mandate as well as the emergence of new centers of Jewish life in the Diaspora, Ahad Ha-Am has proven to be what he had both hoped for and dreaded—a prophet in his own time, convinced of the prescient truth of his assertions yet despised by many of his contemporaries and forgotten by later generations.

The reasons for Ahad Ha-Am's relative obscurity today are not hard to discern. Like many members of the transitional generation, the cultural Zionist displayed strong elitist sentiments. Concerned primarily with intellectual endeavors and distrustful of political activism, he was unwilling to create a mass movement to realize his goals. Unlike the followers of Herzl in the Zionist movement, few individuals could meet the demands that Ahad Ha-am required of the future leaders of the Jewish people—a deep commitment to na-

Ahad Ha-Am

tional renewal coupled with a thorough grounding in Jewish tradition and culture.

Though he occasionally dabbled in philosophical issues, Ahad Ha-Am was primarily an essayist and left no clear exposition of his major ideas. Much of his writing consisted of sophisticated commentaries on the passing Jewish scene that were targeted to a small but devoted group of readers. In contrast to other Jewish intellectuals, Ahad Ha-Am claimed to have little interest in engaging in scholarship for its own sake.[2] The only value of Jewish knowledge, he argued, was as a tool to revitalize Jewish life in the modern world. The result was that Ahad Ha-Am was more often seen as a critic of the innovations of others than as an innovator himself, attempting in the words of a contemporary "to correct what others built or had begun to build rather than [to] construct on his own."[3] His most influential essay, after all, was "Lo zeh ha-derekh" (This Is Not the Way). Its very title denoted the author's belief in the need to rid oneself of false ideas before developing a new perspective. At best, Ahad Ha-Am could be described as a great synthesizer who, like other members of his generation, struggled to combine the old with the new.

Ahad Ha-Am prided himself on being an individual who was concerned with the ideal rather than the real. Yet, while he boldly called for "the rule of the intellect" over human life, he often responded emotionally and sentimentally to the Jewish plight. Despite his cold and dispassionate public demeanor, he was capable of expressing strong feelings of anger and enthusiasm in private moments among close friends.[4] The two seemingly contradictory personality traits combined to create what one contemporary observer called a "stiff-necked and soft-hearted" nature that made Ahad Ha-Am unable to effectively and clearly respond to changing conditions and circumstances.[5]

The contradictions in Ahad Ha-Am's thought and behavior extended into other spheres of his life as well. Deprived of companionship within his own family as a result of the tragic deaths of a sister and brother and lacking friends in his early life, the mature Ahad Ha-Am much preferred solitary contemplation to social interchange.[6] He even seemed to take a perverse delight in the contempt of others for his ideas, regarding it as a mark of his unwavering devotion to the Jewish people.[7] Yet Ahad Ha-Am constantly craved attention. His decision to enter the communal arena in the 1880s, for example, was largely shaped by his desire to gain public recognition.

Whatever Ahad Ha-am may have felt privately, his writings reveal an almost obsessive concern with the public response of his peers to his ideas. The result was a conflicted personality that made Ahad Ha-Am appear to those who knew him well as distant and obsequious at the same time.

Belittled as a child by his father for his intellectual shortcomings, Ahad Ha-Am was haunted by a sense of his own inadequacy throughout his life.[8] His self-doubts may have also resulted from a chronic neurological disorder that doctors diagnosed as melancholia and that afflicted both his father and his eldest daughter, Leah. Despite his continual expressions of disdain for pure scholarship, Ahad Ha-Am seemed especially frustrated by the fact that his responsibilities as an editor and a businessman prevented him from devoting time to serious study. The few "scholarly" works he did manage to publish generally went unread.[9] Yet when offered opportunities to assume an academic position, speak at a scholarly conference, and publish an article in an encyclopedia, Ahad Ha-Am rejected them all. Though publicly claiming that his pressing work schedule and ill health prevented him from devoting the time needed to prepare a serious work, inwardly he feared having his ideas undergo scrutiny.[10] Given his psychological state, Ahad Ha-Am's followers were never quite sure whether his major essays on the Jewish condition represented guides to future activity or philosophical codas to his own life.

Despite (or maybe because of) his inner doubts, Ahad Ha-Am managed to convey an aura of absolute self-confidence to his most ardent admirers. To all appearances, he seemed an individual unwavering in his commitment and certain of the triumph of his ideas.[11] Like the biblical Prophets, the cultural Zionist was convinced that he could probe the depths of the Jewish people's soul. Like the Prophets, he felt surrounded by intellectual "midgets" who unknowingly benefited from the richness of his thought while publicly denouncing him as an insane fool.[12] Under the circumstances, few observers took seriously Ahad Ha-Am's constant complaints that his pronouncements fell on deaf ears. They knew that such statements masked a fervent belief that his ideas would serve as a lasting legacy to future generations of Jews.

Not surprisingly, therefore, the legacy of Ahad Ha-Am was an ambiguous one. As the renowned Zionist historian David Vital has remarked in commenting on the cultural Zionist's role in Hibbat Zion, while he was generally on the margin of events, his ideas went to the very heart of the issues that concerned Jewry. An uncertain activist, Ahad Ha-Am was "above all a major, perennially looming moral and intellectual presence" who both delighted and despaired over his lofty position.[13]

More than any other member of the transitional generation, Ahad Ha-Am was keenly aware of the insecure position his contemporaries held in a Jewish society that was rapidly moving from tradition to modernity. He was convinced that although his peers had begun the difficult process of reconstructing the Jewish people, they had made sure not to lose sight of the sense of intimacy, loyalty, and security that religious tradition had provided for the Jewish people in the past. Not so with subsequent generations that ignored the past in their headlong race to adopt the current political and economic ideologies in the larger society. As Ahad Ha-Am commented cynically to one of his disciples in 1906, while his parents' generation were open to "their Father in Heaven before whom they could pour out their broken hearts and find a little comfort," the present generation offered nothing "except 'abbreviations' (PZ, SS, SR, SD, etc.) whose common denominator is enslavement and fawning to the 'proletariat' and 'the revolution' and for whom all living sentiment and true desire is missing with regard to our internal national issues."[14]

Caught between the past and the future, Ahad Ha-Am saw himself destined to be "the source of all thoughts that remain trapped in many hearts as unclear dreams."[15] His own fate, as he described it, was to minister to all those who were made heartsick by the moral and physical servitude of Jewry but who could no longer seek solace and liberation through the inner power of religious faith. All he asked of future generations was to recognize that "the first steps, the hardest ones, have already been taken by those who preceded you."[16]

Of the three individuals under study, Ahad Ha-Am most clearly understood the need for a modern Jewish society to root itself in the values of the past. His espousal of "cultural Zionism" was a deliberate attempt to respond to the desire of many Jews at the turn of the century to find concrete expression for their identity in the ethics and ideals that had traditionally justified and explained the drive for Jewish distinctiveness. Not surprisingly, therefore, Ahad Ha-Am could not ignore the divisions between religionists and secularists that were beginning to emerge in the struggle over modern Jewish identity. In his critique of Herzl, for example, he worried that political Zionists did not give serious consideration to the spiritual ideals that formed the basis of their experiment in Jewish autonomy. Similarly, in his call for a synthesis of traditional Jewish ethical principles and universalist values, Ahad Ha-Am recognized the need to find common ground between Orthodox and freethinkers in the modern Jewish community. As the Hebrew literary critic I.L. Klausner has described the cultural Zionist's vision: "He saw the 'Jewish problem' in the fact that the Orthodox Jew, who piously preserved all the national and religious values of his people, rejected everything universally human, while the Jew who adopted universal culture shunned everything specifically national and Jewish. This, as he saw it, was the tragedy of a people without a national policy, and without a national-historical spoken language."[17]

In the end, Ahad Ha-Am's tireless effort to find a meaningful synthesis among the conflicting forces in Jewish life meant that he often found himself, in his own terms, "of two opinions." In general, however, he seemed to relish his awkward role. What others saw as a sign of weakness, Ahad Ha-Am would transform into the bold credo of his own distinctive generation. As he stated assertively albeit awkwardly in his essay "Hiyuv u-shlilah" (Positive and Negative), written in 1891: "There is a need for some third system, an intermediary [position] that will stand between the new and the old, tearing away from the former that which needs to be torn away and restoring to the latter that which was removed without understanding. One must also clothe both of them in one new form as befits the age, thereby bringing parity between them—the 'spiritual matters' inherited from the past and those born by the new that have already managed to take deep root in every heart."[18]

Asher Hirsch Ginsberg was born on August 18, 1856 in the city of Skvira, about 120 kilometers southwest of Kiev, in the Ukraine.[19] The Jewish population of Skvira at the turn of the century was approximately 9,000, nearly half the total population. Relatively poor and unsophisticated, the Jews of Skvira were an undistinguished group of mainly petty merchants whose only claim to fame was their strong commitment to Hasidism. Indeed, the town was a battleground between two important Hasidic dynasties in the Ukraine, the Chernobyl and the Ruzhiner. Ahad Ha-Am's family was no exception. Both his father's and mother's families were devotees of the Ruzhiner Rebbe, while his father, Isaiah, played an important role as the local and regional spokesman for the heir to the Ruzhiner clan, the Sadegorer Rebbe.[20]

In 1869, the Ginsberg family moved to Gopitshitza, a small village near Berdichev, where his father served as a lessor for an absentee aristocratic landlord. Here Asher continued his traditional education. He soon became so well versed in Talmud that local rabbis would often turn to him to answer difficult halakhic or legal questions. Because of his precociousness, Ginsberg was assigned a private tutor at the age of ten to study religious texts. At the age of fifteen, he began to study on his own.

It did not take long for Asher to rebel against traditional Judaism. Given his rigid personality and severe intellectualism, it seems unlikely that he ever felt fully comfortable in the mystical and antirational environment of Hasidism that dominated the religious life of Skvira during his youth. In his memoirs, Ahad Ha-Am recalls that as a young child he would constantly argue over biblical and talmudic interpretation with members of the Sadegora sect who came to visit the Ginsberg home. He also had difficulty accepting the laxness and informality of Hasidic behavior and observance. Shortly before his move to Gopitshitza, for example, the young Ginsberg visited the court of the Tsadik of Sadegora with his father and was appalled by the vulgar language and behavior of the spiritual leader's followers. Not yet having reached the age of bar mitzvah, he now decided to break away from Hasidism and become a misnagid, an opponent of Hasidism.[21]

It was during this period that Golda Ginsberg began to read to her son the literature of the Musar movement, which stressed the importance of self-improvement and morality in religious study and thought. Having secretly learned the Russian alphabet at the age of eight by reading storefront signs and then later teaching himself German, Asher now began purchasing books and "borrowing" volumes from his father's library. At night, he secretly devoured the works of central European maskilim. The fact that Isaiah Ginsberg, whom Ahad Ha-Am himself described as "a bit of a maskil," kept "secular" books in his library and approved of his son's reading translations of European works suggests that, despite his religious upbringing and his father's intense desire to raise his son as a Torah scholar, Ahad Ha-Am was exposed at an early age to modernizing ideas.[22]

There were other signs of the influence of modern ideas in the Ginsberg household. Golda Ginsberg's interest in the literature of "modern" Orthodoxy may have been derived in part from her father who, despite his fervent commitment to Hasidism, wrote and spoke Russian.[23] Ahad Ha-Am's mother traveled throughout the Ukraine and New Russia to buy new clothes and jewelry, while his father frequently hosted local and regional government officials in his home.[24] During the 1870s, his parents would take annual trips to the spas of central Europe.[25] Like many of his contemporaries, Ahad Ha-Am would later exaggerate the nature of his alienation from Orthodoxy in order to demonstrate the courageous nature of his decision to accept and defend modern ideas.

Despite his fascination with the writings of the Berlin Haskalah, however, the young Ginsberg soon wearied of the egotism and haughtiness of its contemporary proponents in eastern Europe. His attitudes were reinforced by an unpleasant experience with a group of pretentious and smug maskilim in Warsaw in 1878. In later years, he would praise the Jewish Enlightenment for its attempt to modernize the Jewish community but would criticize it for its imitativeness of non-Jewish thought and its literary formalism. In their desperate effort to gain acceptance in the larger society, he would later argue in recalling his visit to Warsaw, maskilim had emphasized the externals of Jewish life and had ignored the "internal soul and spirit" that defined Jewry as a separate people. In Ahad Ha-Am's view, Yehuda Leib Gordon's famous phrase, "Be a man in the street and a Jew in one's tent," typified the shortsightedness of the generation of the Haskalah. The task of the modern generation was not to separate the Jew from the human being but rather to develop a full and self-confident individual who would be proud and knowledgeable enough to assert his distinctive heritage in both the public and private sectors.[26]

In the end, Ahad Ha-Am would argue, for all its commitment to change, the Haskalah remained wedded to the worst of Jewish tradition. In its desperate attempt to create a literary style that would find acceptance among the European intelligentsia, it mirrored the rabbis' slavish attachment to the written word. In contrast to the maskilim, Ahad Ha-Am believed that language was not an end in itself but merely a tool for the dissemination of ideas. A writer should not seek to impress the reader with his intelligence and wit. Instead, he should clarify his understanding so that he could act rationally and effectively.[27]

Ginsberg's disappointing experiences with maskilim led him to look beyond Jewish literature for further "enlightenment." Like

Simon Dubnow, he seems to have been introduced to general European literature and history though the translations of Kalman Shulman's romantic novels. Yet Ahad Ha-Am remained highly selective in his reading throughout his life. Already at an early age, he displayed little interest in belles-lettres. (Ahad Ha-Am would later dismiss the writings of one modern European writer as "secrets and allegories" that generally hid a "simple idea in the clouds."[28]) Nor did he care much for French philosophy, which he derided as flowery and pedantic. While others reveled in the romanticism of nineteenth-century German literature, he could only regard it as obtuse.[29] Instead, the young Ginsberg chose to read the works of practical British philosophers such as Jeremy Bentham, John Locke, and John Stuart Mill. In contrast to German idealism with its emphasis on emotionalism and personal insight, British empiricists seemed to offer an objective method for discovering "truths" about society and human behavior.[30]

It was during this period as well that Ginsberg became acquainted with the writings of Charles Darwin. Darwin's theory of biological evolution, especially its concern with the struggle between innate and historical forces and its scientific validation of progress, fascinated him. He was also taken with the works of such diverse thinkers as Auguste Comte, Ludwig Feuerbach, and Dimitri Pisarev, all of whom had stressed the importance of psychological factors in shaping human behavior. Such notions appealed to the young Russian Jewish intellectual whose childhood experiences with Hasidic groups sensitized him to the power of ideas and the ability of the charismatic leader to sway the masses. Later in his life, they would also provide him with a means of explaining religious belief and practice in "scientific" terms. Indeed, psychological issues pervade all of Ahad Ha-Am's writings and inform many of the key elements of his analysis of Jewish life, including most notably the role of prophets and prophecy in Jewish history. One also finds important influences of psychological theories of the late nineteenth century in Ahad Ha-Am's constant references to the contradiction between the ideal and real in Jewish development, and his demand that spiritual rejuvenation precede the physical revival of the nation.

Though keenly aware of the main currents of general European thought, Ahad Ha-Am remained an eclectic thinker, borrowing bits and pieces from philosophers and scholars to fit his own immediate needs. Throughout his life he expressed a strong dislike for Jewish intellectuals with decided worldviews borrowed from European philosophy. Enslaved to alien thought, they were blind to the distinctiveness of Jewish thought and tradition.[31] Not surprisingly, therefore, already at a relatively early age Ahad Ha-Am searched out Jewish intellectual sources for insight and understanding. He especially admired the medieval thinker Maimonides and the poet Yehuda ha-Nasi, who he claimed not only provided him with a pattern of clear and decisive thought but also served as models of individuals who could absorb general culture without losing sight of the genius of Jewish philosophy.[32] In time, Ginsberg would also be attracted to the writings of Nachman Krochmal (The Ranak), the early nineteenth-century Hegelian Jewish philosopher and historian, who had defined the Jewish nation as an evolving "spiritual organism" whose history reflected the unfolding of some higher ideal. Like Krochmal, Ahad Ha-Am would later emphasize the centrality of religious values for the survival and growth of the Jewish people and would share his conviction that the belief in one God gave the Jews a distinctive role to play among the world's nations.

Despite his "heresies," the young Ginsberg continued to be regarded in his father's Hasidic circles as an *ilui* (a child prodigy) and thus a desirable husband. In 1873 at the age of seventeen, in the custom of Hasidim and out of respect for his parents, he was married to a relative of the Lubavitcher Rebbe. The marriage seems to have been a happy if not an intellectually stimulating one. In his extensive writings, Ahad Ha-Am says very little about his wife, Rivka. Like many other wives of Russian Jewish intellectuals of the period, she was generally familiar with "secular" writings of the period. Nevertheless, she seemed content to remain at home with their three children, thereby freeing Ginsberg to engage in his literary and political pursuits.[33]

Asher had originally hoped to attend a university and made plans to enter a gymnasium to prepare for his entrance examinations. His plans were thwarted in 1880, however, when Rivka suddenly became ill. Soon afterward, his ailing father asked him to help rescue his failing business. Despite the immense pressures placed upon him to succeed, Ginsberg had always looked at his father with awe. Now, in his time of need, Asher could not bring himself to rebel against Isaiah Ginsberg's wishes.[34] He was also relieved not to have to enter public school. Questioning his intellectual abilities in a more cosmopolitan environment, the young Ginsberg was unsure that after years of private tutoring he would be able to adapt to the discipline of formal schooling.[35] The issue became moot in any case in 1881 after the outbreak of pogroms forced the Ginsberg family to flee to Brody, a city in the bordering region of Galicia in the Austro-Hungarian Empire.

Like Zhitlowski and Dubnow, the young Ginsberg was not deeply perturbed by the pogroms. The bloody events had thrown him into a state of confusion for a full three weeks, he would later note matter-of-factly in his memoirs.[36] Despite the fact that he was surrounded in Brody by families and individuals eager to migrate to the West and remained in daily contact with officials of the Alliance israélite universelle who supervised emigration, he never gave serious thought to permanently leaving Russia. Instead, Ginsberg seemed mainly concerned that his hasty departure from his home had prevented him from pursuing his preparations for the entrance examinations to the university. It was his quest for a general education as much as the experience of pogroms that led him to decide to study abroad.

After numerous unsuccessful attempts to enroll at universities in Vienna, Breslau, Berlin, and Leipzig, Ginsberg returned home. Like Dubnow, he now realized that he would have to give up on the idea of formal higher education. Attempting to make a virtue out of necessity, Asher announced to his parents that he would be an autodidact, seeking out the company of like-minded intellectuals in general society who were free of the stuffiness and pretense of academic life. In 1884, after living mainly at home the first thirty years of his life, Asher Ginsberg set out on his own to seek his fortune and fame.

Though he would later describe his home as a "furnace of iron . . . that destroyed all the best that nature had bestowed upon me,"[37] Ahad Ha-Am's early upbringing had a profoundly positive impact upon his life. Despite his later rejection of Orthodoxy, he never lost the values and ideals inculcated in childhood, including a love of the Jewish people, a fascination with the Bible, a reverence for Hebrew, a deep belief in the importance of commitment to an ideal, and a profound respect for religious ritual. Many of Ahad Ha-Am's fundamental notions, such as his emphasis on the spiritual alienation of the Jewish people in the Diaspora and their cultural revival in the Land of Israel, were drawn from traditional religious concepts concerning *galut* (Exile) and messianic redemption. Ahad Ha-Am's writings are replete with allusions to and citations from the biblical and talmudic sources that he studied in his youth, while his writing style with its constant invocation of divine support and its allusion to the role of destiny and fate betrays his many years of religious study. Ahad Ha-Am's comfortable surroundings and the respect he was given at an early age for his intellect also help to explain his elitism and general disregard for social and economic issues. Finally, the fact that Ahad Ha-Am developed his new attitudes gradually while still living in a traditional Jewish environment meant that he never experienced adolescent rebellion and the pull of the larger society. The result would be a view of Jewish nation building that stressed the importance of evolutionary change from within Jewish society and that generally ignored external factors.[38]

In 1884, after a short stay in Berdichev, Ginsberg moved to Odessa. As with Dubnow before him, the southern Russian seaport provided him with a comfortable social milieu populated by similarly minded Jewish intellectuals in search of new forms of individual and collective expression. Culturally assimilated yet not politically emancipated, the small group he found there including Simon Dubnow, Mendele Moykher Sforim, and Yehuda Leyb Peretz represented a unique collection of divergent viewpoints united by an unwavering commitment to the future of the Jewish people. The relatively open society of Odessa Jewry also offered Ginsberg the opportunity to develop a small but loyal coterie of supporters. Friday nights at his household were a major event for Jewish intellectuals of all types, from Zionists to assimilationists, from secular Jews to the religiously observant. For many young Jews in Odessa, Ginsberg soon emerged as a new authority figure to replace the father, grandfather, teacher, or rabbi they had rejected in their youth.[39] Free from his father's control, he soon developed enough self-confidence to express his opinions openly in public. Not without some exaggeration, Ahad Ha-Am would later describe his twenty-three years in Odessa as "the most precious period in my life."[40]

Almost immediately upon his arrival in Odessa, Ginsberg became involved with the proto-Zionist organization Hibbat Zion. In its beginning stages, the major thrust of Hibbat Zion was "practical" rather than ideological. Its members pressed for the establishment and support of colonies in the Land of Israel and generally avoided debates over the future of Jewry. Hibbat Zion's emphasis on settlement and its disdain for theoretical abstraction reflected the pioneering idealism of its supporters (known as Hoveve Zion, or Lovers of Zion), who deliberately sought to disassociate themselves from the philosophical musings of maskilim. Leaders of the group were also averse to engaging in ideological debate because of the diverse nature of its membership that included both religious and secular elements and of the severe restrictions placed on political activity by the tsarist regime.[41]

Ginsberg immediately set about to change Hibbat Zion's focus and direction. Calling upon the movement to develop a theoretical framework for its activity, he soon assumed the role as its chief ideologue. Elected to the board (*vaad ha-poel*), he used his position to attack the organization's philanthropic orientation and what he believed was its blindness to the concerns of the Jewish community as a whole. Increasingly, members called upon him to arbitrate disagreements and to evaluate ideas and programs that were introduced at meetings. Ginsberg's relative wealth, connections with Hasidic dynasties, and wide learning clearly impressed younger members of Hibbat Zion who looked upon him as both a dynamic counterforce to the staid leadership of the organization and as an articulate intercessor with the Odessa Jewish community, led largely by Russified Jews.[42]

Ginsberg's insistence on the need for Jewish cultural revival and his uncompromising nature soon brought him into conflict with many of Hibbat Zion's early supporters and leading lights, including Moshe Leib Lilienblum and Rabbi Shmuel Mohilever. To the young idealist, the movement's leadership seemed concerned mainly with avoiding government censorship and maintaining the delicate balance that had been created between Orthodox and secular members. In particular, Ginsberg opposed Lilienblum's insistence that agricultural colonization had to precede spiritual reform.[43] As his biographer Leon Simon notes, Ginsberg remained too much of an aristocrat to believe in the idea of a Jewish agricultural proletariat.[44] He was also firmly convinced that the movement's obsession with physical settlement was little more than an attempt to pacify religious elements who were suspicious of the intentions of Palestinophiles. Nor was Ginsberg impressed by what he regarded as Hibbat Zion's halfhearted attempts to link physical labor and cooperative settlement with spiritual renewal. He longed for a new Jewish vision that would signal a return not only to the land but to the core ideals that he believed had enabled Jewry to develop and grow over the centuries.

Ginsberg could hardly be pleased with the decision to appoint the early Zionist theoretician Leon Pinsker as chairman of Hibbat Zion. In his view, it smacked of a desire by the movement's leadership to ingratiate itself with the established Jewish community. Despite Pinsker's efforts to incorporate some of Ginsberg's concerns into the movement's "platform" at its unifying congress in Katowice in 1884, the young ideologue remained unimpressed. Shortly after the congress, Ginsberg attempted to create a counterorganization of young activists who would press for the adoption of his proposals. The effort proved unsuccessful. Yet Ginsberg refused to give up his dream of transforming Hibbat Zion into a movement of cultural renewal. He would remain in the organization as the leader of the "loyal opposition."[45]

In 1885, the impending birth of a second child and the decision by his father to sell off his business led Ginsberg to move back to Gopitshitza. A year later, he returned with his family to Odessa. Though he longed to rejoin the community of Jewish intellectuals in the city, he was consumed by family business affairs. Nevertheless, he devoted his evenings to study. On Friday nights, Ginsberg met with other like-minded young Jews to discuss contemporary Russian and Jewish affairs. Within a short time, his home had again become a central meeting place for intellectual discussion and debate among the Jewish intelligentsia. It was a remarkable turn of events for a young man who had yet to publish a word and who was regarded as a quiet and reserved individual.[46]

Despite his growing reputation, it would take Ginsberg another three years before he was ready to present his ideas to the public. His decision to openly defend his views was motivated in large part by the noticeable decline of Hibbat Zion in the late 1880s. Loyal to the goals of the movement, youthful supporters in Russia had moved to Palestine to establish new settlements. It did not take long, however, before poor management and internecine quarrels threatened their existence. In 1889, an especially bitter controversy erupted when Orthodox members of Hibbat Zion demanded that Palestinian settlers adhere to the biblical commandments of *shmita*, which prohibited the growing and sale of crops every seven years and annulled all monetary obligations among Jews. Secular supporters countered that such policies would destroy the settlements, which were already threatened with economic collapse.[47] Those colonies that were still in existence at the end of the decade grew increasingly dependent on the philanthropy of western Jews like Baron Edmond de Rothschild, who were more interested in ensuring that the settlers could sustain themselves economically than in supporting their efforts to create a new Jewish society in Palestine. For many of the early supporters of Hibbat Zion, such internal and external pressures threatened to destroy the very raison d'être of the movement.

In 1889, in response to growing demands that he make his position clearly known, Ginsberg published his first article, which he entitled "Lo zeh ha-derekh" (This Is Not the Way).[48] Writing in the Hebrew journal *Ha-Melits* for the first time under the pseudonym "Ahad Ha-Am" (One of the People), he pleaded for a gradual revival of the Jewish people based not on colonies of pioneers but on the spiritual rejuvenation of Jewry as a whole. Colonization was bound to disappoint its supporters, he argued, since it overemphasized selfish material needs and ignored the inner yearnings of the nation that had initially fired enthusiasm for settlement in the Land of Israel. Ahad Ha-Am also lashed out at what he believed was the brazenness of Orthodox members of Hibbat Zion. Religious traditionalists within the movement were wrong to impose their outworn ideas on the young Zionist experiment. Judaism in the Diaspora had emphasized individual salvation. The national ideal, though never completely absent, had considerably diminished in importance within Jewish communities. The continuing influence of Orthodoxy in Hibbat Zion, Ahad Ha-Am maintained, would only weaken the idealism and fortitude of pioneers in Palestine, which were necessary for the success of their bold experiment. Ultimately, the struggle to establish a Jewish presence in the Holy Land would have to be built on new ideological foundations. Though Ahad Ha-Am was careful not to break completely with traditional Judaism — the essay was replete with biblical citations to support the author's major arguments — he was insistent that new forms of Jewish identity based on cultural renewal, or *techiyat ha-levavot* (revival of the hearts), would have to be created to ensure Jewish survival and growth. Rejecting both materialists and narrow-minded rabbis as the leaders of the new Palestine, Ahad Ha-Am proclaimed that only "the heart of the nation can serve as the basis upon which to build the land."

In 1891, Ahad Ha-Am reiterated his major themes in an essay published in *Ha-Melits*, which he titled "Ha-kohanim veha-am" (Priests and Nation).[49] Once again, he ridiculed the growing association of the activities of Hibbat Zion with philanthropy and practical business. In denouncing the tendency of the movement to accede to the will of assimilated Diaspora Jews, Ahad Ha-Am recalled the devotion of the first generation of the movement, the poor but committed youth who served as a model for future generations of settlers in the Land of Israel. In his conclusion, he called for the creation of a new generation of priests—the "one in a hundred truly worthy of the name 'Lover of Zion'"—that would provide the necessary spiritual guidance, moral rectitude, and inner strength necessary to lead the nation.

It has become a generally accepted belief that Ginsberg chose the name "Ahad Ha-Am" as a sign of his humility and his commitment to the Jewish people. The source of this explanation was Ginsberg himself, who discussed the origin of the name in his memoirs. In contrast to other activists in the community, he claimed, he was not a professional writer and had no intention of becoming one. Ginsberg deliberately chose the name to demonstrate that he had no desire to become a spokesman for Jewry as a whole; he was merely "one of the people" with a strong interest in national issues.[50] Ginsberg's supporters would later claim that he was so self-effacing and unassuming during this early period that it took quite a while for even the most dedicated activists in Hibbat Zion to discover the true identity of "Ahad Ha-Am."[51]

The reality was much more complicated, however. As one of Ahad Ha-Am's recent biographers, Yosef Goldstein, wryly comments: "Someone who sees himself as one of the people should not have to announce it publicly."[52] In actuality, like many of his generation, Ahad Ha-Am generally had little regard for the will of the "people." Instead, he clearly saw himself as the leader of the intellectual vanguard that would lead the Jewish masses to enlightenment. In order to forge a distinct role within the emerging Jewish nationalist movement, Ginsberg deliberately set out to fashion a distinct persona. Central to the image was the emphasis on introspection and aloofness, which not only fit his reclusive personality but also enabled him to appear to transcend the petty squabbles of everyday life. Ahad Ha-Am was, in the words of one of his most ardent supporters, Haim Nahman Bialik, one "who walks alone."[53]

In public lectures, Ahad Ha-Am assumed an aristocratic demeanor and purposely distanced himself from his listeners. In private "audiences" with his followers, he was careful to cultivate the image of an intellectual seer. A frail individual, Ginsberg's expressive features and stern demeanor conveyed an overwhelming impression of thoughtfulness and self-sacrifice that humbled those in his presence.[54] In discussions, Ahad Ha-Am was careful to wait until others had spoken before sharing his views. When he finally did speak, his words were carefully chosen to have the maximum effect with a minimum of discussion. The result was generally the complete defeat of all opposing views.[55] Even after decisions were made, Ahad Ha-Am generally refused to allow his supporters to act without his direct involvement.[56] The effect of such meetings on those in attendance was nothing short of cataclysmic. It was like "a sin for which there is no penitence," one enthusiast commented, not to have made a special journey to Odessa to have an audience with the great man.[57]

Ahad Ha-Am clearly wished to be regarded as a man of modest background who was called upon by destiny to guide the Jewish people on the right path to redemption. In deliberately attempting to mask his persona in mystery, however, he only fueled wild rumors among the Jewish masses of eastern Europe about his true nature and program. One such rumor suggested that he was a new Maimonides who spent most of his time at home, garbed in prayer shawl and phylacteries, preparing a new *Guide to the Perplexed*. Another claimed that he was actually a priest or missionary seeking to convert his fellow Jews.[58] Such notions could only help to massage Ginsberg's fragile ego while reinforcing his belief that the Russian Jewish masses were in dire need of direction and leadership.

Within the Zionist movement, Ahad Ha-Am saw his nom de plume as a useful propaganda tool that would affirm his right to lead the struggle for national renewal. While he remained loyal to the interests of the Jewish people as a whole, his opponents were selfish and shortsighted.[59] As "one of the people," he could portray himself as an objective observer of the Jewish condition whose concern was always tempered by rationalism and sensibility.[60] This self-fashioning also served Ahad Ha-Am well in his efforts to gain support among youthful Jewish intellectuals who were themselves searching for a way to demonstrate their new self-appointed role within the Jewish community. Even before the publication of "Lo zeh ha-derekh," Ginsberg had gained a reputation among many young Jews in Odessa as a great scholar and seer who stood above the crowd. Here was an individual who was not only well versed in Jewish and secular learning but was also imbued with an unshakable moral character that made him strive for the truth no matter what the cost. The fact that

Ahad Ha-Am did not begin publishing his ideas until he was almost thirty-five years old only reinforced his image as a distinctive personality and a penetrating intellect. In the words of Bialik, he was "a man who . . . had grown so strong as to attain . . . his full powers in one sweep."[61] Given such fits of hyperbole, it is probably not surprising that none of his followers dared suggest that the Zionist thinker may have simply chosen to use a pseudonym that defined him as "one" among many in order to avoid censorship problems.

It did not take long for Ginsberg's efforts to bear fruit. Within months after the publication of "Lo zeh ha-derekh," his coterie of disciples had concluded that his choice of the pseudonym was clearly meant to demonstrate his unique ability to embody the concerns of Jewry itself. As one admirer would later comment, Ahad Ha-Am's own heartbeat was at one with "the heartbeat of the people as a whole, with its sorrows, its anguish over its wretchedness, its defeat, and its destruction!"[62]

In 1889, in response to growing support for his ideas and his leadership role within Hibbat Zion, Ahad Ha-Am helped found a semisecret society of activists called Bnei Moshe (Sons of Moses).[63] Bnei Moshe combined two of the central ideals that Ginsberg had enunciated in "Lo zeh ha-derekh": intellectual elitism and the dominance of the collective spirit over the material needs of the individual. Hibbat Zion had degenerated into a colonization society dependent on the charity of wealthy Jews and a vehicle for individual upward social mobility. In contrast, Bnei Moshe was to be a movement to train an intellectual vanguard that would be responsible for developing a vibrant national Jewish intellectual and cultural life. As the historian Steven J. Zipperstein points out, like the yeshivas and Hasidic courts of the religious community, Ahad Ha-Am saw the movement as "a focal point which would inspire Jews everywhere by virtue of the austere and exemplary behaviour of its members, and especially, its leaders."[64] It was a view that would later also shape Ahad Ha-Am's vision of a spiritual center in Palestine.

Influenced by Ahad Ha-Am's personal contacts with members of Kadimah, a Zionist organization founded by Jewish students in Vienna in 1892, the ideology of Bnei Moshe reflected a blending of Russian revolutionary and romantic nationalist philosophy.[65] Those who joined the movement pledged themselves to work ardently and tirelessly for the cause of Jewish national revival, no matter what their specific party or political affiliations. Mirroring the ideas of "Lo zeh ha-

derekh," participants proclaimed the primacy of national consciousness over religious sentiment and national interest over individual
pursuits.[66] In addition, members were required to contribute two
percent of their annual income to the organization. The rituals surrounding induction were borrowed from Masonic tradition, German
fraternities, and the Jewish marriage ceremony. In imitation of biblical priests and Nazirites, members called each other *ach* (brother)
and pledged to abstain from all "frivolous" activity such as card play-
ing, "family matters," and drinking.

Many of the rules and rituals of Bnei Moshe were formulated to
recall the biblical hero who gave the movement its name — the "Master Prophet" Moses. The organization was founded on the seventh
of Adar, the traditional Hebrew date of Moses' birth and death.
Members greeted each other in Hebrew with the phrase "And his
eyes were undimmed and his vigor unabated," the biblical description of Moses at the time of his death. In swearing allegiance to the
movement, initiates pledged themselves to follow in the footsteps of
the great biblical leaders whose central mission in life was "the revival of Israel in the Land of Israel." The ceremony concluded with
the recital of an oath that obligated participants to support the Mo-
saic characteristics of "truth, justice, peace, spiritual strength, full-
heartedness, and purity of the soul."[67]

Ahad Ha-Am himself regarded Moses as an eponymous hero whose
existence could not be proven but whose "historical truth" was evident
by the manner in which he served as an example for Jews throughout
the generations.[68] In his writings, the cultural Zionist seemed personally obsessed with the biblical figure. Like Moses, Ahad Ha-Am saw
himself as a symbol of truth, one who persevered in spite of reversals
and displayed throughout his life a stern, unyielding allegiance to basic
ideals. Especially in his later life, Ahad Ha-Am may also have personally identified with the tragedy of a leader who led his people to the
Promised Land but could not participate in its conquest and settlement.[69] As with the biblical Moses, the realization of Ahad Ha-Am's
ideals in everyday life was to be left to others in the Jewish community—political activists, businessmen, and diplomats.

Ahad Ha-Am was careful not to model the organization too closely in
his image for fear of being regarded by his enemies as a megalomaniac
or, even worse, a self-proclaimed messenger of God. According to the
founding document of Bnei Moshe, the organization was to be decen-

tralized. As a modified federation modeled in part after the illegal organizations of Russian revolutionaries, each branch would choose a "leader" who would periodically convoke a meeting to inform members of his actions and decisions and to solicit their advice. In turn, branch leaders would appoint a "chief leader" or *ach ha-gadol* (Big Brother) who would make decisions binding upon all members. At get-togethers of Bnei Moshe that were held on Friday evenings at his home, Ahad Ha-Am was referred to as *nasi*, a biblical term denoting a leader of the Jewish community that suggested something less than a prophet or ruler but considerably more than a mere administrative official.[70]

By 1890, Bnei Moshe had established branches throughout Russia and had begun to make inroads into the East European emigré communities of Germany and England. Support for the movement was bolstered by the membership of Lilienblum and the active support of Pinsker (who could not join because he was unable to fulfill its prerequisites for membership: a knowledge of Hebrew and the ability to settle in Palestine).[71] Though few in number—there were never more than 200 members at any one time—Bnei Moshe loyalists were drawn from the cream of Hibbat Zion's activists and soon assumed a dominant role in the central committee of the Odessa branch of the organization. Within a short period of time they had made their mark on almost every aspect of Zionist activity. In the period between 1892 and 1896, members of the Berlin branch were in the forefront of discussions for convening a general congress of Jewish nationalists. Following the guidelines of Ahad Ha-Am, participants in Bnei Moshe set about publishing Hebrew literature for children and adults and were instrumental in the founding of one of the first Hebrew publishing houses in eastern Europe, Achiasaf. In Palestine, they helped to establish a number of important institutions, including the first Hebrew school in Jaffa and the first modern Zionist charitable organization, Keren Kayemet Le-Yisrael (Jewish National Fund). Having deliberately chosen to exclude all "rich and powerful" elements in the community from participation in the movement, Bnei Moshe branches took it upon themselves to assist colonists in Palestine in their struggle with the Rothschild administration. Members of the Warsaw branch, for example, helped to found the colony of Rehovot, which refused to accept support from western philanthropists and insisted that its members speak only Hebrew.[72]

Despite its early successes, Bnei Moshe soon fell on hard times. As Ahad Ha-Am had feared, the movement's secretive nature drew bitter criticism from rabbinic authorities. In their view, Bnei Moshe's "pagan-like" rituals and freethinking ideas were a menace to Jewish society. Ahad Ha-Am did not help his cause by proclaiming that the ideals of the nationalist movement and of Bnei Moshe in particular should be the basis of a new Jewish liturgy.[73] Orthodox leaders were especially incensed by his assertion that religious tradition was merely a reflection of the national spirit and not divinely ordained. Much like the response of Orthodoxy to the rise of religious reform in the West, traditional rabbis in eastern Europe clearly saw Bnei Moshe as a formidable threat. Here was a movement that sought not to destroy Judaism but to create a new spiritual ideal borrowed from religious tradition.[74] The hostility of traditionalists toward Bnei Moshe and Ahad Ha-Am was exacerbated by the tendency of many young Zionist activists to define their commitment to settlement in Palestine and their return to Jewish life in religious terms. Members of Bnei Moshe presented themselves as a new caste of high priests who alone would determine the fate of the Jewish people. As one of the movement's ardent supporters, Elchanan Leib Levinsky, would claim: "To go to Palestine meant to become a whole Jew, to reconvert to Judaism the apostate parts of us. And it is an old law, that if any stranger come to the Jews, and wishes to convert, he must not be received too lightly. On the contrary, he must be warned that our way is a hard one, and that the life of our people is a bitter one. It is only when he has passed through his test of fire that he may be received."[75]

Criticism also arose from within Hibbat Zion on the part of members who were convinced that Ahad Ha-Am was using Bnei Moshe to gain control of the Zionist movement and its Palestinian activities. In a scathing article titled "Derekh bat-ami" (The Way of My People), published in 1889, Lilienblum attacked the cultural Zionist for overemphasizing spiritual renewal at the expense of colonization. It was dangerous nonsense, Lilienblum argued, to believe that the Jewish people were capable of developing a "national spirit" without settlement in Palestine.[76] Such sentiments were reinforced by the often clumsy efforts by Ahad Ha-Am to outmaneuver the veteran leadership of Hibbat Zion and to create a more loyal membership by expelling individuals from Bnei Moshe who publicly criticized his ideas.[77]

In 1891, Bnei Moshe suffered a series of reversals. A serious financial scandal all but bankrupted the movement and led to a noticeable falling off in the organization's colonization efforts in Palestine. Troubled by the increasingly bitter internecine struggles and the decline in the quality of membership, Ahad Ha-Am resigned from the leadership of the movement. Shortly thereafter, the headquarters of Bnei Moshe was moved from Odessa to its most active branch in Warsaw, which effectively removed Ahad Ha-Am from the day-to-day control of the organization. Ahad Ha-Am had never been interested in the movement's administrative affairs. He was also burdened by recurring physical illness and financial problems that consumed most of his energy and attention. In bowing out, however, he made sure that he remained the organization's "spiritual adviser," a position that more closely reflected his own view of leadership. Typically, Ahad Ha-Am sought to downplay his desire to continue to maintain control over the movement. He had never actively pursued a leadership role in Bnei Moshe, he claimed; it was only in response to the incessant pleas of ardent admirers that he had grudgingly agreed to remain on as a spiritual adviser.[78]

In early 1893, Ahad Ha-Am solidified his position in Bnei Moshe by transferring its offices to the Palestinian port city of Jaffa. By moving the organization's activity to Palestine, he hoped to accommodate his many loyalists who had immigrated to the Land of Israel. The move also signaled the transformation of Ahad Ha-Am's ideological goal from the vague notion of spiritual revival fostered by an elite in the Diaspora to the ideal of a Jewish spiritual center in Palestine.[79]

The decision to transfer the activity of the movement to Palestine did little to mollify the critics of Bnei Moshe, however. The fact that Ahad Ha-Am was now convinced that the opportunity to create a new Jewish culture in Palestine lay within his grasp put him on a collision course with the religious and lay establishment of the so-called Old Yishuv, who represented the centuries-old Jewish community that antedated Zionist settlement. He did not have long to wait. Within a few months after the organization's move, leaders of the Old Yishuv attacked the young Hebraist and Zionist Eliezer Ben-Yehuda for allegedly inciting Jews in Palestine to revolt against Turkish rule. Ben-Yehuda's subsequent indictment and imprisonment led Ahad Ha-Am to launch a personal tirade against religious Orthodoxy. In a letter written in 1894 to the editor of the Odessa annual *Ha-Pardes* (Paradise), which he later included in his collected writings under the title "Torah she ba-lev" (Torah of the Heart), he derided traditionalists for enslaving Jewish life to the written word. In the past, enlightened thinkers had been afraid to confront the rabbinate. Yet "the guardians of the written word" were an evil force in Jewish society. "[F]or the sake of every dot and tittle (*kotso shel yod*)," Ahad Ha-Am cynically remarked, they "find it easy to destroy house and home without any feeling of pain." The time had come, he concluded, to boldly confront the "Nineveh" of religious authority with a new vision of Jewish life based on spiritual renewal and freedom.[80]

The same year saw Ahad Ha-Am involved in another struggle that involved Bnei Moshe. This time his adversaries were the leaders of the French philanthropic organization Alliance israélite universelle who opposed the Jewish curriculum of the school founded by Bnei Moshe's Jaffa branch. While Ahad Ha-Am demanded that the school stress Jewish studies, the Alliance insisted upon the need to inculcate European culture among young members of the *yishuv*.[81] The Bnei Moshe curriculum also ran into opposition from ultra-Orthodox elements of the Old Yishuv and religious Zionists like Yehiel Pines who were angered by its insistence on the need to create a new "freethinking" national Jew. Relations were soured further by the decision of Bnei Moshe to drop a clause in its constitution that asked members to respect the dictates of Judaism even when they conflicted with their own views.[82] In the end, the Alliance chose to withdraw its support from the Jaffa school. Without the French organization's financial backing, the school quickly folded, bringing bitter humiliation to Ahad Ha-Am and further weakening the credibility of Bnei Moshe.[83]

By the mid-1890s, Bnei Moshe had become a political anachronism. Its vague appeals for cultural and spiritual revival among Palestinian colonists clashed with the demands of philanthropists for more responsible settlement, while its separatism and elitism were increasingly out of touch with the urgings of modern Jewish nationalists for pluralistic, public, and rational organizational activity. By 1895, Ahad Ha-Am's original enthusiasm for Bnei Moshe had disappeared. He had become convinced that the movement lacked the unity and drive that had characterized its early activity. Once a select group of idealistic youths, it had become a closed circle of friends who were mainly concerned with shoring up existing settlements in Palestine. If Bnei Moshe was to be saved, he now maintained, there was a need to break down what he called the "Chinese Wall" that separated the movement from the Jewish public, especially as it began to branch out into the more open societies of Palestine and the West. Significantly, however, Ahad Ha-Am offered no specific suggestions as to how to end the movement's isolation.[84]

In any event, such advice came too late to save the organization. In 1896, the Jaffa branch disbanded amid a wave of criticism and further rumors of corruption. By the time of the meeting of the First Zionist Congress in 1897, Bnei Moshe had all but ceased to exist. Eight years later, Ahad Ha-Am looked back at the movement and was forced to admit that it had accomplished little in its short lifetime. He seemed utterly oblivious to the fact that his own lack of clear leadership and his refusal to compromise had been instrumental in its failure. All he could say was that he was tired and depressed. Having lost faith in "the sons of our generation," he would again have "to stand alone."[85]

Ahad Ha-Am's involvement in Bnei Moshe had been fueled in large part by his skepticism concerning the value of mass colonization in Palestine. His doubts were reinforced by trips to Palestine in the winter and early spring of 1891 and again in the summer of 1893. On a personal level, the visits were immensely gratifying and spiritually uplifting. "I am in the world of the past and I cannot relate to you even a small portion of what came over me in the few days I have been here," he wrote to his parents and his children during his first visit; "every step, every rock, is a piece of history flowing with blood; one sees historical sites wherever one looks, and what sites!"[86] As the foundation of a new national identity and purpose, however, Palestine proved to be a profound disappointment. The pitiful economic state of the colonies and their impoverished cultural life convinced Ahad Ha-Am that Palestine could never absorb a significant number of Jews. The least likely candidates for aliyah, or immigration to Palestine, he noted ironically, were petty merchants and artisans who formed the backbone of the Palestinophilic movement. In the face of the limited economic opportunities in the Land of Israel, the Jewish middle class would simply have to look for refuge in the United States. Yet the economic problems facing the *yishuv* only reinforced Ahad Ha-Am's commitment to national renewal. What Palestine lacked in numbers, it would make up for in the quality of its Jewish colonizers. Palestinian settlers could become models of the dedicated Jewish pioneer who was not only committed to agricultural labor but would also devote his energy to the cultural revival of the Jewish people.[87]

In 1895, Ahad Ha-Am published his most important work, *Al parshat derakhim* (At the Crossroads). The publication of a collection of all of his articles that had appeared in print since 1889 coincided with a bitter battle over control of the Jaffa branch of Hibbat Zion. Once again, Ahad Ha-Am found himself pitted against both defenders of the original ideals of the organization such as Lilienblum and proponents of Orthodoxy like Pines.[88] There was little doubt in his mind that the publication of the corpus of his writings would solidify his position within Hibbat Zion and serve as useful ammunition against his opponents. In the Introduction, Ahad Ha-Am outlined the purpose of the collection. For the first time in its history, Jewry faced a choice between assimilation and national revival. Hibbat Zion had clearly lost its way. The time had come for Ahad Ha-Am and his supporters to forge a new direction in the Palestinophilic movement that would restore its credibility and influence among world Jewry. In his tendency to personalize the plight of Jewry as a whole, Ahad Ha-Am saw himself at a "crossroads" in his own ideological development as well. The fact that his perspectives were being used by all sides to buttress their arguments, he maintained, necessitated the presentation of his ideas in a coherent and clear form.

In 1902, Ahad Ha-Am decided to republish *Al parshat derakhim*. He now had a new series of opponents to contend with. The collection contained significant additions that incorporated the Zionist thinker's response to the attacks leveled against him as a "negativist" and a "dreamer" by both young Hebrew writers and political Zionists. A third edition, published in 1920, was meant as a coda to Ahad Ha-Am's Zionist activity and represented his final major effort to counter the growing influence of political Zionism in the wake of the Balfour Declaration. It included essays from the previous two editions as well as all of his major writings through World War I. Though rarely read in its entirety today, *Al parshat derakhim* nevertheless serves as a useful compendium of Ahad Ha-Am's perspectives on the major issues facing world Jewry during the most crucial period of his political and literary activity.[89]

In 1896, Ahad Ha-Am faced further disappointments. Much to his shock, not all of the branches of Hibbat Zion chose to support him in the struggle for leadership of the Jaffa branch. The betrayal of his supporters and his failing business interests in Odessa led Ahad Ha-Am to take a position in Warsaw as the editor of the Hebrew-language publishing company Achiasaf. He was delighted with the new appointment. He could assuage the bitter disappointments over the fate of Bnei Moshe by participating directly in the inculcation of "a new spirit in the Jewish people."[90] From his new vantage point he could reaffirm his role as intellectual leader without having to dirty his hands with petty politics. Ahad Ha-Am continued to maintain editorial control over Achiasaf's publications when a short time later he moved to Berlin to become the editor of *Ha-Shiloach*, a new Hebrew-language monthly. The name of the journal referred to a small river in Palestine cited in the sixth chapter of the Book of Isaiah that was known for its quiet, calm stream. It was deliberately chosen by Ahad Ha-Am to reflect his own philosophy of gradualism as well as the commitment of the journal to clear and moderate thought. The criteria for acceptance of submissions were stringent and *Ha-Shiloach* quickly gained a reputation for the quality of its articles. To appear in the monthly meant that a writer had arrived.[91] Ahad Ha-Am clearly meant *Ha-Shiloach* to be a cultural forum for Hebrew writers much in the manner of other European literary publications of the day. Nevertheless, he insisted that the journal concentrate almost exclusively on Jewish matters in contrast to what he regarded as the slavish imitativeness of western journalism and the vulgarity of the popular Jewish press.[92]

By the end of the year, Ahad Ha-Am had moved the entire operation back to Odessa to be closer to cultural developments in Russia and to his family who had remained behind. It was a difficult time for the Zionist thinker, marked by significant financial and ideological reversals. The start of a new century saw the first public expressions by Ahad Ha-Am of his belief that Jewish life was passing him by. It was an attitude that he had previously discussed privately with friends but that took on new meaning after the death of his father in April 1899. Despite the fact that he was less than fifty years old, Ahad Ha-Am increasingly was haunted by fears that he was rapidly aging and would be unable to accomplish his goals before his death.[93]

One of the reasons for Ahad Ha-Am's growing despair at the turn of the century was the challenge posed by Theodor Herzl and his movement for a Jewish state. Unlike many of his contemporaries, the cultural Zionist was singularly unimpressed by the convocation of the First Zionist Congress in Basel in 1897. Much of Ahad Ha-

Am's antagonism to Herzl stemmed from his all-consuming ego. Even before the convening of the congress, he had expressed bitter disappointment that an inexperienced young activist had been sent by the organizers to solicit the support of Hibbat Zion. He had also felt slighted that his old nemesis Lilienblum was the only member of the movement to be formally invited.[94]   When he finally did receive an invitation, Ahad Ha-Am chose to attend as a journalist rather than as a delegate. To do otherwise would compromise his principles; his greatest fear was that others might misperceive him as giving his approval to Herzl's program. From his vantage point in the gallery, the "journalist" kept a close eye on the activity of the congress. He quickly grasped the threat that Herzl's growing appeal posed to his own program for national renewal. Describing himself as "a mourner at the wedding," he attacked the meeting as ill-timed, largely ceremonial, and controlled by "young men whose enthusiasm is greater than their understanding."   In a mixture of jealousy and fear over the appearance of a formidable rival in the Jewish nationalist movement, he denounced Herzl for dominating the proceedings and for his cavalier dismissal of cultural issues. While agreeing in the end to play a minor role in a Hebrew language committee established during the congress, Ahad Ha-Am adamantly refused to officially join the Zionist movement. To do so, he maintained, would force him to accept the view of the masses for a political "quick fix" at the expense of his own intellectual independence.[95]

Ahad Ha-Am gained a short-lived victory at the meeting of the first All-Russian Conference of the Zionist movement held in Warsaw in August 1898. Political maneuvering by his supporters resulted in the passage of a resolution making culture rather than political activism central to Zionist activity. Though the cultural Zionist gloated over his victory—the resolution marked the first step in the effort to "open the eyes of the blind," he explained to one of his close associates[96]—he seemed unwilling or unable to follow up his success with concerted actions against the supporters of Herzl who dominated the movement. Indeed, only a month after the congress, he was already expressing strong fears that Russian Jewish nationalists would not be able to withstand the pressures of western political Zionists and that the resolutions passed at the Warsaw conference would have little practical effect.[97]   Whatever his doubts at the time, in refusing to take an active role in the Russian congress and then later in failing to attend the Second Zionist Congress held in August 1898, Ahad Ha-Am effectively forfeited his control over the Russian Zionist faction. He had only himself to blame when the Russian bloc voted along with other participants at the congress for a watered-down version of the Warsaw proposals that effectively tabled his agenda.[98] The more astute diplomat Herzl had cleverly outflanked the politically naive and "undiplomatic" leader of cultural Zionism who adamantly refused to compromise his principles.

Ahad Ha-Am's curious relationship with the Russian Zionist movement would continue at its Second Congress held in Minsk in September 1902. Asked to speak at the meeting, at first he seemed genuinely excited and enthused. He was flattered that many of the delegates eagerly looked to him as a potential counterforce to the growing influence of religious Zionists in the Russian movement. Upon his entrance, Ahad Ha-Am was greeted with shouts and applause. Speaker after speaker lauded him as the movement's spiritual leader and begged him to take an active role in the movement. Yet Ahad Ha-Am's speech was a profound disappointment to many of those in attendance. His warning that Zionism would not solve the economic, political, or social plight of Jews drew strong opposition from Herzl's supporters, while his insistence that Jewry could find spiritual renewal only in Palestine angered the religious leaders who were present. Even Ahad Ha-Am's most loyal supporters could not accept his proposal to create a committee to foster cultural activity outside the framework of Herzl's Zionist organization. In presenting a dogmatic and uninspiring speech, Ahad Ha-Am again failed to take advantage of the opportunity offered him.[99] As in the past, he seemed more comfortable being the lone (and powerless) voice of righteous opposition—the prophet—amid what he regarded as the howling mob of political beasts.[100]

Toward the end of 1899 Ahad Ha-Am made his third trip to Palestine in his capacity as representative of the Odessa branch of Hibbat Zion's Colonization Society. He returned in April 1900 in a terrible state of health. Personal reversals and public misgivings about the Zionist experiment combined to bring on yet another bout of depression. In 1901 Ahad Ha-Am published a series of articles in *Ha-Shiloach* in which he voiced renewed concern over the development of the *yishuv*. Soon after, he quit the executive committee of Hibbat Zion when a delegation from the Zionist organization sent to Paris to ask Baron Edmond de Rothschild to end his support of colonies in

Palestine backed down from pressing their demand. In one of his rare public displays of anger and emotion, Ahad Ha-Am lambasted the delegation for their timidity. Instead of displaying the pride and fortitude of East European Jews, he argued, they had turned their visit into "a heart-rending joke" by acting like beggars pleading for a handout.[101] He was "disgusted" with political activity, he commented to his friend Yehosuha Ravnitsky after the delegation returned. He would much prefer to concentrate on literary matters than to waste time on "useless meetings and hastily planned events."[102] The Palestine experiment may have been at a "crossroads," as Ahad Ha-am had argued in *Al parshat derakhim*, but he seemed strangely incapable of leading the movement in a new direction.

By 1903, continuing personal financial burdens, a declining readership, and anger over criticisms of his editorial work by contributors led Ahad Ha-Am to resign from the editorship of *Ha-Shiloach*.[103] His decision to leave Hebrew publishing undoubtedly was also influenced by his growing conviction that interest in Hebrew literature within the Russian Jewish community was rapidly losing ground to the more immediate issues of the struggle against anti-Semitism and the movement to gain civil equality.[104] Despite his personal and public reversals, however, Ahad Ha-Am doggedly refused to leave Russia. He would not consider settling in Palestine without gainful employment and an improvement in the economic and cultural life of the *yishuv*. His attitude toward America, on the other hand, was remarkably ambivalent. He had hoped to visit the United States after his third trip to Palestine in 1899.[105] Depression and homesickness forced him to cancel his plans. In 1903 and again in 1907, he again made plans to travel to America. Yet once more, he proved unable to take the step. When offered the presidency of Dropsie College in Philadelphia, Ahad Ha-Am declined, arguing that he was not qualified to assume such an important position. Though he looked with favor on the development of Jewish cultural life in America—he was especially excited by the establishment of the Jewish Theological Seminary of America in 1902, for example—he claimed that as a Zionist he could never agree to emigrate to the United States. Ahad Ha-Am's inability even to visit America suggests more than self-doubt and a faithful adherence to Zionist principles. Like others of his generation, the American experience fascinated and confused Ahad Ha-Am. Was he afraid that he might find in the United States the seeds of a viable Jewish community in the Diaspora? Was it only flattery that led him to describe the United States in a letter to the New York Yiddish writer Abraham Reisin in 1900 as "the future center of Judaism"?[106]

Unwilling to leave Russia, Ahad Ha-Am turned his attention to the plight of the Jews of the Pale of Settlement. In 1903, the brutal pogroms in Kishinev led him for the first time to publicly demand a policy of self-defense against physical attacks on the Jewish community. It was Ahad Ha-Am who was responsible for the issuance of a flyer signed by the Union of Hebrew Writers, an informal group of the leading Jewish nationalist intellectuals of the day in Odessa, which denounced anti-Semitism. In its Conclusion the group called for a general meeting of community representatives to prepare an aggressive counterresponse and to coordinate an orderly emigration from what the flyer described as "the land of blood." So incensed was Ahad Ha-Am by the events that he demanded that each individual sign the document personally. He was livid when his proposal was rejected.[107]

Yet Ahad Ha-Am's militancy had severe limits. Shortly after the outbreak of the pogroms he left on a trip, in part because he wished to take his mind off the bloody events.[108] The flyer that he composed bore his distinctive mark. Though aggressive in tone, it opposed intercession with tsarist government officials and described internal rejuvenation and eternal vigilance as the most important means of Jewish self-defense.[109] Ahad Ha-Am took part in the elections to the Duma that followed the Revolution of 1905, yet he refused to run for office himself. He also rejected an invitation to participate in a special committee established by the Kadet party to choose a candidate for his district. The candidate he eventually supported who ran as an independent received only seventy-seven votes.[110]

Ahad Ha-Am's behavior in the period after 1905 reflected both his willful ignorance of and his disdain for politics and political compromise. In contrast to most other Jewish communal leaders, he opposed alliances with any of the general Russian parties or with any of the other national minorities that were struggling for civil equality. The Jewish plight was a distinctive one, he had argued in an essay entitled "Nishkakhot" (The Forgotten Ones), written in 1903.[111] Only the Jews were humiliated and reduced in their moral status as a result of the loss of independence. Thus, their situation could not be improved by the simple acquisition of political or legal rights. Furthermore, alliances with non-Jewish organizations and movements would create the impression that the general struggle for democracy in Russia was a Jewish invention and would lead to further outbreaks of anti-Semitism. In any event, Ahad Ha-Am concluded in a typically pessimistic manner, it was unlikely that anyone would pay attention to the plight of a small and insignificant people. The dissolution of the Duma in July 1906 seemed to corroborate his doubts. The only solution for the Jewish people, Ahad Ha-Am stated at a meeting held in Homel near his summer retreat in Reshitsa shortly after the collapse of the Russian parliament, lay in the establishment of "an independent national existence in the land of their fathers."[112]

It was Ahad Ha-Am's underlying pessimism after the Kishinev pogrom that also explains his stepped-up attacks against Herzl. He was deeply concerned that Herzl would seek to take advantage of Jewish fears by presenting a bold initiative to solve the problem of anti-Semitism. He did not have long to wait. In May 1903, one month after the bloody events in Kishinev, Herzl responded positively to a British proposal to establish an autonomous Jewish colony in East Africa (today Kenya). Ahad Ha-Am reacted with horror to the so-called Uganda Plan proposed at the Sixth Zionist Congress in late August. In its willingness to dispense with Palestine for any safe refuge, the cultural Zionist argued, the scheme only demonstrated Herzl's lack of sensitivity toward the Jewish people and his failure to understand the true meaning of the Kishinev pogroms. East European Zionists who had originally supported Herzl in 1897 should now realize the true nature of the "westerners'" program for the Jewish people. Their only recourse, Ahad Ha-Am maintained, was to demand a "bill of divorcement" from political Zionism.[113]

Herzl's East Africa proposal was qualified significantly at the congress, thanks to the protestations of the so-called Democratic Faction led by Chaim Weizmann. Nevertheless, Ahad Ha-Am's influence waned after the congress. When the Uganda proposal was first raised, the cultural Zionist had voiced the hope that the Democratic Faction would become the kernel for a movement of cultural revival directed against Herzl's program.[114] Two years earlier, he had agreed to serve as a spiritual adviser to the new group. Did he secretly hope that Weizmann's movement would become the heir to Bnei Moshe? Nevertheless, the faction's growing political savvy and influence at the Fifth Zionist Congress in late 1901 disturbed him greatly.[115] By the time of their successful struggle against the Uganda Plan in 1903, Ahad Ha-Am had reached the bitter conclusion that Weizmann and his followers had been seduced and corrupted by political power. In becoming merely another political movement, the Democratic Faction had lost its credibility as a moral force for national cultural revival.

In retrospect, it seems clear that Weizmann and his supporters were not nearly as initimidated as Ahad Ha-Am by Herzl's program. As members of a new generation of nationalist activists, they were more sensitized to the political realities of mass movements and were far more willing to ride the wave of the growing strength of East European Zionists in the hope of eventually conquering the movement from within. Increasingly, the Democratic Faction became convinced that it had to transform itself from a movement of anti-Herzl protest to a movement for concrete change. For Ahad Ha-Am, on the other hand, Uganda demonstrated the utter corruption of the Zionist movement in its political form. Yet the Democratic Faction had failed to issue it a death blow. In choosing to concentrate on practical settlement in Palestine, it had betrayed Ahad Ha-Am's dream of a generation of "new men" who would resurrect the nationalist ideal.[116] Rejected by younger activists in the group who dismissed his ideas as "transcendental nationalism" that had little relevance to political reality,[117] Ahad Ha-Am retreated to his comfortable and familiar stance of self-righteous isolationism. He summed up his attitude in the following comment taken from a rambling and vitriolic letter to Abraham Lubarsky in October 1903: "It is better for me to be alone in my own world where I am free to speak and do what is necessary; and if people choose to listen or to ignore me, it is all the same to me. If they do not listen now, they will listen eventually. I believe in the power of the truth and I am convinced that I do not speak idly. Thus my spirit will not sink even if the fools shame me a thousand times . . . and even if the hypocrites and sycophants leave me to go someplace where they will soon realize their hopes of becoming a wheel or a cog in the community machinery."[118]

Ahad Ha-Am's bitter experiences in both Russian and Jewish political life had only reinforced his profound distrust of all forms of public activity. He envied Simon Dubnow who after the failure of the struggle for civil rights was able to retreat from public life and devote himself to scholarship.[119] On a more fundamental level, he rejected the predilection of liberal Jews (and political Zionists) for precipitous action and their underlying assumptions that external events should determine the nature of Jewish thought and behavior.[120] His central and only concern was internal revival, which could only come about gradually and was not dependent on the response of the larger society in which Jews lived. Even outbursts of anti-Semitism, Ahad Ha-Am now bitterly concluded, however repellent, should not automatically trigger a Jewish response. In 1902, he had rejected a proposal to include a monthly column in *Ha-Shiloach* chronicling anti-Semitic incidents as nothing but "useless notes about ills that affect and befall us."[121] Ultimately, it was not the physical survival of Jews but the survival of Judaism that was at stake.

This was a view that Ahad Ha-Am had first espoused in 1891 in a blistering attack on French Jewry and then again seven years later during the Dreyfus Affair.[122] For the Zionist thinker, the French Jewish community's concern with the rise of anti-Semitism betrayed an obsessive fear of the attitudes of non-Jews. More tragically, it reflected their moral and intellectual "slavery" in their relations with the outside world. Why, he wondered, did western Jews think it was necessary to couch the struggle against anti-Semitism in the guise of universalism? Couldn't they find enough inner strength and self-confidence to defend their own values and thus surmount the challenge to their existence? In insisting that the assault on Jewry endangered humanity as a whole, Ahad Ha-Am argued, French Jews, and western Jewry in general, seemed to be questioning whether Jews were members of the human race. If Jews were to develop as a proud and noble nation, he had stated previously in an article written in 1893, they needed to rid themselves of the idea that they were the lowliest of creatures.[123]

Not surprisingly, therefore, Ahad Ha-Am's response to the pogroms in Odessa in October 1905 was markedly different from his reaction to Kishinev two years earlier. In 1903 he had called for militant self-defense. Two years later, he seemed mainly concerned with ensuring that he and his family be spared any physical harm. Ahad Ha-Am's letters during the period, though occasionally referring to the bloody nature of the anti-Jewish attacks, were relatively dispassionate. Much of his concern centered on travel matters associated with the position he had taken in 1903 as an accounting manager for the Wissotsky Tea Company. In his memoirs Ahad Ha-Am notes that he played a card game with his son on the night of the Odessa pogrom to drown out the shots fired by local troops and to take his mind off the riots that were occurring outside.[124] As a sign of his displeasure with the political activism of the Russian Jewish leadership, in 1905 Ahad Ha-Am resigned from the Society for the Promotion of Enlightenment among Jews in Russia. Three years earlier, he had joined with Dubnow to help the society create a modern Jewish curriculum. He now claimed that it had lost sight of its original goal in its clamor for political rights.[125] Nor did he evince much interest in the Beilis case in 1913. Commenting on the trial of a young Russian Jew accused of ritual murder, Ahad Ha-Am complained that it took up too much of the Jewish community's time. The result was that there was little opportunity to discuss any other issues of Jewish concern.[126]

After a short trip to Palestine in December 1907 to rest and to visit his daughter Leah, Ahad Ha-Am took a job as the manager of Wissotsky's branch in London. Odessa was already losing its magical attraction for the young Jewish writers who had been his disciples. In addition, many of the members of his generation, including his close friends Dubnow and Mordecai Rabinowitch (Ben-Ami), had left the city. Ahad Ha-Am was also motivated to leave Russia by the growing repressiveness of the government in the aftermath of the failed Revolution of 1905 and by the outbreak of anti-Semitic violence that followed the assassination of a police official. In May, a member of the dreaded Black Hundreds had attacked him while he was waiting for a carriage to take him home. During his stay in Palestine, tsarist police had entered his apartment (as well as those of his friends Bialik and Haim Tchernowitz) in search of firearms.[127]

At first, Ahad Ha-Am looked upon his move to the British capital with enthusiasm. After years of struggling to eke out a living, he would finally achieve a modicum of financial stability. At the very least, his move to London would allow him to escape from the personal and communal disappointments he had experienced in Russia. He was eagerly looking forward to living in a dynamic city filled with culture and interesting sites. Besides, he had always admired British intellectual life for its civility and levelheadedness. London would also afford Ahad Ha-Am an opportunity to observe close-up an East European immigrant community in the West.

Yet the Zionist thinker's fourteen years in London proved to be the bleakest and loneliest period in his life. Almost immediately upon his arrival, Ahad Ha-Am was depressed by the dank climate. His job in what he described as "the hell of London known as 'the City'" proved to be boring and tedious. Exhausted after a full day's work, he had no patience to do any serious scholarship. He was especially angered that his work prevented him from doing research in the British Museum.[128]

From the beginning of his stay, Ahad Ha-Am also developed a strong dislike for British Jews. Their gross materialism and ignorance of Jewish culture only served to reinforce his views about the degenerative nature of western Jewish assimilationism. Nor did he find much solace in the small East European immigrant Jewish community of the East End. Ahad Ha-Am had hoped to replicate in London the community of intellectuals he had left behind in Odessa. Instead, he found an undistinguished mass of revolutionaries and religionists who were more concerned with economic betterment than with enlightenment. Even the Zionist movement in London proved a great disappointment. Its leadership was largely dominated by supporters of Herzl who had little interest in participating in movements of cultural revival. The immigrant community in London, he remarked in a letter written to Yosef Klausner in 1909, was made up of "ignoramuses immersed in Yiddish socialism" and "Lithuanian 'guardians of the Torah' of the 'driest' sort." As for the Zionists of the East End, he concluded, "it is better if I don't say anything."[129]

Even the significant improvement in Ahad Ha-Am's financial situation did little to alter his mood. For the first time in his life, he was free from financial responsibilities toward his parents. Yet the physical and emotional distance from his family and old friends continued to haunt him. He was not the same person who had held court in Odessa, Bialik would later write about Ahad Ha-Am during his stay in London; "the divine presence (*shekhinah*) had departed from him."[130] As Leon Simon has remarked, for all his vaunted cosmopolitanism, Ahad Ha-Am only felt truly at home among the maskilim of Odessa who combined a respect for European culture with a deep love for traditional Judaism.[131] In reaction to his growing sense of isolation, he began to use Hebrew as his daily language. He also found solace in the religious ritual that he slowly reintroduced into his home life.

In the midst of his despair, Ahad Ha-Am's thoughts harked back to Russia. His voluminous correspondence during this period to friends he had left behind reflect both his growing concern with their fate and the impotence he felt in the face of the crises facing his native Jewish community. Many of Ahad Ha-Am's writings centered on the rise of competing ideologies and groups that were quick to take advantage of the crisis within the Zionist movement that arose after the death of Herzl in 1904. Bitterly critical of the organizers of the Czernowitz Conference in 1908, he dismissed Yiddishism as a futile effort to bolster Diaspora Jewish life. Similarly, in an essay entitled "Shlilat ha-galut" (Negation of the Diaspora) written in 1909, he attacked Simon Dubnow's autonomist theories and his defense of continued life in the Diaspora. Two years later, Ahad Ha-Am became embroiled in a bitter controversy over the espousal of Christianity by young Hebrew writers, including most notably Yosef Haim Brenner. In the same year, he continued his diatribe against efforts to place the New Testament on equal footing with the Bible and the Talmud in a review of Claude Montefiore's commentary on the Synoptic Gospels. Given Ahad Ha-Am's sense of isolation in London, the fact that Montefiore was a member of a distinguished British Jewish family must have seemed bitterly ironic. Montefiore's ideas, Ahad Ha-am argued, were only the logical extension of the western Jewish perspective, which saw Judaism merely as a religious faith that was interchangeable with any other.[132]

Ahad Ha-Am's first response to the passing of Herzl in 1904 was mild optimism. The death of the "Messiah," he noted hopefully, would return Zionism to its true path as a "movement of historical national revival." In time, however, he was forced to admit that he had been wrong. He now became convinced that the demise of Zionism's charismatic leader would actually lead to the weakening of nationalist idealism.[133] True, there were still formal differences among the various factions within the movement, Ahad Ha-Am argued, but they no longer seemed relevant in the face of the loss of leadership and Zionism's exclusive emphasis on practical settlement.[134] For all his hostility toward Herzl, the cultural Zionist clearly recognized how linked he himself was to the founder of political Zionism. In the end, they were of the same generation of dreamers who claimed to speak for the Jewish people as a whole. More important, the death of Herzl signaled the end of ideological debate within the movement. Without a formidable figure such as Herzl to oppose him, who would bother to listen to the ramblings of Ahad Ha-Am?

Ahad Ha-Am's despair over the fate of Zionism was compounded by the marriage of his second daughter, Rachel, to the Russian writer Mikhail Osorgin in 1912. As a cultural Zionist, he had always feared assimilation more than anti-Semitism. In a perverse way, his ideology had been confirmed. Yet in the face of the "betrayal" of his own daughter, how could he continue to speak out as a representative of the Zionist ideal? Ahad Ha-Am's reaction was extreme, reflecting both the depth of his personal tragedy and his unwillingness to compromise his ideals and goals. Much like the traditional Jew who sat in mourning after the conversion of a child, he could no longer regard his daughter as his own. In a letter written to the Zionist activist Moshe Smilansky on September 3, 1912, Ahad Ha-Am reaffirmed his belief in the primacy of the collectivity over the individual: "We must stand against this enemy in the name of national survival and be pitiless and unremitting in our attitudes to ourselves and to our offspring. *There can be no pity when our national survival is in danger.* The state has no daughter . . . and that is all there is to it."[135] For a while, he even stopped using the name Ahad Ha-Am and insisted that he be called Asher Ginsberg. He also ceased writing the magnum opus he had been preparing on the nature of Jewish morality.

In 1913, Ahad Ha-Am's hopes were briefly buoyed by what appeared to be a clear ideological victory over political Zionism. At the Eleventh Zionist Congress held in Vienna in 1913, the majority of the delegates all but abandoned Herzl's ideal of establishing a Jewish homeland and chose to concentrate instead on cultural issues such as the establishment of a Hebrew University in Jerusalem. Ahad Ha-Am saw it as a personal triumph. From his earliest days in London, he had helped formulate plans for the creation of a school of technology in Palestine and had actively supported the development of universities in the *yishuv*.[136] The cultural Zionist took great pride in the fact that Haim Nahman Bialik, one of his most devoted admirers, spoke at the closing session of the congress. Things were so topsy-turvy, Ahad Ha-Am gleefully remarked in a letter written soon after the congress, that the political Zionists were now accusing the majority of "Ahad Ha-Amism"![137] For the first time in his life, he even thought of becoming a member of the Zionist movement.

It was a momentary euphoria, however. The following year brought the onset of the war and the cessation of all public Jewish activity. At first, Ahad Ha-Am was too caught up in his writing to take serious note of the outbreak of war. Within a month, however, he was "in absolute despair" and could not work.[138] It was not coincidental that between 1914 and 1916, Ahad Ha-Am's only written effort aside from his voluminous correspondence was a Hebrew translation of Leon Pinsker's deeply pessimistic essay *Autoemancipation*. Like many of

his generation, Ahad Ha-Am was convinced that European civilization was in danger of collapse. The war was nothing less than "the
complete profanation of the most sacred values of civilization in the
name of national interest."[139] To the Zionist thinker, the world seemed
divided into two camps—"crazy people and those in despair."[140] Even
England, the nation that had given birth to Spencer and Mill, had
become jingoistic and bloodthirsty.[141] Although Ahad Ha-Am enter-
tained thoughts of escaping Europe and going to live in Palestine, he
hesitated out of fear that he would be unable to support himself and
that the Wissotsky branch he was managing would go bankrupt.[142]

Ahad Ha-Am was particularly concerned about the effect of the
war on Jewry. The fact that he was in London, far removed from the
devastation and from the masses of Jews in Russia, only increased his
frustration and sense of helplessness. In his loneliness, he recalled
the heroic vision of Moses and Isaiah who denounced the
assimilationism of past Jewish slaves and rulers in the name of spiritual values. Ahad Ha-Am could not understand the stampede of
European Jews to defend their nations' honor in battle. Such efforts "to be more royalist than the king," he argued, meant that few
Jews were prepared to hold up "the banner of truth and justice that
was bequeathed to us by the Prophets."[143] Unlike both Dubnow
and Zhitlowski, Ahad Ha-Am opposed the convening of an international Jewish conference as a useless exercise in public relations. In
rote-like manner and with little conviction, he continued to insist
that only an internal Jewish revival would save the Jewish people.[144]
At the same time, he was bitterly critical of Jewish leaders who refused to speak the truth in public out of fear for their positions or
institutions. What the world longs for, Ahad Ha-Am wrote to a supporter in 1919, was a powerful leader who would stand up and tell
the truth regardless of the consequences.[145] Despite pleas from his
supporters, however, he felt unworthy of the task. The "holy spirit"
had left him and he could not muster the energy and courage to "go
out and prophesy in the [Jewish] camp."[146] During the entire war,
Ahad Ha-Am adamantly refused to speak in public. Instead, he insisted on maintaining what he called "a sickness of silence."[147]

Unlike his fellow Zionists, Ahad Ha-Am did not believe that the
war would bring the fulfillment of their dream. Despite his conviction that the plight of Jewry deserved a central place in the world's
moral consciousness, he did not expect that a postwar peace confer-

ence would devote any time to the "Jewish question." Nor did he place much faith in the willingness of the British government to grant Jews favors in recognition for their active involvement in the war effort.[148] Nevertheless, at the urging of Weizmann, who continued to regard the cultural Zionist as his mentor, Ahad Ha-Am played an important role in shaping the policy of the British Zionist movement in its negotiations with the English government. He was quick to recognize the profoundly ironic nature of his activity. After years of bitter opposition to Herzl's program, he was now openly working toward a political solution to the "Jewish problem."[149]

Ahad Ha-Am's efforts seemed to find fruition with the issuance of the Balfour Declaration in 1917. Yet he continued to voice doubts that the Jewish people were prepared for the task of establishing a Jewish homeland in Palestine. His pessimism was also motivated by the conflicting designs of the Great Powers on the Middle East, the hostility of anti-Zionist elements within the Jewish community, and the generally negative response of the native Arab population. In the face of the numerous obstacles that stood in the way of the fulfillment of the political Zionist's dream, Ahad Ha-Am remained convinced that those who envisioned the building of a Jewish state after the cessation of hostilities were committing the same fatal error as the original proponent of a political solution to the plight of Jewry. Like Herzl, they were guilty of engaging in "messianic" delusions.[150]

Like Dubnow, Ahad Ha-Am enthusiastically welcomed the March Revolution in Russia. It was his fondest hope that the "wonderful events" in his homeland would spread peace and justice throughout the world. By the summer of 1917, however, Ahad Ha-Am was already troubled by the impact of a federal structure, with its ominous intimations of centralized control, upon the rights of Jews. Though geographical distance and lack of firsthand information prevented him from commenting directly on the events of the Bolshevik Revolution, he correctly predicted that the violence in Russia in the aftermath of the Communist takeover would trigger further pogroms.[151]

By 1921, Ahad Ha-Am had become totally disenchanted with Jewish life in Europe. When the German edition of *Al parshat derakhim* was published to rave reviews in the early part of the year, he could only respond weakly. His only comment was that at least his ties with the public had not been severed. In December, Ahad Ha-Am decided that the time had come for him to settle in Palestine.[152] By now, he was gravely ill with a severe neurological disorder that prevented him from working or reading for any length of time. His friend Dubnow had hoped that the "sun of the Land of Israel" would relieve both his physical ailment and his debilitating pessimism. Ahad Ha-Am displayed little emotionalism about his aliyah, however, viewing Palestine more as a final resting place than as a source of physical and psychological renewal. "I wish to live in Erets Yisrael and to die there," he had written in 1916, "so that in my last moments I will know in my soul that I have finished my work in the place where my heart has been all of my life."[153] This was in sharp contrast to his reactions toward his first trip to Palestine in 1891, when he had expressed awe and wonderment with its natural beauty and talked hopefully about the future of Jewish colonization.

Unlike many of his fellow Zionist activists, Ahad Ha-am chose to live in Tel Aviv. He had always enjoyed urban life and Tel Aviv offered the promise of living in the first modern Jewish city. Like Odessa, Tel Aviv also provided him the opportunity to live by the sea. He never considered settling in Jerusalem. While recognizing its pivotal role as a spiritual center, he regarded it as too provincial and dominated by religious fanatics. Collective farms and villages, many of which had been created originally by Hibbat Zion, appealed to him even less.

Yet life in the *yishuv* offered Ahad Ha-Am little sense of self-fulfillment. His cultural programs were no match for the proposals of socialist and practical Zionism whose ranks swelled as a result of the Second Aliyah that occurred between 1905 and 1914. What solution could his lofty ideals of spiritual renewal offer to the pressing needs of struggling agricultural settlements in Palestine? Never particularly supportive of socialism, Ahad Ha-Am found it difficult to identify with the radical perspectives of the young settlers. At the same time, memories of his earlier attack on Brenner and his vitriolic debates with members of Ha-Poel ha-Tsa'ir (Young Worker's Movement) during a visit to Palestine in 1911 made the socialist community distrustful of his overtures.[154]

Ahad Ha-Am was also troubled by the growing tensions between Arabs and Jews in Palestine. It was a conflict that he was convinced had deep roots and that was fundamentally irreconcilable. Already in the 1890s he had questioned the early Jewish colonists' insistence on hiring Arab labor. Yet he was no more supportive of the Second Aliyah's trumpeting of "Jewish labor" in the period before World War

I. All such attempts to create a "new Jewish type" in Palestine, he wrote, were merely "childish actions and quixotic heroism" that in excluding Arab workers from gainful employment would only alienate the native population.[155] Ahad Ha-Am was convinced that only British military control prevented the two populations from attacking each other. If there was a solution, he maintained, it lay in achieving a modus vivendi with the Arabs through the sharing of sovereignty and land. True to his convictions, in 1920 Ahad Ha-Am advocated the establishment of a binational confederation after the expiration of the British mandate.[156]

With each passing year, the aging ideologue grew more convinced that he could no longer contribute to the revival of Jewry. Increasingly, he found it difficult to do any serious writing. Unable to compose the great work on Jewish ethics that he had so desperately wished to publish all of his life, Ahad Ha-Am spent most of his time in his small Tel Aviv apartment preparing his letters for publication. Certain that he was growing old and useless, he stopped reading books and only glanced at newspapers. In moments of deep depression, he would even long for London, "her streets and markets teeming with people." For Ahad Ha-Am, such desires were manifestations of "a clear sign of a sickness nestled in my spirit."[157] In many ways, as Bialik would later remark sadly, during the last decade of his life Asher Ginsberg had ceased to be Ahad Ha-Am.[158]

In 1923, a physically frail and demoralized Ahad Ha-Am returned to Europe for what he was convinced would be his last visit with friends and relatives. He had hoped to see Dubnow in Berlin but was warned that Communist-led riots made it too dangerous to journey to the German capital. For the first time, Ahad Ha-Am now felt strangely aloof from the world he had left behind. Yet his return to Palestine brought him little comfort. His writings on Zionism became more and more pessimistic as his own health declined. Overwhelmed by the development of new colonies and the continued influx of radical elements during the Third Aliyah of 1919–20, Ahad Ha-Am continued to express fears that the Zionist dream was rapidly losing out to the struggle for socialism and Communism within the *yishuv*.[159] In an attempt to counter the growth of radical movements, the aging Zionist activist even went so far as to run unsuccessfully for the municipal council of Tel Aviv under the banner of the rightist General Zionist party. Conflating personal and collective concerns as he had done so many times in the past, Ahad Ha-Am viewed the socialist Zionists' emphasis on material concerns as a direct threat both to his authority as a founder of modern Jewish nationalism and to the spiritual vitality of the Jewish people. As he commented to a group of comrades who visited him in Tel Aviv shortly before his death: "Rekindle the holy fire, for if it goes out, the young people will leave you, flee from you, even spit upon you. Without the sacred fire burning in their heart, what is there for them here and who is to hold them? If this fire is extinguished, what use will they have for this wasteland? Did they come here to earn fifteen *grush*[pennies] a day and to eat black bread?"[160]

Well-wishers continued to flock to Ahad Ha-Am's home in Tel Aviv on his birthdays, so many in fact that police had to close off the street where he lived to traffic. Yet as always he remained terribly isolated and alone. By the summer of 1926, Ahad Ha-Am's physical condition had deteriorated and he was now having difficulty walking. He was, in the words of Bialik, "a broken and shattered vessel."[161] For a while, he took slim hope in Dubnow's promise that the Jewish historian would visit him in Palestine in 1928. He would barely live to see the new year, however. On January 1, 1927, Ahad Ha-Am died peacefully at his home in Tel Aviv at the age of seventy-one.

Ahad Ha-Am shared with both Zhitlowski and Dubnow the firm conviction that the Jewish people could not successfully confront the challenges of modern life without first creating a new basis for Jewish existence. Like his two contemporaries, he drew primarily on the sociobiological theories of Herbert Spencer and other positivists of the late nineteenth century to find an alternative to a religious definition of Jewish life. In his view, the Jewish people were not some metaphysical "chosen" nation but a living organism whose physical survival over the course of the centuries could be explained by what he described as its innate "will to live." Yet Ahad Ha-Am was far too wedded to the distinctiveness of Jewry to be satisfied with an explanation that attributed its triumph over adversity to immutable universal laws and processes. Nor could he accept a definition of Jewish existence that was largely instinctual and that limited itself to the struggle for physical survival. Most important, Ahad Ha-Am recognized that an emphasis on biological determinism would eliminate the need for any ideological or cultural principle in defining Jewish identity and would deny the importance of creative leadership in guiding the nation toward the realization of its goals.

Not surprisingly, therefore, Ahad Ha-Am was viscerally opposed to all materialist explanations of Jewish life. Marxist notions of "economic interests" and "material conditions," he argued, could never explain the survival of the Jewish people in the face of persecution and oppression.[162] For the same reasons, he displayed remarkably little interest in the structural and behavioral dynamics of the Jewish community over the ages. Even Dubnow's analysis of the historical evolution of the Jewish community as the source of its inner strength and resilience struck Ahad Ha-Am as too contingent and too focused on the temporal exigencies of Jewish life. Though he was enamored of social evolutionist thought, he could not accept its deterministic view that the maturing of any society inevitably led first to its growing heterogeneity and then to its eventual demise. For Ahad Ha-Am, Jews were an eternal people who could never die as long as they remained true to their spiritual ideals. More than a mere physical organism, economic force, or social grouping, Jewry contained within it a "national creative power." Like a tree that continued to bear fruit even when it was planted in foreign soil, he maintained, the Jews' inner strength enabled the people not only to survive but to continue to develop its ideals and character, even in the face of adversity.[163]

It was Ahad Ha-Am's ambivalence about the subjective and objective elements of Jewish survival that explains why he never clearly explained his concept of the "will to live." The issue was not simply theoretical. Ahad Ha-Am clearly recognized that the question of the dynamics of Jewish survival was an important bone of contention in the ongoing debate between religious traditionalists and assimilationists within the Jewish community. In offering an explanation that allegedly incorporated both internal and external factors, he hoped to demonstrate the underlying untruth of the two extreme views as well as to forge a distinctive position of his own. The result was that Ahad Ha-Am generally tailored his definition of the Jewish "will to live" to fit his immediate needs. At times, he seemed to refer to it as an instinctual reflex similar to the animal's innate struggle for survival. Jewish identity was a biological reality whose purpose was to guarantee the collective future, not a question of individual belief, he had argued in an essay written in 1891 that attacked the western religious reform movement.[164] More often than not, however, Ahad

Ha-Am stressed the role of the conscious will of individual Jews in ensuring the nation's continued existence. No people could survive merely through the influence of external forces such as biology or a divine being, he had claimed in an essay written in 1898 attacking both political radicalism and Orthodoxy.[165]

In the end, Ahad Ha-Am insisted that Jewish identity was a matter of both biology and psychology, a form of the collective unconscious characterized by shared beliefs that linked Jews in both space and time but that could only be actualized by the willful decision of individuals. Nation building depended not only on the objective conditions associated with physical well-being but also on the development of a common memory and the shaping of a shared dream for the future. In turn, the nation's firm hold on its past and future would enable it to absorb creative ideas in neighboring societies without sacrificing its own integrity and distinctiveness. Through a process that Ahad Ha-Am never fully explained, the collective Jewish will would monitor the absorption of external cultural elements, incorporating those that complemented the values and ideals of the nation and rejecting those that contradicted them.[166]

In adopting a view of Jewish survival that stressed the central role of both the collective unconscious and individual will, Ahad Ha-Am called for the need to differentiate between those elements in contemporary Jewish life that fostered national development and those that were no longer relevant to the nation's continued growth. In so doing, he was able to reject many aspects of tradition as outdated without necessarily condemning the Jewish past in toto.[167] At the same time, he seemed to wish to retain the certainty and permanency of Jewish identity that a religious explanation of Jewish survival afforded while dispensing with its theological trappings.[168] Like the traditional Jew, he was convinced of the deeply rooted nature of a collective Jewish consciousness. Lacking a belief in revelation, however, he could not clearly explain its origins and development. Nor did Ahad Ha-Am express much interest in discussions of the origins of Jewish society. Rejecting both traditional and scientific explanations for the genesis of Jewish peoplehood, he could never adequately answer the question of why the "will to live" was stronger in Jews than in other peoples who had not survived. As he stated in the conclusion to his article "Al shte ha-se'ipim" (Of Two Opinions): "No history has yet been written that can explain in a convincing manner how it can happen that a distinctive religious and cultural perspective could arise within a small nation in a corner of Asia, a perspective that had such a significant influence on the rest of the world while at the same time remaining so alien to the rest of the world that to this day it is unable to conquer the world or to be conquered by it. This entire historical vision, despite the many explanations that have been offered, remains a question mark."[169]

Ahad Ha-Am's theory of Jewish development not only had to explain the survival of the Jewish people in the past. It also had to justify its continued collective identity in the future. The key was the Jewish inner spirit, the compendium of Jewish wisdom and ethical precepts that both sustained the Jewish people and explained its distinctiveness among the peoples of the world. For much of their history, Ahad Ha-Am argued, Jews had embodied their "national creative power" in the beliefs and practices of Judaism. Ultimately, however, religious beliefs were nothing but a reflection of the inner hopes and dreams of the Jewish people translated into the language and form of biblical Israel.[170] Such attitudes had become so deeply obscured by the overpowering nature of religious tradition that individual members of the Jewish people were often unconscious of their existence. What lay beneath the "trappings" of religious belief and practice, Ahad Ha-Am maintained, was an existential core, a "national ethic" that placed morality at the center of human existence. "True" Judaism thus was not a specific belief but rather a special relationship to life's values that had meaning and relevance for all of humanity.[171]

For Ahad Ha-Am, the purest reflection of the "national ethic" was to be found in the writings and actions of biblical leaders and Prophets. Individuals like Moses, Isaiah, and Jeremiah had taught the Jewish people to honor the spirit rather than physical strength. In preaching commitment to both absolute righteousness and the nation, Ahad Ha-Am claimed, they had ensured the survival of Jewry throughout the centuries and had validated its claim to be a "special" people. At the same time, the actions of the biblical leaders illustrated the complex interplay between individual desires and the general will of the people that was necessary for the survival of the Jewish people in the future. It was the powerful personality of the Prophets, which was directed not toward the realization of selfish desires but toward ensuring the well-being of the nation, that explained their honored place in Jewish tradition.[172]

Ahad Ha-Am's analysis of the development of Jewish culture and thought rested on a highly selective and often tenuous reading of the Bible and the Prophets. In his desire to distance himself from the views of religious Orthodoxy, he insisted that the origins of Judaism lay not in its belief in God but in its adherence to absolute justice. At most, he was willing to accept the concept of a "God idea" that embodied the purest form of Jewish values and ideals. The principle of monotheism, he maintained, which was the Jews' major contribution to humanity, was significant not for its theological implications but because it served as an underpinning for the demand for one standard of justice. Ahad Ha-Am was equally insistent that the biblical Prophets stressed ethical behavior over religious ritual, an interpretation that paralleled the view of both nineteenth-century Christian biblical scholars and Jewish religious reformers. Yet he went even further than individuals like Julius Wellhausen and Abraham Geiger in deliberately ignoring the Prophet's self-professed role as the expostulator of God's truth. Instead, he imposed a "secular" interpretation that stressed the Prophets' ability to unerringly reflect the deepest sentiments of the Jewish people.[173]

Like both Zhitlowski and Dubnow, Ahad Ha-Am associated the rise of Judaism with the Diaspora. In similar terms, he argued that the Jewish people's "will to live" and "national creative power" were most severely tested after their exile from the Holy Land. For the first time, Jews not only faced the danger of physical disappearance; they had also suffered the loss of those very ideals that had sustained them in the past. What resulted was the creation of a rigid code of laws and rituals that enabled Jewry to maintain its status as a separate people living among an often hostile majority culture.

Whatever one's personal beliefs, Ahad Ha-Am argued, one could not deny that religious law provided the foundation for traditional Judaism. The problem was that Jews in the Diaspora had come to associate religious belief and practice with the essence of Jewish life. The result was that the decline of religious belief and practice in the nineteenth century necessarily led to a weakening in Jewry's commitment to the national ideal. According to Ahad Ha-Am, modern Jews had to recognize that religion was only an instrument for national survival and not the purpose of Jewish existence. Religious belief and practice thus had no intrinsic value; they were merely a means to an end. In one of his most famous statements, Ahad Ha-Am illustrated the role of religious ritual by emphasizing the importance of the Sabbath in maintaining Jewish collective consciousness and a commitment to Jewish ideals: "One can say without any exaggeration that more than Israel has kept the Sabbath, the Sabbath has kept [the Jewish people]. Without a weekly respite, Jews would have sunk into intellectual and moral depths and descended into the basest form of materialism."[174]

Thus while it was impossible to be a Jew in the religious sense without acknowledging one's nationality, Ahad Ha-am maintained, one could still be a Jew in the national sense without necessarily accepting religious belief.[175] Indeed, he was convinced that in many ways the freethinking Jew was more committed to the national spirit than the religious one. Unlike the Orthodox Jew, the atheist recognized that the creative power of the nation derived from inner forces rather than from the benevolence of a higher power. While the observant Jew sought to rigidly maintain the religious traditions of the past, Ahad Ha-Am argued, the freethinker understood that the responsibility for the Jewish future rested with the present generation. Nevertheless, despite their differences over the source and development of the Jews' unique national spirit, Ahad Ha-Am concluded, both the believer and the nonbeliever shared the same goal—the need to love and respect their people's "national treasures."[176]

Like many of his contemporaries, Ahad Ha-Am fervently believed that Jewish rituals and practices would not long survive the confrontation of Jews with modernity. Like the Prophets who envisioned the "end of days," he was convinced that the progress of humanity would ultimately lead to the divorcement of the Jewish ethical idea from its religious core. Borrowing from the ideas of John Stuart Mill whom he so admired, Ahad Ha-Am maintained that it was the continued development of a moral sense among Jews that would transform religious belief and practice. The result would be that both the religious and the freethinking Jew would eventually unite in their commitment to the Jewish people. It was a reality that Ahad Ha-Am believed was already evident in the rise of nationalist sentiment among both traditionalists and secular Jews within the East European Jewish community but that had been largely ignored among the polarized populations of Orthodox and assimilating Jews in the West.[177]

Yet Ahad Ha-Am was too wedded to his own religious background, too much of a believer in the power of the past over the present, and too concerned about the danger of alienating the rabbinical establishment in both Russia and Palestine to reject Judaism outright. For all his hostility toward what he was he was convinced was the numbing effect of religious tradition on the struggle for national renewal, Ahad Ha-Am was insistent on the need to recognize the role of Judaism as a powerful influence in the development of the Jewish people. Judaism could not be reduced to an infallible dogma as the Orthodox believed, however. It was not enough to observe religious commandments. One also had to understand the underlying spirituality that informed ritual and belief. In keeping with the teachings of the Musar movement that his mother had shared with him in his childhood, Ahad Ha-Am praised those Russian rabbis like Rabbi Mordechai Eliasberg who supported Hibbat Zion and who sought to convince nonbelieving Jews of the need for religious belief and practice through model behavior rather than through coercion. At the same time, he welcomed the attacks leveled by the anti-Zionist Orthodox rabbinate against his proposals. Unlike most Jews who ignored the call of Jewish nationalism, they clearly recognized the true significance and importance of the Zionist experiment.[178]

Despite his opposition to much of Jewish tradition, Ahad Ha-Am was insistent that Judaism could not be changed piecemeal to fit changing external realities. The only alterations he could accept in religious belief and practice were those that arose naturally out of the "developing ethical spirit" of the people.[179] As with the development of halakhah itself in the period after the Exile, religious reform could only come about spontaneously and not through rational decision making or the desperate attempt to imitate the majority culture. In any case, Ahad Ha-Am insisted that such changes should never interfere with those who wished to maintain traditional belief and ritual.[180]

Like Zhitlowski and Dubnow, Ahad Ha-Am's links with classical Judaism and his desire to unite religious and secular Jews in the national effort led him to redefine rather than to dismiss core religious beliefs. Thus, for example, he explained the Jewish idea of the Chosen People as implying a distinctive moral obligation rather than the need to dominate others. It was the Jewish people's reliance on moral values, not the hand of God or political authority, that had given power to a powerless people.[181] Ahad Ha-Am was unwilling to tamper with Jewish ritual, however. For the time being at least, the "shell" of Judaism had to be maintained along with its ethical core. In a community wracked with ideological divisions and confused about its direction, he argued, traditional beliefs and practices could serve as important unifying symbols. Under certain circumstances, they could also be used by committed nationalists to create new forms for the expression of Jewish ideals and values.[182]

Though sharing the Reform movement's concern with the ethical principles of Judaism, Ahad Ha-Am nevertheless made sure to distance himself from its notion of a Jewish "mission" to humanity. As noted earlier, he could not accept the idea that the Prophets were messengers of God who had chosen the Jewish people to be a "light unto the nations." Yet how could Ahad Ha-Am speak about the exemplary nature of Jewish values without linking the fate of Jewry with humanity as a whole? Like Dubnow, the cultural Zionist attempted to avoid the paradox by seeking refuge in historicism. No nation is preordained for a specific purpose, he maintained, though historical development could shape a distinct role for a people in the community of nations. As in the individual case of Ahad Ha-Am, Jewry had been defined by history as "a people who stand alone," a nation that fulfilled its historical task by separating itself from the rest of the world in order to defend its own distinctive vision of humanity. The Prophets had instinctively understood this; hence their prediction of an end of days when the nations would come to Zion. There was no need for the Jews to actively proselytize. The criterion for evaluating the success of the spiritual ideal was not its dissemination to the world at large but the survival of the Jewish nation.[183]

Given the troubled history of Bnei Moshe, it is unlikely that Ahad Ha-Am ever believed that his guarded attempt to "secularize" religious beliefs and practices would mollify Orthodox opposition. What he was clearly unprepared for, however, was the negative response to his views from a group of his own potential supporters within the Russian Jewish intelligentsia. The debate between Ahad Ha-am and the *tse'irim*, or "Young Ones" as they were called, lasted almost two decades. It deserves to be examined in detail since it highlights the profound contradictions in the cultural Zionist's own thought concerning the relationship between religious tradition and modern Jewish identity. At the same time, the debate points up the inability of transitional thinkers like Ahad Ha-Am to create an effective cadre among the next generation of Jewish nationalists to carry on their ideas.

Ahad Ha-Am first met the members of the *tse'irim* in Odessa in 1893 at a meeting of young Jewish writers who were interested in founding a Hebrew journal. Many of the young activists, including most notably Micha Berdichevsky and Yosef Haim Brenner, responded enthusiastically to his call for cultural revival through the Hebrew language and Hebrew literature. A year earlier, Berdichevsky had praised Ahad Ha-Am's collection of essays entitled *Perurim* (Fragments) as a model of clarity that could be compared to the classic works of Jewish literature.[184] Yet the agenda of the *tse'irim* was decidedly different from that of the cultural Zionist. While Ahad Ha-Am sought to find the core ideals embedded in Jewish tradition, individuals like Berdichevsky and Brenner desired nothing less than the transformation of Jewish values.

Desperately searching for a receptive audience for his ideas, Ahad Ha-Am seems to have misunderstood or deliberately misread the true intentions of the *tse'irim* almost from the beginning. In a highly emotional piece he wrote in *Ha-Shiloach* after their first meeting, for example, he praised the desire of young intellectuals "who recognize . . . that the solution to the cultural problem in our midst will not come from an external mingling of Jewishness and humanistic ideas and the granting of 'equal rights' to the latter in our literature but rather through the incorporation of general culture into the core of Judaism." In so doing, he claimed, they recognized that European culture can serve "as a helpmate . . . in the development of our independent understanding and knowledge of our mission in the future." Though recognizing the radical implications of the program of individuals like Berdichevsky and Brenner, Ahad Ha-Am congratulated them for their willingness to "speak politely and humbly" in support of the centrality of Jewish values in any program of national rejuvenation.[185]

It took a while for the *tse'irim* to muster enough courage to break with the Zionist thinker. Ahad Ha-Am firmly believed that he had found in the group yet another worthy replacement for Bnei Moshe. As his many letters written to Berdichevsky during this period attest, he insisted on seeing himself as a spiritual mentor to members of the rebellious group, a position that struck many of them as overly paternalistic. Relations between the Zionist thinker and the *tse'irim* were exacerbated still further after Ahad Ha-Am assumed total editorial control over *Ha-Shiloach*. He now urged them to moderate their criticism of traditional Judaism and to present their ideas in a clearer, more structured, and grammatically correct form. It was an approach that was bound to anger young writers eager to find their ideas in print yet unwilling to compromise their principles.[186]

In time, the *tse'irim* began to distance themselves from Ahad Ha-Am's fundamental philosophical views as well. Especially irksome was the Zionist thinker's constant emphasis on traditional Jewish values. In contrast to Ahad Ha-Am's obsession with the religious and ethical principles of early Jewish civilization, the young writers saw the biblical period as an age of activism and paganism whose events and ideas had been distorted and sanitized by later prophetic and rabbinic teaching. It was for this reason that Berdichevsky dismissed Ahad Ha-Am's notion of a distinctive and absolute Jewish national ethic. As the historian of Zionism Anita Shapira has argued, for members of the younger generation "[i]deas about a Chosen People smacked of misplaced complacency, especially in reference to a people universally scorned and abused."[187] The times called not for a redefinition of a Judaism, the *tse'irim* argued, but for the eradication of traditional beliefs in order to liberate the vitalist forces that lay within the Jewish "soul." In the view of Berdichevsky and his circle, Jewish history had to be seen as a chronicle of naked power rather than a reflection of innate spiritual values.

Carrying Ahad Ha-Am's "evolutionist" theories to their logical extreme, the *tse'irim* maintained that there was no such thing as a set body of principles that defined Jewry. History clearly demonstrated that Jews had constantly reinterpreted their collective ideals over the course of centuries in often diametrically opposed ways. To define Judaism in terms of an ancient set of immutable principles, they maintained, was to deny Jews the limitless freedom that lay before them as they emerged from the ghetto.[188] The result was that the Young Ones conceptualized their identity in a totally different manner than the members of the transitional generation. As Bialik described the division between the two generations, whereas individuals like Ahad Ha-Am employed concepts from "the dictionary of the past," such as Judaism, culture, nation, history, science, and progress, Brenner and Berdichevsky used terminology taken from "the dictionary of the present," including art, creativity, individualism, mysticism, and revolution.[189]

Ultimately, writers like Berdichevsky saw Ahad Ha-Am as mired in confusion and contradiction. On the one hand, the Zionist thinker expressed disdain for many aspects of modern European culture and derided those Jews who sought to incorporate non-Jewish values into Jewish life. On the other, his obsession with the centrality of ethics, much like the perspective of religious reformers, would seem to lead inevitably to the affirmation of universalist values. After all, the *tse'irim* cynically maintained, didn't Ahad Ha-Am constantly harp on the distinctive contribution of Jewry to humanity?[190]

In the view of the Young Ones, Ahad Ha-Am's insistence on the uniqueness of the Jewish "spirit" created a false dichotomy between Jewish and human concerns and thus restricted Jewish creativity and spontaneity. In contrast, the *tse'irim* preferred to rest Jewish nationalism on the only distinctive criteria that did not demand conformity with communal norms at the expense of the concerns of humanity as a whole—land and language. Yet Berdichevsky and his colleagues had little in common with Jewish political radicals like Haim Zhitlowski. Their trumpeting of universalism in Jewish life served merely as a backdrop for their true concern—a Nietzschean reaffirmation of the self. Ultimately, their goal was not the replacement of Judaism with a modern Jewish identity but the creation of a new Jew who defied all conventions in the name of individualism and activism. As Brenner proclaimed defiantly in 1909: "Have we still not recognized that God, all the gods, have died? Yes, they have died . . . and are gone forever and with them their laws, their commandments, their ordinances."[191]

Ahad Ha-Am's response to the attacks by the *tse'irim* was at once bitter and wistful. It was also marked by a characteristic contradiction in his view of his relationship to the Jewish community. Ahad Ha-Am's exaggerated sense of self-importance had originally led him to overestimate the young rebels' response to his calls to join in a program of cultural renewal. Realizing his mistake, the Zionist thinker was now convinced that a generation that had once sat at his feet had deserted its master. At the same time, however, Ahad Ha-Am feared that the writings of such young upstarts speaking in the language of cultural renewal threatened the gains he had made in introducing his ideas into communal life. For all his talk of prophetic isolation, Ahad Ha-Am clearly prided himself on his editorship of Achiasaf and *Ha-Shiloach*, his work on behalf of the Society for the Promotion of Enlightenment among Jews in Russia, and his participation in the special committee on culture established by the First Zionist Congress.[192]

Ahad Ha-Am initiated his counterattack in 1895 in an article entitled "Shinui ha-orkhin" (Transformation of Values). In the essay, he attacked the *tse'irim* for their slavish imitation of faddish ideologies in European society and for their rejection of traditional Jewish culture and values.[193] In two later articles—a critique of Jewish "Nietzscheans" published in 1899 and a review of Claude Montefiore's book *The Synoptic Gospels* published in 1910—the Zionist thinker rejected the underlying view of the younger generation that Jewish values had little relevance to human concerns. The only way in which Jews could achieve their humanity, Ahad Ha-Am maintained, was by first discovering their distinctiveness as a separate people. Judaism, after all, was nothing but "humanity in a Jewish form."[194]

Ahad Ha-Am's polemical attack was countered by the poet Yosef Brenner in an article that appeared at the end of 1910 in *Poel ha-Tsa'ir* (The Young Worker), a socialist Hebrew newspaper published in Tel Aviv.[195] Brenner had been one of the most vociferous opponents of Ahad Ha-Am among the *tse'irim*. At a meeting between the two men held in London shortly before the publication of Brenner's article, the young intellectual had purposely arrived late and had scornfully dismissed Ahad Ha-Am's suggested emendations.[196] Brenner was also motivated to respond to the Zionist thinker as part of a general debate that was currently raging in the *yishuv* over the question of whether Christianity was an advancement over Judaism. In 1897, a group of Jewish converts to Christianity had asked to participate in the First Zionist Congress but were rejected by Herzl. In 1908–9, two Jewish intellectuals in Palestine, Shai Hurwitz and Shimon Menachem Lazar, created a scandal when they suggested that in many ways Christianity was superior to Judaism.

Brenner decided to use his article to lash out at all those including Ahad Ha-Am who insisted on synthesizing traditional Jewish religious values with the quest for a modern Jewish identity. The essay was highlighted by a scathing attack on Jewish religious practice and belief as creations of the "rotten" Diaspora. For both practical and principled reasons, Brenner argued, the Zionist movement should not shun those Jewish supporters who had converted to Christianity. It was certainly no worse than traditional Judaism, which restricted individual creativity and limited the development of national consciousness. While denouncing opportunistic converts as traitors to the nation, Brenner insisted that only the committed individual could define his Jewish identity. There could be no limitations or obligations placed on such an intensely personal decision.[197]

In his caustic response to Brenner written in *Ha-Shiloach*, Ahad Ha-Am reiterated his contention that religion was a central factor in

the survival of the Jewish people.[198] The existence of God might not
be a literal truth but its mythic significance was undeniable and in-
controvertible for all nationalist Jews. Even an atheistic nationalist
had to recognize the centrality of the Jewish deity, "that historical
force that has given life to our nation and has influenced its spiritual
character and development over thousands of years." All Jewish nationalists had to recognize that religious writings were not simply
literature; they were part of the "national sancta" that transcended
the time in which they were written. To argue otherwise was to play
into the hands of Christian missionaries who were eager to gain a
foothold in the *yishuv*. Ahad Ha-Am was also bitterly critical of what
he regarded as the irresponsible demand of the *tse'irim* for "free
speech" at all costs. In denigrating Judaism, radical freethinkers in
the *yishuv* were biting the hand of the practicing Jews in the Diaspora
that "fed" them. Vicious attacks on traditional Judaism within the
Palestinian Jewish community, Ahad Ha-Am argued, would only serve
the interests of the Turkish government which would point to their
diatribes as proof of the *yishuv*'s inability to govern itself. The revolutionary idealism of the Young Ones, he maintained, was a sham. In
the end, Brenner and his supporters were as corrupt as the Jewish
official in Kiev who was ready to take money from the kosher meat
tax fund in order to strengthen the local police.[199]

Ahad Ha-Am claimed to find support in his struggle against the
ideological extremism of both traditionalists and youthful Nietzscheans
in the writings of Maimonides, known as the Rambam. In an article
written in 1905, he attempted to apply the medieval Jewish thinker's
perspective to the wave of irrationalism that he believed was sweeping
over the Jewish community at the turn of the century.[200] In contrast
to modern-day Orthodox rabbis, Ahad Ha-Am argued, Maimonides
was solely concerned with the purpose of truth and how it could be
used to help individuals attain their true potential as rational human
beings. Unlike end-of-century prophets of radical individualism like
Friedrich Nietzsche who were so popular among young Jewish intellectuals, however, the Rambam believed that the search for truth could
take place only within the context of a collectivity. Only participation
in the nation could allow the individual to realize his true purpose in
life, in part because it was the only sphere in which meaningful intellectual activity could take place, in part because it offered posterity for
the individual. Like Ahad Ha-Am himself, Maimonides thus stood

midpoint in the wrenching debate between traditionalists and modernizers, between those who emphasized the power of collective authority and those who stressed the importance of the individual.

Ahad Ha-Am was clearly uncomfortable with the fact that for all his defense of rationalism, Maimonides remained throughout his life a fervent believer in biblical Judaism. His weak response was that the medieval thinker may simply have been too young to attempt to create a new religious form that would embody his new approach to Judaism. With an eye to his own situation, Ahad Ha-Am also suggested that the Rambam's continued reliance on rabbinic Judaism reflected his recognition of the need to guard himself against the vengeful wrath of traditionalists in the community. In his most important works such as the *Mishneh Torah*, for example, Maimonides had cleverly introduced his ideas about the "true," that is, rational, meaning of Judaism into traditional textual analyses of a sacred text. Ultimately, Ahad Ha-Am argued, the Rambam believed that religion was subordinate to reason. As the Zionist thinker tendentiously summarized the central message of Maimonides's work *Moreh Nevukhim* (Guide to the Perplexed): "Pursue . . . reason on its own terms. And interpret religion in a manner that is compatible with reason. Because [the pursuit of] reason is the goal of man and religion is only a means to that end."[201]

As with the biblical Moses, Ahad Ha-Am saw significant parallels between his own views and those of Maimonides. Like the Zionist thinker, Maimonides remained neutral on the issue of the "truth" of Judaism. In contrast to other Jewish medieval scholars (and Ahad Ha-Am's modern-day Orthodox critics), the Rambam did not believe that it was possible to explain why the Jews were chosen by God. His major concern was to demonstrate how religion served as a "fortress," uniting the Jewish people in the Diaspora by embodying the basic principles of Jewish thought in a simplified form.[202] Ultimately, Ahad Ha-Am claimed, Maimonides believed that the purpose of Judaism was to provide the means whereby the masses could understand the fundamental ethical truths of the Jewish people that were first preached by the Prophets. Such truths were eternal and could not be changed by individuals according to their own personal whims. Through them, the Jewish people would create a society in which the "rule of the intellect" would dominate. In this manner, Ahad Ha-Am argued, Maimonides resolved an important dilemma confronting many late-nineteenth-century Jewish nationalists—how to combine a belief in elitist leadership with a commitment to the community. In his conclusion, Ahad Ha-Am summarized the medieval thinker's goals in terms that mirrored his perception of his own role in late-nineteenth-century Russia: "[T]o make Judaism worthy of its dual mission: . . . on the one hand, to reveal to the entire nation in a clear manner 'the true ideas' contained in the Torah; and on the other—to extricate the practical commandments (mitzvot) from the 'sea' of Talmudic debate and to teach them in a simple and concise manner so that they would be easy to remember and familiar to the nation."[203]

Ahad Ha-Am's visceral response to the *tse'irim* pointed up the profound debt that the transitional generation owed to religious tradition. The cultural Zionist's understanding of religion rested upon the freethinker's sentimental attachment to and underlying respect for the Jewish beliefs and practices of one's childhood, attitudes that had little relevance to a younger generation unschooled in Judaism. Similarly, Ahad Ha-Am inherited from traditional Jewish life the principle of the primacy of the community over the individual. As a result, despite his rejection of Orthodoxy, he was compelled to seek out a unifying ideal to maintain Jewish solidarity. Such sentiments were bound to conflict with the attitudes of the Young Ones whose central concern was the search for self in what they perceived as a world of numbing conformity and mediocrity.

Despite his rejection of the atheism of the *tse'irim*, however, Ahad Ha-Am could not accept Maimonides' philosophical justification of religious belief. He would have undoubtedly liked to find a more "sophisticated" explanation for the power of tradition, one which would have clearly demonstrated his mastery of the methodology of modern-day social science. In the end, however, Ahad Ha-Am again was led to conclude that religion was more a matter of feeling than of rational thought. After all, hadn't he always maintained that the religious "truth" of his beloved Prophets derived not from their confrontation with the divine but from their keen psychological awareness of the true destiny of the Jewish people? Similarly, his deep conviction that the power of ritual lay in its symbolic and emotive meaning for the practitioner had led him to the realization that it was possible to observe biblical commandments even if one no longer was a believing Jew.[204]

It was a view that was clearly reflected in Ahad Ha-Am's approach toward his own religious belief and practice. When asked directly by an admirer if he believed in God, he was deliberately evasive. Like Immanuel Kant, the Zionist thinker had concluded that it was not a question that could be rationally discussed. For the most part, he simply did not think about the matter.[205] In his writings, Ahad Ha-Am had argued that in the absence of a clear exposition of Jewish morality, Jewish ethical precepts could best be expressed on a daily basis through participation in collective ritual. Nevertheless, in his own daily life it was emotion rather than intellect that informed his religious activity. At times, Ahad Ha-Am's religious observance was little more than a response to personal crisis. Thus he made sure to say Kaddish (the memorial prayer) after his father's death and held seders (Passover meals) in his London home in order to reaffirm his attachment to the East European Jewish community in an alien environment. In other cases, Ahad Ha-Am's religious observance seemed strangely eclectic and unfocused. While keeping a kosher home, for example, he used the free time he had on holidays and the Sabbath to write letters and essays. Though a chain smoker, he nevertheless refrained from cigarettes in public on Saturdays in deference to his more observant friends. Similarly, while claiming that he would never force his children to observe religious practices, he insisted on sending his son to a yeshiva in Odessa.[206] Ahad Ha-Am undoubtedly was referring to his own attitudes toward Judaism when he commented that while the religious Jew says "I believe," the freethinker says "I feel."[207] It was a sign of the Zionist thinker's own inner ambivalence toward Judaism that he suggested that it might be best if Jews simply eliminated the word "religion" from their vocabulary. The term not only created confusion and misunderstanding between the generations, he concluded; it also smacked of the desire of Jews to win favor in the eyes of non-Jews.[208]

Such arguments did little to mollify Ahad Ha-Am's traditionalist and radical opponents. Both groups continued to insist that he explain how "modern" Jews could accept the primacy of religious values without accepting the tenets and obligations of traditional Judaism. The Zionist thinker had originally hoped to clarify his position by chronicling the development of the Jewish "national spirit" in a general work on Jewish ethics. His intention was to demonstrate how the deeply rooted value system in Jewish life—the "national ethic," he called it— had expressed itself in different forms throughout Jewish history. "Events" kept getting in his way, however. More than likely, Ahad Ha-

Am could never fully synthesize the ambiguous and often self-contradictory elements of his weltanschauung. The numerous references to the subject of the ethical foundations of a modern Jewish identity in Ahad Ha-Am's essays reveal an unformed and at times contradictory view that reflected his continual inability to clearly delineate the role of subjective and objective factors in shaping Jewish life. On the one hand, Ahad Ha-Am regarded the development of an ethical perspective as an indication of the growing power of reason in shaping individual thought. On the other, he placed morality at the center of the national "will to live," which transcended individual desire and reasoning. As a result, he never clearly explained why a Jewish identity based on "a national ethic" would be any more binding upon individual Jews than one that rested on religious obligation.[209]

Despite his emphasis on the developmental nature of the Jewish "national ethic," Ahad Ha-Am was insistent that the Jewish concept of justice was absolute and unmediated. As a result, he did not share Zhitlowski's and Dubnow's fascination with the ethical principles of Christianity. Jewish principles of morality were quite different from both Christian and modern secular notions of right and wrong. While the former were derived from rational thought, the latter, he claimed with some exaggeration, were based merely on love, individual self-fulfillment, and altruism. Unlike Christianity, Jewish ethics was not a matter of individual choice and could not be defined by a specific issue or be associated with one specific religious figure. Nor was it dependent on "selfish" notions of reward and punishment or "nonexistent" differentiations between body and soul.[210]

Ahad Ha-Am applied his understanding of the "national ethic" to solving the various crises facing Jewry in his own time. Of special concern to him was the impact of assimilation on Jewish identity. Political Zionists and Jewish socialists, he maintained, were wrong to argue that anti-Semitism or economic and material deprivation were the major threats to Jewish life in the modern era. Such challenges were as old as the Jewish people itself. As external dangers, they could be fended off through coordinated communal action. Far more damaging in Ahad Ha-Am's view was the disappearance of the distinctive ideals of Jewry through Jewish integration into the larger society. For the Zionist thinker, assimilation threatened the very existence of the Jewish people. In rejecting the fundamental ideals that defined Jewry, the assimilated Jew weakened the people's very "will to live." Without a strong value system, the Jewish nation could not exist as a separate entity.

For Ahad Ha-Am, assimilationism was first and foremost a moral failing, a sapping of the Jewish people's inner strength through a denial of its distinctive ethical ideals. It was for this reason, he could argue, that although it was physically and psychologically possible to assimilate, the drive to integrate into the larger society was a fundamentally immoral act. His most blistering critique of assimilationism could be found in his article "Avdut be-tokh herut" (Slavery in Freedom), published in 1891. Written in response to an essay by Simon Dubnow that contrasted the enlightened attitudes of western Jewry with the parochialism of the East European Jewish community, Ahad Ha-Am argued that western Jews had achieved formal freedom at the cost of their enslavement to the values and ideals of the dominant society. Russian and Polish Jews, on the other hand, lacked political freedom. In their commitment to Jewish national identity and culture, however, they demonstrated an inner liberation as morally upright and autonomous individuals.[211] As bearers of the "national ethic," only Russian and Polish Jewry could bring salvation to the Jewish people. As the Zionist thinker noted in one of his many comments that simultaneously attacked western Jews and defended his East European coreligionists: "Not you but we 'the believing poor' from the East will come and liberate you from your internal slavery in which you are sunk without realizing it; we will come and fill the emptiness of your heart with Jewish sensitivities—not the meaningless Judaism of nice phrases that you carry on your lips but the living Judaism of the heart, full of will and power to develop and renew its youth."[212]

In extolling the virtues of East European Jews, Ahad Ha-Am deliberately chose to ignore the attitudes of the larger society that prevented their assimilation. Like the degeneration of Jewish life, the maintenance of strong Jewish ties was to be explained solely by the internal dynamics of the Russian Jewish community. Unlike the western Jew, Ahad Ha-Am argued, the East European Jew was far too rooted in Jewish life to succumb to the temptations of the larger society. So strong was the latter's attachment to his people that even those who left the fold could not truly assimilate. They would be unnatural creatures, Ahad Ha-Am claimed, trying "to be what they are not." Russian and Polish Jews were simply unable to rid themselves of "the will to national existence and love of national culture that fill their hearts."[213]

Thus the assimilated Jew's attempt to "solve" the Jewish problem through a change in external conditions was bound to fail. Only an inner revival marked by a reaffirmation of the "national ethic" in modern terms could save Jewry from its present-day crisis.

Ahad Ha-Am's insistence on the degenerative nature of assimilation and his call for spiritual renewal led him to espouse a distinctive form of Zionism. In his view, the concept of the centrality of Zion had preceded monotheistic Judaism as the core belief of the Jewish people. In the nation's formative years, the Jewish God embodied the collective ideals and hopes of the nation and was intimately associated with the land and specifically with the Temple in Jerusalem. Judaism, in the sense of a system of religious thought, became a dominant force in national life only after the destruction of the Second Temple. It was in exile that love of God became disassociated from the Promised Land and became an end in itself.

In Ahad Ha-Am's view, the key figures in the transformation of Judaism from a cultic and tribal religion to a faith system were the Prophets. Their redefinition of the collective ideal allowed Jews to survive the trauma of exile. Nevertheless, Ahad Ha-Am was convinced that Isaiah and Jeremiah never envisioned the survival of Jewry in the Diaspora. They clearly understood that if Jewry were to remain true to its origins, it could only flourish on its native soil.[214] Diaspora, after all, meant not only physical exile. It was also a form of spiritual alienation, a concept that Ahad Ha-Am likened to the traditional religious notion of the Galut ha-shekhinah, the self-imposed exile of the Divine Presence.[215] Unlike his friend Dubnow, Ahad Ha-Am insisted that the hope for national return remained a deeply rooted faith that survived over the centuries in "the dark and narrow chamber of [Jewish] hearts."[216]

Ahad Ha-Am fervently believed that the Diaspora had a debilitating effect on the Jewish spirit. In assessing Jewish life in exile, he borrowed creatively from the Prophets' view of the corruption and degradation resulting from the Jews' interaction with the nations around them. The recent history of Diaspora Jews bore out the painful reality that had been prophesied by the spiritual leaders of the Bible: the inability of the community to defend itself against anti-Semitic attack, the juggernaut of assimilation, and the growing gap between old and new generations.[217] In a more profound sense, Ahad Ha-Am argued, living as a minority in a majority culture created a split personality among Jews. As a participant in the larger society, the Jew strove to minimize his attachment to his people. At the same time, as a member of a persecuted nation, he sought to ensure Jewish collective survival. Such divisions also led individual Jews to differentiate between human and Jewish values. Ultimately, Ahad Ha-Am maintained, the history of the Diaspora demonstrated that it was impossible to serve two masters at the same time. Only a return to Zion would restore the wholeness of the Jewish people and end its schizophrenic existence.[218]

Unlike most other Zionists, however, Ahad Ha-Am was not a radical negator of the Diaspora. At the least, he argued, one had to face the reality that most Jews would not immigrate to Palestine. As demonstrated by his attitude toward America, Ahad Ha-Am could even look favorably upon the development of new centers of Diaspora life. More than anything else, however, it was his ambivalent attitude toward Judaism that led him to downplay his criticism of the Diaspora. To reject Jewish life in the Diaspora completely would have led Ahad Ha-Am to renounce the rich heritage of Jewish tradition as it had developed over the centuries, something which we have seen over and over again he could not do. Despite his conviction that life in the Diaspora was ultimately unhealthful for Jewry, Ahad Ha-Am could not deny the element of continuity that allowed for the survival of Jewish ideals despite the separation of Jewry from the source of its creativity in the Land of Israel.

Ahad Ha-Am's generally negative attitude toward the Diaspora brought him into direct conflict with his close friend Simon Dubnow. In part, the conflict between the two men stemmed from their different personalities. As Robert Seltzer has noted, despite Ahad Ha-Am's profound respect for Dubnow, he lacked the Jewish historian's optimism and willingness to accept partial solutions to the Jewish plight.[219] Though accepting Dubnow's contention that Diaspora Jewry had succeeded in maintaining Jewish values over the centuries, Ahad Ha-Am could never embrace the notion that its continued existence was a positive experience upon which one could build a national future. The Diaspora was an objective fact that could not be denied, he wrote in response to the publication of Dubnow's *Letters on Old and New Judaism*, but it was neither an immutable condition nor a positive good in an absolute sense.[220]

Ahad Ha-Am was especially critical of Dubnow's autonomism. In both public essays and private letters, the cultural Zionist scathingly attacked the Jewish historian for believing that the nations of the world would grant Jews within their midst full national rights. He likened such notions to a discussion of "whether the cows of Pharaoh's dream should be eaten roasted or boiled."[221] Ultimately, the Jewish minority had little or no control over its fate. Even the most tolerant of nations would demand total integration, that is unless Jews would be willing to return to the ghetto. Of course, Ahad Ha-Am grudgingly admitted, autonomism was "better than nothing at all." Nevertheless, he was insistent that the demand for autonomy could only be a step in the development of national consciousness that must eventually lead all Jewish nationalists to recognize the ultimate goal of establishing a Jewish majority in its own land. Any attempt to create a viable Jewish life in the Diaspora in the long run, he warned Dubnow, was a "labor of Sisyphus."[222]

While Ahad Ha-Am did not reject the attempt by Jews to improve their lives in the Diaspora, he urged them to concentrate their energy in the realization of a "full solution"—the establishment of a Jewish cultural center in Palestine. Such a solution did not negate the Diaspora. On the contrary, Ahad Ha-Am maintained, a spiritual center in Israel would serve to strengthen the resolve of Jews wherever they lived. Even autonomists would have to admit that the only true solution to Jewish life in the Diaspora lay outside the boundaries of the Diaspora itself. Only the Land of Israel, he maintained, could combine the "unadulterated Jewishness of the ghetto with the breadth and freedom of modern life." As the birthplace of Jewish ideals, only Israel could provide the important spiritual leaven for national revival.[223]

The idea of the Land of Israel as a Jewish spiritual center did not originate with Ahad Ha-Am. Its roots lay in the biblical notion of Zion as the locus of Jewish loyalties and commitments. For centuries, religious Jews had prayed for the coming of the Messiah, which would bring about the speedy return of Jewry to their ancient homeland and the rebuilding of the Temple in Jerusalem. In modern times, the need for a Jewish spiritual center as a solution to the plight of Diaspora Jewry had been first broached by Leon Pinsker in his work *Autoemancipation* published in 1882, though the proto-Zionist had not specifically emphasized the importance of Palestine.[224] In the 1880s, Ahad Ha-Am undoubtedly saw the idea of a "spiritual center" in Palestine as a way out of the fruitless debate in Hibbat Zion over the nature and future of the Jewish settlement in the Land of Israel. The concept of a spiritual center could serve as a middle path between Lilienblum's demand for physical settlement and his own early emphasis on the need for spiritual revival.[225] Ahad Ha-Am's interest in a spiritual center may also have been influenced by Italian nationalism in the latter half of the nineteenth century with its call for a Risorgimento or cultural renaissance as a key to national strength.

In a letter written to a supporter in 1909, Ahad Ha-Am outlined his plans for the Jewish spiritual center. It would include a national library, museum, publishing house, press, and, most important, "a Hebrew academy where fifteen to twenty scholars and writers of the highest level would live and would receive an appropriate salary that would enable them to live simple lives without any concerns."[226] Ahad Ha-Am made no effort to explain the center's day-to-day functioning, however. He seems to have believed that its mere existence would provide the spiritual direction and purpose necessary for collective Jewish survival. He was firmly convinced that the center would help to break down ideological and religious differences among Jews. As Ahad Ha-Am stated in the preface to the first edition of *Al parshat derakhim* published in 1895: "A circle has millions of points on its circumference but the central point alone is the 'soul' that gives life to them all."[227] By uniting Jews around the world, a spiritual center would serve the role previously played by the Sanhedrin, the supreme political, religious, and judicial body in Palestine during the Roman period. At times, Ahad Ha-Am seemed to assume that the center would be a successor to the Temple as well. During his visit to Palestine in 1891, for example, he invoked the prayer of King Solomon after the construction of the First Temple. Speaking in eschatological terms, he envisioned the fulfillment of the biblical prophecy of the construction of a central spiritual shrine not only for Jews but for all the nations of the world.[228]

Ahad Ha-Am was insistent that one of the central roles of a Jewish spiritual center would be to create new forms of collective Jewish consciousness. Yet he deliberately avoided the question of when the institution could begin its historic task. Was it simply a matter of the development of a critical mass of intellectuals in Palestine, or did the foundation of the center necessitate some cataclysmic event akin to the messianic coming? Given his strong emphasis on evolutionary development and his inability to gain a sizable following in the Zionist movement, Ahad Ha-Am generally seemed content to place his vision of a Jewish spiritual center in the distant future. In the meantime, Jews had to live in a state of perpetual expectation, while preparing the groundwork for the future restoration of Zion. In contrast to the utopianism of political Zionists and radicals, however, he cautioned against any attempt to "hurry the Messiah."[229] "Do not rush the end of days as long as the conditions for its realization have not been attained," Ahad Ha-Am wrote in the conclusion to his Preface to the third edition of *Al parshat derakhim*, "yet do not belittle the value of realizable work at any time, even if it will not bring the Messiah today or in the future."[230]

Fearful of alienating the Orthodox Jewish establishment in Palestine, Ahad Ha-Am was also deliberately vague about the relationship between the spiritual center and the political and religious leadership of the existing *yishuv*. In his most radical proposal, the Zionist thinker had envisioned the replacement of synagogues in Palestine by *bate midrash* (houses of learning), where Jewish values would be discussed and inculcated and where prayers would be supplementary. It was not by accident, however, that he chose to share his proposal in a private letter to the sympathetic American Zionist and Reform rabbi Judah Magnes rather than in a public statement.[231] As we have seen, when Ahad Ha-Am attempted to establish Hebrew-language schools in Palestine as a preliminary step in the development of a new Jewish culture in the Land of Israel, he was roundly denounced by leaders of the Old Yishuv and by religious Zionists. Even secularists wondered about the relevance of such study to the concrete needs of the existing *yishuv*. The issue becomes even more clouded when one considers that Ahad Ha-Am did not believe that teachers in Palestine were adequately trained to take on the burden of cultural revival or that the Hebrew language was sufficiently developed to handle the teaching of sophisticated subjects such as science. No wonder that his critics in Palestine accused him of creating a perverse vision of Zion that ignored its inhabitants and catered instead to the "spiritual" needs of those who remained in the Diaspora.[232]

Ahad Ha-Am's vision of a spiritual center was a logical outcome of his work in Hibbat Zion and Bnei Moshe. He had always believed that the masses of Jews were far too much concerned with the here and now, the material and physical conditions of life, to create a new

Jewish culture and national identity. Even if the majority of Jewry in the Diaspora were eventually to reject Judaism in the name of economic enrichment and social acceptance, Ahad Ha-Am claimed, a small group of faithful intellectuals based in Palestine would be able to maintain the rich tradition of the past and provide the conditions for the ultimate redemption of the Jewish people in the future. "As long as the thread does not fall from the hands of 'these last Jews,'" he wrote in an essay published in 1907, the Jewish people has the potential to once again "become a 'great nation.'"[233]

Such statements suggest that those critics who argued that Ahad Ha-Am had ignored the interests of the *yishuv* in the name of Diaspora Jewry misread the true intentions of the cultural Zionist. For all his concern with those Jews who lived beyond the borders of Palestine, Ahad Ha-Am's vision of a Jewish spiritual center was that of a sui generis institution. In the end, its links with world Jewry were as tenuous as those with the Jews of Palestine. Ahad Ha-Am was convinced that history had demonstrated time and time again that the secret of Jewish survival lay not in appeals to the masses but in the maintenance of its ideals by a small group of devoted scholars and intellectuals.[234] Thus, he never bothered to explain how the Palestinian-based facility would disseminate its ideas to a Diaspora made up of culturally illiterate Jews. Nor did he clearly define the role of the Diaspora in cultural renewal. Was it to be an active participant in national revival or merely a passive recipient of the new "Torah from Zion"? Given his rejection of messianism and his concerns over the fate of the Diaspora, Ahad Ha-Am's program for a spiritual center seemed more closely modeled after the experience of Yavneh, the rabbinical school hurriedly founded by Yochanan ben Zakkai after the destruction of the Second Temple and the fall of the Judean state, than of Mount Zion and the Temple, where Jews from all over the Diaspora would come to offer sacrifices during the period of the First and Second Commonwealths.

Such concerns were reinforced by Ahad Ha-Am's insistence that it was not necessary for all Jews to live in Israel. In contrast to other Zionist thinkers, he adamantly maintained that the settlement of all Jews in the Land of Israel was not physically possible. Though Ahad Ha-Am supported the establishment of a concrete Jewish settlement in Palestine that would provide the economic sustenance for the rejuvenation of Jewish culture, he warned that the land could not absorb more than a few hundred thousand immigrants. In the end, he argued, the creation of one Hebrew university was far more significant than the establishment of a hundred colonies. In contrast to those who claimed that through mass immigration the *yishuv* could become the model of a new Jewish society, Ahad Ha-Am insisted that Jewish settlement must develop gradually in response to developing economic conditions.[235]

Ahad Ha-Am's views of the limitations of Jewish settlement, his intellectual elitism, and his insistence on gradualism placed him on a collision course with Theodor Herzl and his supporters within the Zionist movement. Ahad Ha-Am's disagreements with the founder of political Zionism arose from his most fundamental beliefs. Like Dubnow, he was convinced that political Zionism (or "Zionismus" as he disparagingly referred to it in an allusion to the central European background of its founder) represented a "quick fix," a desperate attempt to solve Jewish problems that lacked adequate planning and grounding in Jewish tradition and history. Like messianic movements before it, Zionism in its Herzlian form was hopelessly unrealistic. The stark reality, Ahad Ha-Am argued, was that the hope for "the ingathering of the exiles" was a fantasy; the Diaspora "in its physical sense" would always exist. Thus political Zionism's claim that the establishment of a Jewish state would solve the problem of anti-Semitism was preposterous. What, after all, Ahad Ha-Am wondered, would it accomplish for those Jews who chose to remain in the Diaspora? Did Herzl and his followers believe that the Land of Israel would be able to send "a naval battalion" to save Diaspora Jews in their time of need?[236]

Ahad Ha-Am's questioning of the significance of a Jewish homeland could already be detected in his struggles with the leaders of Hibbat Zion in the late 1890s. In his early writings, he had underscored the importance of sovereignty in the Land of Israel for ensuring Jewish survival. It was only during the period of the ancient Jewish state, Ahad Ha-Am had noted in an article written in 1890, for example, that Jews had been able to live normal lives.[237] His trip to Palestine in 1891, however, convinced him that the Palestinophiles' emphasis on the rebuilding of the land ignored the true "catastrophe," the destruction of the Jewish people. Questions of geographical concentration, social and economic construction, and political sovereignty were diversionary issues that enabled Jewish leaders to ignore the spiritual crisis that was gnawing at the very soul of the Jewish people. As the cultural Zionist remarked after visiting the

Wailing Wall in Jerusalem: "These stones testify to the destruction of our land, these people—to the destruction of our nation. Which of these two catastrophes is greater? Over which one should we shed more tears? In a situation in which the land is destroyed but our nation is still full of life and power, the people will follow a Zerubbabel and a Nehemiah who will build it again; but who will arise and where will our help come if the nation itself is destroyed?"[238]

The struggle with Herzl in the late 1890s led Ahad Ha-Am to reassert his earlier views even more forcefully. Like Hibbat Zion's support of colonization, Herzl's insistence on a political solution to the "Jewish problem" represented an effort to rest the fate of Jewry solely on external conditions. Herzl was obsessed with Jews, Ahad Ha-Am claimed, but thought little of the needs of Judaism. Yet the physical degradation of the Jew was nothing when compared to his inner spiritual and moral crisis. In putting off questions of the "Jewishness" of the Jewish homeland, Ahad Ha-Am argued, political Zionism deliberately ignored the source of Jewish existence and creativity over the centuries. In insisting that a Jewish collectivity could not exist without territorial sovereignty, it also denied the millennia of Jewish communal and intellectual history. Only after the Jewish people had been spiritually rejuvenated, Ahad Ha-Am contended, could a state be established. In contrast to Herzl's entity, the culturally enriched settlement would "not only be a state for the Jews but a true Jewish state."[239]

In his effort to prevent Herzl from making inroads among Russian and Polish Jewish nationalists, Ahad Ha-Am stressed the hollowness and superficial nature of the political Zionist's commitment to the Jewish people. Ignoring the fact that the same arguments could be used against many of the founders of East European Zionism, the cultural Zionist dismissed Herzl and his supporters as Jewish nationalists of "the first hour" and "children of anti-Semitism."[240] Newly committed to the task of national renewal, western and central European Jews had formulated their programs, organizations, and procedures largely in response to the non-Jewish world around them. As Ahad Ha-Am cynically commented after the conclusion of the First Zionist Congress in 1897: "Anti-Semitism gave birth to Herzl, Herzl gave birth to 'The Jewish state,' 'The Jewish state'—to 'Zionismus,' and 'Zionismus'—to the Congress."[241] Political Zionists believed that Jews merely had to express their love of the Jewish people. Inwardly, however, they could continue to ignore Jewish culture and to mimic European society. It was clear to everyone, Ahad Ha-Am argued, that the goal of Herzl and his supporters was not to create a Jewish homeland. What they actually desired was "a European colony that lifts its heart and eyes only to the European continent and tries to emulate . . . [European culture] in its own way of life."[242]

Ahad Ha-Am was convinced that Herzl's rejection of assimilation was insincere. In contrast to East European Jewish nationalists, the western Zionist's change of heart stemmed from his disappointment with assimilation's ineffectiveness as a solution to the "Jewish problem" rather than from a concern with its impact on Jewish survival. Despite his overtures to Russian Jewry, Ahad Ha-Am maintained, Herzl was actually more interested in the fate of western Jews who could not assimilate than in the plight of those Russian and Polish Jews who chose to live independent and autonomous lives.[243] The Jewish masses should not be carried away by Herzl's charisma, Ahad Ha-Am argued. In the end, the political Zionist would be revealed for what he really was—a feuilletonist, adept at using words to disguise his lack of principles and his superficial understanding of the Jewish reality.[244]

Ahad Ha-Am was especially disturbed by Herzl's focus on politics and political power. Herzl's fascination with party congresses and diplomacy, he claimed, was nothing but "paper Zionism." For all his grandiose political designs, the political Zionist was mainly concerned with the trappings of power—bureaucracy and administration—that left little time for a serious evaluation of the larger and more pressing issues affecting the community.[245] Even more troubling to Ahad Ha-Am was what he believed to be Herzl's willingness to compromise basic principles for short-term gains. The true purpose of Jewish nationalism was not to demonstrate the power and strength of the Jewish people, as political Zionism contended, but to highlight the ethical and spiritual values of Judaism that would enable the individual to link himself with humanity as a whole.[246] In his desperate desire for immediate results, Ahad Ha-Am maintained, Herzl denied the importance of absolute justice and truth that underlay Jewish national identity. In pandering to the masses, the leader of political Zionism appealed to the basest aspects of human thought and behavior. Ahad Ha-Am claimed to have personally experienced Herzl's duplicity at a series of meetings he had with the Zionist leader in 1898 that dealt with the creation of a national fund to aid settlement in Palestine. When the cultural Zionist voiced concerns over the appropriateness of presenting the proposal at the Zionist Congress before any money had actually been raised, Herzl allegedly replied: "So what? We won't tell anyone if the amount is small." Herzl thought little of the incident. For a moral absolutist like Ahad Ha-Am, however, such comments clearly demonstrated the political Zionist leader's dishonesty and raised serious doubts about his trustworthiness.[247]

As a strict moralist, Ahad Ha-Am believed that politics and diplomacy were synonymous with lying and deception and had no place in the "holy" work of Jewish revival.[248] Nowhere was Herzl's "profanation" of the Jewish national ideal more evident than in the latter's defense of Uganda as a Jewish asylum in 1903–4. The fundamental appeal of Herzl's proposal, Ahad Ha-Am maintained, rested on its claim to solve the immediate physical need for a place of refuge. In its desire for short-term diplomatic success, however, political Zionism was willing to compromise one of the most fundamental ideals of Jewry—the return to Zion.[249] Such an approach would transform an ancient and proud nation into a plaything in the hands of the Great Powers. The quest for Zion did not need to be legitimized by others, Ahad Ha-am argued; it lay at the very foundation of Jewish life. Ultimately, he concluded in a not-so-subtle allusion to his own role in the Jewish nationalist movement, Jewry would be saved by prophets and not by diplomats.[250]

Despite his often trenchant attacks upon Herzl, Ahad Ha-Am generally found himself outflanked by the Zionist leader. Though the cultural Zionist often bent over backward to appease rabbinical leadership, even going so far as to recognize the need for a separate religious educational system in the *yishuv*,[251] it was Herzl who gained the support of those traditional religious elements in the Jewish community who chose to support Zionism. While Ahad Ha-Am's insistence on the need to create a new Jewish worldview was seen as a threat to religious Orthodoxy, Herzl was clever enough to recognize that any discussion of the nature of Jewish life in the Land of Israel would divide secularists and religionists and weaken the movement. Paradoxically, Ahad Ha-Am suffered as a result of his familiarity with traditional Jewish culture, whereas Herzl's relatively assimilated Jewish background actually gained him support among religious leaders. In contrast to Ahad Ha-Am whose programs they denounced as a clever attempt by a knowledgeable Jewish heretic to usurp the authority of traditional religion, many Orthodox Jewish leaders saw

Herzl's assumption of the leadership of the Zionist movement and his public deference to rabbinic authority as undeniable proof that he was a true *hozer be-tshuvah* (one who has returned to the faith).[252] Ironically, it was the political Zionist rather than the founder of Bnei Moshe who assumed the role of the new Moses to lead the children of Israel through the desert of the Diaspora to the Promised Land.

Nor did Ahad Ha-Am make much headway among the younger generation of Zionist activists in eastern Europe who came into their own in the first decade of the twentieth century. Despite his opposition to Herzl, his agenda remained as in the past far too esoteric and elitist to have appeal beyond a narrow group of enthusiasts. More significantly, while Herzl pledged bold and immediate action to deal with anti-Semitism and economic immiserization, Ahad Ha-Am's concern with slow and gradual change seemed to ignore the pressing problems facing Russian Jewry, especially after the Kishinev pogroms. Ironically, despite his belief in the power of the prophetic individual, Ahad Ha-Am could not compete with the charisma of Herzl. Nor did he possess the public relations and managerial skills necessary to transform the Zionist dream into a day-to-day reality. If anything, Ahad Ha-Am's failure to offer institutional and practical alternatives to congresses and diplomatic maneuverings only weakened the fledgling Russian Jewish nationalist movement in its effort to maintain its independence from the leader of political Zionism. Burdened by political oppression and economic crisis, most Russian Zionists were forced to acknowledge the dependence of East European Jews on elements outside the community for assistance.[253] It was only after the death of Herzl that Russian and Polish Zionists could begin to assert themselves within the movement. By then, of course, few were willing to listen to the appeals of an aging intellectual and writer like Ahad Ha-Am.

As a cultural nationalist, Ahad Ha-Am shared Haim Zhitlowski's conviction that language had the unique ability both to embody and to transmit the values and ideals of a people from generation to generation. In contrast to the Yiddishist, however, he stressed the importance of the Hebrew language. Already in the early 1890s, Ahad Ha-Am had been in the forefront of the struggle to defend Hebrew against supporters of Yiddish, Russian, and German within Jewish nationalist circles. Interestingly, he accepted the criticism of those who argued that Hebrew was an "aristocratic" language known only to a select few. Unlike Yiddishists and other Hebraists, however, he believed that its limited audience was a source of pride rather than of shame and obloquy. What better proof could there be that Hebrew was both a faithful reflection of the distinctive national spirit that had evolved over generations and an indispensable tool for the intellectual elite to transmit it to future generations?

Given his elitist sentiments, Ahad Ha-Am's response to Yiddish could only be negative. In his only published article in Yiddish, written in 1899, he denounced the language as a "mishmash" geared to the most vulgar elements of the Jewish people. How could a "jargon" that emerged millennia after the creation of the ethical core of Jewish life transmit the basic values of Jewry to the ignorant masses?[254] For the cultural Zionist, Yiddish was a pale reflection of the cultures that oppressed Jewry in the Diaspora and was doomed to disappear within a few generations. Despite its pretensions of being a language of cultural revival, Yiddish had no intrinsic value or resonance in Jewish life. It was an artificial tongue, Ahad Ha-Am insisted, concocted by autonomists and socialists who needed a tool to communicate their Diasporist demands to the Jewish masses.[255] Why struggle to give birth to a new Jewish language and culture, he had written to Simon Dubnow in 1909, when Hebrew offered a rich heritage of form and content that could be adapted to the new challenges facing a revived Jewish people? The creation of a so-called democratic language, as the Yiddishists demanded, thus would only diminish Jewry's status as a proud and self-sustaining nation. Should Yiddish triumph over Hebrew, Ahad Ha-Am concluded, "I see no purpose or reason for such a base national existence. . . . [I]t would be better if we wrote finis to the book of our history rather than add such empty pages."[256]

Despite his strong support of Hebrew, Ahad Ha-Am was hardly obsessive about the matter. Though he is generally credited with introducing important innovations in modern Hebrew literature, he actually did not write in Hebrew until he arrived in Odessa. According to one scholar who has studied the matter, Ahad Ha-Am never developed an interest or facility in the spoken language. During his visits to Palestine in 1891 and 1900, for example, he generally refused to speak Hebrew. It was only after 1908 and largely in response to his sense of isolation in London that Ahad Ha-Am began to use Hebrew in conversation. Even after settling in Tel Aviv in 1920, he continued to speak Russian at home to his wife, who knew little Hebrew.[257]

For all his insistence on the centrality of Hebrew, Ahad Ha-Am distanced himself from Hebrew "chauvinists." Thus, for example, he rejected their demand that the use of Yiddish be banned at Jewish public gatherings. For the time being, at least, activists had to recognize that "jargon" remained the language of the masses. As long as it was being used for propaganda purposes rather than as a vehicle for cultural revival, it could do little harm. Ahad Ha-Am also insisted that Jewish intellectuals learn foreign languages in order to remain current with the literature and thought of European civilization. In his struggle for the introduction of Hebrew into the curriculum of Palestinian schools, for example, he recognized that in the short run at least, German would probably be a more appropriate language of instruction for scientific and technological subjects. Throughout his life, he prided himself on his ability to read and speak most of the major western and central European languages. Ahad Ha-Am's fervent hope was that Jewish ideals would one day take their place in the pantheon of civilized thought. As Bialik stated at a memorial service for the Zionist thinker six years after his death, his ultimate goal was to create a linguistic and philosophical "synthesis that enabled him to express a Jewish idea that would become European and a European [idea]—that would become Jewish."[258]

While minimizing the importance of spoken Hebrew, in his mature years Ahad Ha-Am stressed the importance of the written word.[259] Like the maskilim before him, he insisted that Jewish ideals could only be transmitted to future generations through Hebrew prose. In reaction to the flowery style of the Haskalah, however, Ahad Ha-Am's own written works display a close attention to detail and an obsession with the economy of words. The Hebrew writer Aharon Kabak did not exaggerate when he wrote that it was impossible to remove even one sentence from any of the cultural Zionist's writings without ruining the content of the essay.[260] But Ahad Ha-Am's concern with detail reflected more than a belief in the importance of formal presentation. The task of the modern Hebrew writer, he would tell his followers, was akin to that of the codifiers of the Torah and Talmud. His purpose was not to amuse or engage his readers but rather, as Bialik stated at Ahad Ha-Am's funeral in 1927, to "create the national embodiment of God and to explain the nature of . . . [the nation's] responsibility."[261] Hebrew thus was inextricably tied to Hebrew culture. As one author has aptly written, Ahad Ha-Am firmly believed that "Hebrew was both the medium and the message."[262]

Nevertheless, like many other aspects of his thought, Ahad Ha-Am never clearly explained what he meant by a distinctively "Hebrew culture." It was obvious from his writing that he intended Hebrew education to be more than linguistic instruction. He constantly chided those Jewish educators who insisted on teaching the "dry laws" of Hebrew grammar. The study of language and literature was only valuable as a means of linking the individual Jew with the ethical and aesthetic ideals of his people. At the same time, however, he had little tolerance for those who wished to use Hebrew to create personal statements about the world. Anyone whose "soul is enslaved to the beauty of nature and the pleasure of love," he had written in an editorial in the first issue of *Ha-Shiloach*, would find his needs sufficiently met in other languages.[263] Ahad Ha-Am was equally insistent that classical Hebrew writings should not merely be used to instill patriotism and false pride. An overemphasis on Hebrew literature to the exclusion of other writings could only lead to a division within the student's mind between general and Jewish learning. The cultural Zionist's great dream was to create a new compendium of Jewish thought in Hebrew that would encapsulate the central ideals and values of Jewish religious belief, philosophy, history, and literature in a form that was easily accessible to the modern reader. Such a work would serve to realize the central purpose of Ahad Ha-Am's educational program—"to rear complete human beings whose self-consciousness as men and Jews would be united in one undivided purpose."[264]

Yet Ahad Ha-Am often voiced the hope that the revival of the Hebrew language would ultimately lead to a distinctively "Hebrew" approach to all secular subjects. Jewish students had to be girded with Jewish values to confront the difficult task of ensuring collective survival that lay ahead. Without the integration of Hebrew culture and universal knowledge, however, young Jews might well begin to wonder about the relevance of Judaism to their lives. What was necessary, Ahad Ha-Am argued, was the "liberation of Jewish education in the Land of Israel from the influence of the alien spirit that necessarily accompanied the rule by a foreign tongue."[265] Such a view suggested a curriculum in which language and thought would unite to reinforce the student's commitment to the Jewish people and to humanity as a whole. Thus, for example, Ahad Ha-Am envisioned courses in "Hebrew geography" that would emphasize the topography of the Land of Israel as both an end in itself and a model for understanding earth science. More questionable was his proposal for an approach to arithmetic that would use examples taken from daily life in the *yishuv*. As the modern Hebrew scholar Yaakov Shavit has remarked, all too often, the result of Ahad Ha-Am's conflations of Hebrew language and culture was the "reductio ad absurdum of the principle of 'Hebrewness.'"[266]

Yet Shavit's criticism fails to take into account the severe limitations under which Ahad Ha-Am developed his plan for national cultural renewal. Today, Israelis (and many Diaspora Jews) recognize Hebrew as a natural vehicle for the expression of all facets of life. What Ahad Ha-Am was grappling with, of course, was the attempt to make Hebrew and "Hebrew" culture a vital part of the daily life of the *yishuv* in a period in which the struggle for economic survival overwhelmed all other concerns. The cultural Zionist was also limited by his elitist tendencies and his relative unfamiliarity with the day-to-day life of Jewish settlers. Most important, the fact that he refused to recognize the role that Jewish sovereignty could play in facilitating these developments all but doomed his effort to failure.

Today, Ahad Ha-Am's struggle to create a modern Jewish culture in the Land of Israel that would link Jews around the world continues to resonate in both Israel and the Diaspora. Yet in his own time, Ahad Ha-Am remained largely a marginal figure. Even his most avid supporters at the turn of the century were forced to admit that his immediate influence was limited. By 1914, an admirer of Ahad Ha-Am could write a laudatory essay that nevertheless argued that the cultural Zionist's most famous writings were passé and his causes no longer relevant.[267] On the most basic level, Ahad Ha-Am's insistence on the need for an ideological foundation for future action contrasted sharply with the activist and pragmatic bent of most Jewish nationalist movements of his era. Though he had hoped to bridge the gap between Diasporists and Zionists with his notion of a spiritual center in Zion, he only succeeded in alienating both camps. Among autonomists, his refusal to view the Diaspora as anything more than a necessary evil gained him little support. Within the Zionist movement itself, the death of Herzl led to a renewed commitment to gradual and "systematic" development, while the growing visibility and influence of Jewish nationalism meant that it no longer felt the need for intellectual seers to guide it.[268] Though the retreat from the maximalist and utopian demands of political Zionism could be seen in some sense as a victory for Ahad Ha-Am, he reaped very little personal benefit from it in his own lifetime. The result was that though he was clearly recognized as a profound critic of the movements and ideas of his day, he was incapable of clearly and concisely expressing his own positions. In the end, as a recent biographer has insightfully noted, it was the myth rather than the practical influence of Ahad Ha-Am that defined his place among his contemporaries.[269]

Ultimately, Ahad Ha-Am's signal failure to create a mass following for his message of national renewal lay in his desperate effort to synthesize the old and the new. Despite his much vaunted goal of re-evaluating the Jewish past, the Zionist thinker proved unable or unwilling to discard the traditions of previous generations. Indeed, in his emphasis on the various components that contributed to the nation's survival—land, culture, and language—he only succeeded in blurring the lines between the sacred and the profane. Ahad Ha-Am's efforts to incorporate elements of Judaism into his new worldview angered both religionists who viewed him as a dangerous subversive and secularists who denounced him as halfhearted and cowardly. His pretensions of speaking in the name of the people as a whole rested more upon the vision of ancient kings and Prophets than upon the techniques of modern administrators and politicians. Unlike ancient leaders, however, he lacked the certainty of divine inspiration.

In two contrasting letters to the Hebrew writer Shmuel Ben-Ami, Ahad Ha-Am reflected upon his legacy in Jewish life. Like the Prophets of old, he wrote to Ben-Ami in 1906, he was convinced that he had been destined to "pour out" his "spirit" in some form or another. Six years later, however, he would comment that he now realized that his ultimate fate was to proclaim "the most horrible vision of the moral degradation within his nation," while his "calls for repentance went unheeded."[270] Contemporaneous observers would be quick to dismiss such sentiments as yet another example of the Zionist thinker's unremitting egotism. Yet Ahad Ha-Am's self-portrayal as a visionary whose ideas of national revival occasioned little support in his own lifetime aptly describes the fate of the founder of cultural Zionism. In a more general sense, it can also serve as a fitting description of the legacy of the transitional generation as a whole.

The Contemporary Relevance of the Transitional Generation

AMONG THE myriad proposals offered by contemporary Jews to solve their personal and collective angst, one rarely hears any discussion of the ideology of the transitional generation. It is not difficult to explain why the names of Haim Zhitlowski, Simon Dubnow, and Ahad Ha-Am are almost unknown in modern Jewish life. The historical conditions that generated the movements of Yiddishism, autonomism, and cultural Zionism, including the presence of national minorities within powerful Austro-Hungarian and Russian empires, the maintenance of strong Jewish communal institutions and identities in eastern Europe, and the uncertain future of Jewish settlement in Palestine, no longer exist. The few examples of autonomism and Yiddishist culture in the interwar period, such as those in the Ukraine in 1918 and Poland during the 1920s and '30s, did not long survive the rise of radically nationalist and authoritarian regimes, which frowned upon ethnic difference and demanded total adherence to the society and state on the part of all its citizens. In addition, the decimation of East European Jewry during the Holocaust brought an end to the rich and vibrant communities that provided Zhitlowski, Dubnow, and Ahad Ha-Am with their most loyal adherents. Finally, the establishment of the State of Israel, in realizing the goals of political Zionism, seemed to eliminate the need for any "theoretical" discussion of the nature of Jewish life in the Diaspora or of future Jewish cultural revival. It is no wonder that even contemporary Jewish scholars have dismissed the work of transitional thinkers as little more than a "piously remembered relic."[1]

Today, the underlying concern of Zhitlowski, Dubnow, and Ahad Ha-Am—the creation of a well-defined Jewish identity that was consistent with the demands of modern life and true to the cultural and spiritual heritage of the Jewish past—no longer seems to resonate among the decidedly nonideological Jews of the Diaspora and Israel. The bitter struggles over the fate of Jewry, which so deeply divided the communities of eastern Europe at the turn of the century and which fueled the writings and activities of the transitional generation, have little relevance for young American and Israeli Jews who generally define their future in terms of "situational ethics" and whose loyalties are parceled out among many competing identities. Those in the Diaspora who think seriously about their commitments to Jewish life generally begin their quest with deeply felt and often inexpressible personal experiences and only at the end of their journey, if at all, embrace the norms of the Jewish people.[2] In contrast, most Israeli Jews simply accept their Jewishness as a part of their political identity as citizens of a Jewish state with little or no thought of its relevance to their personal lives. Even those rabbis, scholars, and communal leaders in the Diaspora and Israel who are paid to think seriously about the problem of a "modern" Jewish identity tend to view the issue in denominational terms (Orthodox versus Reform) or political concepts (liberal versus conservative) which are borrowed from the experiences of nineteenth-century western societies rather than those of eastern Europe.

Zhitlowski, Dubnow, and Ahad Ha-Am often spoke approvingly about the development of a vibrant Jewish community in the United States. Yet they could hardly foresee the dramatic and revolutionary implications of the shift in the center of Diaspora life from the threatened and ideologically charged environment of eastern Europe to the relatively comfortable and fiercely pragmatic community of America. If Jewish leaders in the United States continue to voice the same concerns as Zhitlowski, Dubnow, and Ahad Ha-Am about the decline of Jewish commitment, they do not share the view of these transitional thinkers that the problem is to be explained in terms of individual betrayal or moral failure. Instead, assimilation has come to be seen as a natural sociological process in a democratic society that cannot be thwarted by a simple act of collective will or commitment. With the exception of certain elements of Orthodoxy, Jews in the Diaspora no longer define their condition as *galut*, an exile imposed from without, but rather as *tfutsot*, a freely chosen dispersion where each person may create his or her form of Jewish identification or, alternatively, simply disaffiliate from the Jewish community. Zhitlowski, Dubnow, and Ahad Ha-Am may have differed strongly over how to be Jewish. Only rarely, however, did they have to confront the question "Why be Jewish?" Could the transitional generation ever have envisioned a society in which some Jews would proudly wear their ethnicity both literally and figuratively as a superficial ornament while others would share their non-Jewish spouse's joy in raising their children in two religious traditions or as part of the "race of none"?[3]

Another important factor in the contemporary era that would seem to demonstrate the irrelevancy of the ideas of Zhitlowski, Dubnow, and Ahad Ha-Am has been the creation of the second "hegemonic community," the State of Israel. Clearly, the major argument leveled against political Zionism by all three thinkers—that the "ingathering of exiles" was a utopian dream—has lost much of its significance. Zionism is no longer the ideology of a few dedicated idealists; instead, it has become the central focus of contemporary Jewish concern. While Zhitlowski, Dubnow, and Ahad Ha-Am appealed to economically, geographically, educationally, and linguistically defined audiences, the Zionist cause has been able to incorporate all elements of the Jewish community into its orbit. So powerful has been the emotional impact of the Jewish state on world Jewry that today it would be unthinkable for any Jewish community in the Diaspora to define its own future in terms that ignore the survival of Israel. The result has been that most Jews view the ties between Israel and the Diaspora as self-evident and rarely subject them to rational scrutiny.

Other developments in the process of modernization that were unforeseen by Zhitlowski, Dubnow, and Ahad Ha-Am a century ago have also appeared to weaken the power of their ideas. The existence of intermediary institutions such as clubs and associations has broken down the sharp division between the individual and the state that informed the transitional thinkers' assessment of both the "Jewish problem" and its solution. So, too, the increased mobility of modern life has attenuated the attachment of the individual to place and to community. The sense of loyalty to the collectivity and the view of settlement as an existential decision, which underlay many of the debates between Zhitlowski, Dubnow, and Ahad Ha-Am and their opponents, have become less important with advances in transportation and electronic communication. With the significant narrowing of the physical and psychological gap between Israel and the Diaspora, Jews have been able to participate in and feel part of both communities at the same time.

True, many of the tensions between the communities of the Diaspora and the Land of Israel, which were first noted by members of the transitional generation at the turn of the century, still exist. In contrast to the pre-state period, however, relations between Jews living in Israel and in the Diaspora are increasingly defined in terms of concrete realities rather than ideals. As a result, contemporary Jews generally do not see their future in terms of the triumph of one community's weltanschauung over the other's. If anything, increased mobility and communications have tended to blur the cultural lines between the Diaspora and Israel. The result has been the emergence of a growing consensus between the two communities to live and let live. In place of the hegemonic and exclusivist notions of Zionists and Diasporists in late nineteenth-century Russia, contemporary Jews have adopted the concept of bicentrism, in which both communities are viewed as valid and viable frameworks for the development of Jewish life.

Finally, the decline of interest in the theories of Zhitlowski, Dubnow, and Ahad Ha-Am can be attributed to their failure to resolve a number of basic problems that haunted the three thinkers from the beginning of their literary and political activity. As I have attempted to demonstrate throughout the book, each of them vainly attempted to find appropriate methods to fulfill the three major tasks that had previously been assumed by traditional Judaism: the explanation and justification of Jewish survival in the past; the definition of Jewry and of the nature of communal authority in the present; and the development of appropriate methods of transmission of belief and loyalty to ensure the Jewish future.

The efforts by Zhitlowski, Dubnow, and Ahad Ha-Am to replace the Bible and rabbinical Judaism with other systems of authority, such as history, Jewish ethics, language, and culture, that would bind Jewry together ultimately proved unsuccessful. All too often, they were forced to rely on pseudoscientific theories and apologetics that merely "humanized" rather than supplanted religious beliefs to explain the basis of Jewish life and the key to its survival. Despite their concern with the fate of Jewry as a whole, Zhitlowski, Dubnow, and Ahad Ha-Am generally targeted their ideas to specific elements in the Jewish population, whether intellectuals, political activists, or Yiddish speakers. As elitists and self-professed prophets, they distrusted mass politics and insisted on maintaining tight control over all decision making. The result was that only a limited audience of devoted supporters ever heard their ideas, while those outside their small following either ignored or misunderstood their proposals. Nor were the transitional thinkers able to develop appropriate means of transmitting their ideas to future generations. Their scattered attempts at developing secularized rituals proved to be only pale imitations of religious belief and practice with little impact on the general Jewish population. More important, Zhitlowski's, Dubnow's, and Ahad Ha-Am's views of the future of the Jewish community rested upon a naive belief that subsequent generations would share their veneration for and knowledge of the cultural and spiritual heritage of the Jewish past.

Obsessed with balancing tradition and modernity, Zhitlowski, Dubnow, and Ahad Ha-Am ended up alienating both religionists and staunch secularists, both conservatives and progressives. As in other national movements of the twentieth century, control over policy making in the Jewish community during the modern era would lie not with ideologues but with pragmatic activists skilled in methods of public relations and willing to effect compromises with competing segments of the general population to gain the maximum support and influence.

Yet before contemporary Jews dismiss the members of the transitional generation entirely, they would do well to take a second look at their ideas in light of the serious problems that continue to beset the communities of Israel and the Diaspora. Specifically, the life and writings of Zhitlowski, Dubnow, and Ahad Ha-Am deserve reconsideration for two important interrelated reasons: first, the vacuum left by the inability of their political Zionist opponents to fully realize their ideals; and second, the absence of a strong contemporary defense of life in the Diaspora.

Within Israel itself, the achievement of political sovereignty in 1948 left the issue of the Jewish nature of the society unresolved. Unlike members of the transitional generation, political Zionists deliberately chose to ignore the fact that the most difficult and challenging task of nation building is not the establishment of the state but the creation of national consciousness.[4] One has only to look at the ongoing debates in Israel over "Who is a Jew" and the continued tensions between the nation's religious and secular communities to recognize that the central questions of personal and collective identity raised by Zhitlowski, Dubnow, and Ahad Ha-Am a century ago have yet to be decided. Even the bitter quarrels within Israel over peace negotiations with its Arab neighbors may be seen at least in part as resulting from vastly different views of the nature of Jewish values and ideals and their role in the shaping of state policy. In their firm conviction that Jewish political sovereignty and Jewish identity were coterminous, the heirs to Herzlian Zionism have proven to be no more successful in developing a collective Jewish ethos in their own "community" than were their early opponents among the transitional generation of eastern Europe.

Despite the hopes of the creators of the Jewish state, the majority of world Jewry continue to live outside its borders. In doing so, they express their belief in the possibility of maintaining a viable Jewish life as a minority in a majority non-Jewish culture. Yet secular Zionists were unable to replace traditional religious ties and beliefs with a set of meaningful ideals that would link Jews around the world no matter where they lived. Today, Israeli leadership has not responded aggressively to the growing differences in perception within the world Jewish community over the nature and needs of Jewish life. Its attempt to create a unified ethos by centering Jewish commitment and concern on issues of the survival of Israel has only exacerbated the problem. Whether consciously or unconsciously, by diverting attention from the problems of assimilation and anti-Semitism, which the establishment of Israel did little to resolve, leaders of the Jewish state have generally ignored the special challenges facing Jews living in the Diaspora.

At the same time, the decline of Diasporist ideologies has left many members of Diaspora communities without an adequate language of their own to define their continued existence as Jews. While Jews in the modern Diaspora represent the most sophisticated and educated Jewish community in history, they remain generally ignorant of Jewish life and culture. The results are only too well known. Though displaying strong self-confidence in their economic strength and political influence, Jewish leaders in America and elsewhere are continually beset by uncertainty over their fate as a distinctive community. The Diaspora Jew's self-understanding is made more difficult by his or her acceptance of a simplistic and highly tendentious view of Jewish historical development in the modern era that is defined by the polarities of the Holocaust in Europe on the one hand and the creation of the State of Israel on the other. The attempts by at least some Jews to seek refuge in movements such as the Lubavitcher Hasidim, which reaffirm the traditional bases of Jewish identification, point up the inability of established Jewish communal leadership to clearly define and defend meaningful Jewish life outside the State of Israel.

From time to time, contemporary issues have served to temporarily rekindle the turn-of-the-century debate between Zionism and Diasporism. The controversy over the emigration of Soviet Jews in the 1980s, which pitted Israeli authorities against American Jewish leaders, was one such example. While most Diaspora Jews adopted a bicentric view that emphasized both the ability and the right of Russian immigrants to live full and rich Jewish lives in either the United States or Israel, others, including representatives of the Israeli and Zionist establishment, demanded that Russian Jews settle exclusively in Israel. (There was even a small group of Jews in America and Europe who reaffirmed the extreme "Diasporist" view of the need for Russian Jews to struggle for religious and civil rights in their own homeland.) The agreement among Diaspora and Israeli leaders to direct most Russian immigrants to Israel while allowing those who refused to migrate to the United States effectively put an end to the debate. Over the past decade, Jews throughout the world have watched with justifiable pride as hundreds of Russian Jews arrive daily at Ben-Gurion Airport. Yet the larger question of the viability of the Diaspora vis-à-vis Israel, which the issue of Russian Jewry unexpectedly raised, remains without clear resolution.

What then do the perspectives of Zhitlowski, Dubnow, and Ahad Ha-Am offer contemporary Jews in the Diaspora and Israel? Of the three individuals, Zhitlowski would appear to have the least relevance today. Unlike Dubnow and Ahad Ha-Am, he had an opportunity to test his ideas and policies in America itself. With the exception of helping to develop Yiddishist schools and the American Jewish Labor movement, both of which flourished during the interwar period and then quickly died in the aftermath of World War II, however, he had little success. Nevertheless, though Zhitlowski's emphasis on Yiddish proved to have little lasting relevance to American Jewry, his fierce commitment to the language points up the continuing need for the development of shared forms of communication and a common "method of speaking" among a dispersed people. The Jewish socialist's fascination with Christianity and the boundaries of Jewish identification also anticipate contemporary debates in Israel and in the United States over the appropriate communal response to intermarriage.[5] Similarly, his insistence on the need for Jews to link their fate with humanity as a whole, though framed in terms of a radical political agenda, nevertheless speaks to the challenge of contemporary Jews in the Diaspora who seek to define the nature of their loyalty to their people and to the larger society in which they live. Finally, Zhitlowski's belief in the need to concentrate on building the Diaspora while not losing sight of the distant goal of a Jewish homeland represented a foreshadowing of the bicentric ideal.[6]

And what of the Jewish historian Simon Dubnow? Despite the development of Jewish studies on university campuses throughout the world, few contemporary Jews share his concern with searching the past for clues to Jewish survival. Indeed, the study of history in general appears to have little meaning for a generation of Jews made up largely of individuals whose view of reality is, like that of most Americans, largely ahistorical. As the popular fascination with the Holocaust attests, at best contemporary Jews see history as a means of reinforcing their own visceral feelings about Jewry as the eternal victim of persecution. Nor do modern Jewish historians trained in general historiographical methodology and research techniques find much value in the manipulative manner in which Dubnow used history to illuminate contemporaneous concerns.

Yet Dubnow's attempt to transform the objective reality of the Diaspora into a source for Jewish revival could well aid those in the United States and elsewhere who are sincerely convinced that Jewish life outside the State of Israel has its own integrity and authenticity. His conviction that the source of Jewish strength lay in communal institutions offers a useful framework for an examination of the role of such contemporary institutions as the synagogue and the Jewish community center in the maintenance of Jewish life in the Diaspora. Further, the encouragement of ethnic difference in a number of different societies including Canada, France, and to a limited extent, the United States could well provide significant opportunities to establish forms of Jewish collective life that, although falling short of Dubnow's much vaunted autonomism, nevertheless could strengthen the role of communal structures in the development and the defense of commonly held values and beliefs.

Of the three transitional thinkers, it is Ahad Ha-Am who has emerged as the most relevant to contemporary Jewish life. It is not an exaggeration to say that most Diaspora Jews are crypto-Ahad Ha-Am'ists. With few exceptions, they define their commitment to Jewish life at least in part in terms of vaguely felt spiritual and cultural ties to the "Holy Land." While only a handful of Jews in America and elsewhere would ever consider relocating to Israel, most regard it a personal obligation to visit the Jewish state at least once in their lives. For all its faults, Israel remains the yardstick with which most Jews measure Jewish authenticity, even for those who choose not to settle there. If most Israelis cannot be said to be crypto-Ahad Ha-am'ists, it is nevertheless true that the ideas of the cultural Zionist have direct relevance to the experience of the formation of Israel's national consciousness in the period after 1948. Though modern-day Israel is justifiably consumed by immediate political and economic concerns, the resilience and strength of the Jewish state during its nearly fifty years of existence owes much to the power of Ahad Ha-Am's vision of a unified culture with ties to the past that can break through ideological and ethnic barriers to form an ongoing collective commitment to the Jewish future. Finally, Ahad Ha-Am's willingness to recognize that the Diaspora would survive despite the creation of a significant Jewish settlement in Palestine has proved to be remarkably prophetic. The cultural Zionist's "spiritual center" remains an unrealized (and probably an unrealizable) ideal. Yet there seems little question that if they are to remain strong and vital, relations between the Jewish State and the majority of world Jewry must be based as much on the shared ideals of a common heritage and a common culture as on concerns over Israeli security, economic development and growth, and the allocation of limited financial resources.

In their writings, Zhitlowski, Dubnow, and Ahad Ha-Am spoke to the needs of a society in which traditional religion no longer served as a binding loyalty for a growing number of its members. They were firmly convinced that without the intervention of a bold new personal and collective agenda, the modernization of Russian Jewry and of Russian society might well lead to the loss of communal solidarity and of Jewish distinctiveness. In contemporary America, the ease of assimilation has indeed led to an alarming rise in the number of unaffiliated Jews. Some have found spiritual meaning in cults and "New Age" movements. For a few young men and women, religious Orthodoxy has offered a way back to Jewish life. For the majority of committed Jews, however, the bonds of loyalty to the community, if they exist at all, rest on vaguely felt sentiments about a common Jewish fate. In many cases, even these ties are rapidly losing their power, whether because of the fading memory of the Holocaust or the "normalization" of the State of Israel.

Recently, Jewish sociologists have begun to talk about the development of a Jewish "civil religion" in both the American Jewish community and Israeli society. Briefly defined, the term refers to a system of secularized beliefs, values, and rituals through which Jews define their ultimate destiny, which is said to be replacing traditional Judaism. According to Charles Liebman and Eliezer Don-Yehiya who have studied the phenomenon in the Jewish state, one of the central purposes of Israeli "civil religion" is to unite the society by involving its members in a series of shared ceremonies and myths that express a common past and a common destiny.[7] Similarly, Jonathan Woocher, who has written about the "civil religion" of American Jews, suggests that its purpose is to produce in its adherents "the sentiment that the society or group is tied to a sacred order, that its history and activity point beyond themselves to a higher realm of purpose and significance."[8]

One senses in these developments the powerful echoes of ideas expressed by Zhitlowski, Dubnow, and Ahad Ha-Am almost a century ago. As the studies of secularization in the modern era clearly reveal, individuals and groups continue to search for transcendental meaning in their lives despite the loss of religious belief. In this sense, the desire of the transitional generation to find new bases for personal and collective Jewish identity while retaining the aura of tradition can be seen as not only a response to contemporaneous historical conditions but as a prescient insight into the deeply felt psychological needs that all men and women living in the modern era manifest in their attempt to examine their place in a rapidly changing and largely anonymous society.

There are those who might argue that the transitional generation has little to say to communities that have either developed in an environment of religious and cultural diversity or have achieved Jewish political sovereignty. Yet despite important differences, the challenges confronting contemporary Jewry remain essentially the same as those framed by Zhitlowski, Dubnow, and Ahad Ha-Am at the beginning of the twentieth century—the bitter struggles between religious and secular Jews, the alienation of younger Jews from the community, the fears of a growing divergence between the Diaspora and the Land of Israel, the quest for a common ground among the multiplicity of Jewish identities and commitments, and the continual pursuit of an appropriate role for the Jewish people in the world community.

Once, the ideologies of Zhitlowski, Dubnow, and Ahad Ha-Am spoke to a small but devoted group of Russian Jewish youth who responded to their invitation to assist in the creation of a new Jewish identity based upon a shared history, language, and culture. Once, their call for a new Jewish identity provided an exciting challenge for thoughtful young men and women desperately seeking to reconnect with their heritage and to find personal meanings in their lives. Given the crying need for leadership and direction that continues to frustrate the efforts by many Jews in both the Diaspora and Israel to define their common and distinct futures, is it too much to suggest that the voices of Zhitlowski, Dubnow, and Ahad Ha-Am deserve to be heard again in our own generation?

FOREIGN TERMS

aliyah - literally, ascension; the act of immigrating to the Land of Israel

galut - Exile

Geistesgeschichte - literally, spiritual history; a view of Jewish history that emphasizes the role of ideas and values

halakhah - Jewish religious law that defines daily rituals and observances

Hasidism - a popular religious movement that originated in eastern Europe at the end of the eighteenth century which stressed the importance of individual spirituality and was characterized by an emphasis upon personal ecstasy and charismatic leadership

Haskalah - movement of Jewish Enlightenment which began in Germany in the 1770s and spread to Russia beginning in the 1840s

Hibbat Zion - literally, Love of Zion; Jewish movement that arose in Russia in the 1880s pledged to colonization in Palestine; its supporters were know as Hoveve Zion (Lovers of Zion)

kahal - Jewish communal structure in Poland established in the thirteenth century which maintained itself in those areas incorporated into the Russian Empire at the end of the eighteenth century

Leidensgeschichte - literally, lachrymose history; a view of Jewish history that places primary emphasis upon the persecution of Jewry

maskilim - Jewish Enlighteners

matzah, plural *matzot* - unleavened bread eaten during Passover

misnagid - literally, an opponent; religious opponent of Hasidism in eastern Europe

mitzvah, plural *mitzvot* - a biblical commandment incumbent upon all Jews

Shulchan Aruch - literally, Set Table; a sixteenth-century book of Jewish laws written by Joseph Caro

tsadik - literally, the righteous one; charismatic leader associated with the Hasidic movement

yishuv - Jewish settlement in Palestine

NOTES

In citing works in the Notes, Hebrew and Yiddish titles have been translated and short titles have been used after the first mention in each chapter. Works frequently cited have been identified by the following abbreviations:

EJ   *Encyclopedia Judaica.* Jerusalem: Keter, 1971-72.

GS   Chaim Zhitlowski, *Gezamelte shriftn* (Collected Writings), 10 vols. New York:Yubelyum Oysgabe, 1912–17, 1919.

IAH   Asher Ginsberg, *Igrot Ahad Ha-Am* (The Letters of Ahad Ha-Am), 6 vols. Tel Aviv: Dvir, 1956–60.

KKAH   *Kol kitve Ahad Ha-Am* (The Collected Writings of Ahad Ha-Am). Tel Aviv: Dvir, 1965.

LJAN   Simon Doubnov, *Lettres sur le judaïsme ancien et nouveau* (Letters on Old and New Judaism), translated and annotated by Renée Poznanski. Paris: Éditions du Cerf, 1989.

Introduction: The Transitional Generation

1. Eli M. Lederhendler, "Religious Reform in Russian Haskalah," *1830–1880* (unpublished essay, 1979), p. 1.

2. Thus, for example, the Jewish historian Michael Meyer has defined the impact of modernization upon Jewish identity as "the historical process whereby increased exposure to non-Jewish ideas and symbols progressively erodes the given generational continuities, first in one location, then another, first among certain classes of Jews, then among others. Its product is Jewish modernity: the ongoing situation where internal continuity stands in potential or actual conflict with forces exterior to Jewish tradition." See Michael A. Meyer, *Jewish Identity in the Modern World* (Seattle: University of Washington Press, 1990), pp. 6–7.

3. A typical example of this approach is that of the historian of Russian Jewry Jonathan Frankel, who equates the pogroms with a political revolution, creating a sudden upsurge of opposition to established authority and ideology in the Jewish community. See "The Crisis of 1881–82 as a Turning Point in Modern Jewish History" in *The Legacy of Jewish Migration: 1881 and Its Impact*, edited by David Berger (New York: Social Science Monographs, Brooklyn College Press, 1983), pp. 9–22.

4. Robert Wohl, *The Generation of 1914* (Cambridge, Mass.: Harvard University Press, 1979), p. 210.

5. Among other figures of the transitional generation were the Labor Zionist A. D. Gordon and the socialist Zionist Nahman Syrkin. For information on Gordon, see David Kenani, *Ha-aliyah ha-shniyah ha-ovedet vi-yehasehah le-dat u-le-masoret* (The Second Labor Aliyah and Its Relationship to Religion and Tradition) (Tel Aviv: Sifriyat Poalim, 1976), pp. 56–70; for Syrkin, see Marie Syrkin's study of her father, *Nachman Syrkin, Socialist Zionist: A Biographical Memoir* (New York: Herzl Press, 1961).

6. See, for example, the comments by Nathan Rotenstreich in *Tradition and Reality: The Impact of History on Modern Jewish Thought* (New York: Random House, 1972), p. 115.

7. As the Israeli sociologist Shmuel Eisenstadt has argued: "[I]t is quite clear that once intellectuals have contributed to the shaping of new symbols of collective identity, they are taken up by other elites. Intellectuals are then relegated to a more specialized and less central role, culturally and politically." See "Intellectuals and Tradition" in *Intellectuals and Tradition*, edited by S.N. Eisenstadt and S.R. Graubard (New York: Humanities Press, 1973), p. 7.

8. It is interesting to note, for example, that Ahad Ha-Am suffered greatly during his sojourn in London, in large part because the East European immigrant population in the British capital was so small. In turn, Zhitlowski was drawn to America mainly because of its growing Russian Jewish population. Similarly, the Hebrew writer David Frischman, who resided in Berlin at the same time as Dubnow, is said to have made the following comment about the parochialism of the Russian Jewish emigré community living in the German capital: "When you come to Germany you have to know the language of the country, that is, Russian, Polish, and Yiddish." Cited in Mordechai Noruk, "Pegishato im Dubnov" (A Meeting with Dubnow), *He-Avar* (The Past) 8 (1961): 23.

9. Typical of their response to non-Ashkenazic or Sephardic Jews of the Middle East and North Africa was the following observation by Dubnow: "[T]he entire East slumbered on the eve of the stormy nineteenth century. Eventually—only at the end of the century— the rumble of the seething European movements would manifest themselves here; and a new life would echo among the ancient tombs." See Simon Dubnow, *History of the Jews*, translated by Moshe Spiegel (New York: Thomas Yoseloff, 1967-73), vol. 4, p. 491.

10. In the spring of 1917, Simon Dubnow commented on World War I in the following terms, typical of his generation: "From my earliest youth, I saw the idea of peace as the foundation of progress: as long as men fought they would never be able to escape from a condition of barbarism. And now in my old age I have arrived at the most barbaric war in all three of its manifestations: a war of nations, a war of peoples within nations, and a war of classes within peoples. It is a deluge and it would be horrible to die without the security of knowing that this deluge will not return, that a rainbow of peace will shine among nations, peoples, and classes." Cited in Yom-Tov Hellman, "Rabi Shimon Dubnov" (Rabbi Simon Dubnow), *He-Avar* 8 (1961): 16.

11. See, for example, the comments of Ahad Ha-Am in the first article of his collection, "Al dvar otsar ha-yahadut be-lashon ivrit" (On the Matter of a Treasury of Jewish Thought in the Hebrew Language), published in 1894, in *KKAH*, p. 105.

12. For a discussion of the concepts of fathers, sons, and grandsons as they apply to the Russian intelligentsia, see Martin Malia, "What is the Intelligentsia?" in *The Russian Intelligentsia*, edited by Richard Pipes (New York: Columbia University Press, 1961), pp. 12, 17. For a general discussion of the impact of the discovery of adolescence on late-nineteenth-century intellectual developments in Europe, see Wohl, *Generation of 1914*, p. 206.

13. David Vital, *Zionism: The Formative Years* (Oxford: Clarendon Press, 1988), p. 454.

14. Robert J. Brym, *The Jewish Intelligentsia and Russian Marxism: A Sociological Study of Intellectual Radicalism and Ideological Divergence* (London: Macmillan, 1978), pp. 4–6, 45.

15. One historian insightfully describes the year 1905 as the "1848" of Jewish nationalism, both in the excitement it raised and the attendant disappointment. See Camillo Dresner, "Haim Zhitlovsky: Teoretikan 'ha-leumiyut ha-galutit' be-zikotah le-sotsializm" (Haim Zhitlowski: Theoretician of 'Diaspora Nationalism' and Its Relationship to Socialism), (unpublished Ph.D. dissertation, Hebrew University, 1975), p. 260.

16. Simon Doubnov, *LJAN*, Twelfth Letter, p. 397.

17. For a discussion of the differing responses of the transitional generation to the events of 1881 and 1905, see Dubnow's prefatory remarks to Ahad Ha-Am's flyer entitled "Megilat-

starim shel Ahad Ha-Am" (The Secret Tract of Ahad Ha-Am), published in 1905 and reproduced in *KKAH*, p. 501.

18. Robert N. Bellah, "The Historical Background of Unbelief" in *The Culture of Unbelief*, edited by Rocco Caporale and Antonio Grumelli (Berkeley: University of California Press, 1971), p. 39.

19. Haim Zhitlowski, "Di natsional-politishe vidergeburt fun der idisher religie" (The National-Political Renaissance of the Jewish Religion), in *GS*, vol. 4, p. 250.

20. Thus, for example, in the fashion of the time, all three individuals used the term "rare" to denote deeply ingrained national traits rather than biologically predetermined ones. For a short discussion of the problem, see Joshua Fishman, *Ideology, Society, & Language: The Odyssey of Nathan Birnbaum* (Ann Arbor: Karoma Publishers, 1987), p. 90.

21.The statement by Ahad Ha-Am is taken from his essay "Ha-kongres ha-tsiyoni harishon" (The First Zionist Congress), written after the First Zionist Congress in 1897 and reproduced in *KKAH*, p. 276. Similarly, Simon Dubnow described the role of the prophets (and by implication Jewish historians such as himself) in the following terms: "The power of the prophetic message lay in the graphic lesson of history, in the repeated hammering away at the idea that moral law is dominant in the histories of nations" (*History of the Jews*, vol. 1, p. 213). In turn, the prominent American Zionist Judah Magnes described Zhitlowski as "a preacher who calls men back to repentance, and who seeks to urge them on to higher ideals and new achievements." Cited in Dresner, "Haim Zhitlovsky," pp. 189–90.

22. See, for example, Jacques Kornberg's "At the Crossroads: An Introductory Essay," in *At the Crossroads: Essays on Ahad Ha-am* (Albany: SUNY Press, 1983), p. xv.

23. Avraham Zarzuvsky, "Mihanekh ha-dor" (Educator of a Generation), Ha-Shiloach 30 (1914): 296. See also Moshe Kleinman, "Meh hayah lano Ahad Ha-Am?" (What Did Ahad Ha-Am Mean to Us?), ibid., 297–301; and Chaim Nachman Bialik,"On Ahad Ha-Am," *Jewish Frontier* 21, no. 10 (November 1964): 19–21. See also Bialik's comments in *Devarim sheh be-al peh* (Oral Statements) (Tel Aviv: Dvir, 1935), vol. 2, pp. 192, 201, 205–6.

24. Followers of these modern-day prophets often described them in hagiographic terms. Thus, for example, Zhitlowski's leadership abilities led to the hyperbolic comment by one of his supporters that he was "the Moshe Rabenu (Moses Our Teacher) of our generation." See also Yom-Tov Hellman's comments on Dubnow's followers in St. Petersburg in his article "Rabi Shimon Dubnov," pp. 10–16. For an interesting discussion of the manner in which Ahad Ha-Am cultivated his role as a leader, see the unpublished essay by Steven Zipperstein, "Ahad Ha-Am as a Leader: Elitism and the Coming of Mass Jewish Politics" (1988).

25. The sociologist and linguist Joshua Fishman correctly describes these groups as "congeries of individuals in search of common threads and structures to bind them together effectively into operative forces." See *Ideology, Society, & Language*, p. 124.

26. For a typical discussion of the generation's view of the publicist's role, see Ahad Ha-Am's essay "Teudat Ha-Shiloach" (The Mission of *Ha-Shiloach*), *KKAH*, pp. 126–28.

27. Erik Erikson, *Young Man Luther* (New York: W. W. Norton, 1958), p. 103.

28. For an interesting discussion of this phenomenon as it applies to intellectuals in general, see Richard K. Fenn, "Toward a Theory of Secularization," *Society for the Scientific Study of Religion, Monograph Series Number 1* (Ellington, Conn.: K & R Publishers, 1978), p. 61.

29. See, for example, Dubnow's description of the Prophets in his *History of the Jews*, vol. 1, pp. 14–17.

30. Surprisingly, none of the three expressed much interest in Zechariah Frankel's Positive Historical Judaism. In its emphasis upon continuity and change and its recognition of the role of the Jewish collectivity in shaping history and culture, Frankel's position seemed

to closely mirror that of the generation under study. Nevertheless, the founder of the Conservative movement was generally lumped together with other western religious reformers as an apologist to non-Jews and a traitor to the Jewish people. See, for example, the comments of Ahad Ha-Am in his article "Tehiyat ha-ruach" (Revival of the Spirit), published in 1902, *KKAH*, p. 188.

31. For an interesting comparison between the attitudes of the Haskalah and the transitional generation, see Michael Stanislawski's discussion of Judah Leib Gordon and Ahad Ha-Am in *For Whom Do I Toll?: Judah Leib Gordon and the Crisis of Russian Jewry* (Oxford: Oxford University Press, 1988), p. 228.

32. For further information, see Tchernowitz's memoir *Pirke haim* (Chapters in My Life) (New York: Bitzaron, 1954), pp. 188–91.

33. See, for example, Simon Dubnow's comments on the deleterious impact of hellenization upon Jewry in his *History of the Jews*, vol. 1, p. 516.

34. Eli M. Lederhendler, *The Road to Modern Jewish Politics: Political Tradition and Political Reconstruction in the Jewish Community of Tsarist Russia* (New York: Oxford University Press, 1989), pp. 85–86.

35. Evgenii Lampert, *Sons Against Fathers: Studies in Russian Radicalism and Revolution* (Oxford: Clarendon Press, 1965), p. 42.

36. Bernard Meland, *The Secularization of Modern Cultures* (New York: Oxford University Press, 1966), p. 11. See also the comments by Antonio Grumelli in his essay "Secularization: Between Belief and Unbelief" in *The Culture of Unbelief*, edited by Rocco Caporale and Antonio Grumelli (Berkeley: University of California Press, 1971), p. 86.

37. Leopold H. Haimson, "The Parties and the State" in *The Transformation of Russian Society: Aspects of Social Change since 1861*, edited by Cyril E. Black (Cambridge, Mass.: Harvard University Press, 1960), p. 115.

38. Vladimir C. Nahirny, *The Russian Intelligentsia: From Torment to Silence* (New Brunswick, N.J.: Transaction Books, 1983), pp. 154–69.

39. Kornberg, "At the Crossroads," p. xvi.

40. For further information on the views of the two Austrian socialists, see Otto Bauer, *Die Nationalitätenfrage und die Sozialdemokratie* (The Nationalities Question and Social Democracy) (Vienna: I. Brand, 1907); and Karl Renner (Rudolf Springer), *Der Kampf der osterreichischen Nationen um den Staat* (The Struggle for a State of Austrian Nations) (Leipzig/Vienna: Duticke, 1902). See also the discussion of their theories in Oscar I. Janowsky, *The Jews and Minority Rights, 1898–1919* (New York: Columbia University Press, 1933), pp. 30–31.

41. See, for example, Dubnow's comments in *History of the Jews*, vol. 1, p. 516; vol. 3, p. 739; and vol. 4, p. 123.

42. Talcott Parsons, *On Institutions and Social Evolution: Selected Writings*, edited and with an Introduction by Leon H. Mayhew (Chicago: University of Chicago Press, 1982), pp. 106–14.

43. Leon Simon, *Ahad Ha-Am* (New York: Herzl Press, 1960), p. 308.

44. "Mi-masaotai be-erets yisrael" (From My Travels in the Land of Israel), *KKAH*, p. 474.

Chapter 1: The Secularization of Russian Jewry in the Nineteenth Century

1. See, for example, Jacob S. Raisin's *The Haskalah Movement in Russia* (Philadelphia: Jewish Publication Society, 1913); Louis Greenberg's *The Jews in Russia: The Struggle for Emancipation* (New York: Schocken, 1976), part 1, chap. 3, and part 2, chaps. 6 and 7; and Simon Dubnow's own *History of the Jews in Russia and Poland*, translated by I. Friedlander (Philadelphia: Jewish Publication Society, 1916–20), vol. 2.

2. One such effort is Steven Zipperstein's *The Jews of Odessa: A Cultural History, 1794–1881* (Stanford: Stanford University Press, 1985), which argues that objective conditions played a greater role than ideology in Russian Jewry's receptivity to modernity and its rejection of tradition. Odessa was an important center for the development of modernizing Jewish thought and activity and provided the backdrop for the intellectual development of two of the thinkers under study—Dubnow and Ahad Ha-Am. As a relatively open city situated in the region known as New Russia, however, Odessa was far more tolerant of Jews than most other areas of the Pale and it is doubtful that the experience of its Jewish community in the nineteenth century can be applied to many other communities in Russia.

An extreme example of a structuralist analysis of Jewish society in the modern era is Calvin Goldscheider and Alan S. Zuckerman's *The Transformation of the Jews* (Chicago: University of Chicago Press, 1984). See also the essay by Y. Trivush, "Partsufah shel odessa ha-yehudit" (The Face of Jewish Odessa), *He-Avar* (The Past) 1 (1953): 58–64.

3. Owen Chadwick, *The Secularization of the European Mind in the Nineteenth Century* (New York: Cambridge University Press, 1975); David Martin, *A General Theory of Secularization* (Oxford: Basil Blackwell, 1978); Susan Budd, *Varieties of Unbelief: Atheists and Agnostics in English Society* (London: Heinemann, 1976).

4. See, for example, the selections from the writings of socialist Zionists in Arthur Hertzberg's *The Zionist Idea* (New York: Atheneum, 1970), pp. 329–95; Lucy Dawidowicz's overview of East European secular Jewish thought in *The Golden Tradition* (New York: Holt, Rinehart & Winston, 1967); and Saul Goodman's anthology of Jewish secularism, *The Faith of Secular Jews* (New York: Ktav, 1976).

5. Isaac Deutscher, *The Non-Jewish Jew and other essays* (London: Oxford University Press, 1968); John Murray Cuddihy, *The Ordeal of Civility: Freud, Marx, Lévi-Strauss, and the Jewish Struggle with Modernity* (New York: Basic Books, 1974); Hannah Arendt, *The Jew as Pariah: Jewish Identity and Politics in the Modern Age*, edited with an Introduction by Ron H. Feldman (New York: Grove Press, 1978).

6. Information on the size of the Jewish population in Russia is extrapolated from the following sources, which offer widely divergent figures: Salo W. Baron, *The Russian Jew Under Tsars and Soviets* (New York: Macmillan, 1976), p. 64; Robert J. Brym, *The Jewish Intelligentsia and Russian Marxism: A Sociological Study of Intellectual Radicalism and Ideological Divergence* (London: Macmillan, 1978), pp. 30–31; Isaac Levitats, *The Jewish Community in Russia, 1844-1917* (Jerusalem: Posner and Sons, 1981), pp. 1–4; Richard Pipes, *The Formation of the Soviet Union: Communism and Nationalism, 1917–1923* (Cambridge, Mass.: Harvard University Press, 1970), pp. 2–3; Isaac Rubinow, "Economic Condition of the Jews in Russia," *Bulletin of the United States Bureau of Labor* 72 (September 1907): 488; Robert M. Seltzer, "Simon Dubnow: A Critical Biography of His Early Years" (unpublished Ph.D. dissertation, Columbia University, 1970), pp. 3–4; David Vital, *The Origins of Zionism* (Oxford: Oxford University Press, 1980), pp. 30–33; Shmuel Ettinger, "Russian Society and the Jews," *Bulletin on Soviet and Eastern European Jewish Affairs* 5 (1970): 36–42.

7. Simon Kuznets, "Immigration of Russian Jews to the United States: Background and Structure," *Perspectives in American History* 9 (1975): 67. Michael Aronson has attempted to take a middle position by arguing that the increase in population can be explained by high birth rates and relatively low child mortality rates, which resulted from medical advances and the special concern that Jewish parents and community organizations showed toward children. See his *Troubled Waters: The Origins of the 1881 Anti-Jewish Pogroms in Russia* (Pittsburgh: University of Pittsburgh Press, 1990), pp. 38-39.

8. Rubinow, "Economic Condition of the Jews," 496; Yehuda Slutsky, "Sikum agum" (A

Somber Summary), *He-Avar* 19 (1972): 6.

9. See, for example, the comments of Lev Levanda, a writer who served as the Jewish expert to the governor general of Vilna from 1860 to his death in 1888, in *Rassvet* (Dawn) 1 (1860): 8, cited in Greenberg, *Jews in Russia*, p. 160. See also the comments on Vilna Jewry by a member of the British Royal Commission on Alien Immigration, cited in Vital, *Zionism: The Formative Years* (Oxford: Clarendon Press, 1988) p. 170.

10. Levitats, *Jewish Community in Russia*, p. 163.

11. Figures cited in "Russia," in *EJ* , vol. 14, col. 443.

12. Baron, *The Russian Jew*, p. 73; Stephen M. Berk, *Year of Crisis, Year of Hope: Russian Jewry and the Pogroms of 1881–1882* (Westport, Conn.: Greenwood Press, 1985), p. 29. For a detailed study of Russian Jewish immigration to the United States between 1881 and 1914, see Simon Kuznets' "Immigration of Russian Jews to the United States," 93, 100. Kuznets concludes from an examination of the statistical evidence that the tendency to emigrate was greater among men than among women, among able-bodied types rather than children and the elderly, among lower-income groups, and among those more adversely affected by legal restrictions and persecution. At the same time, there was a greater tendency for Russian Jews as opposed to non-Jewish immigrants to the United States to bring their families with them.

13. Yaakov Lestschinsky, "Ha-reka ha-kalkali shel tehom ha-moshav la-yehudim berusyah" (The Economic Background of the Russian Jewish Pale), *He-Avar* 1 (1953): 41. The area of Poland annexed to the Russian Empire after the Congress of Vienna retained separate status as the Kingdom of Poland or "Congress Poland" as it was popularly known. Jews living in this area were treated differently than Jews in the Pale and their history is not incorporated in the present study. For a thorough discussion of the development of the Pale of Settlement and its relationship to tsarist policies toward Russian Jews in the nineteenth century, see Shmuel Ettinger, "Ha-yesodot veha-megamot be-itsuv mediniyuto shel ha-shilton ha-rusi klape ha-yehudim im halukot polin" (The Foundations and Goals of Russian Policy Toward Jews After the Polish Partitions), *He-Avar* 19 (1972): 20–34.

14. Kuznets, "Immigration of Russian Jews," 69–70.

15. Ezra Mendelsohn, *Class Struggle in the Pale: The Formative Years of the Jewish Workers' Movement in Tsarist Russia* (Cambridge: Cambridge University Press, 1970), p. 3.

16. For information on Jewish populations in specific cities in the nineteenth century, see Lestschinsky, "Ha-reka ha-kalkali," 39; and Rubinow, "Economic Condition of the Jews," 491, 493. Rubinow cites a study by the Jewish Colonization Study in 1898 which concluded that 77.8 percent of Russian Jews lived in urban areas.

17. Edward C. Thaden, ed., *Russification in the Baltic Provinces and Finland, 1855–1914* (Princeton: Princeton University Press, 1981), p. 459.

18. As the Russian historian Marc Raeff notes: "At no point was it [the Russian Empire] conscious or aware of the dynamic force of nationalism and nationality. Yet the Russian government did not aim at eradicating or destroying nations or nationalities. It simply felt that their way of life would change in a process of natural evolution which their membership in the Empire could speed up and help along. That this might at the same time lead to the destruction of traditional customs, language, or sense of identity which people held very dear did not seem to enter into governmental expectations." See "Patterns of Russian Imperial Policy," in *Soviet Nationality Problems*, edited by Edward Allworth (New York, Columbia University Press, 1971), pp. 37–38.

19. Hélène Carrère d'Encausse, *The Great Challenge: Nationalities and the Bolshevik State, 1917–1930* (New York: Holmes & Meier, 1992), pp. 5–6.

20. John Klier, "The Ambiguous Legal Status of Russian Jewry in the Reign of Catherine

II," *Slavic Review* 39, no. 3 (September 1976): 513.

21. Hans Rogger, "The Jewish Policy of Late Tsarism: A Reappraisal," *Wiener Library Bulletin* 25 (1971): 43.

22. Pipes, *Formation of the Soviet Union*, pp. 5–6.

23. Hans Rogger, *Jewish Policies and Right-Wing Politics in Imperial Russia* (Berkeley/ Los Angeles: University of California Press, 1986), p. 27.

24. Rogger, "Jewish Policy of Late Tsarism," 43.

25. John Klier, *Russia Gathers Her Jews:The Origins of the"Jewish Question" in Russia, 1772–1825* (DeKalb: Northern Illinois University Press, 1986), pp. 28, 30.

26. For a representative example of such sentiments, see the synopsis of three articles written by the journalist I. Aksakov in 1862 and 1864 in Shmuel Ettinger's essay "Ha-reka ha-ideologi le-hofa'atah shel ha-sifrut ha-antishemit ha-hadasha be-rusyah" (The Ideological Background to the Appearance of the Literature of the New Anti-Semitism in Russia), *Zion* 35, nos.1–2 (1970): 214–16. In the article written in 1864, Aksakov summarized the threat that Jews posed to Russian Christian values in the following terms: "Consciously, the believing Jew continues to crucify the Messiah and to struggle against His ideas, in a forceful and desperate manner, in order to gain the right to the spiritual chosenness that he lost, and in reaffirming the Torah [he ventures out] to do battle against He who came to annul it." Cited in ibid., 216.

27. See, for example, Evgenii Lampert, *Sons Against Fathers: Studies in Russian Radicalism and Revolution* (Oxford: Clarendon Press, 1965), p. 114.

28. Hugh Seton-Watson, *The Decline of Imperial Russia, 1855–1914* (New York: Frederick A. Praeger, 1952), pp. 17–18.

29. For a thorough discussion of Russian policy toward Jews in the period before and immediately after the partition of Poland, see Klier, *Russia Gathers Her Jews*, pp. 22-80, and his article "Ambiguous Legal Status of Russian Jewry," 504–17.

30. For information on Jewish agricultural colonization in nineteenth-century Russia, see Y. N. Steinberg, "Yidishe kolonizatsie" (Jewish Colonization), *Algemayne Entsiklopedie*, Yidn A (New York: CYCO, 1950), col. 490.

31. Cited in Ettinger, "Ha-reka ha-ideologi," 194.

32. For an insight into the attitudes and behavior of the small group of middle-class Jews who lived outside the Pale during this period, see Oskar Gruzenberg's *Yesterday: Memoirs of a Russian-Jewish Lawyer*, edited by D.C. Rawson (Berkeley: University of California Press, 1981).

33. Levitats, *Jewish Community in Russia*, pp. 13–14; Greenberg, *Jews in Russia*, p. 80.

34. Aronson, *Troubled Waters*, p. 21.

35. Ettinger, "Ha-reka ha-ideologi," 201.

36. Barbara A. Engel, *Mothers and Daughters: Women of the Intelligentsia in Nineteenth-Century Russia* (London/New York: Cambridge University Press, 1983), p. 47.

37. For further information on the increase in anti-Semitic attitudes among Russian intellectuals in the wake of the Polish uprising, see Ettinger,"Ha-reka ha-ideologi," 193–225.

38. Rubinow, "Economic Condition of the Jews," 507.

39. Ibid., 521.

40. Greenberg, *Jews in Russia*, pp. 95–97. Individual Jewish participants in *Narodnaya Volya* figure prominently in Barbara Engel's discussion of the involvement of women in the organization. See *Mothers and Daughters*, pp. 173–90.

41. Dubnow, *History of the Jews in Russia*, vol. 2, p. 342.

42. Sidney S. Harcave, *First Blood: The Russian Revolution of 1905* (New York: Macmillan, 1964), p. 21.

43. Ben-Tsion Katz, "Ha-yahadut ha-rusit be-shnat ha-mahapekha veha-peraot 1905" (Russian Jewry During the Revolution and Riots of 1905), *He-Avar* 4 (1956): 3–10.

44. For further information on the deputies, see Sidney S. Harcave, "The Jewish Question in the First Russian Duma," *Jewish Social Studies* 6 (1944): 156–57.

45. For a personal account of the impact of the assassination of Stolypin and the onset of the Beilis case on the Jewish community, see Simon Dubnow's edited version of the memoirs of A. N. Goldenstein, a young Russian Jewish soldier, published in French as *Histoire d'un soldat juif, 1881–1915* (History of a Jewish Soldier, 1881-1915) (Paris: Editions du Cerf, 1988), pp. 44–45.

46. Ibid., pp. 49–50, 62–67, 75–78.

47. For a discussion of the circumstances surrounding the granting of civil rights to Jews after the February 1917 revolution, see Shaul Ginsburg, *Amolike petersburg: Forshungn un zikhroynes vegn yidishn lebn in tsarishn rusland* (St. Petersburg of Yesteryear: Studies and Recollections Concerning Jewish Life in Tsarist Russia) (New York: CYCO, 1944), pp. 247–56.

48. I[rwin] Michael Aronson, "Nationalism and Jewish Emancipation in Russia: The 1880s," *Nationalities Papers* 5, no. 2 (1977): 178. See also the comments by John Klier in *Russia Gathers Her Jews*, pp. 183–84.

Recent scholarship has attempted to portray a more nuanced picture of tsarist policy toward Jews, particularly during the reigns of Catherine II, Nicholas I, and Alexander III, which traditionally have been associated with brutal anti-Semitism. For a discussion of Catherine II, see Richard Pipes, "Catherine II and the Jews: The Origins of the Pale of Settlement," *Soviet Jewish Affairs* 5, no. 2 (1975): 3–20; on Nicholas I, see Michael Stanislawski, *Tsar Nicholas I and the Jews: The Transformation of Jewish Society in Russia, 1825–1855* (Philadelphia: Jewish Publication Society, 1983); on Alexander II, see I[rwin] Michael Aronson's two articles, "The Attitudes of Russian Officials in the 1880s Toward Jewish Assimilation and Emigration," *Slavic Review* 34, no. 1 (March 1975): 1-18; and "The Prospects for the Emancipation of Russia Jewry during the 1880s," *Slavonic and East European Review* 55 no. 3 (1977): 348–69; and Rogger, "Jewish Policy of Late Tsarism," 42–51.

49. Kuznets, "Immigration of Russian Jews," 55.

50. Figures from the study conducted by the Jewish Colonization Society in 1898 and cited in Kuznets, "Immigration of Russian Jews," 79.

51. Rubinow, "Economic Condition of the Jews," 538–39.

52. By 1900, more than 60 percent of the rail network was under state control. See Karl C. Thalheim, "Russia's economic development," in *Russia Enters the Twentieth Century, 1894–1917*, edited by Erwin Oberländer et al. (New York: Schocken Books, 1971), p. 105.

53. Kuznets, "Immigration of Russian Jews," 79.

54. Aronson, *Troubled Waters*, p. 37.

55. Ibid.; Goldscheider and Zuckerman, *Transformation of the Jews*, pp. 95-96; Rubinow, "Economic Condition of the Jews," 520, 524.

56. Werner E. Mosse, *Alexander II and the Modernization of Russia* (New York: Macmillan, 1958), pp. 78–79. For a general discussion of the impact of the abolition of serfdom on the Russian countryside, see Harry T. Willetts, "The agrarian problem," in *Russia Enters the Twentieth Century, 1894-1917*, edited by Erwin Oberländer et al. (New York: Schocken Books, 1971), pp. 114-19.

57. Baron, *The Russian Jew*, p. 86; Klier, "Ambiguous Legal Status of Russian Jewry," 509.

58. Berk, *Year of Crisis, Year of Hope*, p. 25. See also Steven J. Zipperstein, "Russian Maskilim and the City," in *The Legacy of Jewish Migration: 1881 and Its Impact*, edited by David Berger (New York: Social Science Monographs, Brooklyn College Press, 1983), p. 34.

59. Aronson, *Troubled Waters*, p. 39.

60. Rubinow, "Economic Condition of the Jews," 524–25, 529–30.

61. For a discussion of the development of a Jewish proletariat in late-nineteenth-century Russia, see Mendelsohn, *Class Struggle in the Pale*, pp. 1-26.

62. Rogger, *Jewish Policies and Right-Wing Politics*, p. 17.

63. Seltzer, "Simon Dubnow," p. 3; Baron, *The Russian Jew*, p. 94. In "Immigration of Russian Jews," 79, Kuznets estimates that between one-fifth and one-quarter of the Jews of the Pale lived "at miserably low economic levels." For a complete discussion of the occupations of Russian Jews based upon figures from the 1897 government census, see Rubinow, "Economic Condition of the Jews," 498–502.

64. As a secret memorandum that accompanied the establishment of the Crown schools stated, the purpose of the new educational institutions was to "bring them [the Jews] nearer to the Christians and . . . uproot the harmful beliefs which are influenced by the Talmud." Cited in "Russia," *EJ*, vol. 14, col. 440.

65. Alexander Orbach, *New Voices of Russian Jewry: A Study of the Russian-Jewish Press in the Era of the Great Reforms, 1860–1871* (Leiden: E.J. Brill, 1980), p. 161.

66. Ibid.

67. Levitats, *Jewish Community in Russia*, p. 47.

68. Yehuda Slutsky, *Ha-itonut ha-yehudit be-toldot ha-yehudim be-mizrach eropah ad 1881* (The Jewish Press in the History of East European Jewry Until 1881) (Jerusalem: Mossad Bialik, 1971), p. 27.

69. Zvi Halevy, *Jewish Schools Under Czarism and Communism* (New York: Springer Library, 1976), p. 60; Zipperstein, *Jews of Odessa*, pp. 129–30; Levitats, *Jewish Community in Russia*, pp. 118–20; Shmaryahu Levin, *Forward from Exile* (New York: Jewish Publication Society, 1967), p. 95; Yakov Lestschinsky, "Moreshet ha-yahadut ha-rusit mi-lifne ha-mishtar ha-sovieti" (The Russian Jewish Heritage Before the Advent of Soviet Rule), He-Avar 4 (1956): 14.

70. For further information, see the article "Shtetl," *EJ*, vol. 14, cols. 1466–73. For a romanticized view of shtetl life, see Mark Zborowski and Elizabeth Herzog, *Life Is with People: The Culture of the Shtetl* (Philadelphia: Schocken, 1972).

71. Bernard Weinryb, *The Jews of Poland, 1500–1800* (Philadelphia: Jewish Publication Society, 1973), pp. 179–205; Robert M. Seltzer, *Jewish People, Jewish Thought: The Jewish Experience in History* (New York, Macmillan, 1980), p. 482.

72. Slutsky, "Sikum agum," 8.

73. Klier, *Russia Gathers Her Jews*, p. 65. For a detailed discussion of relations between government authority and *kahal* leadership during this period, see Eli M. Lederhendler, *The Road to Modern Jewish Politics: Political Tradition and Political Reconstruction in the Jewish Community of Tsarist Russia* (New York: Oxford University Press, 1989), pp. 47–52.

74. For further information on the nature and methods of tax collection, see Levitats, *Jewish Community in Russia*, pp. 23–35. For a detailed discussion of the origin and development of the *korobka* and other taxes, see Mordechai Berger, "Mas nerot shabat be-rusyah" (The Sabbath Candles Tax in Russia), *He-Avar* 19 (1972): 127–31.

75. For more information on the institution of the "Crown" rabbinate, see Azriel Shochat's work *Mosad "ha-rabanut mi-taam" be-rusyah* (The Institution of the Crown Rabbinate in Russia) (Haifa: University of Haifa Press, 1975). For the experiences of a young intellectual who assumed a position as crown rabbi in Vilna, see Shmaryahu Levin, *Forward from Exile*. According to Levitats, in the city of Novgorod a Christian was appointed to the position. Levitats, *Jewish Community in Russia*, p. 88.

76. See, for example, the letter sent to the minister of the interior in 1853 by the poor of Chichelnik protesting the abuse of the collection of the *korobka* tax by communal leaders,

cited in Levitats, *Jewish Community in Russia*, pp. 26–27.

77. Lederhendler, *Road to Modern Jewish Politics*, pp. 52, 68. As Lederhendler notes: "Political representation, as such, passed completely into the hands of individuals of local, regional, or sometimes national reputation, almost all of whom acted out of their own sense of civic responsibility or personal capability and ambition, none of whom was accountable to some higher Jewish authority and most of whom defined the Jewish interest in more or less narrowly subjective terms." See ibid.

78. For a discussion of the nature of communal authority after the abolition of the *kahal* structure, see Levitats, *Jewish Community in Russia*, pp. 56–68, 129–46.

79. Stanislawski, *Nicholas I and the Jews*, pp. 127–31, 149–53. See also Stanislawski's essay "The Transformation of Traditional Authority in Russian Jewry: The First Stage," in *Legacy of Jewish Migration: 1881 and Its Impact*, edited by David Berger (New York: Social Science Monographs, Brooklyn College Press, 1983), pp. 23–30.

80. In his book on Polish Jewry, Bernard Weinryb claims that Hasidism also shared certain attitudes with some of the radical and mystical Russian Ukrainian sects of the period, including opposition to traditional sacred books and religious service, spiritualization of faith, and emphasis upon oral traditions through the telling of legends, stories, and songs. See Weinryb, *Jews of Poland*, p. 272.

81. Lederhendler, *Road to Modern Jewish Politics*, pp. 41–43.

82. Levitats, *Jewish Community in Russia*, pp. 99–102. For highly provocative discussions of the general impact of denominationalism upon traditional societies that have relevance to the Russian Jewish community in the early nineteenth century, see Chadwick, *Secularization of the European Mind*, pp. 40–45; and Bryan Wilson, *Religion in a Secular Society: A Sociological Comment* (London: Watts, 1966), pp. 30–45.

83. For Peter Berger's definition of "plausibility structure," see *A Rumor of Angels: Modern Society and the Rediscovery of the Supernatural* (Garden City, N.Y.: Anchor-Doubleday, 1970), p. 32; *The Sacred Canopy* (Garden City, N.Y.: Doubleday, 1967), pp. 45–51; and his collaborative work with Thomas Luckmann, *The Social Construction of Reality* (Garden City, N.Y.: Doubleday, 1966), pp. 106–7. See also Luckmann's essay "Belief, Unbelief, and Religion" in *The Culture of Unbelief*, edited by Rocco Caporale and Antonio Grumelli (Berkeley: University of California Press, 1971), pp. 21–37.

84. Wilson, *Religion in a Secular Society*, p. 184.

85. For information on the development of such associations, see Levitats, *Jewish Community in Russia*, pp. 69–84.

86. See, for example, David Vital's analysis of the membership of the proto-Zionist organization Hibbat Zion in *Zionism: The Formative Years*, pp. 479–94.

87. Statistics from Ilya Trotzky, "Jewish Institutions of Welfare, Education, and Mutual Assistance," in *Russian Jewry (1860–1917)*, edited by Jacob Frumkin et al. (New York: Thomas Yoseloff, 1966), p. 417; Brym, *Jewish Intelligentsia and Russian Marxism*, pp. 55–57; Levitats, *Jewish Community in Russia*, p. 48; and Ehud Luz, *Makbilim nifgashim: Dat veliumiyut ba-tnuah ha-tsiyonit be-mizrach eropah be-reshitah (1882–1904)* (When Parallels Meet: Religion and Nationalism in the Early Zionist Movement in Eastern Europe, 1882–1904) (Tel Aviv: Am Oved, 1985), pp. 39–40. Luz's work has also been published in English under the title *Parallels Meet: Religion and Nationalism in the Early Zionist Movement 1882–1904* (Philadelphia: Jewish Publication Society, 1988).

88. Of the 360 Russian students at the University of Berlin in 1905, for example, 261 were Jewish. Nevertheless, no more than 1,000 Jewish students from Russia lived in Germany at any given time before World War I. Figures from Robert C. Williams, *Culture in Exile: Russian Emigrés in Germany, 1881–1941* (Ithaca: Cornell University Press, 1972),

pp. 25, 34, and 49. According to the economist and statistician Arthur Ruppin, at the beginning of the twentieth century there were 655 Russian Jewish students in Germany, between 850 and 1,270 in Switzerland, and between 280 and 370 in France. During the same period, 1,757 Jewish students attended universities in Russia. Cited in Yisrael Klausner, *Opozitsiyah li-Herzl* (Opposition to Herzl) (Jerusalem: Achieved, 1960), p. 7.

89. Paula E. Hyman, "Culture and Gender: Women in the Immigrant Jewish Community," in *The Legacy of Jewish Migration: 1881 and Its Impact*, edited by David Berger (New York: Social Science Monographs, Brooklyn College Press, 1983), pp. 157–68.

90. Engel, *Mothers and Daughters*, p. 159.

91. Simon Dubnow, *Sefer ha-hayim* (Autobiography), vol. 1 (Tel Aviv: Dvir, 1936), p. 89. See also Rubinow, "Economic Condition of the Jews," 581.

92. Yehoshua Barzilay, "Ekh naaseh Asher Gintsberg le-Ahad Ha-Am (zikhronot)" (How Asher Ginsberg Became Ahad Ha-Am [Remembrances]), *Ha-Shiloach* 30 (1914): 303.

93. For further information on Zina Dizengoff, see Yosef Goldstein, *Ahad Ha-Am* (Jerusalem: Keter, 1992), p. 247.

94. Orbach, *New Voices of Russian Jewry*, p. 55.

95. Ibid., p. 89.

96. The terms are taken from Effie Ambler, *Russian Journalism and Politics: 1861-1881* (Detroit: Wayne State University Press, 1972), p. 27.

97. See, for example, the comments by Alexander Zederbaum, the founder of both *Ha-Melits* (The Interpreter) and *Kol Mevasser* (The Voice of the Messenger), cited in Orbach, *Voices of Russian Jewry*, p. 81.

98. For a discussion of the circumstances surrounding the development of *Ha-Melits* and *Kol Mevasser* with special reference to the role of their founder Alexander Zederbaum, see Orbach, *New Voices of Russian Jewry*. For a general discussion of the development of the Russian press in the eighteenth and nineteenth centuries, see Ambler, *Russian Journalism*, pp. 13–35.

99. Information on newspapers is taken from the article "Press," *EJ*, vol. 13, cols. 1044–45. For a specific discussion of the foundation and development of the Russian Jewish press, see Shaul Ginsburg, *Amolike petersburg*, pp. 155–69.

100. For an interesting insight into this phenomenon, see Chaim Aronson's memoirs *A Jewish Life Under the Tsars* (Totowa, N.J.: Allanheld, Osmun, 1983), pp. 95–96, 111.

101. Luz, *Makbilim nifgashim*, pp. 39–40. See also Levitats, *Jewish Community in Russia*, pp. 180–81.

102. Jacob Katz, "Yahadut ve-notsrut al reka ha-hiloniyut ha-modernit" (Judaism and Christianity in Light of Modern Secularism), *Leumiyut yehudit: masot u-mehkarim* (Jewish Nationalism: Essays and Research Articles) (Jerusalem: Ha-sifriyah ha-tsiyonit, 1983), p. 111.

103. See, for example, Simon Dubnow's comments about Russian society after the Kishinev pogrom of 1903, in *LJAN*, Twelfth Letter, pp. 394–96.

104. Yosef Eliahu Heller, "Le-dmuto ha-nafshit viha-ruhanit shel Ahad Ha-Am" (On Ahad Ha-Am's Practical and Spiritual Vision), *Melilah* 5 (1956): 261.

105. Franco Venturi, *Roots of Revolution* (New York: Grosset & Dunlap, 1960), p. 456. For a useful analysis of the concept and nature of the Russian intelligentsia, see George Fischer, "The Intelligentsia and Russia," in *The Transformation of Russian Society: Aspects of Social Change Since 1861*, edited by Cyril E. Black (Cambridge, Mass.: Harvard University Press, 1960), pp. 253–74.

106. For further information on Lavrov's views concerning the relationship between intellectuals and the masses, see Philip Pomper, *Peter Lavrov and the Russian Revolutionary Movement* (Chicago: University of Chicago Press, 1972), pp. 47, 66, 92–93, 101–2, 106.

107. See, for example, the discussion of Vilna yeshivas in Israel Cohen,*Vilna* (Philadelphia: Jewish Publication Society, 1943), p. 290.

108. B. Orlov, "A Statistical Analysis of Jewish Participation in the Russian Revolutionary Movement in the 1870s," *Slavic and Soviet Series* 4 (1979): 7; Greenberg, *Jews in Russia*, p. 149.

109. For information on Ukrainian support of a federalist state, see Carrère d'Encausse, *The Great Challenge*, pp. 19–22.

110. See, for example, the comments of Violet Conolly on Ukrainian nationalism in her article "The 'nationalities question' in the last phase of tsardom," in *Russia Enters the Twentieth Century, 1894–1917*, edited by Erwin Oberländer et al. (New York: Schocken, 1971), p.161; and by Seton-Watson on Polish and Ukrainian nationalist movements in *The Decline of Imperial Russia*, pp. 79–82.

111. According to the demographer and economist Jacob Lestschinsky, Jews constituted an absolute or relative majority of between 50 and 59 percent of the population in the main towns of the provinces of Minsk, Vitebsk, Grodno, Mohilev, Volhyn, Kielce, Siedlice, and Radom. The first four provinces were situated in White Russia, the fifth in the Ukraine, and the last three in Poland. See "Dubnow's Autonomism and His 'Letters on Old and New Judaism,'" in *Simon Dubnow, The Man and His Work*, edited by Aaron Steinberg (Paris: World Jewish Congress, 1963), pp. 88–89.

112. Ibid., p. 88.

113. See, for example, the debate between the Ukrainian historian and nationalist N. Kostomarov and the Ukrainian editor Belozerski and the editors of the Russian-language Jewish journal *Sion* (Zion), in 1861–62, cited in Ettinger, "Ha-reka ha-ideologi," 216–23. In an editorial in a Ukrainian-language paper, Belozerski argued that "[u]ntil now the Jewish tribe has lived apart in the midst of the population of southern Russia; until now it has not had anything in common with our nation and has not taken one step to interrelate with it; on the contrary, not infrequently it acts against the spirit and the welfare of our nation." Cited in Ettinger, 219.

In response, the editors of S*ion* derided the nationalism of "Little Russia," arguing that the Ukrainian language was inferior to Russian and that Ukrainian culture was merely *derivative of Russian culture*. See Orbach, *New Voices of Russian Jewry*, pp. 49–51.

114. See, for example, Ahad Ha-Am's comments on Lithuanians and Slovaks in his essay "Shlilat ha-galut" (Negation of the Diaspora), *KKAH*, p. 401; and Haim Zhitlowski's comments on Bulgarians and Finns in his article "A por verter vegn inteligents un am harates" (A Few Words Concerning Intelligence and Stupidity), *GS*, vol. 10, p. 144.

115. For an example of the penetration of themes of non-Russian nationalism into Jewish collectivist consciousness, see Shmaryahu Levin's discussion of Ukrainian nationalist movements in *Forward from Exile*, p. 133. For a general discussion of nationalist movements among Russia's ethnic minorities in the late-nineteenth and early twentieth centuries, see Conolly, "The 'Nationalities Question,'" pp. 155–81.

116. For information on Jewish autonomy demands in the Austro-Hungarian Empire, see Oscar I. Janowsky, *The Jews and Minority Rights, 1898–1919* (New York: Columbia University Press, 1933), pp. 136–44. For a discussion of the growth of Jewish nationalism in the Austro-Hungarian Empire, see Robert Wistrich, *Socialism and the Jews: The Dilemmas of Assimilation in Germany and Austria-Hungary* (East Brunswick, N.J.: Associated University Presses, 1982), pp. 207–14.

117. Cited in Carrère d'Encausse, *The Great Challenge*, p. 16.

118. See, for example, the statements cited in Lederhendler, *Road to Modern Jewish Politics*, p. 87.

119. Lederhendler argues provocatively if not altogether convincingly that in relying upon state support for their programs, the maskilim were merely continuing the practice of both traditional religious authorities and *shtadlanim* in the community. See ibid., pp. 89, 100.

120. Stanislawski, *Nicholas I and the Jews*, p. 53.

121. Cited in Orbach, *New Voices of Russian Jewry*, p. 29.

122. Gordon himself was not a Russifier per se but preached the importance of incorporating modernist values into Jewish life. For an intensive discussion of his ideas, see Michael Stanislawski, *For Whom Do I Toll?: Judah Leib Gordon and the crisis of Russian Jewry* (Oxford: Oxford University Press, 1988).

123. Figures from Alexander Orbach, "The Russian-Jewish Leadership and the Pogroms of 1881–1882: The Response from St. Petersburg," *The Carl Beck Papers in Russian and East European Studies*, paper no. 308 (Pittsburgh: University of Pittsburgh, 1984), p 10; and from "Moscow," *EJ*, vol. 12, cols. 363–64.

124. Orbach, *New Voices of Russian Jewry*, p. 31.

125. Yehuda Slutsky, *Tnuat ha-haskalah be-yahadut rusyah* (The Enlightenment Movement Among Russian Jews) (Jerusalem: Merkaz Zalman Shazar, 1977), p. 6; Michael Seltzer, *The Wineskin and the Wizard* (New York: Macmillan, 1970), pp. 139–40; Halevy, *Jewish Schools*, pp. 111–15; Goldstein, *Ahad Ha-Am*, p. 290.

126. Max Lilienthal, cited in Raisin, *The Haskalah Movement*, p. 177.

127. Rogger, "Jewish Policy of Late Tsarism," 50. See also M.S. Agurskij, "Die Judenchristen in der Russisch-Orthodoxen Kirche," *Ostkirchliche Studien* 23, no. 2/3 (September 1974): 155–56.

128. Rogger, *Jewish Policies and Right-Wing Politics*, p. 35; and "Jewish Policy of Late Tsarism," 48–49. See also Shmaryahu Levin's observations about the dilemma of Jewish converts in Ekaterinoslav in his *Forward from Exile*, pp. 351–53. For information on some of the more famous Jewish converts to Russian Orthodoxy, see Baron, *Russian Jew*, pp. 33–136.

129. Baron, *Russian Jew*, p.156; Steven J. Zipperstein, "Heresy, Apostasy, and the Transformation of Joseph Rabinovich," in *Jewish Apostasy in the Modern World*, edited by Todd M. Endelman (New York: Holmes & Meier, 1987), p. 208; Jacob Lestschinsky cited in David Kenani, *Ha-aliyah ha-shniyah ha-ovedet vi-yehasehah le-dat u-le-masoret* (The Second Labor Aliyah and Its Relationship to Religion and Tradition) (Tel Aviv: Sifriyat poalim, 1976), p. 73; Rogger, *Jewish Policies and Right-Wing Politics*, p. 35; and "Jewish Policy of Late Tsarism," 48. See also the comments by Kuznets in "Immigration of Russian Jews," 66.

130. Cited in Raisin, *The Haskalah Movement*, p. 248.

131. Zipperstein, "Joseph Rabinovich," pp. 223–24.

132. Berk, *Year of Crisis, Year of Hope*, p. 138; "Gordin, Jacob," *EJ*, vol. 7, cols. 787-89.

133. Baron, *Russian Jew*, p. 23.

134. For more information on the Kadets' attitudes toward Jews, see ibid., p. 20.

135. For a general discussion of the attitudes of Russian liberals towards Jews, see Yitzchak Maor, "Ha-liberalim ha-rusiyim be-meah ha-19 u-she'elat ha-yehudim" (Russian Liberals in the 19th Century and the Jewish Question), *He-Avar* 5 (1957): 90–103. See also the statements by Y.P. Karnovitch and S. Grumke in articles on the Jewish question published in the journal *Sovremennik* (The Contemporary) in 1858, cited in Ettinger, "Ha-reka ha-ideologi," 204-7.

136. Moshe Mishkinsky, "Al emdatah shel ha-tnuah ha-mehapkhanit ha-rusit le-gabe ha-yehudim be-shnot ha-70 shel ha-meah ha-19" (On the Position of the Russian Revolutionary Movement Toward Jews in the 1870s), *He-Avar* 9 (1962): 45; and Yitzchak Maor, *She'elat ha-yehudim be-tnuah ha-liberalit veha-mahapkhanit be-rusyah: 1890–1914* (The Jewish Question in the Liberal and Revolutionary Movements in Russia, 1890–1914) (Jerusa-

lem: Mossad Bialik, 1974), p. 106.

137. Cited in Maor, *She'elat ha-yehudim*, p. 111.

138. Lederhendler, *Road to Modern Jewish Politics*, pp. 137–38.

139. For further information on Brafman's work and the publication of anti-Semitic literature in Russia in the 1870s and '80s, see Norman Cohn, *Warrant for Genocide: The Myth of the Jewish World Conspiracy and the Protocols of the Elders of Zion* (New York: Harper & Row, 1969), pp. 51–59; and Levitats, *Jewish Community in Russia*, pp. 190–99.

140. Berk, *Year of Crisis, Year of Hope*, pp. 50–53, 74–75.

141. Aronson, *Troubled Waters*, pp. 217–19, 223–25.

142. Information from "Pogroms," *EJ*, vol. 13, cols. 695–97. For an exhaustive examination of the pogroms in their historical context, see the volume *Pogroms: Anti-Jewish Violence in Modern History*, edited by John D. Klier and Shlomo Lambroza (Cambridge: Cambridge University Press, 1992). For a forceful refutation of the argument that the Russian government supported the pogroms, see Aronson, *Troubled Waters*, pp. 82–144.

143. For further discussion of the hardening of government attitudes toward Jews in the 1880s, see I. Michael Aronson, "Nationalism and Jewish Emancipation in Russia," 167–82.

144. "Am Olam," *EJ*, vol. 2, cols. 861–62.

145. Cited in Berk, *Year of Crisis, Year of Hope*, p. 103.

146. For a discussion of the foundation of and contributors to *Voskhod*, see Ginsburg, *Amolike petersburg*, pp. 170–83. Beginning in 1901, the paper became the organ of the Jewish supporters of the Kadets.

147. For a detailed description of the founding and early development of the Jewish labor movement in Russia, see Mendelsohn, *Class Struggle in the Pale*.

148. For a discussion of Kishinev in the general context of Jewish responses to catastrophe, see David Roskies, *Against the Apocalypse: Responses to Catastrophe in Modern Jewish Culture* (Cambridge, Mass.: Harvard University Press, 1984), pp. 83–92.

Chapter 2: Haim Zhitlowski: Language, Political Radicalism, and Modern Jewish Identity

1. Emanuel S. Goldsmith, *Architects of Yiddishism at the Beginning of the Twentieth Century* (Rutherford, N.J.: Fairleigh Dickinson University Press, 1976), pp. 229, 240–41.

2. As Abraham Liessin, a Russian Yiddish poet and editor and Bundist supporter who moved to New York at the turn of the century, stated: "In 'Jargonism,' whose purpose was also to fight capitalism, I saw something new, an overturn in Jewish society, an intimation that the common man would come to demand his share in intellectual life. . . . The more the Jewish masses awakened, all the more would builders of our literature emerge." Cited in Lucy Dawidowicz, *The Golden Tradition: Jewish Life and Thought in Eastern Europe* (New York: Holt, Rinehart & Winston,1967) p. 425.

3. As Ruth Wisse has written somewhat hyperbolically about the dilemma of leftwing Yiddishists: "A Jew who lived in accordance with the religious tradition could presumably maintain his Jewishness in Spanish as well as English, or even modern Hebrew. A secular Zionist could abandon religious practice and many of the 'trappings' of Jewish culture, secure in the belief that statehood would generate a new national identity. The Jewish Left, however, had only its culture to set it apart from the Polish Left and the Russian Left, and that culture, stripped of its religious content, added up to Yiddish—the language, the folklore, the literature." See Ruth Wisse, "The Politics of Yiddish," *Commentary* 80, no. 1 (July 1985): 32.

4. Despite their similar backgrounds and perceptions, there were significant differences in the views of Syrkin and Zhitlowski, most notably on the viability of Palestine as a Jewish homeland. Syrkin summed up his disagreements with Zhitlowski in the following terms:

"We have divided the world between us. Zhitlovsky has taken everything that exists; I have taken everything that still does not exist. Zhitlovsky has chosen the Yiddish which we have; I, the Hebrew which we still do not have; Zhitlovsky has chosen the Diaspora which we have; I, the homeland which we still do not have." Cited in Marie Syrkin, *Nachman Syrkin, Socialist Zionist: A Biographical Memoir* (New York: Herzl Press, 1961), p. 158.

5. Shimen Dubnov, "Zhitlovskis autonomizm" (Zhitlowski's Autonomism), in *Zhitlovski zamlbukh* (Zhitlowski Anthology) (Warsaw: Farlag Ch. Brzoza, 1929), p. 190.

6. See especially the comments by Jonathan Frankel in *Prophecy and Politics: Socialism, Nationalism, and the Russian Jews, 1862–1917* (Cambridge: Cambridge University Press, 1981), p. 258. Frankel's chapter on Zhitlowski is an extremely insightful introduction to the role of the eclectic thinker in the Russian Jewish socialist movement at the turn of the century.

7. Camillo Dresner, "Haim Zhitlovsky: Teoretikan 'ha-leumiyut hagalutit' be-zikotah le-sotsializm" (unpublished Ph.D. dissertation, Hebrew University, 1975), p. 2.

8. Haim Zhitlowski, *Zikhroynes fun mayn lebn* (Remembrances of My Life) (New York: Posy-Shoulson Press, 1935), vol. 1, p. 119. The memoirs were published in three volumes and cover the period from Zhitlowski's birth through his stay in Switzerland.

9. Dresner, "Haim Zhitlovsky," p. 7.

10. Zhitlowski, *Zikhroynes*, vol. 1, p. 160.

11. Ibid., pp. 96, 262. For a specific discussion of Zhitlowski's attitudes concerning the economic activity of his family, see *Zikhroynes*, vol. 2, p. 38.

12. *Zikhroynes*, vol. 1, pp. 125, 210; vol. 2, p. 38.

13. In the 1930s, for example, Zhitlowski's attacks on Jewish "parasitism" occasioned especially bitter opposition within the American Jewish immigrant community. One of his fiercest critics was Hayim Lieberman, a former Yiddishist and socialist who in the 1930s joined the religious Zionist movement. Lieberman attacked Zhitlowski for pro-Communist and anti-religious views in two polemical works entitled *Doktor Haim Zhitlovski un zayne fartaydiker* (Doctor Haim Zhitlowski and His Defenders) (New York: 1944, n.p.); and *Idn un idishkayt in di shriftn fun Doktor Ch. Zhitlovski* (Jews and Judaism in the Writings of Doctor H. Zhitlowski) (New York: 1944, n.p.).

14. Zhitlowski, *Zikhroynes*, vol. 1, p. 48.

15. Fifty years later, Zhitlowski would express his continued deep respect for Chernyshevski by devoting more than twenty pages to him in his memoirs.

16. Zhitlowski, *Zikhroynes*, vol. 1, p. 259.

17. *Zikhroynes*, vol. 2, p. 216.

18. Ibid., p. 122. Zhitlowski also claimed to have been influenced by a story published in a Russian liberal magazine about a wolf who is hated by the local peasants and can only find respite from his tragic fate by committing suicide. Zhitlowski was convinced that the writer was referring to Jews who could only end anti-Semitism by assimilating into the general population. Cited in *Leksikon fun der nayer yidisher literatur* (Biographical Dictionary of Modern Yiddish Literature) (New York: CYCO, 1960), vol. 3, pp. 687–88.

19. For a synopsis of Lilienblum's earlier writings and the reaction to them within the Russian Jewish community, see Alexander Orbach, *New Voices of Russian Jewry: A Study of the Russian-Jewish Press in the Era of the Great Reforms, 1860–1871* (Leiden: E.J. Brill, 1980), pp. 134–45.

20. Zhitlowski, *Zikhroynes*, vol. 2, pp. 38–39.

21. Cited in Frankel, *Prophecy and Politics*, p. 259.

22. Zhitlowski, *Zikhroynes*, vol. 2, p. 39.

23. Ibid., p. 126; Frankel, *Prophecy and Politics*, p. 263.

24. Zhitlowski, *Zikhroynes*, vol. 2, p. 205.

25. Melech Epstein, *Profiles of Eleven* (Detroit: Wayne State University Press, 1965), p. 306.

26. Zhitlowski, *Zikhroynes*, vol. 3, pp. 127–30, 133.

27. For a discussion of the Jewish emigré community in Germany at the end of the nineteenth century, see Robert C. Williams, *Culture in Exile: Russian Emigrés in Germany, 1881–1941* (Ithaca: Cornell University Press, 1972), pp. 32–34, 49–51.

28. Zhitlowski, *Zikhroynes*, vol. 3, pp. 144, 218.

29. Dresner, "Haim Zhitlovsky," p. 25; Epstein, *Profiles of Eleven*, p. 307.

30. Frankel, *Prophecy and Politics*, p. 268.

31. The tract is reproduced in *GS*, vol. 6, pp. 13–55. See, also, Frankel's comments in *Prophecy and Politics*, pp. 268–70.

32. Frankel, *Prophecy and Politics*, p. 271.

33. For information on the SRs' position on the nationalities question, see Yitzchak Maor, *She'elat ha-yehudim be-tnuah ha-liberalit veha-mahapkhanit be-rusyah: 1890–1914* (Jerusalem: Mossad Bialik, 1974), pp. 194–95, 212–20.

34. The essay is reproduced in *GS*, vol. 5, pp. 31–43.

35. The essay is reproduced in ibid., pp. 47–76.

36. Cited in Frankel, *Prophecy and Politics*, p. 259.

37. See, for example, Zhitlowski's retrospective comments in the article "A por verter vegn inteligents un am haratses" (A Few Words Concerning Intelligence and Stupidity), published in 1910, *GS*, vol. 10, pp. 125–30. For a discussion of the Bund's position on the national question after its crucial Fourth Congress in 1901, see Henry J. Tobias, *The Jewish Bund in Russia: From Its Origins to 1905* (Stanford: Stanford University Press, 1972), pp. 160–76.

38. For further information on Zhitlowski's troubled association with the Bund, see Frankel, *Prophecy and Politics*, pp. 276–78.

39. "Saboni ki-dvoyrim" (They Surround Me Like Bees), published in 1914, *GS*, vol. 9, p. 47. For Zhitlowski's recollections of his meeting with Herzl, see "Eynige shoeh mit Dr. Teodor Herzl" (A Few Hours with Dr. Theodor Herzl), published in 1915, *GS*, vol. 9, pp. 7–40.

40. Dresner, "Haim Zhitlovsky," pp. 134–35.

41. Haim Zhitlowski, "Der kamf far idish-natsionale rekht (1900–1907)" (The Struggle for Jewish National Rights, 1900–1907), *Zukunft* 38 (December 1933): 713.

42. Gregor Aronson, "Ideological Trends Among Russian Jews," in *Russian Jewry (1860–1917)*, edited by Jacob Frumkin et al. (New York: Thomas Yoseloff, 1966), p. 163. For Zhitlowski's views on territorialism during this period, see his "Teritorializm — bemzumn oder oyf borg?" (Territorialism in Cash or on Credit?), published in 1906, *GS*, vol. 5, pp. 122–31.

43. Zhitlowski spoke of his interest in Swiss cantonism in a retrospective article, "Di problemn fun dem golus-natsionalizm" (The Problems of Diaspora Nationalism), *Zukunft* 38 (November 1933): 652–53.

44. Frankel, *Prophecy and Politics*, p. 270. In her memoirs, the anarchist Emma Goldman claimed that in 1904 Zhitlowski frequently visited her New York apartment to urge her to devote herself to the Jewish people. She refused, claiming that social injustice was not confined to one "race." Cited in Emma Goldman, *Living My Life* (New York: AMS Press, 1970) p. 370.

45. Leopold H. Haimson, "The Parties and the State," in *The Transformation of Russian Society: Aspects of Social Change since 1861*, edited by Cyril E. Black (Cambridge, Mass.: Harvard University Press, 1960), pp. 120–121; Zhitlowski, "Der kamf far idish-natsionale rekht," 714.

46. For a discussion of the development of the SERP program, see Frankel, *Prophecy and Politics*, pp. 282–83, 324; and Maor, *She'elat ha-yehudim*, pp. 221–27. For Zhitlowski's

critique of Dubnow's position, see his "Hern Dubnovs 'gaystiger' natsionalizm" (Mr. Dubnow's Spiritual Nationalism), published in 1908, *GS*, vol. 7, pp. 211–38.

47. In 1917 at a meeting in New York City, SERP and SS joined together as the so-called "*Fareinigte* " or United Jewish Socialist Workers Party. After the Russian Revolution, the Fareinigte would disband and unite with the Communist Party. For further information, see Michael Astur, *Geshikhte fun der frayland-lige un funm teritorialistishn gedank* (A History of the Free Land League and of the Territorialist Idea) (Buenos Aires/New York: Freiland Lige, 1967), vol. 1, pp. 20–21.

48. See, for example, Zhitlowski's comments in "Di Problemn fun dem golus natsionalizm," 655–57.

49. Maor, *She'elat ha-yehudim*, p. 225. For Zhitlowski's view of the situation in Russia, which he wrote upon arrival in the United States in 1909, see his "Vegn faraynigung" (Concerning Unity), parts 1 and 2, *GS*, vol. 4, pp. 47–75.

50. Cited in Dresner, "Haim Zhitlovsky," p. 88.

51. Oscar I. Janowsky, *The Jews and Minority Rights, 1898–1919* (New York: Columbia University Press, 1933), pp. 145–46.

52. "A idishe dorf un a idishe folks-bank" (A Jewish Village and a Jewish People's Bank), published in 1911, *GS*, vol. 10, pp. 184–86.

53. See, for example, Zhitlowski's comments in "Simonim fun a nayem lebn bay di idn in amerika" (Signs of a New Life among Jews in America), published in 1909, *GS*, vol. 10, pp. 171–72. It should be noted that Zhitlowski claimed in a later gloss published in 1918 that his "unreserved optimism" in the farmers' movement had disappeared but that he still believed in its significance for Jewish national revival. See ibid., vol. 10, p. 178n.

54. Ibid., pp. 176–79.

55. "Der ingster sheyvet" (The Youngest Tribe), published in 1915, *GS*, vol. 9, p. 84.

56. For an insight into Zhitlowski's disagreements with Cahan, see the article "A por verter vegn inteligents un apikoyres," *GS*, vol. 10, pp. 136–65.

57. See, for example, Zhitlowski's two-part essay "Di tsukunft fun di felker in amerika" (The Future of Nationalities in America), published in 1912, *GS*, vol. 2, pp. 189–286.

58. "Das program fun 'Das Naye Lebn'" (The Program of *Das Naye Lebn*), published in 1909, *GS*, vol. 3, pp. 13–19.

59. Joshua Fishman, *Ideology, Society, & Language: The Odyssey of Nathan Birnbaum* (Ann Arbor: Karoma Publishers, 1987), p. 50.

60. For more information on Zhitlowski's view of the nature of progressive Yiddish schools in America, see the article "A bisl nakhes" (A Little Satisfaction), published in 1910, *GS*, vol. 10, pp. 197–200. For information on Zhitlowski's role in the development of Yiddish education in America, see Epstein, *Profiles of Eleven*, pp. 275–78.

61. Dresner, "Haim Zhitlovsky," pp. 50–53.

62. As Zhitlowski noted in an article published in 1909: "Palestine and the neighboring lands are the Where of the Jewish homeland. The steady colonization of Palestine and Mesopotamia is the How of our existence and life. From now and evermore, that is the answer to the When." See "Simonim fun a nayem lebn," *GS*, vol. 10, pp. 171–72.

63. For an insight into Zhitlowski's views of Zionism and the *yishuv* during this period, see the articles "Der tsionizm un der 'nayer yishuv' in erets yisroel" (Zionism and the New Jewish Settlement in the Land of Israel) and "Di klayn-kolonizatsie in erets-yisroel un ir politishe badaytung" (The Small Colonization Effort in the Land of Israel and Its Political Significance), both published in 1915, *GS*, vol. 9, pp. 73–76 and 85–90.

64. For Zhitlowski's views on the war and the appropriate Jewish response, see the collections of articles "In shverer tsaytn" (In Difficult Times) and "Di Interesn fun idishn

folk" (The Interests of the Jewish People), both published between 1914 and 1915, *GS*, vol. 8, pp. 7–78 and 81–122.

65. For further information, see the article "Mayne oysgemishte program" (My Eclectic Program), published in 1915, *GS*, vol. 9, pp. 207–13.

66. For further information, see "Unzer vendung tzu dem internatsional" (Our Démarche to the International) and "A idishe sektsie inm internatsional" (A Jewish Section in the International), both published in 1915, ibid., pp. 196–206.

67. Dresner, "Haim Zhitlovsky," pp. 339–340. See also Zhitlowski's retrospective comments in the article "Bimkom tsionizmn un das sotsiale lebn in erets-yisroel" (Substitute Zionisms and Society in the Land of Israel), *Zukunft* 38 (July 1933): 406–11.

68. "Der mandat oyf erets yisroel" (The Mandate in Palestine), *Das Naye Lebn* 1, no. 1 (October 1922): 2–4. See also Zhitlowski's comments in the article "Hebrayizm un idishizm" (Hebraism and Yiddishism), *Das Naye Lebn* 1, no. 10, (July-August 1923): 8.

69. "Di russishe revolutsie un dos idishe folk" (The Russian Revolution and the Jewish People), published in 1917, *GS*, vol. 10, pp. 9-48.

70. Cited in Dresner, "Haim Zhitlovsky," p. xix.

71. Zhitlowski, "Bimkom tsionizmn un das sotsiale lebn," 408.

72. Zhitlowski, "Tsu der krizes fun der idisher natsionaler autonomiye" (On the Crisis in Jewish National Autonomism), *Das Naye Lebn* 1, no. 4 (January 1923): 1–6.

73. Dubnov, "Zhitlovskis autonomizm," p. 194.

74. Zhitlowski, "Tsu dem ershter mai" (On May First), *Das Naye Lebn* 1, no. 8 (May 1923): 4.

75. Dresner, "Haim Zhitlovsky," p. 410.

76. See, for example, Zhitlowski's analysis of the Soviet Constitution of 1937, "Di naye konstitutsie in rusland" (The New Constitution in Russia), *Zukunft* 42 (May 1937): 260–72.

77. Frankel, *Prophecy and Politics*, pp. 258–59.

78. Zhitlowski, "Dray periodn in unzer golus-geshikhte" (Three Periods in Our Diaspora History), published in 1906, *GS*, vol. 5, p. 102.

79. "A bisl nakhes," *GS*, vol. 10, pp. 198–200; and "Der entviklung fun dem natsional-bevustzayn" (The Development of National Consciousness), vol. 8, p. 221.

80. "Tsvay farlezungn vegn id un mensh, tsvayter artikl" (Two Lectures Concerning the Jew and Humanity, Second Article), published in 1912, *GS*, vol. 2, pp. 147–49; "Toyt un vidergeburt fun geter un religonen" (Death and Rebirth of Gods and Religions), published in 1911, vol. 4, p. 199; "A brif fun a idishn sotsialist" (A Letter from a Jewish Socialist), published in 1906, vol. 5, pp. 13–14; and "Natsional-klerikel" (National-Clerical), published in 1915, vol. 10, p. 212.

81. *GS*, vol. 2, pp. 123-24.

82. "Historishe ideyen-farbindungn" (Historically Connected Ideas), published in 1908, *GS*, vol. 3, p. 60; and "Materializm un di natsionale frage" (Materialism and the National Question), published in 1908, vol. 6, p. 62.

83. See, for example, the compilation essay "Der biterer emes" (The Bitter Truth), published between December 1911 and September 1912, *GS*, vol. 6, pp. 163–251.

84. "Di geshikhts-filosofiye un der end-tsil" (Historical Philosophy and the Final Goal), published in 1908, *GS*, vol. 3, p. 169; Epstein, *Profiles of Eleven* , p. 305.

85. Zhitlowski, "Di geshikhts-filosofiye un der end-tsil," *GS*, vol. 3, p. 144; and *Zikhroynes*, vol. 3, p. 59.

86. "Dr. Max Nordau un der politisher tsionizm" (Dr. Max Nordau and Political Zionism), *GS*, vol. 3, p. 244. Zhitlowski's positive view of elements of Christianity were a considerable source of embarrassment to his supporters. It is interesting to note that despite his

voluminous writing on Jesus, the essays included in his collected writings contain only scattered references to the founder of Christianity.

87. Zhitlowski, *Zikhroynes*, vol. 3, pp. 62–63, 179–80. It was Zhitlowski's overarching concern with national unity that explains why, though he expressed toleration for Jewish converts to Christianity, he was often skeptical of their motives. In many cases, he argued, their intention was to gain favor among non-Jews rather than to realize their own spiritual yearnings. See, for example, his comments in "Di asimilatsie, vos zee zogt tsu un vos zee git" (Assimilation: What It Claims to Do and What It Actually Accomplishes), originally published by Poale Zion in 1914, *GS*, vol. 8, pp. 211–12.

88. For a full discussion of Zhitlowski's view of the effect of assimilation on Jewish identity, see ibid., pp. 175–216.

89. "Di russishe revolutsie un dos idishe folk," *GS*, vol. 10, pp. 14–15.

90. A typical example of Zhitlowski's use of such terminology is the following convoluted definition of the contemporary state of the Jewish people living in the Diaspora, written in 1914: "[Jewry is] a 'folk-organism,' that has a higher brain and a bundle of veins and nerves, [that has become] twisted together with a foreign brain, foreign veins and nerves, foreign spinal fluids, rooted in foreign muscles, held up by a foreign skeleton … [It] should develop its own muscles, its own bone structure, its own spinal fluid." "Kekhol ha-goyim" (Like All the Nations), published in 1914 and reproduced in *GS*, vol. 8, p. 113.

For a similar confusion in terms, see the article by Nahman Syrkin, entitled "Geza, amamiyut, ve-liumiyut" (Race, Nationality, and Nationalism), originally published in *Ha-Dor* (The Generation) in 1901, *Kitve Nachman Syrkin* (The Writings of Nahman Syrkin) (Tel Aviv: Davar, 1938–39), pp. 263–72.

91. Zhitlowski, *Zikhroynes*, vol. 1, pp. 82–83.

92. "Historishe ideyen-farbindungn," *GS*, vol. 3, pp. 43–44.

93. The debate is discussed in detail by Zhitlowski in *Zikhroynes*, vol. 1, pp. 80–84. For further information on Anski's attitudes on the Jewish question, see Maor, *She'elat ha-yehudim*, pp. 203–4.

94. "Religie un natsie" is reproduced in *GS*, vol. 4, pp. 187–200; "Tzvay farlezungn vegn id un mensh," vol. 2, pp. 103–86; "Toyt un vidergeburt fun der idisher religie," vol. 4, pp. 187–217; and "Di natsional-poetishe vidergeburt fun der idisher religie," in vol. 4, pp. 221–78. See also "Di entviklung fun dem natsional-bevustzayn," in vol. 8, pp. 217–21.

95. "Tsvay farlezungn vegn id un mensh," *GS*, vol. 2, p. 125. Zhitlowski's anticlerical and anti-Orthodox rhetoric continued to surface in his polemical discussions and articles long after he had rejected many of the basic suppositions that lay behind them. In an article written in 1915, for example, he could still describe traditional Jewish life in the following terms: "A profound ignorance toward everything related to nature and to human life; a belief in spirits, devils, miracles, rabbis, and Hasidic masters, enchanters and sorcerers, potions and incantations; a blind neglect of housekeeping, clothing, cleanliness, and external affairs; a childish helplessness in the face of the cosmos and of all worldly matters; an economic life of dust and wind, a hand-to-mouth existence of idleness and squeezing together on benches in houses of prayer and study; at best, a life of parasitism…[in which one lives] off the body of the goy [non-Jew]." See "Di asimilatsie," *GS*, vol. 8, p. 181.

96. *GS*, vol. 4, p. 228.

97. Ibid., p. 233.

98. "Di asimilatsie," *GS*, vol. 8, pp. 204, 270.

99. "Dray periodn in unzer golus-geshikhte," *GS*, vol. 5, pp. 101–10; *Zikhroynes*, vol. 2, p. 167; and vol. 3, pp. 65–71.

100. "Toyt un vidergeburt fun geter un religionen," *GS*, vol. 4, p. 217.

101. *Zikhroynes*, vol. 2, pp. 151–52.

102. Ibid., p. 157.

103. Ibid., pp. 164–65.

104. Dresner, "Haim Zhitlovsky," p. 51.

105. "Toyt un vidergeburt fun geter un religionen," *GS*, vol. 4, pp. 203-17; and "A brif fun a idishn sotsialist," vol. 5, p. 16.

106. "Natsional-klerikel," *GS*, vol. 10, p. 209.

107. "Di natsional-poetishe vidergeburt fun der idisher religie," *GS*, vol. 4, pp. 240–41.

108. "Toyt un vidergeburt fun geter un religionen," *GS*, vol. 4, pp. 216.

109. "Di natsional-poetishe vidergeburt," *GS*, vol. 4, pp. 249–59.

110. "Der arbayter ring" (The Workman's Circle), published in 1915, *GS*, vol. 10, p. 285.

111. "Di geshikhts-filosofie un der end-tsil," *GS*, vol. 3, p. 173; "Di kritik fun dem natur-filosofishn materializm" (The Criticism of Philosophical Materialism), published in 1912, *GS*, vol. 2, p. 78; and the article "Materializm un di natsionale frage,"*GS*, vol. 6, p. 78.

Zhitlowski's disdain for theoretical abstraction is evident in his evaluation of the three individuals whom he regarded as the most influential thinkers of the late nineteenth century —Tolstoy, Nietzsche, and Marx. It was Zhitlowski's contention that despite their radical differences, all three rejected the notion of "ideas for ideas' sake" and constantly sought to ground their theories in reality. See his article "Tolstoy, Nietzsche un Karl Marx," published in 1912, *GS*, vol. 1, pp. 12–14.

112. For a detailed discussion of Zhitlowski's views on materialism and idealism, see his two articles "Tsvay farlezungn vegn dem natur-filosofishn materializm" (Two Lectures Concerning Natural-Philosophical Materialism), published in 1912, *GS*, vol. 2, pp. 7–100. See also his analysis of the philosophical debate between Karl Marx and Ferdinand Lassalle in *GS*, vol. 3, pp. 25–35; and his essay "Di geshikhts-filosofie un der end-tsil," vol. 3, pp. 133–91.

113. For a further discussion of this point, see Dresner, "Haim Zhitlovsky," p. 179.

114. Victor Tchernov, "Hayim Zhitlovski un der 'farband fun di russishe sotsial-revolutsionarn,' 1900–1903" (Haim Zhitlowski and the "Union of Russian Social Revolutionaries," 1900–1903), *Zhitlovski zamlbukh* (Warsaw: Farlag Ch. Brzoza, 1929), p. 102.

115. See, for example, Zhitlowski's comments about the Jewish worker in "Tsionizm oder sotsializm" (Zionism or Socialism), *GS*, vol. 5, p. 61.

116. "Di klayn-kolonizatsie in erets-yisroel," *GS*, vol. 9, p. 87.

117. *Di Veker* (The Call), November 20, 1937, cited in Lieberman, *Doktor Haim Zhitlovski*, p. 12.

118. As Zhitlowski remarked in one of his earliest works: " [The] stuffy factory...daily belches forth volcanoes of black smoke and...makes a worker a dial on a machine." See "Tsionizm oder sotsialism," *GS*, vol. 5, p. 71.

119. Zhitlowski, *Zikhroynes*, vol. 2, p. 143.

120. "Der beginen fun der idisher videroyflebung" (The Beginning of the Jewish Revival), published in 1907, *GS*, vol. 5, pp. 135–141. See also the article "Simonim fun a nayem lebn," *GS*, vol. 10, pp. 170–71.

121. Frankel, *Prophecy and Politics*, pp. 285–86.

122. See, for example, Zhitlowski's comments in the article "Di arbayter un dos folk" (The Worker and the People), published in 1915, *GS*, vol. 10, p. 217.

123. See, for example, Bauer's comments on Jews in his *Die Nationalitätenfrage und die Sozialdemokratie* (Vienna: I. Brand, 1907), pp. 318–26.

124. Robert M. Seltzer, "Simon Dubnow: A Critical Biography of His Early Years," (unpublished Ph.D. dissertation, Columbia University, l970), p. 217.

125. See, for example, Zhitlowski's comments in "Di problemn fun dem golus-

natsionalizm," 655.

126. See, for example, Haim Zhitlowski, "Shayles un tshuves in hilkhes idishizm" (Responsa Concerning the Laws of Yiddishism), *Zukunft* 36 (October 1931): 641–42.

127. "Alter un nayer natsionalizm" (Old and New Nationalism), published in 1915, *GS*, vol. 8, p. 224.

128. "Tsionizm un erets-yisroel" (Zionism and the Land of Israel), published in 1915, *GS*, vol. 10, p. 147.

129. For a further discussion of Dubnow's views, see Chapter 3.

130. The review was entitled "Hern Dubnovs 'gaystiger' natsionalism" and is reproduced in *GS*, vol. 7, pp. 211–38. See also Zhitlowski's comments in the article "Hebrayizm un idishism," 4–5.

131. Birnbaum is often credited with being the major force behind the convening of the Czernowitz Conference. In his writings, he spoke glowingly of Ukrainian nationalism, which aroused the ire of many Jews who associated the latter with vicious anti-Semitism. For more on Birnbaum, see Fishman, *Ideology, Society, & Language.*

132. For a full exposition of Herder's thought on language and national identity, see his *Outlines of a Philosophy of the History of Man*, translated by T. Churchill (New York: Bergman Publishers, nd). See also the work by F. M. Barnard, *Herder's Social and Political Thought: From Enlightenment to Nationalism* (Oxford: Clarendon Press, 1965).

133. Barnard, *Herder's Social and Political Thought*, pp. 140–41, 172; Isaiah Berlin, *Vico and Herder: Two Studies in the History of Ideas* (New York: Viking Press, 1976), p. 159n.

134. As Matisyohu Mieses, a prominent Yiddishist at the turn of the century, remarked in an article written in 1907: "If Yiddish is abandoned, its true adversary, the language of the country, will be victorious and complete assimilation, the destruction of our nation, which our traitors anticipate, will come about." Cited in Goldsmith, *Architects of Yiddishism*, p. 142.

135. For information on Zamenhof, see the entry "Zamenhof, Ludwik Lazar," in *EJ*, vol. 16, cols. 925–26.

136. Zvi Halevy, *Jewish Schools under Czarism and Communism* (New York: Springer Library, 1976), p. 95n.

137. Tudor Parfitt, "Ahad Ha-Am's Role in the Revival and Development of Hebrew," in *At the Crossroads: Essays on Ahad Ha-am*, edited by Jacques Kornberg (Albany: SUNY Press, 1983), p. 12; Dan Miron, *Bodedim be-moadam* (When Loners Come Together) (Tel Aviv: Am Oved, 1987), pp. 59–60, 92–93.

138. Wisse, "Politics of Yiddish," 31.

139. Shaul Ginsburg, *Amolike petersburg: Forshungn un zikhroynes vegn yidishn lebn in tsarishn rusland* (St. Petersburg of Yesteryear: Studies and Recollections Concerning Jewish Life in Tsarist Russia) (New York: CYCO, 1944), p. 185. At first, Tsar Alexander II thought that a "Judeo-German" paper would be useful in assimilating Jewry into Russian society by serving as a "cure" for "their sickness of fanaticism." Cited in B.Z. Goldberg, "The American Yiddish Press at Its Centennial," in *Never Say Die: A Thousand Years of Yiddish in Jewish Life and Letters*, edited by Joshua Fishman (The Hague: Mouton, 1981), pp. 517–18.

140. Max Weinreich, *History of the Yiddish Language*, translated by Shlomo Noble (Chicago: University of Chicago Press, 1980), p. 26.

141. Violet Conolly, "The 'nationalities question' in the last phase of tsardom," in *Russia Enters the Twentieth Century, 1894–1917*, edited by Erwin Oberländer et al. (New York: Schocken Books, 1971), pp. 161–162. Interestingly, the Ukrainian language was often attacked by Russian officials as a jargon with little or no literary or intellectual merit. See ibid.

142. Ginsburg, *Amolike petersburg*, p. 230.

143. See, for example, Goldsmith's comments on Peretz in *Architects of Yiddishism*, pp.

134–35.

144. For details on the creation of *Der Fraynd*, see Ginsburg, *Amolike petersburg*, pp. 184–220.

145. For information on the conference, see Joshua Fishman, "Attracting a Following to High-Culture Functions for a Language of Everyday Life: The Role of the Tshernovitz Language Conference in the 'Rise of Yiddish,'" *Never Say Die*, p. 387; and Goldsmith, *Architects of Yiddishism*, p. 197.

146. Zhitlowski, "Iz der hebrayizm progresiv?" (Is Hebraism Progressive?), published in 1915, *GS*, vol. 8, pp. 159–165; "Alter un nayer natsionalizm," vol. 8, p. 226; "Di russishe revolutsie un dos yidishe folk," vol. 10, p. 29; and "Unzer tsukunft du in land" (Our Future Here in the United States), published in 1915, vol. 10, p. 90.

147. As Zhitlowski noted in a short poem published in *Der Fraynd* in 1904:
>Lovelier than all the images
>Is my mother's face.
>More loved than all of the languages
>Is my mother-tongue.
>Cited in "Shayles un tshuves in hilkhes idishizm" (October 1931), 640.

148. "Vos iz asimilatsie?" (What Is Assimilation?), published in 1915, *GS*, vol. 8, p. 173.

149. "Das idishe folk un di idishe shprakh" (The Jewish People and the Yiddish Language), published in 1904, *GS*, vol. 5, p. 81.

150. Haim Zhitlowski, *Yid un velt* (New York: Farlag IKUF, 1945), p. 191, cited in Goldsmith, *Architects of Yiddishism*, p. 255.

151. See especially "Vos iz asimilatsie?" *GS*, vol. 8, pp. 169–75.

152. As Ruth Wisse describes the views of Yiddishists on the role of the language in the revival of Jewish culture: "[A]s the community had once generated an independent language to express its cultural autonomy, so that same language would now cement a culturally autonomous community." See Wisse, "Politics of Yiddish," 30.

153. Zhitlowski, "Di entviklung fun dem natsional-bevustzayn," *GS*, vol. 8, pp. 218–19; and "Di russishe revolutsion un di yidn," vol. 9, p. 47.

154. "Hebrayizm un idishizm," 9.

155. Goldsmith, *Architects of Yiddishism*, pp. 172–173. See also the article "Idish un hebrayish" (Yiddish and Hebrew), published in 1911, *GS*, vol. 4, pp. 125–61. Like many Yiddishists, Zhitlowski dismissed other Jewish folk languages such as Ladino, spoken by Sephardic Jews. In the previously cited article, he candidly admitted that he knew very little about Judeo-Spanish but doubted that the Jewish people would fight to maintain it. See ibid., pp. 130–31.

156. "Iz der hebrayizm progresiv?," *GS*, vol. 8, pp. 162–63.

157. "Hebrayizm un idishizm," 9; "Di russishe revolutsie un dos idishe folk," *GS*, vol. 10, p. 32.

158. "Dos idishe folk un di idishe shprakh," *GS*, vol. 5, p. 92.

159. Ibid., p. 94.

160. "Shayles un tshuves in hilkhes idishizm," (September 1931), 573.

161. "Simonim fun a nayem lebn," *GS*, vol. 10, pp. 174–75.

162. See, for example, Lieberman, *Idn un idishkayt*, p. 23.

163. Zhitlowski, "Tsvay farlezungn vegn id un mensh," *GS*, vol. 2, p. 134.

164. "Di russishe revolutsie un dos idishe folk," *GS*, vol. 10, pp. 29–31; and "Di idishe kultur un di idishe shprakh" (Jewish Culture and the Yiddish Language), published in 1911, *GS*, vol. 4, p. 181.

165. "Teritorializm — bemzumn oder oyf borg?" *GS*, vol. 5, p. 126. See also Zhitlowski's

article "Hebrayizm un idishizm," 4.

166. "Di idishe shprakh-beveygung un di tschernovitzer konferents" (The Yiddish Language and the Czernowitz Conference), published in 1909, *GS*, vol. 4, pp. 114–17; and "Shayles un tshuves in hilkhes idishizm," 572, 641–42.

Chapter 3: Simon Dubnow: History and Modern Jewish Identity

1. For an elaboration of this theme, see Yosef Hayim Yerushalmi's provocative work *Zachor: Jewish History and Jewish Memory* (Seattle: University of Washington Press, 1982).

2. Cited from the Russian edition of Dubnow's memoirs in Robert M. Seltzer, "Simon Dubnow: A Critical Biography of His Early Years" (unpublished Ph.D. dissertation, Columbia University, l970), p. 179. Dubnow's memoirs were published in Russian, German, and Hebrew. Dubnow also published selections from his autobiography in Yiddish in *Zukunft*, a New York–based journal, in the 1930s. I have examined the German, Hebrew, and Yiddish translations that are abridgements of the complete three-volume Russian original edition, which was entitled *Kniga jizni* (Book of My Life). For material covered in the Russian version as well as for synopses of Dubnow's articles in the Russian-language journal *Voskhod*, I have depended on both Robert Seltzer's dissertation and Renée Poznanski's insightful Introduction and footnotes in her edited and annotated French translation of Dubnow's *Lettres on Old and New Judaism, Lettres sur le judaïsme ancien et nouveau (LJAN)*, pp. 11–70. Selections from Dubnow's writings in *Rassvet* and *Voskhod* can also be found in Yehuda Slutsky, "Kritikus," *He-Avar* 8 (1961), 43-64 and B. Dinberg, "Shimon Dubnov: Le-yovelo ha-shivim ve-hamesh" (Simon Dubnow: In Honor of His Seventy-fifth Birthday), *Zion* 1, no. 2 (1936): 95–128.

3. Simon Dubnow, *Jewish History: An Essay in the Philosophy of History* (Freeport, N. Y.: Books for Libraries Press, 1972), p. 174.

4. Noah Rosenbloom, "Ahad Ha-Am veha-yeda ha-histori" (Ahad Ha-Am and Historical Understanding), *Salo Wittmayer Baron Jubilee Volume* (Jerusalem/New York: American Academy for Jewish Research, 1975), vol. 3, p. 333.

5. Dubnov, *History of the Jews*, translated by Moshe Spiegel (New York: Thomas Yoseloff, 1967-1973), vol. 1, p. 388.

6. Figures cited in *Simon Dubnow (1860–1941): The Life and Work of a Jewish Historian—Catalogue of the Exhibition* (New York: YIVO Institute for Jewish Research, 1961), p. 9.

7. Sophie Erlich-Dubnov, *Shimon Dubnov: Toldot hayav* (Simon Dubnow: The Story of His Life) (Tel Aviv: Hanhalat ha-yisraelit shel ha-kongres ha-yehudi ha-olami, nd), p. 7.

8. For a discussion of the genealogy of the Dubnow family that traces back its ancestry to Rabbi Judah Loeb, the so-called Maharal of Prague, see S. A. Horodetzky, "The Genealogy of Simon Dubnow," *YIVO Annual of Jewish Social Science* 6 (1951): 9–18.

9. Dubnow would later describe the Talmudic sage in the following terms that clearly reflected his own image of his grandfather and quite possibly his vision of his own future as an aging scholar: "This white-haired old man, with a stormy past full of experiences and thought, would not mingle with the scatterbrained crowd, would not descend to the level of neophytes dominated by fleeting, youthful enthusiasm. Loyally this weather-bronzed, inflexible guardian of the Law stuck to his post—and, faithful to his duty, held fast to the principle: *j'y suis, j'y reste*" (italics in the original). See Dubnow, *Jewish History*, p. 92.

A number of writers have suggested, not terribly convincingly, that Dubnow's reserved and methodical approach to study stemmed from his Lithuanian or "Litvak" background. See, for example, Samuel Niger (Niger-Charny), "Simon Dubnow as a Literary Critic," *YIVO Annual of Jewish Social Science*, 1 (1946): 316–17.

10. Shimon Dubnov, *Sefer ha-hayim* (Tel Aviv: Dvir, 1936), vol. 1, pp. 31-32.

11. Ibid., p. 46. As a mature historian, Dubnow would later claim that he found Shulman's "historical" writings "ridiculous." Cited in Rosenbloom, *Ahad Ha-Am veha-yeda ha-histori*, p. 341.

12. Dubnov, *Sefer ha-hayim*, p. 51. See also Dubnow's caustic comments about a wandering *maggid* or itinerant preacher, who during his youth visited Mstislav and railed against the Haskalah, in ibid., p. 43.

13. Lionel Kochan, *The Jew and His History* (New York: Schocken, 1977), p. 90. Dubnow's first piece in Yiddish, a propaganda tract on behalf of the Folkspartei, was not published until 1907. For a general discussion of Dubnow's use of Russian, Hebrew, and Yiddish, see Sh[muel] Niger, "Shimen Dubnov—un yidish" (Simon Dubnow and Yiddish), *Zukunft* 56, no. 10 (December 1951): 456–60.

14. Dubnov, *Sefer ha-hayim*, pp. 80–95. For further information on the fate of Jewish externs, see Simon Doubnov's *Histoire d'un soldat juif, 1881–1915* (Paris: Les Editions du Cerf, 1988), pp. 30–31.

15. Dubnov, *Sefer ha-hayim*, p. 174.

16. Ibid., p. 122.

17. Ibid., p. 81.

18. As Dubnow commented in a letter written to Haim Zhitlowski in March 1936 upon receiving the latter's memoirs: "Several years before you I had gone through the same process of development in my Mogilev district, with the following difference—I was impelled more by individual than social problems." Cited in *Simon Dubnow: Catalogue of the Exhibition*, p. 34n.

19. See, for example, Dubnow's analysis of Marxism in *History of the Jews*, vol. 5, pp. 110–11.

20. Despite his indebtedness to Buckle, Dubnow rejected the British historian's emphasis on the role of physical and geographical factors in history in his own treatment of Jewish historical development. See Shimen Dubnov, "Fun mayn lebns-bukh" (From My Autobiography), *Zukunft* 38 (June 1933): 357. See also the comments by Salo Baron in his article "Emphases of Jewish History," *Jewish Social Studies* 1, no. 1 (1939): 22.

21. Dubnov, *Sefer ha-hayim*, pp. 105, 135.

22. See, for example, Dubnow's analysis of the reign of King Herod as an illiberal regime in *History of the Jews*, vol. 1, p. 674.

23. Dubnov, "Fun mayn lebns-bukh," 417–18.

24. Erlich-Dubnov, *Shimon Dubnov: Toldot hayav*, p. 11.

25. Dubnov, "Fun mayn lebns-bukh," 477.

26. Zev Dubnow eventually returned to Russia in 1915, complaining of physical exhaustion. See Yosef Klausner, "Shimon Dubnov u-tnuat hibat tsiyon" (Simon Dubnow and the Hibbat Zion Movement), *He-Avar* 8 (1961): 33. The essay is republished in Yosef Klausner, *Be-darkhe tsiyon* (On the Road to Zion) (Jerusalem: Reuben Mass, 1978), pp. 304–20. For Zev Dubnow's letter to his brother explaining the reasons for his return, see *Ketavim le-toldot hibat-tsiyon ve-yishuv erets-yisrael* (Documents on the History of Hibbat Zion and the Settlement in Palestine), edited by Shulamit Laskov (Tel Aviv: Tel Aviv University, 1987), vol. 3, pp. 16–17.

27. Cited in Shimen Dubnov, *Fun "zhargon" tsu yidish* (From "Jargon" to Yiddish) (Vilna: Vilner farlag fun B. Kletzkin, 1929), p. 12. See also Niger, "Shimen Dubnov—un yidish," 458–59.

28. Niger-Charny, "Simon Dubnow as a Literary Critic," 311. For a discussion of Dubnow's literary analyses, see ibid., 305–17; and Slutsky, "Kritikus," 43–64. See also Dubnow's own comments in *Sefer ha-hayim*, p. 147.

29. Dubnov, "Fun mayn lebns-bukh," 476.

30.*Voskhod*, July-August, 1885, p. 26, cited in Dinberg, "Shimon Dubnov . . . ha-shivim ve-hamesh," 100; and Klausner, "Shimon Dubnov u-tnuat hibat tsiyon," 35–36.

31. *Rassvet* 34, 35 (August 21, 28, 1881), cited in Dinberg, "Shimon Dubnov," 102; and Klausner, "Shimon Dubnov," 33. On the misperceptions of Russian Jews about the United States, see Stephen M. Berk, *Year of Crisis, Year of Hope: Russian Jewry and the Pogroms of 1881–1882* (Westport, Conn.: Greenwood Press, 1985), p. 126.

32. Dubnov, *Sefer ha-hayim*, p. 138.

33. The article is cited in Poznanski's Introduction to *LJAN*, p. 20.

34. Thus, for example, in his general history of the Jews, Dubnow described the demise of the movement led by the sixteenth-century false messiah Samuel Molcho in the following terms: "Thus came to a tragic end the distinctive 'Zionist' movement of the 16th century—a movement in which Messianic-mystical elements merged with political affairs; and dreams of visionaries combined with projects of practical workers and shrewd diplomacy." See Dubnov, *History of the Jews*, vol. 3, p. 540.

35. Dubnov, *Sefer ha-hayim*, p. 145.

36. Even in his later life, Dubnow would voice sympathy for Spinoza though his view was now filtered through the optic of Jewish autonomism. As he noted in his *History of the Jews*, for example, the seventeenth-century heretic was excommunicated because he ignored the fact that in his own era, Jewish national consciousness was interwoven with Judaism. In the modern era, Dubnow maintained, Spinoza would undoubtedly have been accepted in the community since "secularized Jewry recognized the fact that it was possible to remain in the nation though one harbored complete religious freethinking." See Dubnov, *History of the Jews*, vol. 3, p. 644.

37. Dubnov, *Sefer ha-hayim*, p. 162; Klausner, "Shimon Dubnov," 33. The Voltairean statement concerning the masses is cited without reference to the French *philosophe* in *Sefer ha-hayim*, p. 153.

38. *Voskhod* 5 (1883): 226, cited in Yehuda Slutsky, "Kritikus," *He-Avar* 8 (1961): 47.

39. *Voskhod* 8 (1884): 9, cited in ibid.

40. *Voskhod* 5–8 (1883), cited in Josef Fraenkel, "Simon Dubnow and the History of Political Zionism," in *Simon Dubnow: The Man and His Work*, edited by Aaron Steinberg (Paris: World Jewish Congress, 1963), p. 146. In his work on the Jews of Russia and Poland published between 1916 and 1920, Dubnow expressed a more reasoned view of Pinsker. Though criticizing *Autoemancipation* for narrowly defining the Jewish nation in territorial and political terms and ignoring its cultural unity in the Diaspora, Dubnow praised the "close reasoning" of Pinsker's essay and noted its powerful impact on a despairing population. See Dubnov, *History of the Jews in Russia and Poland*, translated by I. Friedlander (Philadelphia: Jewish Publication Society, 1916–20), vol. 2, p. 332. See also Dubnow's comments about Pinsker's work in his Sixth Letter in *LJAN*, pp. 239–42.

41. Cited in Klausner, "Shimon Dubnov," 37, 42. See also Dubnov, *Sefer ha-hayim*, p. 154; and Dinberg, "Shimon Dubnov," p. 102.

42. Dubnov, *Sefer ha-hayim*, p. 166.

43. Ibid., p. 170. See also Dubnow's comments on Elisha in *History of the Jews*, vol. 2, p. 105*n*.

44. Slutsky, "Kritikus," 50–53.

45. See, for example, Dubnow's article in *Voskhod* 1 (1887): 13, cited in Slutsky, "Kritikus," 51.

46. Dubnow, *Kniga jizni*, vol. 1, pp. 206–7, cited in Seltzer, "Simon Dubnow," p. 133.

47. Dubnov, *Sefer ha-hayim*, p. 192.

48. Ibid., p. 174. See also Erlich-Dubnov's comments in *Shimon Dubnov: Toldot hayav,*

p. 14.

49. Cited in Seltzer, "Simon Dubnow," p. 125.

50. Dubnov, *Sefer ha-hayim*, pp. 218–19.

51. Shimon Dubnov, *Toldot ha-hasidut* (History of Hasidism) (Tel Aviv: Dvir, 1944), Preface.

52. Dubnov, ibid., Introduction.

53. One writer even suggests that Dubnow secretly regarded himself as a pantheist. See Y. Meisel, "Haye Shimon Dubnov" (The Life of Simon Dubnow) in *Sefer Shimon Dubnow* (The Book of Simon Dubnow), edited by Simon Rawidowicz (London: Ararat Publishing Company, 1954), p. 42n. See also the comments of Aaron Steinberg in his *History as Experience: Aspects of Historical Thought—Universal and Jewish* (New York: KTAV, 1983), pp. 101–2.

54. In his autobiography, Dubnow poignantly described his last visit to Mstislav in 1901. Life in his native town and the surrounding small Jewish towns was desperate, he wrote, as Jews found themselves caught between grinding poverty and the disruptive inroads of modern Jewish political movements. See Dubnow, *Mein Leben* (My Life), edited by Elias Hurwicz (Berlin: Jüdische Buchvereinigung, 1937), p. 128.

55. Robert Seltzer, "Ahad Ha-Am and Dubnow: Friends and Adversaries," in *At the Crossroads: Essays on Ahad Ha-am*, edited by Jacques Kornberg (Albany: SUNY Press, 1983), p. 62.

56. For a discussion of the image of Odessa among young Jewish intellectuals, see Dan Miron, *Bodedim be-moadam* (Tel Aviv: Am Oved, 1987), pp. 341–46. For Dubnow's reminiscences concerning the group which met regularly between 1891 and 1894 and then periodically thereafter under the spiritual leadership of Mendele Moykher Sforim, see Dubnov, *Fun "zhargon" tsu yidish*, pp. 107–27.

57. For Dubnow's influence among intellectuals in Odessa, see Chaim Tchernowitz, *Pirke haim* (New York: Bitzaron, 1954), pp. 21-22, 187.

58. Ibid., p. 192.

59. For the English publication of the work, see note 3 above.

60. See especially the comments by S. Levenberg in his article "The Historian of Russian Jewry," in *Simon Dubnow: The Man and His Work*, edited by Aaron Steinberg (Paris: World Jewish Congress, 1963), p. 187.

61. Dubnow, *Mein Leben*, p. 97; Dubnov, *Sefer ha-hayim*, p. 268.

62. In her introduction to her annotated edition of Dubnow's *Letters on Old and New Judaism*, Poznanski incisively examines the effect of crucial events within Russian Jewish society between 1897 and 1907 on the formulation of Dubnow's Letters, which were first published in 1907. See *LJAN*, Introduction, pp. 25–30.

63. Dubnov, *History of the Jews*, vol. 5, p. 111.

64. Fraenkel, "Simon Dubnow and the History of Political Zionism," p. 159.

65. Dubnov, *History of the Jews*, vol. 5, p. 686.

66. Cited in *Simon Dubnow: Catalogue of the Exhibition*, p. 11n.

67. Josef Fraenkel, *Dubnow, Herzl, and Ahad Ha-Am* (London: Ararat Publishing Society, 1963), p. 23; and Dubnov, *Fun "zhargon" tsu yidish*, pp. 121–22. For the text of the speech that Dubnow gave before the society in 1902 in which he outlined his proposal for introducing Jewish studies into the curriculum of the subsidized schools, see "Ha-limudim ha-ivriim" (Jewish Studies), in *Ha-lashon veha-hinukh, neumin be-hevrat "mefitseihaskalah be-yisrael"* (Language and Education: Speeches Delivered at the Society for the Promotion of Enlightenment Among Jews [in Russia]) (Cracow: Yosef Fisher, 1907), pp. 20–28.

68. For an English translation of the proclamation, see David Roskies, *Against the Apoca-*

lypse: Responses to Catastrophe in Modern Jewish Culture (Cambridge, Mass.: Harvard University Press, 1984), pp. 156–59.

69. Dubnow, Preface to the German translation of the first two Letters (1903), *LJAN*, p. 468; Poznanski, Introduction, *LJAN*, p. 60.

70. Dubnow, *Mein Leben*, p. 39.

71. "Vilna," in *EJ*, vol. 16, cols. 144–47.

72. Shmaryahu Levin, the Zionist activist, visited Dubnow in his Vilna home and described the atmosphere in the following reverential terms: "Simon Dubnow lived the classical life of a scholar. In his house, there was peace. It was like a temple dedicated to research and meditation." See Shmaryahu Levin, *Forward from Exile* (New York: Jewish Publication Society, 1967), p. 391.

73. Cited in Sofia Dubnow-Erlich, *Das lebn un shafn fun Shimen Dubnov* (The Life and Work of Simon Dubnow) (Mexico City: Mendelson Fund, 1952), p. 19. The work has been published in English as *The Life and Work of S. M. Dubnow: Diaspora Nationalism and Jewish History* (Bloomington: Indiana University Press, 1991).

74. Dubnow, *Mein Leben*, p. 149.

75. Erlich-Dubnov, *Shimon Dubnov: Toldot hayav*, p. 18. Dubnow himself would later dismiss his activity during the period, claiming in his memoirs that he never really cared for mass action because "the voices of individuals are not heard." See Dubnow, *Mein Leben*, p. 172.

76. Dubnow, *History of the Jews in Russia and Poland*, vol. 3, p. 112.

77. *LJAN*, Twelfth Letter, p. 410.

78. For a discussion of Jewish political participation in the three Dumas that sat between 1905 and 1914, see Jacob G. Frumkin, "Pages from the History of Russian Jewry," in *Russian Jewry (1860–1917),* edited by Jacob Frumkin et al. (New York: Thomas Yoseloff, 1966), pp. 47–57. For a discussion of the response of the various nationality groups to the Revolution of 1905, see Hugh Seton-Watson, *The Decline of Imperial Russia, 1855–1914* (New York: Frederick A. Praeger, 1952), pp. 231–45.

79. *LJAN*, Fourteenth Letter, pp. 443–56. See also Dubnow's comments on the platform of the party in his letter to the Yiddish scholar and Folkspartei activist N[ahum] Shtiff (also known as Bal-Dimyon) in June 28, 1923, cited in *Simon Dubnow: Catalogue of the Exhibition*, p. 26n, and his discussion of the foundation of the party in *History of the Jews*, vol. 5, p. 771.

80. Dubnow, *History of the Jews in Russia and Poland*, vol. 3, pp. 144–45; Oscar I. Janowsky, *The Jews and Minority Rights, 1898–1919* (New York: Columbia University Press, 1933), pp. 91–113. According to the Jewish historian Jacob Lestschinsky, Dubnow's *Letters on Old and New Judaism* helped shape the Zionists' decision concerning Diaspora activity at the Helsingfors conference. See Lestschinsky, "Dubnow's Autonomism and his 'Letters on Old and New Judaism,'" in *Simon Dubnow, The Man and His Work*, edited by Aaron Steinberg (Paris: World Jewish Congress, 1963), p. 79.

81. Seton-Watson, *Decline of Imperial Russia*, pp. 303–10. A third Duma, largely controlled by reactionaries and under the close watch of Tsar Nicholas, sat from November 1907 to June 1912.

82. For an intensive discussion of the activity of the territorialists during this period, see Michael Astur, *Geshikhte fun der frayland-lige un funm teritorialistishn gedank* (Buenos Aires/New York: Freiland Lige, 1967), vol. 2, pp. 10–20.

83. One student who attended Dubnow's lectures, the historian Mark Wischnitzer, would later claim that Dubnow's volume on Jewish history and his articles in *Voskhod* were "widely read by the younger generation." See Wischnitzer, "Reminiscences of a Jewish Historian,"

in *Russian Jewry (1860–1917)*, edited by Jacob Frumkin et al. (New York: Thomas Yoseloff, 1966), p. 473.

84. Simcha Kling, *Joseph Klausner* (Cranbury, N.J.: Thomas Yoseloff, 1970), p. 45.

85. *Kniga jizni*, vol. 2, pp. 54–55, cited in Poznanski's Introduction to *LJAN*, p. 30n..

86. Isaiah Trunk, "Historians of Russian Jewry," in *Russian Jewry (1860–1917)*, edited by Jacob Frumkin et al. (New York: Thomas Yoseloff, 1966), p. 463. See also Baruch Karu, "Be-mehitsato shel Dubnov" (The Distinctiveness of Dubnow), *He-Avar* 8 (1961): 17.

87. Poznanski, Introduction to *LJAN*, p. 30.

88. Erlich-Dubnov, *Shimon Dubnov: Toldot hayav*, p. 19.

89. Dubnov, *History of the Jews*, vol. 5, p. 833. See also Dubnow's letter to Ahad Ha-Am dated November 22, 1915, "Igrot el Ahad Ha-Am" (Letters to Ahad Ha-Am), in *Sefer Shimon Dubnow*, edited by Simon Rawidowicz (London: Ararat Publishing Company, 1954), p. 279.

90. *Kniga jizni*, vol. 2, p. 173, cited in Poznanski's Introduction to *LJAN*, p. 32n. See also Doubnov, *Histoire d'un soldat juif*, pp. 49–80.

91. Erlich-Dubnov, *Shimon Dubnov*, p. 21.

92. Letter to Ahad Ha-Am dated February 9, 1915, "Igrot el Ahad Ha-Am," p. 265.

93. Dubnow, *Mein Leben*, p. 214.

94. Erlich-Dubnov, *Shimon Dubnov*, p. 22.

95. Dubnov, *History of the Jews*, vol. 5, p. 841.

96. Dubnow,"Der tsvayter khurbn fun ukrayn" (The Second Catastrophe in the Ukraine), *Historishe shriftn* (Historical Writings) 1 (1929): 27. See also Dubnow's comments to Ahad Ha-Am in a letter written on August 21, 1924, "Igrot el Ahad Ha-Am," p. 279. For further information on Jewish autonomy in the Ukraine, see M. Belberyszki, "Volkism and the VolksPartei," in *Struggle for Tomorrow: Modern Political Ideologies of the Jewish People*, edited by Basil J. Vlavianos and Feliks Gross (New York: Arts Inc., 1954), p. 238.

97. S*imon Dubnow: Catalogue of the Exhibition*, p. 14n.

98. Mordechai Altshuler, "Ha-nisayon le-argen kinus klal-yehudi be-rusyah achar ha-mahapekha" (The Attempt to Organize a General Jewish Conference in Russia After the Revolution), *He-Avar* 12 (1965): 75–89.

99. Letter dated August 21, 1924, "Igrot el Ahad Ha-Am," p. 279.

100. See, for example, his comments in *Zukunft* published in 1935 and cited in Koppel Pinson, "The National Theories of Simon Dubnow," *Jewish Social Studies* 10, no. 4 (October 1948): 357–58.

101. Cited in Levenberg, "The Historian of Russian Jewry," p. 190.

102. Dubnow, *Mein Leben*, p. 235; Letter from Simon Dubnow to Ahad Ha-Am dated January 22, 1924, "Igrot el Ahad Ha-Am," pp. 274–75.

103. Ibid., p. 274.

104. Cited in *Simon Dubnow: Catalogue*, p. 15n.

105. As he noted in a letter to the Yiddish poet and editor of *Zukunft* Abraham Liessin, written shortly after his arrival in Riga in 1933: "I personally was not harmed in the German zoo with its wild animals, but life among wolves and hyenas was unbearable." Cited in ibid., p. 16n.

106. Letters to Ahad Ha-Am dated April 22 and August 21, 1924, "Igrot el Ahad Ha-Am," pp. 277, 280.

107. Dubnow's archives were destroyed by the Nazis after his death with the exception of small collections that have been preserved in the archives of YIVO in New York and at the Hebrew University in Jerusalem.

108. The league was in the process of being formed when war broke out. S*imon Dubnow: Catalogue*, pp. 27n; 28n.

109. Koppel Pinson, "Dubnovs natsionale teorie in shayn fun unzer tsayt" (Dubnow's

National Theory in the Light of Our Own Times), *Yivo bleter* 34 (1950): 18.

110. Cited in *Simon Dubnow: Catalogue*, p. 28n.

111. See, for example, Dubnow's comments to the journalist, socialist leader, and former political rival Wolf Latzky-Bertholdi, in a letter written in November 1934 and cited in *Simon Dubnow: Catalogue*, p. 16n.

112. Cited in ibid., p. 28n.

113. Dubnow's sentiments are expressed in the article "Vos darf men ton in haymens tsaytn" (What Must One Do in Haman's Times), written in response to the so-called Back to the Ghetto movement, an attempt by a group of European Jewish intellectuals in 1939 to reaffirm the values of pre-Emancipation Jewry. It is reproduced in English translation in *Nationalism and History: Essays on Old and New Judaism*, edited by Koppel S. Pinson (New York/Philadelphia: Meridian/Jewish Publication Society. 1961), pp. 354–59.

114. Letter to Daniel Charney, Riga, February 12, 1940, cited in *Simon Dubnow: Catalogue*, p. 43n.

115. Dov Levin,"Mi-riga ha-sovietit le-yerushalayim be-da'aga: mikhtavo ha-acharon shel Shimon Dubnov le-yedidav be-erets yisrael" (From Soviet Riga to Jerusalem with Concern: The Last Letter of Simon Dubnow to His Friends in Israel), *Shvut* 8 (1981): 112n.

116. Letter to Joseph Meisel, March 5, 1941, cited in Dubnow, *Nationalism and History*, p. 37.

117. Hillel Melamed, "Vi azoy di nazis hobn demordet Prof. Sh. Dubnov" (How the Nazis Murdered Professor Simon Dubnow), *Zukunft* 50 (April 1946): 320.

118. Cited in Erlich-Dubnov, *Shimon Dubnov,* p. 30.

119. Ibid., p. 30.

120. Ibid., p. 31.

121. Seltzer, "Simon Dubnow," pp. l61–64.

122. See especially Dubnow's comments in his *History of the Jews*, vol. 1, p. 26.

123. For a further discussion of differences between Graetz and Dubnow, see Aryeh Tartakower, "Le-vikoret shitato ha-sotsiologit shel Dubnov" (Toward a Critical Analysis of Dubnow's Sociological System), in *Sefer Shimon Dubnov*, edited by Simon Rawidowicz (London: Ararat Publishing Company, 1954), pp. 77–78.

124. Thus, for example, Dubnow described the fate of medieval Jewry in the following manner: "If there had not been a medieval winter of blizzards and frosts, there would have been no spring flood of apostasy. And what, after all, is the spring flood but an interval of havoc between the time of an icebound river and the time in which the same river flows serenely and benevolently between restored banks?" See Dubnov, *History of the Jews*, vol. 4, p. 645.

125. Ibid., p. 645.

126. Cited in Seltzer, "Simon Dubnow," p. 326.

127. Cited in Dinberg, "Shimon Dubnov," 114.

128. For a detailed description of Dubnow's periodization of Jewish history, see his *History of the Jews*, vol. 1, pp. 44–45.

129. Dov Weinryb, "Dubnov veha-historiografiah ha-yehudit" (Dubnow and Jewish Historiography), in *Sefer Shimon Dubnov*, edited by Simon Rawidowicz (London: Ararat Publishing Company, 1954), 73; and Kochan, *The Jew and His History*, p. 95. Dubnow claimed that the study of Jewish history would actually lessen anti-Semitism by revealing the true nature of Jewish life. See Dubnov, *History of the Jews*, vol. 1, pp. 38–39.

130. Gartner, "Diaspora Nationalism and Jewish History," *Midstream* 13 (December 1967): 59.

131. For further information on Danilewski, see Franco Venturi, *Roots of Revolution* (New York: Grosset & Dunlap, 1960), p. 85; and Seton-Watson, *Decline of Imperial Russia*,

pp. 91–92.

132. Kochan, *The Jew and His History*, p. 89. According to Dinberg, Dubnow also derived many of his liberal ideals from Russian intellectual sources, including Peter Lavrov, Vladimir Soloviev, and Alexander Gradovsky. See Dinberg, "Shimon Dubnov," 123. See, also Seltzer "Simon Dubnow," p. 55.

133. See, for example, Dubnow's discussion of the "negative and positive poles of nationalism" in *LJAN*, Third Letter, pp. 151–57.

134. Kochan, *The Jew and His History,* p. 88.

135. Seltzer, "Simon Dubnow," p. 169.

136. Cited in Trunk, "Historians of Russian Jewry," p. 468 (italics in the original).

137. "Shimen Dubnov tsu zayn 75-yokn yoyvl" (Simon Dubnow on His 75th Birthday) Hist*orishe shriftn* 2 (1937): xi.

138. See the comments by the Marxist Jewish historian Raphael Mahler in his "Shitat Dubnov u-mif'alo be-historiografiah ha-yehudit" (Dubnow's Theoretical Approach and Work in Jewish Historiography), in *Simon Dubnow, The Man and His Work*, edited by Aaron Steinberg (Paris: World Jewish Congress, 1963), p. 68.

139. Dubnov, *History of the Jews*, vol. 1, p. 26.

140. Ibid., p. 253.

141. Ibid., p. 31.

142. Ibid., p. 223; Dubnov, *History of the Jews*, vol. 3, p. 540.

143. See especially Dubnov, *History of the Jews*, vol. 1, pp. 80–90.

144. Shimon Dubnov, "Kiyum ha-am ha-yehudi" (The Survival of the Jewish People), *He-Atid* (The Future), 4 (1912): 25.

145. Dubnov, *History of the Jews*, vol. 1, p. 311.

146. In his review of the English edition of the first two volumes of Dubnow's *History of the Jewish People*, Lloyd Gartner intriguingly argues that despite the tendency of modern historians (including Dubnow) to emphasize objective conditions to explain Jewish survival, the nineteenth-century historians of *Geistesgeschichte* may in the end have been correct. As he notes: "And so we are driven back to the Idea: the Jews really believed what they believed and created their institutions and environment and literature to cherish and perpetuate their beliefs until God would deliver them." See Gartner, "Diaspora Nationalism and Jewish History," 61.

147. The essays were first published in collected form in 1907 in Russian and republished with emendations in Hebrew in 1937. For an examination of the differences between the two editions, see Poznanski's Introduction to *LJAN*, pp. 39–43. Since I am unable to read Russian, I have chosen to rely on Poznanski's newly revised and authoritative French translation of the complete original Russian version. In cases where there are substantial differences in the later Hebrew edition, I have referred to Koppel Pinson's abridged English translation, *Nationalism and History: Essays on Old and New Judaism* .

148. *LJAN*, First Letter, pp. 76, 74. See also the extract from Dubnow's introduction to the 1897 edition of the letters in *LJAN*, pp. 473–75.

149. *LJAN*, First Letter, p. 73.

150. Ibid., pp. 85–88.

151. Dubnow, *Jewish History*, pp. 4–5.

152. *LJAN*, First Letter, pp. 85–88.

153. Dubnow, *Jewish History*, p. 19.

154. Ibid., pp. 10, 21. A few pages later in the work, Dubnow argued that because of its distinctiveness, the Jewish past would yield new insights into the philosophy of history and the psychology of nations as well. See ibid., p. 29.

155. Thus, for example, in his *History of the Jews in Russia and Poland*, Dubnow commented on the efforts by tsarist officials to forcibly assimilate Russian Jews in the following manner: "[H]ad the ruling spheres of Saint Petersburg known the history of the Jewish people, they might have realized that the annihilation of Judaism had in past ages been attempted more than once by other, no less forcible, means and that the attempt had always proved a failure." See *History of the Jews in Russia and Poland*, vol. 1, p. 15.

156. Dubnov, *History of the Jews*, vol. 1, p. 25.

157. Dubnow, *Jewish History*, p. 46.

158. Ibid., pp. 52, 55.

159. Ibid., p. 67.

160. Ibid., pp. 20–21. See also Dubnov, *History of the Jews*, vol. 1, p. 259, 312.

161. Dubnov, *Jewish History*, p. 136.

162. *LJAN*, First Letter, p. 92.

163. Cited from Dubnow's article "The Secret of the Survival and the Law of Survival of the Jewish People" published in 1912 and reproduced in *Nationalism and History*, p. 45.

164. *LJAN*, First Letter, p. 88.

165. Dubnov, *History of the Jews in Russia and Poland*, vol. 3, p. 169.

166. Dubnov, *History of the Jews*, vol. 1, p. 455.

167. *LJAN*, Fifth Letter, p. 214.

168. *LJAN*, Second Letter, p. 119.

169. *LJAN*, First Letter, p. 95.

170. *LJAN*, Second Letter, p. 119. Dubnow did accept the notion, however, that over the course of generations the offspring of "physical union" between Jews and non-Jews could become part of the Jewish people. He explained the nature of peoplehood (translated here as "nation") in the following definition of Frenchmen: "In order to be part of the French nation, one must be [either] born French, descended from Gauls or a parent race, or through the course of generations be linked to Frenchmen by the assimilation of their particular traits that result from the historical evolution of the French people." See ibid., p. 120.

171. LJAN, First Letter, p. 101. See also Dubnow's comments about M.Y. Herzenstein, a Jewish convert to Russian Orthodoxy who served in the first Duma, in ibid., p. 114*n*. At one point, Dubnow described the baptism of Jews as "a pestilential whiff of treason" and compared apostates to rats leaving a sinking ship. Cited in Fraenkel, "Simon Dubnow," p. 142.

172. *LJAN*, First Letter, p. 90; Dubnov, *History of the Jews*, vol. 1, p. 395.

173. Dubnov, *History of the Jews*, vol. 1, p. 101.

174. Ibid., pp. 848–54.

175. See, for example, Dubnow's comments on the persecution of Jews under the Seleucids during the Maccabean revolution in *History of the Jews*, vol. 1, p. 488.

176. See, for example, Dubnow's discussion of Hasidism in *History of the Jews*, vol. 1, p. 887; and vol. 4, pp. 394–95.

177. As Dubnow wrote: "The community was protected by a high fence [of religious Orthodoxy]—not against animals, but beast–like human beings who would break in and cause havoc 'in the name of Christ.'" See *History of the Jews*, vol. 3, p. 410.

178. Dubnow, *Jewish History*, p. 120. See also ibid., pp. 86–87, 179. For a representative sampling of Dubnow's views concerning Christian anti-Semitism and the inappropriateness of Christianity as a basis for Jewish national self-development, see *History of the Jews*, vol. 1, pp. 30, 824, 839–66; and vol. 2, pp. 175, 496, 512.

179. Dubnow's critique of Maimonides can be found in his *History of the Jews*, vol. 2, p. 770; and his analysis of Moses Mendelssohn in vol. 4, pp. 330–36.

180. Dubnov, *History of the Jews*, vol. 5, pp. 274, 279.

181. Dubnov, *History of the Jews*, vol. 1, pp. 674, 658.

182. *LJAN*, Second Letter, pp. 135–36; see also *LJAN*, Third Letter, p. 157.

183. *LJAN*, Second Letter, p. 134; Dubnov, *History of the Jews*, vol. 3, p. 288.

184. Dubnov, *History of the Jews*, vol. 2, p. 23.

185. *LJAN*, First Letter, p. 90.

186. *LJAN*, Second Letter, p. 135; and *LJAN*, Fifth Letter, p. 214.

187. *LJAN*, Second Letter, p. 118.

188. *LJAN*, First Letter, p. 98.

189. Shimon Dubnov, "Shalosh madregot be-liumiyut" (Three Stages of Nationalism), *Ha-Olam* (The World) 52 (December 26, 1924): 1047.

190. *LJAN*, Third Letter, p. 149.

191. Ibid., p. 152.

192. *LJAN*, First Letter, pp. 97, 98, 104.

193. Seltzer, "Simon Dubnow," p. 124.

194. Cited in Steinberg, *History as Experience*, p. 95.

195. *LJAN*, Fourth Letter, pp. 175–76.

196. Janowsky, *The Jews and Minority Rights*, pp. 63–64. For a general discussion of Birnbaum's ideas, see Joshua Fishman, *Ideology, Society, & Language: The Odyssey of Nathan Birnbaum* (Ann Arbor: Karoma Publishers, 1987).

197. *LJAN*, Fourth Letter, p. 201, 176–78. See also Dubnow's comments in *Jewish History*, pp. 154–55.

198. Dubnov, *History of the Jews*, vol. 1, p. 296.

199. Ibid., p. 345.

200. Dubnov, *History of the Jews*, vol. 2, p. 19.

201. Dubnow, *History of the Jews in Russia and Poland*, vol. 1, pp. 113, 121.

202. Dubnov, *History of the Jews*, vol. 3, p. 747; Dubnow, *History of the Jews in Russia and Poland*, vol. 1, pp. 59–61, 113, 188. Despite his comments about the role of the Vaad in fostering Jewish cultural life, Dubnow was not always clear about the relationship between autonomy and cultural development. In the case of eastern Europe, for example, he emphasized the importance of a solid institutional structure in shaping the cultural life of the community. In his discussion of Turkish Jews in the nineteenth century, however, he argued that their cultural backwardness caused their autonomy to become an instrument "of stagnation and lifeless conservatism." See *History of the Jews*, vol. 5, p. 393.

203. Dubnow, *History of the Jews in Russia and Poland*, vol. 1, pp. 371–79.

204. Dubnow, *History of the Jews in Russia and Poland*, vol. 2, pp. 111–13, 125, 137; Dubnov, *History of the Jews*, vol. 5, pp. 308, 343–44.

205. *LJAN*, Fourth Letter, p. 175 (italics in the original).

206. *LJAN*, Fourteenth Letter, pp. 447–48.

207. Dubnov, *History of the Jews*, vol. 4, pp. 499, 509, 636, 644; and vol. 5, pp. 250, 362–66; also *LJAN*, Fourth Letter, pp. 191–92.

208. *LJAN*, Second Letter, p. 121 (italics in the original). It was for this reason that Dubnow also insisted on the need to differentiate between citizenship and nationality.

209. *LJAN*, Second Letter, p. 130.

210. Fishman, *Ideology, Society & Language*, p. 121.

211. Information on Dubnow's view of communal autonomy in a restructured Russian society is taken from an article published in *Evreîski mir* 4 (1910): 1–6, written to defend the Folkspartei position on autonomism. The article is synopsized in Poznanski's Introduction to *LJAN*, pp. 51–52. See,also Dubnow's brief discussion of a community organization model in his Twelfth Letter, *LJAN*, pp. 415–17, as well as the analysis of the Folskpartei

program in Seltzer, "Simon Dubnow," pp. 210–12.

212. In his discussion of independent Judea in 140 B.C.E. in his *History of the Jews*, for example, Dubnow argued that it had a choice between becoming an ordinary state engaged in political and diplomatic activity or achieving the status of "a heavenly state" (*Civitas Dei*) . . . zealously guard[ing] its unique spiritual form of communal life which had heretofore constituted the distinctive trait of the 'chosen people.'" See Dubnov, *History of the Jews*, vol. 1, p. 558.

213. *LJAN*, Seventh Letter, pp. 265–268; Dubnov, *History of the Jews*, vol. 5, pp. 677–78.

214. *LJAN*, Sixth Letter, p. 253. See also Dubnov, *History of the Jews*, vol. 1, pp. 569, 803.

215. Cited in *LJAN*, Seventh Letter, p. 278.

216. As Dubnow noted: "Political Zionism is thus a threefold utopia: a utopia with regard to the possibility of creating a Jewish state guaranteed by international law, a utopia with regard to the transference of a large portion of the Jewish people to this state; and finally a utopia as a means of resolving the Jewish problem in its entirety." See *LJAN*, Sixth Letter, p. 253.

217. See, for example, Dubnow's discussion of the correspondence between the political Zionist leader Max Nordau and Moshe Lubetski, a young proponent of cultural Zionism, in *LJAN*, Seventh Letter, pp. 268–73. Dubnow discussed the anti-Semitic perception of Jews as aliens in Europe at length in his Second Letter, found in *LJAN*, pp. 121–27.

218. *LJAN*, Sixth Letter, pp. 234–38, 254, 256–57.

219. See, for example, Dubnow's comments in "Vegn der izolatsie fun 'bund' un der tsionishtisher folks-beveygung" (On the Isolationism of the Bund and the Zionist Movement), *Zukunft* 43 (June 1938): 329.

220. *LJAN*, Sixth Letter, p. 256. For an examination of Dubnow's changing attitude toward Zionism and the *yishuv* in the 1930s, see Arieh Tartakower, "Migration Problems in Dubnow's Theory of Jewish Nationalism," in *Simon Dubnow: The Man and His Work*, edited by Aaron Steinberg (Paris:World Jewish Congress, 1963), pp. 96–103. See also Dubnow's hope for the establishment of a Jewish spiritual center in Palestine in *LJAN*, Fifteenth Letter, p. 467.

221. Letter from Simon Dubnow to Ahad Ha-Am dated March 16, 1904, in "Igrot el Ahad Ha-Am," p. 251. For further information on their meeting in Reshitsa, see Yosef Goldstein, *Ahad Ha-Am* (Jerusalem: Keter, 1992), p. 273.

222. See, for example, Dubnow's article "Shlilat ha-galut ve-hiyuvah be-torat Ahad Ha-Am" (Negation and Affirmation of the Diaspora in the Thought of Ahad Ha-Am), published to commemorate the twenty-fifth anniversary of Ahad Ha-Am's literary activity in *Ha-Shiloach* 30 (1914): 206–10.

223. *Ha-Olam* 25 (January 21, 1927): 41.

224. Dubnov, *Toldot ha-hasidut*, Preface.

225. "Shalosh madregot" (Three Steps), *KKAH*, pp. 250–53. See also the discussion in this book, Chapter 4, p. 277–78.

226. The essay is reproduced in *KKAH*, pp. 499–503.

227. The letter is reproduced in *LJAN*, pp. 265–87.

228. *LJAN*, Sixth Letter, pp. 244, 252; Seventh Letter, p. 286. See also Dubnow's *History of the Jews in Russia and Poland*, vol. 2, pp. 422–23.

229. Dubnov, *History of the Jews*, vol. 5, pp. 696–97. See also Dubnow's comments in his letter to Ahad Ha-Am dated September 6, 1906, and reproduced in "Igrot el Ahad Ha-Am," p. 261.

230. Dubnov, *History of the Jews*, vol. 5, p. 859.

231.The essay is reproduced as the Eighth Letter in Dubnow, *Nationalism and History*, p. 182–191. Dubnow's response to Ahad Ha-Am's critique of Dubnow's autonomism, written in 1909 after the publication of the original version of the Letters, was included in the 1937 Hebrew translation and is found in Pinson's English version as well.

232. The letter is reproduced in *LJAN*, pp. 337–72.

233. Dubnov, *History of the Jews*, vol. 1, p. 709. For further discussion of Dubnow's views of the "politics of class," see his *History of the Jews*, vol. 3, p. 425; and his response to Shlomo Anski in the Thirteenth Letter in *LJAN*, pp. 425–32.

234. Dubnov, "Vegn der izolatsie fun 'bund,'" 329; and *LJAN*, Twelfth Letter, p. 440. See also Dubnow's letter to his son-in-law, the Bundist leader Henry Erlich, written in October 1938 and cited in *Simon Dubnow: Catalogue of the Exhibition*, p. 27n.

235. *LJAN*, Twelfth Letter, pp. 404–5, 430–31.

236. Dubnov, *History of the Jews*, vol. 1, p. 492.

237. *LJAN*, Fifteenth Letter, p. 468.

238. *LJAN*, Eleventh Letter, pp. 377–89. For further statements on emigration, see Dubnow's article "The Mission of the Folkspartei," published in 1907 and included as the Fourteenth Letter in *LJAN*, pp. 443–57; and "A Liberation Movement and an Emigration Movement," published in the same year and included as the Fifteenth Letter in *LJAN*, pp. 459–71.

239. Dubnov, *History of the Jews*, vol. 5, p. 838.

240. Ezra Mendelsohn, *The Jews of Central Europe Between the World Wars* (Bloomington: Indiana University Press, 1983), pp. 247, 254.

241. See, for example, Dubnow's comments about London's East End in his *History of the Jews*, vol. 5, p. 799.

242. *LJAN*, Fourth Letter, pp. 181,194. For Dubnow's general evaluation of the prospects for autonomy in various Jewish communities around the world, including Paris and London, in the interwar period, see Dubnov, *History of the Jews*, vol. 5, pp. 799–808.

243. Cited in Poznanski's Introduction, *LJAN*, p. 53.

244. Dubnov, *History of the Jews*, vol. 3, p. 412.

245. See, for example, Dubnow's comments in his letter to Ahad Ha-Am dated August 21, 1924, "Igrot el Ahad Ha-Am," p. 280.

246. Dubnov, *Fun "zhargon" tsu yidish*, pp. 9–12.

247. Ibid., p. 21.

248. Dubnov, *History of the Jews*, vol. 5, p. 894.

Chapter 4: Ahad Ha-Am: Culture and Modern Jewish Identity

1. A survey conducted by the literary supplement of the Israeli newspaper *Yediot Achronot* (Latest News) in February 1987 found that Israeli high schools no longer required students to read the major essays of Ahad Ha-Am and that interest in his thought and writing was decreasing at both the high school and university level. Cited in Yaakov Shavit, "Ahad Ha-'Am and Hebrew National Culture: Realist or Utopianist?" *Jewish History* 4, no. 2 (fall 1990): 73.

2. See, for example, Ahad Ha-Am's comments in "Al dvar otsar ha-yahadut be-lashon ivrit," published in 1894, *KKAH*, pp. 108-9.

3. Yehoshua Thon, "Lo zeh ha-derekh" (This Is Not the Way), *Ha-Shiloach* 30 (1914): 214.

4. See, for example, the comments of Haim Nahman Bialik in his article "On Ahad Ha-Am," *Jewish Frontier* 21, no. 1 (November 1964): 22-23.

5. Such was the description of Ahad Ha-Am by the Polish rabbi and early Zionist Yehoshua Thon in "Lo zeh ha-derekh," 214.

6. Yosef Goldstein, *Ahad Ha-Am* (Jerusalem, Keter, 1992), p. 25. In his memoirs, Ahad Ha-Am notes that as a child his "dearest friends were books" and that reading them "took

up all his time." See "Reshimot hadashot" (New Notes), *KKAH*, p. 481. In a letter written to the Hebrew journalist and publisher Yehoshua Hana Ravnitzky dated April 22, 1901, he claimed that his greatest desire was to retreat to a small town and to sit alone in a room for two or three days with no one knocking on his door. See *IAH*, vol. 3, p. 44.

7. See, for example, Ahad Ha-Am's comments to the rabbinic scholar Shimon Bernfeld in a letter dated February 13, 1901, *IAH*, vol. 3, p. 13.

8. "Pirke zikhronot" (Chapters from My Memoirs), *KKAH*, p. 468. Ahad Ha-Am blamed his low self-esteem on his father, one of whose pedagogical techniques, he claimed, was "to debase myself in my own eyes." See "Reshimot hadashot," *KKAH*, p. 483.

9. For an example of Ahad Ha-Am's disappointment with the reaction of scholars to his works, see his response to the American rabbi and translator Isaac Friedlander's critique of his article on Maimonides, dated June 13, 1913, *IAH*, vol. 5, p. 53.

10. Noah Rosenbloom, "Ahad Ha-Am vehe-yeda ha-histori" in *Salo Wittmayer Baron Jubilee Volume* (Jerusalem/New York: American Academy of Jewish Research, 1975), vol. 3, pp. 337–40.

11. See, for example, the comments of Shimon Bernfeld in an essay entitled "Sofer ve-dabar" (Storyteller and Spokesman), written on the occasion of the twenty-fifth anniversary of the publication of "Lo zeh ha-derekh," in *Ha-Shiloach* 30 (1914): 202–3.

12. "Kohen vi-navi" (Priest and Prophet), published in 1893, *KKAH*, pp. 90–93.

13. David Vital, "The Zionist as Thinker: Ahad Ha-Am and Hibbat Zion," in *At the Crossroads: Essays on Ahad Ha-am*, edited by Jacques Kornberg (Albany: SUNY Press, 1983), p. 89.

14. Letter written in 1906 to the writer and agricultural pioneer Moshe Smilanski, *IAH*, vol. 4, p. 9. See also Ahad Ha-Am's comments on the death of Elhanan Levinsky, the Hebrew writer and Zionist leader, in the article entitled "Ha-rishon" (The First) published in 1911, ibid., pp. 433–36; and his eulogy to Moshe Leib Lilienblum, entitled "Ha-acharon" (The Last), published in 1910, ibid., pp. 431–33.

15. Letter to the historian and philosopher Yosef Klausner, dated October 28, 1910, *IAH*, vol. 4, pp. 301–2; letter to Ben-Ami (Mordechai Rabinowitch) dated January 31, 1912, *IAH*, vol 5, p. 5.

16. "Le-petihat 'Ha-makhon li-mada'e ha-yahadut' be-yerushalayim" (On the Opening of the Jewish Studies Institute in Jerusalem), published in *Ha-Aretz* (The Land of Israel) in 1925, *KKAH*, p. 464.

17. I.L. Klausner, "Literature in Hebrew in Russia," in *Russian Jewry (1860–1917)*, edited by Jacob Frumkin et al. (New York: Thomas Yoseloff, 1966), p. 373.

18. *KKAH*, p. 78.

19. Steven J. Zipperstein's exhaustive biography *Elusive Prophet: Ahad Ha-Am and the Origins of Zionism* (Berkeley/Los Angeles: University of California Press, 1993), which contains extremely valuable material on Ginsberg's early life, arrived too late for me to make extensive use of its findings in my study. I have examined a number of Zipperstein's published essays, however, that formed the basis for his biography.

20. Goldstein, *Ahad Ha-Am*, pp. 19–21. Ahad Ha-Am would later describe Skvira as "one of the darkest corners in the Hasidic district of Russia." See "Pirke zikhronot," *KKAH*, p. 446. See also "Reshimot hadashot," ibid., pp. 491–92.

21. "Reshimot hadashot," *KKAH*, p. 479.

22. Ibid., pp. 480, 483–84. In his memoirs, Chaim Tchernowitz lists Ahad Ha-Am's father as one of the maskilim who was active in the Bet Midrash ha-Gadol (Rabbinic School of Learning) in Odessa. See Chaim Tchernowitz, *Pirke haim* (New York: Bitzaron, 1954), p. 182.

23. "Reshimot hadashot," *KKAH*, p. 493.

24. Ironically, the tsarist minister of interior Nikolai Ignatiev, who would later be responsible for issuing the May Laws that forced Ahad Ha-Am's family to leave Gopitshitza, had been a neighbor of the Ginsbergs. He and Isaiah Ginsberg would often entertain each other in their homes. See *KKAH*, p. 495.

25. Goldstein, *Ahad Ha-Am*, pp. 48–50.

26. "Ha-adam be-ohel" (A Man in His Tent), published in 1891, *KKAH*, pp. 48-51.

27. "Torah sheh-ba-lev" (Torah of the Heart), published in 1894, *KKAH*, pp. 51–54; "Tehiyah u-briyah" (Revival and Creation), published in 1898, ibid., p. 292. See also Ginsberg's comments on *melitsah*, the flowery style of the maskilim, in "Ha-lashon ve-sifrutah" (Language and Its Literature), *KKAH*, pp. 93–97. For a full discussion of Ahad Ha-Am's relation to the Hebrew language, see Tudor Parfitt, "Ahad Ha-Am's Role in the Revival and Development of Hebrew," in *At the Crossroads: Essays on Ahad Ha-am*, edited by Jacques Kornberg (Albany: SUNY Press, 1983), pp. 12–27.

28. Letter to Shimon Bernfeld dated March 8, 1899, *IAH*, vol. 2, p. 249. It is hardly coincidental that Ahad Ha-Am did not include his only published poem in his collection of writings.

29. "Reshimot hadashot," *KKAH*, p. 495.

30. See, for example, Ahad Ha-Am's discussion of the task of morality in "Hikui ve-hitbolilut" (Imitation and Assimilation), written in 1892 and published in 1893, *KKAH*, pp. 86–89. Despite his disdain for German philosophy, Ahad Ha-Am was fond of using a dialectical approach in his writings, as noted in the titles of such essays as "Positive and Negative," "Priest and Prophet," and "Flesh and Spirit."

31. Rosenbloom, "Ahad Ha-Am," p. 347. For an insight into Ahad Ha-Am's own approach to general philosophy, see his essay "Etzah tovah" (Good Advice), published in 1897, *KKAH*, pp. 132–34.

32. See, for example, Ahad Ha-Am's comments in "Shilton ha-sekhel" (The Rule of the Intellect), written in 1905 on the occasion of the 700th anniversary of the death of Maimonides, *KKAH*, pp. 355–69.

33. "Reshimot hadashot," *KKAH*, p. 483. According to Ahad Ha-Am's sister, Esther, he was especially proud of his wife's ability to read Heine, Schiller, and Spinoza in the original German. See Goldstein, *Ahad Ha-Am*, p. 47; and Goldstein's own comments, ibid., pp. 173–74.

34. Two years later, Ginsberg, now twenty-six, was unable to tell his father of his desire to study abroad, fearing that he would not let him go. See "Pirke zikhronot," *KKAH*, p. 468.

35. "Reshimot hadashot," *KKAH*, p. 494.

36. "Pirke zikhronot," *KKAH*, p. 467.

37. Ibid., p. 469.

38. For additional insights into the effect of Ahad Ha-Am's childhood experiences on his later attitudes, see the comments of Leon Simon in his biography *Ahad Ha-Am* (New York: Herzl Press, 1960), p. 307.

39. Dan Miron, *Bodedim be-moadam* (When Loners Come Together) (Tel Aviv: Am Oved, 1987), p. 344. See also Bialik "On Ahad Ha-Am," 20.

40. Letter to Simon Dubnow dated August 15, 1922, *IAH*, vol. 6, p. 244.

41. For further information on Hibbat Zion, see David Vital, *The Origins of Zionism* (Oxford: Oxford University Press, 1980), pp. 135-200.

42. Steven J. Zipperstein, "Ahad Ha-'Am's Politics," *Jewish History* 4, no. 2 (fall 1990): 92; Yehoshua Barzilay, "Ekh naaseh Asher Gintsberg le-Ahad Ha-Am (zikhronot)," *Ha-Shiloach* 30 (1914): 303-304.

43. "Reshimot hadashot," *KKAH*, p. 489. Lilienblum remained a strong opponent of Ahad Ha-Am's cultural Zionism throughout the period of the founding of the Zionist movement until his death in 1910. For his criticism of spiritual Zionism and Ahad Ha-Am after the First Zionist Congress, see *Kol kitve Moshe Leib Lilienblum* (The Complete Writings of Moshe Leib Lilienblum) (Odessa: Moriah, 1912), pp. 373–75. See also David Vital, *Zionism: The Formative Years* (Oxford: Clarendon Press, 1988), pp. 32–33; and Yosef Salmon, "Tahalikhe kituv be-yishuv ha-yehudi ba-arets be-machatsit ha-rishonah shel shnot ha-90" (The Development of Conflict Within the Jewish *yishuv* in the First Half of the 1890s), *Catedra* 12 (summer 1979): 17–18.

44. Simon, *Ahad Ha-Am*, p. 244.

45. Goldstein, *Ahad Ha-Am*, p. 69.

46. Ibid., p. 73.

47. For further information on the controversy, see S. Zalman Abramov, *Perpetual Dilemma: Jewish Religion in the Jewish State* (Jerusalem: World Union for Progressive Judaism, 1976), pp. 47–49.

48. The article is reproduced in *KKAH*, pp. 11–16.

49. The essay is reproduced in ibid., pp. 19–21.

50. "Pirke zikhronot," *KKAH*, p. 469.

51. Barzilay, "Ekh naaseh Asher Gintsberg," 304.

52. Goldstein, *Ahad Ha-Am*, p. 104.

53. "Le-Ahad Ha-Am" (To Ahad Ha-Am), *Kol kitve H"N Bialik* (The Complete Writings of H.N. Bialik) (Tel Aviv: Dvir, 1954), pp. 33–34. In a telling comment written in 1916 to Samuel Daiches, a rabbi active in the London Jewish community, Ahad Ha-Am explained his decision to work on the Sabbath as a means of saving himself "from enslavement to the masses." The letter, dated April 6, 1916, is in *IAH*, vol. 6, p. 15.

54. Barzilay, "Ekh naaseh Asher Gintsberg," 302–5.

55. Shmaryahu Levin described Ahad Ha-Am's response to his critics at public debates in the following terms: "Woe to the speaker who became tangled up in his thoughts. The word of the master was then like a sharp, quiet blade which cut clean across the tangle, so that the imposing mass of thoughts suddenly collapsed into a helpless heap of shreds and tatters. He made the cut like a skillful surgeon, a minimum of blood-letting, a maximum of effect." See Shmaryahu Levin, *Youth in Revolt* (New York: Harcourt, Brace, and Company, 1930), pp. 203–4.

56. Yehshua Thon, "Lo ze ha-derekh," 215.

57. Simchah Ben-Tsion, cited in Miron, *Bodedim be-moadam*, p. 357. The Zionist leader Menahem Ussishkin described Ahad Ha-am during his first visit to Palestine in 1891 as looking like the "Ras Al Kol Yahud," the traditional leader of the Jewish community recognized by the Ottoman Empire. See Menahem Ussishkin, "Baal dimyon" (Dreamer), *Ha-Shiloach* 30 (1914): 306.

58. Tchernowitz, *Pirke haim*, p. 132. See also the comments by Levin in *Youth in Revolt*, p. 204.

59. See, for example, Ahad Ha-Am's letter to Sh. Alexandrov dated April 11, 1904, in *IAH*, vol. 3, p. 316.

60. Yosef E. Heller, "Le-dmuto ha-nafshit veha-ruhanit shel Ahad Ha-Am," *Melilah* 5 (1956): 250.

61. Bialik, "Le-Ahad Ha-Am," p. 384; "On Ahad Ha-Am," 20; and *Devarim sheh be-al peh* (Oral Statements) (Tel Aviv: Dvir, 1935), vol. 2, p. 206. See also the letter from Yosef Lurie to Leo Motzkin, another Russian Zionist activist, dated March 29, 1896, cited in Yisrael Klausner, *Opozitsiyah li-Herzl* (Jerusalem: Achieved, 1960), p. 11.

62. Zalman Epstein, "Adam ve-yehudi" (Man and Jew), *Ha-Shiloach* 30 (1914): 248.

63. Ahad Ha-Am claimed that it was actually two young settlers from Palestine, Abraham Lubarsky and Yehoshua Eisenstadt (Barzilay), who originated the idea of founding Bnei Moshe and who asked him to help organize it. See "Reshimot hadashot," *KKAH*, p. 488. See also the comments of Yehoshua Barzilay in "Asher Gintsberg," 302–5. In his biography, Yosef Goldstein argues convincingly that Ahad Ha-Am had a more direct role in the creation of the organization than he was willing to admit. See Goldstein, *Ahad Ha-Am*, pp. 93–94. For a general discussion of Bnei Moshe, see Joseph Salmon, "Ahad Ha-Am and Benei Moshe: An 'Unsuccessful Experiment'?" in *At the Crossroads: Essays on Ahad Ha-am*, edited by Jacques Kornberg (Albany: SUNY Press, 1983), pp. 98–105; and Shmuel Tchernowitz, *Bnei Moshe u-tekufatam* (Bnei Moshe and Its Era) (Warsaw:, Ha-tsefirah, 1914). See also Ahad Ha-Am's own comments on the program of Bnei Moshe in his essay "Derekh ha-hayim" (Way of Life), published in 1889, *KKAH*, pp. 438–41.

64. Steven J. Zipperstein, "Ahad Ha'Am and the politics of assimilation" in *Assimilation and Community: The Jews in Nineteenth-Century Europe*, edited by Jonathan Frankel and Steven J. Zipperstein (Cambridge: Cambridge University Press, 1992), pp. 349–50.

65. Josef Fraenkel, *Dubnow, Herzl, and Ahad Ha-Am* (London: Ararat Publishing Society, 1963), p. 31.

66. "Lo zeh ha-derekh," *KKAH*, pp. 12–13.

67. Salmon, "Ahad Ha-Am and Benei Moshe," p. 186*n*:; Goldstein, *Ahad Ha-Am*, p. 94.

68. As Ahad Ha–Am stated in his essay on Moses: "Even if . . . [learned scholars] could succeed in clearly demonstrating that Moses never existed or did not function [as a national leader] . . . it would not have the slightest effect upon the historical reality of the ideal Moses, who walked before us not only during the forty years in the Sinai Desert but also during the thousands of years in the 'deserts' that we have traversed from the time of Egypt to the present." See "Moshe" (Moses), published in 1904, *KKAH*, p. 342.

Interestingly, similar views concerning Moses and the biblical Prophets were expressed by one of Ahad Ha-Am's major influences, Herbert Spencer. See, for example, his *Principles of Sociology*, edited by Stanislav Andreski (Hamden, Conn.: Archon Books, 1969), p. 630.

69. "Moshe," *KKAH*, p. 343. In his work *Fun "zhargon" tsu yidish*, Simon Dubnow recounts an amusing anecdote that points up both Ahad Ha-Am's close identification with Moses and the suspicion it often aroused among his intellectual peers in Odessa. One evening, the cultural Zionist gave a speech to the Beseda Club, a literary group of young Jewish intellectuals, in which he discussed his view that Moses did not have to have been a real person to have had an impact upon Jewish life. After the speech, Dubnow saw the aged Hebrew writer Mendele Moykher Sforim sitting in a corner. The Jewish historian approached him and asked the writer what he thought of Ahad Ha-Am's presentation. The Bible teaches that no one knows where Moses is buried, Mendele responded. Tonight, however, thanks to Ahad Ha-Am, he had finally found Moses's grave—the Beseda Club! See Simon Dubnow, *Fun "zhargon" tsu yidish* (Vilna: Vilner Farlag fun B.Kletzkin, 1929), p. 124.

70. "Derekh ha-hayim," *KKAH*, p. 449.

71. Goldstein, *Ahad Ha-Am*, p. 96.

72. Gershon Swet, "Russian Jews in Zionism and the Building of Palestine," in *Russian Jewry (1860–1917)*, edited by Jacob Frumkin et al. (New York: Thomas Yoseloff, 1966), pp. 187–88; Simon, *Ahad Ha-Am*, pp. 76-82; Jehuda Reinharz, "Ahad Ha-'Am—In the Eye of the Storm," *Jewish History* 4, no. 2 (fall 1990): 51.

73. See, for example, Ahad Ha-Am's comments in "Mukdam u-meuhar ba-hayim" (Anticipations and Survivals in Life), published in 1891, *KKAH*, p. 80.

74. See, for example, the criticism leveled by the religious Zionist Yechiel Michael Pines

cited in Ehud Luz, *Makbilim nifgashim: Dat ve-liumiyut be-tnuah ha-tsiyonit be-mizrach eropah be-reshitah (1882–1904)* (When Parallels Meet: Religion and Nationalism in the Formative Stages of the Eastern European Zionist Movement, 1882–1904) (Tel Aviv: Am Oved, 1985), pp. 135–36. (The work was published in English translation as *Parallels Meet: Religion and Nationalism in the Early Zionist Movement, 1882-1904* by the Jewish Publication Society in 1988.) Pines was a member of the Jaffa branch of Bnei Moshe for a short time before being expelled. See also the comments of the rabbinical scholar in the *yishuv*, Aryeh Leib Frumkin, cited in Shavit, "Ahad Ha-'Am and Hebrew National Culture," 76. For a general discussion of the response of the ultra-Orthodox community to Bnei Moshe, see Yosef Salmon, "Ha-maavak al daat ha-kahal ha-haredit be-mizrach eropah be-yachas le-tnuah ha-liumit ba-shanim 1894–1896" (The Ideological Struggle Within the Ultra-Orthodox Community over the Question of the Nationalist Movement in the Years 1894–1896), in *Prakim be-toldot ha-hevrah ha-yehudit be-yeme ha-benayim uvi-et ha-hadashah* (Chapters in the History of Jewish Society from the Middle Ages to the Modern Era) (Jerusalem: Magnes Press, 1980), pp. 330–68.

75. Cited in Levin, *Youth in Revolt*, pp. 193–94.

76. Goldstein, *Ahad Ha-Am*, pp. 101–2.

77. Salmon, "Ahad Ha-Am and Benei Moshe," p. 103.

78. "Nisayon sheh-lo-hitzliach" (An Unsuccessful Experiment), *KKAH*, p. 437. See also the insightful comments by Steven Zipperstein in his article "Ahad Ha-'Am's Politics," 91.

79. Yosef Salmon, "Ha-maavak al daat ha-kahal ha-haredit," p. 333; Goldstein, *Ahad Ha-Am*, p. 160. A partial insight into the fate of Bnei Moshe in the period between 1891 and 1896 is contained in general correspondance that Ahad Ha-Am sent to the organization's branches, reproduced in *KKAH*, pp. 441–45.

80. *KKAH*, pp. 52–53. For further details on the debate over Ben Yehuda's imprisonment, see Goldstein, *Ahad Ha-Am*, pp. 173–83.

81. Ahad Ha-Am's curriculum can be found in *KKAH*, pp. 198–99.

82. Zipperstein, "Ahad Ha'Am and the politics of assimilation," p. 353.

83. Salmon claims that most of the students at the school actually came from Sephardic families who preferred the Alliance curriculum and had little interest in the ideals of Bnei Moshe. Salmon, "Ahad Ha-Am and Benei Moshe," p. 102. For Ahad Ha-Am's own views on the controversy, see his article "Bate ha-sefer be-yafo" (The Schools in Jaffa) published in 1891, *KKAH*, pp. 187–210.

84. Letter to the Bnei Moshe leadership on the 24th of Adar (March 20), 1895, *IAH*, vol. 1, pp. 77–78.

85. Letter to A. Sokobolsky dated April 28, 1905, *IAH*, vol. 3, p. 348. In 1913, Ahad Ha-Am would describe Bnei Moshe as "an experiment that did not succeed" ("Nisayon sheh-lo-hitzliach"), *KKAH*, p. 437.

86. Letter dated April 27, 1891, *IAH*, vol. 6, p. 195.

87. "Emet mi-erets yisrael" (The Truth from the Land of Israel), published in 1891 and reproduced in *KKAH*, pp. 23–34. See also "Mi-masaotai be-erets yisrael" (From My Journeys to the Land of Israel), personal notes on his visits to Palestine written between 1891 and 1912, *KKAH*, pp. 470–79.

88. For a discussion of the debate see Yosef Goldstein, "Ma'amado shel Ahad Ha-Am ad bo Herzl be-ri'ee 'mishpat dibah' neged Margalit" (Ahad Ha-Am's Position [in the Zionist Movement] before the Rise of Herzl as Reflected in the 'Libel Accusation' Against Margalit), *Zion* 52 (1987): 471–87.

89. For discussions surrounding the publication of the three editions, see Ahad Ha-Am's Prefaces to each of the editions in *KKAH*, pp. 1–10.

90. Letter to the Achiasaf staff dated October 28, 1896, *IAH*, vol. 1, p. 122; letter to the Warsaw branch of Bnei Moshe written in October 1895, *KKAH*, p. 448.

91. Arthur Hertzberg, "100 Years Later, a Jewish Writer's Time Has Come," *New York Times Book Review* March 31, 1991, p. 22.

92. "Teudat 'Ha-Shiloach,'" *KKAH*, pp. 126–34.

93. See, for example, Ahad Ha-Am's letter to the Zionist activist and dramatist Yehoshua Barzilay (Eisenstadt) dated February 23, 1904, in *IAH*, vol. 3, p. 309. For Ahad Ha-Am's reactions to his father's death, see Goldstein, *Ahad Ha-Am*, p. 263.

94. Letter to the political Zionist M[arcus] Ehrenpreis dated July 8, 1897, *IAH*, vol. 1, p. 235.

95. "Ha-kongres ha-tsiyoni ha-rishon" (The First Zionist Congress), *KKAH*, p. 276; Letter to Dr. Z[elig] Michelson dated July 29, 1897, *IAH*, vol. 1, pp. 247–48; Letter to T. Hindus dated August 14, 1898, *IAH*, vol. 2, pp. 128–29.

96. Letter to Sh[imon] Bernfeld dated September 13, 1898, *IAH*, vol. 2, p. 134.

97. Letter to Yehoshua Ravnitsky dated September 9, 1898, *IAH*, vol. 2, p. 131.

98. The resolution emphasized the need for the dissemination of the Hebrew language and provided for an annual subsidy for the publication of textbooks for schools in the *yishuv*. Jehuda Reinharz, *Chaim Weizmann: The Making of a Zionist Leader* (New York: Oxford University Press, 1985), p. 60.

99. Klausner, *Opozitsiyah li-Herzl*, pp. 196–97; Goldstein, *Ahad Ha-Am*, pp. 295–96; Yossi Goldstein, "Ahad Ha-'Am: A Political Failure," *Jewish History* 4, no. 2 (fall 1990): 34–35, 38–39.

100. See, for example, Ahad Ha-Am's bitter comments to L. (Lubarsky?) after the Uganda crisis in a letter dated August 31, 1903, in *IAH*, vol. 3, p. 256.

101. "Shluhe am ani" (The Messengers of an Impoverished People), published in 1901, *KKAH*, p. 305.

102. Letter to Ravnitsky dated April 29, 1901, *IAH*, vol. 3, p. 46.

103. "Predah" (The Parting), published in 1903, *KKAH*, pp. 330–32. See also Ahad Ha-Am's letter to Lubarsky dated May 25, 1902, *IAH*, vol. 3, pp. 156–57.

104. "Tsorekh ve-yekholet" (Need and Ability), published in 1897, *KKAH*, p. 130; "Achar eser shanim" (After Ten Years) published in 1903 on the tenth anniversary of the founding of *Ha-Shiloach*, ibid., pp. 329–30.

105. Letter to the early Zionist activist Z[ev] Gluskin dated October 3, 1899, *IAH*, vol. 2, p. 309.

106. Letter dated August 14, 1900, ibid., p. 369.

107. The flyer is reproduced in "Megilat starim shel Ahad Ha-Am," first published in the journal *Ha-Tekufah* (The Era) in 1925, *KKAH*, pp. 501–3. For Ahad Ha-Am's response to the decision not to include individual names on the flyer, see his letter to Ravnitsky dated June 18, 1903, *IAH*, vol. 3, p. 254.

108. Letter to E[liezer] Kaplan, business manager of Achiasaf, dated May 4, 1903, ibid., p. 241.

109. "Megilat starim shel Ahad Ha-Am," *KKAH*, p. 502. See also Ahad Ha-Am's denunciation of a delegation of Russian Jewish notables sent to the tsar after the Kishinev pogrom in a letter to the writer M[enahem Mendel] Levin dated May 16, 1903, *IAH*, vol. 3, pp. 246–47.

111. Goldstein, *Ahad Ha-Am*, p. 321.

111. The essay is reproduced in *KKAH*, pp. 395–97.

112. Cited in Goldstein, *Ahad Ha-Am*, p. 321.

113. "Ha-bokhim" (The Weepers), published in 1903, *KKAH*, pp. 333–43.

114. Letter to A[braham] L[ubarsky] dated August 31, 1903, *IAH*, vol. 3, p. 268.

115. Goldstein, "Ahad Ha'Am: A Political Failure," 37–38.

116. Letter to Weizmann dated March 17, 1902, *IAH*, vol. 3, p. 27.

117. Letter from Aaron Gurland to Weizmann, cited in Klausner, *Opozitsiyah li-Herzl*, p. 78.

118. Letter to Lubarsky dated October 2, 1903, *IAH*, vol. 3, p. 273. See also Ahad Ha-Am's letter to Lubarsky dated August 31, 1903, ibid., pp. 265–69. For further information on the transformation in the Democratic Faction, see Klausner, *Opozitsiyah li-Herzl*, pp. 236–37.

119. Letter to Simon Dubnow dated January 24, 1904, *IAH*, vol. 3, pp. 295–96.

120. As Ahad Ha-Am stated in a letter written to Dubnow in 1908, he had learned one thing in life: "Everywhere you see many activities suddenly explode at once for no obvious reason and without any previous gradual development; you should know that it is not therapeutic and natural energy but rather merely feverish warmth. . . . [Such a phenomenon] rises up and quickly subsides in a sudden transformation without any obvious explanation." Letter to Simon Dubnow dated December 7, 1908, *IAH*, vol. 4, p. 165.

121. Letter to Shmaryahu Levin dated February 9, 1902, *IAH.*, vol. 3, p. 118.

122. "Avdut be-tokh herut" (Slavery in Freedom), *KKAH*, pp. 64–69; "Ha-progres vi-sin'at yisrael" (Progress and Hatred of Israel), ibid., pp. 162–63. See also Ahad Ha-Am's letter to the young Hebrew writer Micha Berdichevsky dated March 6, 1898, *IAH*, vol. 2, p. 45.

123. "Hatsi nehama" (Small Consolation), *KKAH*, pp. 70–72.

124. "Reshimot hadashot," *KKAH*, p. 492. See also Ahad Ha-Am's letter to the Hebrew writer Mordechai Ben Hillel Hakohen dated November 12, 1905, *IAH*, vol. 3, pp. 355–56.

125. Letter to the militant Zionist Vladimir Jabotinsky dated March 26, 1905, *IAH*, vol. 3, pp. 338–39.

126. Letter to Shmaryahu Levin dated November 5, 1913, *IAH*, vol. 5, p. 192.

127. Letter to Simon Dubnow dated May 22, 1907, *IAH*, vol. 3, p. 90; letter from Dubnow to Ahad Ha-Am dated April 9, 1907, "Igrot el Ahad Ha-Am" (Letters to Ahad Ha-Am), in *Sefer Shimon Dubnow*, edited by Simon Rawidowicz (London: Ararat Publishing Company, 1954), p. 262.

128. Letter to Shimon Bernfeld dated June 30, 1914, *IAH*, vol. 5, p. 299; letter to Y. Sirkes dated January 17, 1910, *IAH*, vol. 4, p. 246.

129. Letter dated June 28, 1909, *IAH*, vol. 4, p. 176. See also the comments of Ben Halpern in "The Disciple, Chaim Weizmann," in *At the Crossroads: Essays on Ahad Ha-am*, edited by Jacques Kornberg (Albany: SUNY Press, 1983), p. 164.

130. Bialik, *Devarim sheh be-al peh*, vol. 2, p. 209. See also his poem "Al-kef yam mavet zeh" (On the Cliff of This Dead Sea), in *Kol kitve H"N Bialik*, p. 44.

131. Simon, *Ahad Ha-Am*, p. 218.

132. "Al shte ha-se'ipim" (Of Two Opinions), *KKAH*, pp. 370–78. The work was published in English under the title "Judaism and the Gospels." See also Ahad Ha-Am's letter to Lubarsky dated May 5, 1910, *IAH*, vol. 4, pp. 265–66. For a discussion of the controversy over Brenner's writings, see later in this chapter.

133. Letter to the literary critic, historian, and Zionist thinker Yosef Klausner dated October 16, 1905, *IAH*, vol. 3, pp. 354–55.

134. See, for example, Ahad Ha-Am's comments in a letter to the Jewish historian and economist Jacob Lestschinsky dated August 22, 1911, *IAH*, vol. 6, p. 223.

135. "Igrot Ahad Ha-Am," *He-Avar* 5 (1957), 160–61 (italics in the original). Osorgin had offered to convert but Ahad Ha-Am opposed it because he was convinced that the Russian writer was not sincere. See his letter to Mordechai Ben Hillel Hakohen dated October 1, 1913, ibid., p. 161. Osorgin eventually converted to Judaism. In the 1930s, Ahad Ha-Am's daughter left her husband and went to live in Palestine.

136. Goldstein, *Ahad Ha-Am*, pp. 329–33, 335–40.

137. Letter to Jacob Lestschinsky dated September 22, 1913, *IAH*, vol. 5, p. 164.

138. Letter to Mordechai Ben Hillel Hakohen dated September 2, 1914, *IAH.*, vol. 5, pp. 304–305; letter to Shalom Dov Ber Maximon, an essayist and educator living in New York, dated October 4, 1914 , ibid., p. 307.

139. Letter to Maximon dated October 4, 1914, *IAH*, vol. 5, p. 307. Similarly, in a letter dated March 5, 1915 to the Yiddish novelist and essayist Zvi Hirsch Cohen, Ahad Ha-Am described the war as "the abomination of all that is dear and holy to human beings." Ibid., p. 322. Cohen was the author of a biographical novel entitled *Ahad Ha-Am*, which was published in 1933.

140. Letter to the Talmudic scholar and Hebrew writer Haim Tchernowitz, dated May 29, 1916, *IAH*, vol. 6, p. 24.

141. Letter to Simon Dubnow dated January 20, 1916, *IAH*, vol. 6, p. 6. See also Ahad Ha-Am's letter to Dubnow dated November 7, 1915, *IAH*, vol. 5, pp. 345–47. For Dubnow's response, see his letter of November 22, 1915 in "Igrot el Ahad Ha-Am," pp. 268–71.

142. Letter to the Zionist leader and diplomat V[ictor] Jacobson dated September 7, 1916, *IAH*, vol. 6, p. 32. See also Ahad Ha-Am's letter to Simon Dubnow dated January 31, 1917, ibid., pp. 57–59.

143. Letter to Dubnow dated April 27, 1916, *IAH*, vol. 6, p. 21.

144. Letter to Dubnow dated November 7, 1915, *IAH*, vol. 5, p. 346.

145. Letter to Rabinowitch (Ben-Ami) dated July 20, 1919, *IAH*, vol. 6, p. 146.

146. Letter to the New York-based Zionist Sh. Melamed dated February 13, 1916, *IAH*, vol. 6, p. 9.

147. Letter to A[braham] Lubarsky dated April 30, 1918, *IAH*, vol. 6, p. 105.

148. For Ahad Ha-Am's skepticism about the postwar conference, see his letter to Simon Dubnow dated November 7, 1915, *IAH*, vol. 5, pp. 345–46; for his views of the British government, see his discussion of the establishment of a Jewish Legion in Palestine in his letter to the military leader in the *yishuv* Yosef Trumpeldor dated November 12, 1916, *IAH*, vol. 6, p. 46.

149. "Reshimot hadashot," *KKAH*, p. 485; Goldstein, *Ahad Ha-Am*, p. 375.

150. "Mikhtav la-asefah" (Letter to the Meeting), published in 1922, *KKAH*, p. 461; Letter to Shmaryahu Levin dated May 22, 1919, *IAH*, vol. 6, p. 136.

151. Letter to Tchernowitz dated April 6, 1917, ibid., pp. 69–70; letter to Weizmann dated August 5, 1917, ibid., p. 77; Letter to Lestschinsky dated October 30, 1917, ibid., p. 91; Letter to Lestschinsky dated November 20, 1919, ibid., pp. 151–52.

152. Letter to Jacobson dated June 10, 1921, *IAH*, vol. 6, pp. 166–67.

153. Letter to Lubarsky dated November 12, 1916, *IAH*, vol. 6, p. 47. For Dubnow's comments, see his letters to Ahad Ha-Am dated January 22 and April 22, 1924, "Igrot Ahad Ha-Am," pp. 275, 276. For other factors affecting Ahad Ha-Am's decision to immigrate to Palestine in the early 1920s, see Goldstein, *Ahad Ha-Am*, pp. 389–92.

154. For information on Ahad Ha-Am's conflicts with members of the Eyn Ganim moshava during his visit in 1911, see Goldstein, *Ahad Ha-Am*, p. 351.

155. "Pirke zikhronot," *KKAH*, pp. 474-75, 479.; "Emet mi-erets yisrael," ibid., p. 24. In his biography of Ahad Ha-Am, Goldstein claims that the Zionist thinker was not always consistent in his attitudes toward Arabs. During a trip to Palestine in 1911, for example, Ahad Ha-Am had expressed the belief that Arabs might participate in the Jewish cultural revival by integrating into the Jewish community. After all, he commented, it was possible that in the past they may have been Jews. See Goldstein, *Ahad Ha-Am*, p. 349.

156. Jacques Kornberg, "At the Crossroads: An Introductory Essay," in *At the Crossroads: Essays on Ahad Ha-am*, edited by Jacques Kornberg (Albany: SUNY Press, 1983),

pp. xxiv–xxv.

157. Letter to Dubnow dated March 28, 1923, *IAH*, vol. 6, p. 252.

158. Bialik, *Devarim sheh be-al peh*, vol. 2, pp. 195–96.

159. Letter to Leon Simon dated January 13, 1925, *IAH*, vol. 6, p. 265. Socialist Zionists in turn had little regard for Ahad Ha-Am's views, dismissing him as a bourgeois Jew unable to break with the past and insensitive to the concrete needs of the Jewish masses. See, for example, the comments of Nahman Syrkin in an editorial in *Ha-Shachar* (The Dawn) published in 1903, in *Kitve Nachman Syrkin* (The Writings of Nahman Syrkin) (Tel Aviv: Davar, 1938-39), pp. 101–25.

160. Cited in Bialik, "On Ahad Ha-Am," 23.

161. Bialik, *Devarim sheh be-al peh*, vol. 2, p. 209.

162. "Higiyah ha-shaah" (The Time Has Come), Second Letter, published in 1909, *KKAH*, p. 385.

163. "Tehiyat ha-ruach" (Revival of the Spirit), *KKAH*, p. 176.

164. "Derekh ha-ruach" (The Way of the Spirit), ibid., p. 151.

165. "Tehiyah u-briyah," ibid., p. 292.

166. "Shte reshuyot" (Two Masters), published in 1892, *KKAH*, p. 85; "Avar ve-atid" (Past and Future), published in 1891, ibid., pp. 81–83; "Shinui ha-orkhin" (The Transformation of Values), published in 1898, ibid., p. 156. See also the comments by Shavit in "Ahad Ha-'Am and Hebrew National Culture," 79.

167. See, for example, Ahad Ha-'Am's comments in the essay "Nachalat avot" (The Legacy of Our Forefathers), published in 1897, *KKAH*, pp. 271–73.

168. As Ahad Ha-Am's biographer Leon Simon has noted: "In effect, he substituted the national will to live for the divine providence, and the nation's moral sense for the divine inspiration." See Simon, *Ahad Ha-Am*, p. 46.

169. "Al shte ha-se'ipim," *KKAH*, p. 397.

170. See, for example, Ahad Ha-Am's comments in a letter written to the British rabbinic and talmudic scholar Israel Abrahams in 1913, cited in Simon, *Ahad Ha-Am*, p. 228.

171. "Ha-musar ha-leumi" (The National Ethic), published in 1899, *KKAH*, p. 152.

172. See, for example, the essays "Midat ha-din u-midat ha-rachamim" (Justice and Mercy) published in 1891, *KKAH*, pp. 74–75; and "Hikui ve-hitbolilut" published in the following year, ibid., pp. 86-89.

173. For further analysis of Ahad Ha-Am's interpretation of the Bible, see the article by Yechezkel Kaufman, "'Yahaduto' shel Ahad Ha-Am" (The "Judaism" of Ahad Ha-Am), *Ha-Shiloach* 30 (1914), pp. 257–64.

174. "Shabbat ve-tsiyonut" (Sabbath and Zionism), published in 1897, *KKAH*, p. 286.

175. Letter to the American Rabbi and Zionist Judah Magnes, cited in Simon, *Ahad Ha-Am*, p. 229.

176. "Tehiyah u-briyah," *KKAH*, p. 292; "Al shte ha-se'ipim," ibid., p. 397.

177. Letter to Rabbi E. Lolli of Padua, Italy, dated April 11, 1898, *IAH*, vol. 2, pp. 62–63.

178. See, for example, Ahad Ha-Am's comments in "Rav Mordehai Eliasberg" (Rabbi Mordechai Eliasberg), published in 1890, in *KKAH*, pp. 40–43; and "Rav leumi" (Nationalist Rabbi), published in 1897, ibid., pp. 265–67. See also his comments about the Grand Rabbin of France, Zadok Kahn, in "Mi-masaotai be-erets yisrael," ibid., p. 472.

179. Letter to Yosef Klausner dated January 27, 1895, *IAH*, vol. 6, pp. 201–2.

180. "Ben kodesh le-hol" (Between the Sacred and Profane), published in 1892, *KKAH*, p. 73; "Divre shalom" (Words of Peace), published in 1895, ibid., p. 58.

181. Aryeh Simon and Yosef Heller, *Ahad Ha-Am: ha-ish, pe'alo vi-torato* (Ahad Ha-Am: His Activity and His Teachings) (Jerusalem: Magnes Press, 1955), pp. 189, 192; "Shinui

ha-orkhin," *KKAH*, p. 156.

182. See, for example, Ahad Ha-Am's remarks to Rabbi Eliasberg, cited in Yosef Goldstein, "Yehaso shel Ahad Ha-Am la-dat be-aspeklariah ha-historit" (Ahad Ha-Am's Relationship to Religion Viewed in a Historical Light), *Tmurot be-historiah ha-yehudit ha-hadashah* (Developments in Modern Jewish History) (Jerusalem: Merkaz Zalman Shazar, 1988), p. 165.

183. See Ahad Ha-Am's comments in "Shinui ha-orkhin," published in 1898, *KKAH*, pp. 154-58.

184. Miron, *Bodedim be-moadam*, p. 358.

185. "Mizrach u-maarav," *KKAH*, p. 333.

186. See, for example, Ahad Ha-Am's letters to Berdichevsky dated January 28, 1898, *IAH*, vol. 2, pp. 22–29; February 3, 1898, ibid., pp. 27–30; and August 21, 1898, ibid., pp. 113–14. See also Tchernowitz, *Pirke haim*, p. 188.

187. Anita Shapira, "Herzl, Ahad Ha-'Am, and Berdichevsky: Comments on Their Nationalist Concepts," *Jewish History* 4, no. 2 (fall 1990): 67.

188. Ibid., 64–65.

189. Cited in Miron, *Bodedim be-moadam*, p. 354. See also ibid., pp. 361–62.

190. See, for example, the comments of Yaakov Klatzkin in his article "Boker shel tekufah" (Dawn of an Age), *Ha-Shiloach* 27 (1911): 259–303.

191. Cited in Jonathan Frankel, *Prophecy and Politics: Socialism, Nationalism, and the Russian Jews, 1862-1917* (Cambridge: Cambridge University Press, 1981), p. 405.

192. Luz, *Makbilim nifgashim*, pp. 36–49; Goldstein, *Ahad Ha-Am*, p. 293.

193. "Shinui ha-orkhin," *KKAH*, pp. 154–58.

194. "Ha-musar ha-leumi," *KKAH*, pp. 159–64; "Al shte ha-se'ipim," ibid., pp. 390–97. See also Ahad Ha-Am's remarks to Yosef Klausner in a letter dated February 19, 1902, *IAH*, vol. 3, p. 124.

195. The most complete treatment of the "Brenner Affair" can be found in Nurit Govrin's *Meorah Brenner: Ha-ma'avak al hofesh ha-bitui* (The Brenner Affair: The Struggle for Freedom of Expression) (Jerusalem: Yad Izhak Ben-Zvi, 1985).

196. Miron, *Bodedim be-moadam*, p. 339.

197. David Kenani, *Ha-aliyah ha-shniyah ha-ovedet vi-yehasehah le-dat u-le-masoret* (The Second Labor Alyah and Its Relationship to Religion and Tradition) (Tel Aviv: Sifriyat Poalim, 1976), pp. 72–74; Govrin, *Meorah Brenner*, pp. 133–39.

198. "Torah mi-tsiyon" (The Law Out of Zion), published in 1911, *KKAH*, pp. 406–9.

199. Letter to Mordehai Ben Hillel Hakohen dated February 26, 1911, *IAH*, vol. 4, p. 359.

200. "Shilton ha-sekhel," *KKAH*, pp. 355–59.

201. Ibid., p. 366.

202. Ibid., p. 369; "Ben kodesh le-hol," *KKAH*, p. 72.

203. "Shilton ha-sekhel," *KKAH*, p. 355.

204. Letter to M.K.B. (?) dated April 12, 1889, *IAH*, vol. 2, p. 275.

205. Goldstein, *Ahad Ha-Am*, p. 122.

206. Letter to M. Samburski, June 30, 1901, in *IAH*, vol. 6, p. 208.

207. "Torah mi-tsiyon," *KKAH*, p. 408.

208. Letter to Shmaryahu Levin dated February 27, 1908, *IAH*, vol. 6, pp. 116–17.

209. See, for example, the comments of Yechezkel Kaufman in his article "'Yahaduto' shel Ahad Ha-Am," 267.

210. "Al shte ha-se'ipim," *KKAH*, pp. 383–87; "Basar va-ruach" (Flesh and Spirit), published in 1904, ibid., p. 350.

211. "Avdut be-tokh herut," *KKAH*, pp. 64–69.

212. "Goel hadash" (A New Savior), published in 1901, *KKAH*, p. 301.

213. "Ha-kongres ve-yotzro" (The Congress and Its Creator), published in 1898, *KKAH*, p. 278.

214. See, for example, Ahad Ha-Am's remarks in "Basar va-ruach," *KKAH*, pp. 348–52.

215. "Higiyah ha-shaah, First Letter," ibid., p. 380.

216. "Mukdam u-meuhar ba-hayim," ibid., pp. 78–80.

217. See the comments by Eliezer Schweid in his work *Ha-yahadut vi-hatarbut ha-hilonit* (Judaism and Secular Culture) (Tel Aviv: Ha-kibutz ha-meuhad, 1981), p. 30.

218. Moshe Glickson, "Ahad Ha-Am," *Ketavim*, vol. 2 (Tel Aviv: Dvir, 1962–63), p. 275.

219. Robert Seltzer, "Ahad Ha-Am and Dubnow: Friends and Adversaries," in *At the Crossroads: Essays on Ahad Ha-am*, edited by Jacques Kornberg (Albany: SUNY Press, 1983), pp. 70–72.

220. "Shlilat ha-galut," published in 1909, *KKAH*, pp. 399–403.

221. Letter to the Hebrew writer A[lter] Druyanov dated September 16, 1906, *IAH*, vol. 4, p. 55.

222. "Shalosh madregot," published in 1898, *KKAH*, pp. 150–53; Letter to Dubnow dated September 22, 1907, *IAH*, vol. 4, pp. 94–96.

223. "Shlilat ha-galut," *KKAH*, p. 403; Tehiyat ha-ruach," ibid., p. 188.

224. In an article written to commemorate Pinsker's death, Ahad Ha-Am attempted to identify the latter with his own views by claiming that toward the end of his life, Pinsker had concluded that Palestine must be a home for Judaism and not simply for Jews. See "Doktor Pinsker u-machbarto" (Dr. Pinsker and His Tract), published in 1892, *KKAH*, p. 45.

225. Goldstein, *Ahad Ha-Am*, pp. 142, 153. See also Ahad Ha-Am's essay "Hikui ve-hitbolilut," *KKAH*, p. 89.

226. Letter to Y. [Zeev?] Zeitlin dated July 11, 1909, *IAH*, vol. 3, p. 216.

227. *KKAH*, p. 3.

228. Cited in Ussishkin, "Baal dimyon," 308.

229. "Nachalat avot," *KKAH*, p. 273.

230. *KKAH*, p. 10.

231. Letter dated September 18, 1910, *IAH*, vol. 4, pp. 283–85.

232. For a contemporary view, see Shavit, "Ahad Ha-'Am and Hebrew National Culture," 82.

233. "Higiyah ha-shaah, First Letter," *KKAH*, p. 383. See also "Milim u-musagim" (Words and Concepts), published in 1907, ibid., pp. 392–94.

234. "Pitze ohev" (A Lover's Wounds) published in 1891, *KKAH*, pp. 20–22.

235. "Higiyah ha-shaah, First Letter," *KKAH*, p. 380.

236. "Doktor Pinsker u-machbarto," *KKAH*, p. 47. See also "Pirke zikhronot," ibid., p. 479. Ahad Ha-Am's most bitter critique of Herzl was contained in the essay "Altneuland" (Old-New Land), published in 1903, and reproduced in *KKAH*, p. 313. The title of the essay referred to Herzl's utopian work in which he outlined his view of the nature of the future Jewish society. Ahad Ha-Am's critique was viciously attacked in an article by Max Nordau, which in turn led to a massive outpouring of support for Ahad Ha-Am on the part of many young Zionist activists. For a discussion of the debate surrounding "Altneuland," see Goldstein, *Ahad Ha-Am*, pp. 299–300.

237. "Heshbon ha-nefesh" (An Accounting of the Soul), *KKAH*, p. 61.

238. "Emet mi-erets yisrael," *KKAH*, p. 30.

239. Ahad Ha-Am, "Le-she'elot ha-yom" (On the Questions of the Day), *Ha-Shiloach* 3 (1898): 103. See also Ahad Ha-Am's comments to L. (Lubarsky?) after the Uganda Affair in a letter dated August 31, 1903, *IAH*, vol. 3, pp. 265–66.

240. Letter to the Zionist activist [Marcus] Ehrenpreis dated December 22, 1897, *IAH*, vol. 1, p. 278.

241. "Ha-kongres ve-yotzro," *KKAH*, p. 276.

242. "Ha-het ve-onsho" (The Sin and Its Punishment), published in 1903, *KKAH*, p. 425.

243. "Medinat ha-yehudim ve-'tsarat ha-yehudim'" (The Jewish State and the "Plight of the Jews"), published in 1898, *KKAH*, p. 138.

244. In a letter to to the journalist and publisher Yehoshua Ravnitsky written shortly after the convening of the First Zionist Congress, Ahad Ha-Am described the participants as akin to "animals in a herd following a leader." See letter dated September 1, 1897, *IAH*, vol. 1, p. 252.

245. "Ha-bokhim," *KKAH*, p. 338.

246. See, for example, Ahad Ha-Am's comments in "Ha-hinukh ha-leumi" (National Education), *Ha-lashon veha-hinukh* (Language and Education) (Cracow, Yosef Fisher, 1907), p. 9.

247. Letter written to the Zionist activist Yechiel Tchelnov dated October 7, 1898, *IAH*, vol. 2, pp. 146–48.

248. "Reshimot hadashot," *KKAH*, p. 495.

249. "Yachid ve-rabim" (The Individual and the Collectivity), published in 1899, *KKAH*, pp. 296–97.

250. "Ha-kongres ha-tsiyoni ha-rishon," *KKAH*, p. 276.

251. Letter to Victor Jacobson dated April 17, 1903, *IAH*, vol. 3, p. 236.

252. Luz, *Makbilim nifgashim*, p. 191. According to Luz, the religious Zionist Pines stated in his eulogy of Herzl in 1904 that if the Zionist leader had not died so young, he would undoubtedly have become an observant Jew. Ibid., p. 134.

253. As David Vital has written, in contrast to the relatively solid organizational structure and clear focus of Herzl's movement, Russian Zionism at the turn of the century was characterized by "huge energies, much individual talent, and great strength in numbers . . . along with an invertebrate institutional structure, deep ideological divisions, and an absence of first-rate (as opposed to very good second-rate) leadership." See Vital, *Zionism: The Formative Years*, p. 182.

254. "Ver iz 'Der Yud'?" (What Is "The Jew"?), *Der Jude* 1, no. 7 (April 1899): 1–3. The cleverly chosen title referred to Ahad Ha-Am's concerns about both the nature of Jewry and the goals of the fledgling Yiddish paper. Ahad Ha-Am signed the article with the three letters A-D-M ("Odem"), Yiddish for "A Man." See also Ahad Ha-Am's letter to Ravnitzky dated April 17, 1910, *IAH*, vol. 4, p. 264.

255. "Tehiyat ha-ruach," *KKAH*, p. 179; Letter to Ravnitsky dated February 12, 1911, *IAH*, vol. 4, p. 352.

256. Letters to Dubnow dated June 16, 1909, *IAH*, vol. 4, p. 211; September 27, 1909, ibid., p. 226; and February 24, 1910, ibid., pp. 254–55. For a full discussion of Ahad Ha-Am's attitudes toward the language question, see his essay "Riv ha-lishonot" (The Debate Over Language), published in 1911, *KKAH*, pp. 403–6.

257. Parfitt, "Ahad Ha-Am's Role," pp. 21–26.

258. Bialik, *Devarim sheh be-al peh*, vol. 2, p. 207.

259. As Ahad Ha-Am wrote: "In all matters pertaining to clarity of thought it is not speech but the written word that is central; and every enlightened nation has a distinctive written language for the expression of its ideas and its spiritual ideas that is often different from the regular spoken language. "Ha-lashon ve-sifrutah," *KKAH*, p. 94.

260. Aharon Kabak, "Li-tsurato ha-ruhanit shel Ahad Ha-Am" (On the Spiritual Approach of Ahad Ha-Am), *Ha-Shiloach* 30 (1914): 240.

261. Bialik, *Devarim sheh be-al peh*, vol. 2, p. 196.

262. Parfitt, "Ahad Ha-Am's Role," p. 14.

263. "Teudat 'Ha-Shiloach,'" *KKAH*, p.128. See also Ahad Ha-Am's remarks in "Ha-hinukh ha-leumi," p. 7.

264. "Ha-hinukh ha-leumi," pp. 8–12, 15; "Al dvar otsar ha-yahadut be-lashon ivrit," *KKAH*, pp. 104-14. The effort to create the anthology came to nought when Ahad Ha-Am's major sponsor and employer Kalman Wissotsky withdrew his support from the project. See Salmon, "Ha-maavak al daat ha-kahal ha-haredit," p. 365.

265. Cited in Glickson, "Ahad Ha-'Am," p. 282. See also Ahad Ha-Am, "Ha-hinukh ha-leumi," p. 14.

266. Shavit, "Ahad Ha-'Am and Hebrew National Culture," 78.

267. Aharon Kabak in *Ha-Shiloach* 30 (1914): 231. In the article, the Hebrew writer likened the rereading of the essays of *Al parshat derakhim* in 1914 to entering a kindergarten filled with "delights of the imagination" and "toys of thought" of times gone by. In the same issue, the Jewish historian and religious philosopher Shimon Bernfeld commented on Ahad Ha-Am's influence by noting that his generation was blessed that there were men "even if not many, who knew and recognized the value of his activity and writings." See Bernfeld, "Sofer ve-dabar," 203.

268. Vital points especially to the impact of the Zionist movement's decision to support *Gegenwartsarbeit* (work within the Diaspora) at its Helsingfors Congress in 1906. This position, he argues, signaled "the withdrawal from the centre of affairs of those whose minds were concentrated essentially on Zionism's original and primary task, as they had understood it, and a corresponding enhancement of the role of those who were less single-minded and whose thinking was less strictly ideological and programmatic, and who had a taste and a talent for management." See Vital, *Zionism: The Formative Years*, p. 415.

269. Goldstein, *Ahad Ha-Am*, p. 410.

270. Letters to Ben-Ami dated September 18, 1906, *IAH*, vol. 4, p. 68; and January 31, 1912, ibid., vol. 5, p. 5.

Conclusion

1. Cited in Lloyd Gartner's review of the English translation of Dubnow's *History of the Jews*, "Diaspora Nationalism and Jewish History," *Midstream* 13 (December 1967): 63. Ahad Ha-Am's recent biographer, Yosef Goldstein, is somewhat more charitable about his subject. As he states in his concluding sentence: "[E]ven while the ideal [of the identification of the majority of Jewry with their nationality] whose basic outlines were outlined over a century ago continue to be realized, its author—through the paradoxical judgment of history—is all but forgotten." See Goldstein, *Ahad Ha-Am* (Jerusalem, Keter, 1992) p. 413.

2. Arnold J. Eisen, "Rethinking Jewish Modernity," *The Albert T. Bilgray Lecture, April 1992* (Tucson: University of Arizona, 1993), p. 10.

3. For the discussion of "race of none," see Barbara Ehrenreich, "Cultural Baggage," *New York Times Sunday Magazine*, April 5, 1992, 16–17. See also the comments by Jonathan S. Woocher in his work *Sacred Survival: The Civil Religion of American Jews* (Bloomington, Ind.: Indiana University Press, 1986), p. 4.

4. For an analysis of the concept of "invented" nationalism, see E. J. Hobsbawm's work, *Nations and Nationalism Since 1980* (Cambridge: Cambridge University Press, 1990).

5. Jonathan Frankel, *Prophecy and Politics: Socialism, Nationalism, and the Russian Jews, 1862-1917* (Cambridge: Cambridge University Press, 1981), p. 259.

6. Zhitlowski clearly embraced a bicentric solution in an article written in 1931. As he stated: "Diaspora nationalism therefore demands that the territorialist idea must never be

removed from our daily agenda and must never be ignored by our people. But this can only occur under the condition that it must never take the place of the national revival in the Diaspora; and this revival must never be blocked or weakened at any time." See "Shayles un tshuves in hilkhes idishizm" (Responsa Concerning the Laws of Yiddishism), *Zukunft* 36 (September 1931): 572.

7. Charles S. Liebman and Eliezer Don-Yehiya, *Civil Religion in Israel: Traditional Judaism and Political Culture in the Jewish State* (Berkeley: University of California Press, 1983), p. 5.

8. Woocher, *Sacred Survival*, pp. 16–17. See also Woocher's extensive discussion of "the civil Jewish faith," ibid., pp. 63–103.

BIBLIOGRAPHY

Aberbach, David. *Bialik*. London: Peter Halban Publishers, 1988.

Abramov, S. Zalman. *Perpetual Dilemma: Jewish Religion in the Jewish State*. Jerusalem: World Union for Progressive Judaism, 1976.

Agurskij, M.S. "Die Judenchristen in der Russisch-Orthodoxen Kirche." *Ostkirchliche Studien* 23, no. 2/3 (September 1974): 137–76.

Agus, Jacob. *Jewish Identity in an Age of Ideologies*. New York: Frederick Ungar, 1978.

Ahad Ha-Am. See Ginsberg, Asher.

Aldanov, Mark. "Russian Jews of the 1870s and 1880s." In *Russian Jewry (1860–1917)*, edited by Jacob Frumkin, Gregor Aronson, and Alexis Goldenweiser, pp. 11-17. New York: Thomas Yoseloff, 1966.

Allport, Gordon. *The Individual and His Religion*. New York: Macmillan, 1950.

Allworth, Edward, ed. *Nationality Group Survival in Multi-Ethnic States: Shifting Patterns in the Soviet Baltic Region*. New York: Praeger, 1977.

_____. *Soviet Nationality Problems*. New York: Columbia University Press, 1971.

Almog, Shmuel. *Tsiyonut vi-historiyah*. Jerusalem: Magnes Press, 1982.

Altbauer, Moshe. "Mered 1863 be-sifrut ube-folklor ha-yehudi." *He-Avar* 11 (1964): 27–36.

Altmann, Alexander. "Le-harakhat mif'alo shel Ahad Ha-Am." In *Panim shel yahadut*, pp. 155–59. Tel Aviv: Am Oved, 1983.

Altshuler, Mordechai. "Ha-nisayon li-argen kinus klal-yehudi be-rusyah achar ha-mahapekhah." *He-Avar* 12 (1965): 75–89.

Ambler, Effie. *Russian Journalism and Politics: 1861–1881*. Detroit: Wayne State University Press, 1972.

"Am Olam." *Encyclopedia Judaica*, vol. 2, cols. 861–62. Jerusalem: Keter, 1972.

Arendt, Hannah. *The Jew as Pariah: Jewish Identity and Politics in the Modern Age*. Edited with an Introduction by Ron H. Feldman. New York: Grove Press, 1978.

Aronson, Chaim. *A Jewish Life Under the Tsars*. Translated and edited by Norman Marsden. Totowa, N.J.: Allanheld, Osmun, 1983.

Aronson, Gregor. "Geographical and Socioeconomic Factors in the 1882 Anti-Jewish Pogroms in Russia." *The Russian Review* 39 (January 1980): 23–26.

_____. "Ideological Trends Among Russian Jews." In *Russian Jewry (1860–1917)*, edited by Jacob Frumkin, Gregor Aronson, and Alexis Goldenweiser, pp. 144–71. New York: Thomas Yoseloff, 1966.

Aronson, I(rwin) Michael. "The Attitudes of Russian Officials in the 1880s Toward Jewish Assimilation and Emigration." *Slavic Review* 34, no. 1 (March 1975): 1–18.

_____. "Nationalism and Jewish Emancipation in Russia: The 1880's." *Nationalities Papers* 5, no. 2 (1977): 167–82.

_____. "The Prospects for the Emancipation of Russian Jewry During the 1880's." *Slavonic and East European Review* 55, no. 3 (1977): 348–69.

_____. *Troubled Waters: The Origins of the 1881 Anti-Jewish Pogroms in Russia*. Pittsburgh: University of Pittsburgh Press, 1990.

Astur, Michael. *Geshikhte fun der frayland-lige un funm teritorialistishn gedank*. 2 vols. Buenos Aires/New York: Freiland Lige, 1967.

Barnard, F.M. *Herder's Social and Political Thought: From Enlightenment to Nationalism*. Oxford: Clarendon Press, 1965.

Baron, Salo. "Emphases of Jewish History." *Jewish Social Studies* 1, no. 1 (1939): 15–38.

———. *History and Jewish Historians*. Philadelphia: Jewish Publication Society, 1964.

———. *The Jewish Community*. Westport, Conn.: Greenwood Press, 1972.

———. *Modern Nationalism and Religion*. Freeport, N.Y.: Books for Libraries Press, 1971.

———. *The Russian Jew Under Tsars and Soviets*. New York: Macmillan, 1976.

———. "World Dimensions of Jewish History." In *Simon Dubnow: The Man and His Work*, edited by Aaron Steinberg, pp. 26–40. Paris: World Jewish Congress, 1963.

Barzel, Alexander. *Li-heyot yehudi*. Tel Aviv: Ha-kibutz ha-meuhad, 1978.

Barzilay, Yehoshua. "Ekh naaseh Asher Gintsberg le-Ahad Ha-Am (zikhronot)." *Ha-Shiloach* 30 (1914): 302–5.

Bauer, Otto. *Die Nationalitätenfrage und die Sozialdemokratie*. Vienna: I. Brand, 1907.

Belberyszki, M. "Volkism and the VolksPartei." In *Struggle for Tomorrow: Modern Political Ideologies of the Jewish People*, edited by Basil J. Vlavianos and Feliks Gross, pp. 236–43. New York: Arts Inc., 1954.

Bellah, Robert N. "The Historical Background of Unbelief." In *The Culture of Unbelief*, edited by Rocco Caporale and Antonio Grumelli, pp. 39–52. Berkeley: University of California Press, 1971.

Ben-David, Joseph, and Terry Nichols Clark, eds. *Culture and Its Creators: Essays in Honor of Edward Shils*. Chicago: University of Chicago Press, 1977.

Berdyczewski, Micha Josef, and Joseph Hayyim Brenner. *Halifat igrot*. Holon: Bet Devora vi-Emanuel, 1984.

Berger, Mordechai. "Mas nerot shabat be-rusyah." *He-Avar* 19 (1972): 127–31.

Berger, Peter L. *A Rumor of Angels: Modern Society and the Rediscovery of the Supernatural*. Garden City, N.Y.: Anchor-Doubleday, 1970.

———. *The Sacred Canopy*. Garden City, N.Y.: Doubleday, 1967.

———, and Thomas Luckmann. *The Social Construction of Reality*. Garden City, N.Y.: Doubleday, 1966.

Berk, Stephen M. *Year of Crisis, Year of Hope: Russian Jewry and the Pogroms of 1881–1882*. Westport, Conn.: Greenwood Press, 1985.

Berlin, Isaiah. *Vico and Herder: Two Studies in the History of Ideas*. New York: Viking Press, 1976.

Bernfeld, Simon. "Sofer ve-dabar." *Ha-Shiloach* 30 (1914): 195-205.

Bialik, Haim Nahman. *Devarim sheh be-al peh*. 2 vols. Tel Aviv: Dvir, 1935.

———. *Kol kitve H"N Bialik*. Tel Aviv: Dvir, 1954.

——— (Chaim Nachman). "On Ahad Ha-Am." *Jewish Frontier* 21, no. 10 (November 1964): 15–23.

Black, Cyril E. *The Dynamics of Modernization: A Study in Comparative History*. New York: Harper & Row, 1966.

Bodin, Louis. *Les Intellectuels*. Paris: Presses universitaires de France, 1964.

Bowler, Peter J. *Evolution: The History of an Idea*. Berkeley: University of California Press, 1989.

Breiman, S. *Ha-pulmus ben Lilienblum le-ven Ahad Ha-Am ve-Dubnov veha-reka shelo*. Jerusalem: 1951, n.p.

Brower, Daniel R. *Training the Nihilists: Education and Radicalism in Tsarist Russia*. Ithaca: Cornell University Press, 1975.

Brym, Robert J. *Intellectuals and Politics*. London: Allen & Unwin, 1980.

———. *The Jewish Intelligentsia and Russian Marxism: A Sociological Study of Intellectual Radicalism and Ideological Divergence*. London: Macmillan, 1978.

Budd, Susan. *Varieties of Unbelief: Atheists and Agnostics in English Society*. London: Heinemann, 1976.

Cannon, Ellen S. "The Political Culture of Russian Jewry During the Second Half of the Nineteenth Century." Unpublished Ph.D. dissertation, University of Massachusetts, 1974.

Carrère d'Encausse, Hélène. *The Great Challenge: Nationalities and the Bolshevik State, 1917–1930*. New York: Holmes & Meier, 1992.

Chadwick, Owen. *The Secularization of the European Mind in the Nineteenth Century*. New York: Cambridge University Press, 1975.

Cohen, Arthur A. *The Natural and the Supernatural Jew*. London: Valentine, Mitchell, 1967.

Cohen, Israel. *Vilna*. Philadelphia: Jewish Publication Society, 1943.

Cohn, Norman. *Warrant for Genocide: The Myth of the Jewish World Conspiracy and the Protocols of the Elders of Zion*. New York: Harper & Row, 1969.

Confino, Michael. "On Intellectuals and Intellectual Traditions in Eighteenth– and Nineteenth-Century Russia." In *Intellectuals and Tradition*, edited by S.N. Eisenstadt and S.R. Graubard, pp. 117-49. New York: Humanities Press, 1973.

Conolly, Violet. "The 'nationalities question' in the last phase of tsardom." In *Russia Enters the Twentieth Century, 1894–1917*, edited by Erwin Oberländer et al., pp. 152-81. New York: Schocken, 1971.

Conquest, Robert, ed. *Soviet Nationalities Policy in Practice*. London: Bodley Head, 1967.

Cox, Harvey G. *Religion in a Secular City: Toward a Post-Modern Theology*. New York: Simon & Schuster, 1984.

_____. *The Secular City*. New York: Macmillan, 1966.

Cuddihy, John Murray. *The Ordeal of Civility: Freud, Marx, Lévi-Strauss, and the Jewish Struggle with Modernity*. New York: Basic Books, 1974.

Davis, Moshe. "Jewry East and West—The Correspondence of I. Friedländer and S. Dubnow." *YIVO Annual of Jewish Social Science* 9 (1954): 9–61.

Dawidowicz, Lucy. *The Golden Tradition: Jewish Life and Thought in Eastern Europe*. New York: Holt, Rinehart & Winston, 1967.

Deutscher, Isaac. *The Non-Jewish Jew and other essays*. London: Oxford University Press, 1968.

Dinberg, B. "Shimon Dubnov: Le-yovelo ha-shivim ve-hamesh." *Zion* 1, no. 2 (1936): 95–128.

Dixon, Simon. "The Russians: the Dominant Nationality." In *The Nationalities Question in the Soviet Union*, edited by Graham Smith, pp. 21-37. London/New York: Longman, 1990.

Dresner, Camillo. "Haim Zhitlovsky: Teoretikan 'ha-leumiyut ha-galutit' be-zikotah le-sotsializm." Unpublished Ph.D. dissertation, Hebrew University, 1975.

Drosdoff, Nachman. *Ahad Ha-Am: Highlights of His Life and Work*. Holon: Beth Avoth, 1962.

Dubnow, Simon. (Dubnov, Shimon). Article in memory of Ahad Ha-Am. *Ha-Olam* 25 (January 21, 1927): 41.

_____ (Dubnov, Shimen). "Fun mayn leybns-bukh." *Zukunft* 38 (May–August 1933): 271–73, 356–59, 413–19, 472–77.

_____ (Dubnov, Shimen). *Fun "zhargon" tsu yidish*. Vilna: B. Kletzkin, 1929.

_____ (Doubnov, Simon). *Histoire d'un soldat juif; 1881–1915*. Paris: Les Editions du Cerf, 1988.

_____ (Dubnov, Simon). *History of the Jews*. Translated by Moshe Spiegel. 5 vols. New York: Thomas Yoseloff, 1967–73.

_____. *History of the Jews in Russia and Poland.* Translated by I. Friedlander. 3 vols. Philadelphia: Jewish Publication Society, 1916–20.

_____ (Dubnov, Shimen). *Idishe geshikhte fun shul un haym.* New York: Morris S. Sklarsky, 1948.

_____. *Jewish History: An Essay in the Philosophy of History.* Freeport, N. Y.: Books for Libraries Press, 1972.

_____ (Dubnov, Shimon). "Kiyum ha-am ha-yehudi." *He-Atid* 4 (1912): 22–27.

_____ (Doubnov, Simon). *Lettres sur le judaïsme ancien et nouveau.* Translated and annotated by Renée Poznanski. Paris: Les Editions du Cerf, 1989.

_____ (Dubnov, Shimon). "Ha-limudim ha-ivriyim." *Ha-lashon veha-hinukh,* p. 20–28. Cracow: Yosef Fisher, 1907.

_____. *Mein Leben.* Edited by Elias Hurwicz. Berlin: Jüdische Buchvereinigung, 1937.

_____. *Nationalism and History: Essays on Old and New Judaism.* Edited by Koppel S. Pinson. New York/Philadelphia: Meridian/Jewish Publication Society, 1961.

_____ (Dubnov, Shimon). *Sefer ha-hayim.* Vol. 1. Tel Aviv: Dvir, 1936.

_____ (Dubnov, Shimon). "Shalosh madregot be-liumiyut." *Ha-Olam* 52 (December 26, 1924): 1047–48.

_____ (Dubnov, Shimon). "Shlilat ha-galut vi-hiyuvah be-torat Ahad Ha-Am." *Ha-Shiloach* 30 (1914): 206–10.

_____ (Dubnov, Shimon). *Toldot ha-hasidut.* Tel Aviv: Dvir, 1944.

_____ (Dubnov, Shimon). "Der tsvayter khurbn fun ukrayn." *Historishe shriftn* 1: 27–54. Vilna: YIVO, 1929.

_____ (Dubnov, Shimen). "Vegn der izolatsie fun 'bund' un der tsionishtisher folks-beveygung." *Zukunft* 43 (June 1938): 329.

_____ (Dubnov, Shimen). "Zhitlovskis autonomizm." In *Zhitlovski zamlbukh.* Warsaw: Farlag Ch. Brzoza, 1929.

Ehrenreich, Barbara. "Cultural Baggage." *New York Times Sunday Magazine,* April 5, 1992.

Eisen, Arnold M. "Rethinking Jewish Modernity." *The Albert T. Bilgray Lecture, April 1992.* Tucson: University of Arizona, 1993.

Eisenstadt, S.N. "Intellectuals and Tradition." In *Intellectuals and Tradition,* edited by S.N. Eisenstadt and S.R. Graubard, pp.1–19. New York: Humanities Press, 1973.

Eisenstein, Miriam. *Jewish Schools in Poland, 1919–1939, Their Philosophy and Development.* New York: Kings Crown Press, Columbia University, 1950.

Elbogen, Ismar. "Von Graetz bis Dubnow: Fünfzig Jahre jüdischer Geschichtsforschung." *Festschrift zu Simon Dubnows siebzigsten Geburtstag,* pp. 7–23. Berlin: Jüdischer Verlag, 1930.

Ellul, Jacques. *The New Demons.* Translated by C. Edward Hopkin. New York: Seabury Press, 1973.

Engel, Barbara A. *Mothers and Daughters: Women of the Intelligentsia in Nineteenth-Century Russia.* London/New York: Cambridge University Press, 1983.

Epstein, Melech. *Jewish Labor in the U.S.A., 1914–1952.* New York: Trade Union Sponsoring Committee, 1953.

_____. *Profiles of Eleven.* Detroit: Wayne State University Press, 1965.

Epstein, Zalman. "Adam ve-yehudi." *Ha-Shiloach* 30 (1914): 246–48.

Erikson, Erik. *Young Man Luther.* New York, W. W. Norton, 1958.

Erlich-Dubnov, Sophie (Dubnow-Erlich, Sofia). *Das lebn un shafn fun Shimen Dubnov* Mexico City: Mendelson Fund, 1952.

_____. *Shimon Dubnov: Toldot hayav*. Tel Aviv: Hanhalat ha-yisraelit shel ha-kongres ha-yehudi ha-olami, nd.

Ettinger, Shmuel. "Jews and Non-Jews in Eastern and Central Europe Between the Wars: An Outline." In *Jews and Non-Jews in Eastern Europe, 1918–1945*, edited by Bela Vago and George L. Mosse, pp. 1–19. New York, Halsted Press, 1974.

_____. "Ha-reka ha-ideologi le-hofa'atah shel ha-sifrut ha-antishemit ha-hadasha be-rusyah." *Zion* 35, nos. 1–2 (1970): 193–225.

_____. "Russian Society and the Jews." *Bulletin on Soviet and East European Jewish Affairs* 5 (1970): 36–42.

_____. "Ha-yesodot veha-megamot be-itsuv mediniyuto shel ha-shilton ha-rusi klape ha-yehudim im halukot polin." *He-Avar* 19 (1972): 20–34.

Falkus, Malcolm E. *The Industrialisation of Russia, 1700–1914*. London: Macmillan, 1972.

Fedotov, George P. *The Russian Religious Mind*. Belmont, Mass.: Norland, 1975.

Feldmesser, Robert A. "Social Classes and Political Structure." In *The Transformation of Russian Society: Aspects of Social Change Since 1861*, edited by Cyril E. Black, pp. 245–52. Cambridge, Mass.: Harvard University Press, 1960.

Fenn, Richard K. "Toward a Theory of Secularization." *Society for the Scientific Study of Religion, Monograph Series Number 1*. Ellington, Conn.: K & R Publishers, 1978.

Fischer, George. "The Intelligentsia and Russia." In *The Transformation of Russian Society: Aspects of Social Change Since 1861*, edited by Cyril E. Black, pp. 253–74. Cambridge, Mass.: Harvard University Press, 1960.

Fishman, Joshua. *Ideology, Society, & Language: The Odyssey of Nathan Birnbaum*. Ann Arbor: Karoma Publishers, 1987.

_____. *Language and Nationalism*. Rawley, Mass.: Newbury House Publishers, 1973.

_____. *Language in Sociocultural Change*. Stanford: Stanford University Press, 1972.

_____, ed. *Never Say Die: A Thousand Years of Yiddish in Jewish Life and Letters*. The Hague: Mouton, 1981.

Fraenkel, Josef. *Dubnow, Herzl, and Ahad Ha-Am*. London: Ararat Publishing Society, 1963.

_____. "Simon Dubnow and the History of Political Zionism." In *Simon Dubnow: The Man and His Work*, edited by Aaron Steinberg, pp. 140-61. Paris: World Jewish Congress, 1963.

Francis, E.K. *Interethnic Relations: An Essay in Sociological Theory*. New York: Elsevier, 1976.

Frank, Herman. "Tsu der frage fun yidishn got-begrif." In *Zhitlovski zamlbukh*, pp. 415–22. Warsaw: Farlag Ch. Brzoza, 1929.

Frankel, Jonathan. "Assimilation and Jews in nineteenth-century Europe: towards a historiography?" In *Assimilation and Community: The Jews in Nineteenth-Century Europe*, edited by Jonathan Frankel and Steven J. Zipperstein, pp. 1–37. Cambridge: Cambridge University Press, 1992.

_____. "The Crisis of 1881–82 as a Turning Point in Modern Jewish History." In *The Legacy of Jewish Migration: 1881 and Its Impact*, edited by David Berger, pp. 9–22. New York: Social Science Monographs, Brooklyn College Press, 1983.

_____. *Prophecy and Politics: Socialism, Nationalism, and the Russian Jews, 1862–1917*. Cambridge: Cambridge University Press, 1981.

Freundlich, Charles H. *Peretz Smolenskin: His Life and Thought*. New York: Bloch Publishing Company, 1965.

Friedman, Theodore. "The Case for Secularism—A Reply." *Forum* 48 (spring 1983): 121–26.

Friesel, Evyatar. "Ahad Ha-Amism in American Zionist Thought." In *At the Crossroads: Essays on Ahad Ha-am*, edited by Jacques Kornberg, pp. 133–41. Albany: SUNY Press, 1983.

Frumkin, Jacob G. "Pages from the History of Russian Jewry." In *Russian Jewry (1860--1917)*, edited by Jacob Frumkin, Gregor Aronson, and Alexis Goldenweiser, pp. 18–84. New York: Thomas Yoseloff, 1966.

Gartner, Lloyd P. "Diaspora Nationalism and Jewish History." *Midstream* 13 (December 1967): 58-63.

————. "Simon Dubnow: The Man and His Work." *American Jewish Historical Quarterly* 54 (1964-65): 358–59.

Gerschenkron, Alexander. "Problems and Patterns of Russian Economic Development." In *The Transformation of Russian Society: Aspects of Social Change since 1861*, edited by Cyril E. Black, pp. 42-62. Cambridge: Harvard University Press, 1960.

Gilbert, Alan D. *The Making of Post-Christian Britain: A History of the Secularisation of Modern Society*. London: Longman, 1980.

Ginsberg, Asher (Ahad Ha-Am). *Essays-Letters-Memoirs*. Translated and edited by Leon Simon. Oxford: East and West Library, 1946.

————. "Ha-hinukh ha-leumi." In *Ha-lashon veha-hinukh*, pp. 5–19. Cracow: Yosef Fisher, 1907.

————. *Igrot Ahad Ha-Am*. 6 vols. Tel Aviv: Dvir, 1956–60.

————. *Kol kitve Ahad Ha-Am*. Tel Aviv: Dvir, 1965.

————. "Le-she'elot ha-yom." *Ha-Shiloach* 3 (1898), 1–11, 97–103, 289–95.

————. *Selected Essays*. Translated by Leon Simon. Philadelphia: Jewish Publication Society, 1912.

————. *Ten Essays on Zionism and Judaism*. Translated by Leon Simon. New York: E.P. Dutton, n.d.

———— (O-D-M). "Ver iz 'Der Yud'?" *Der Jude* 1, no. 7 (April 1899): 1–3.

Ginsberg, Morris. "On Dubnow's Conception of Jewish History." In *Simon Dubnow: The Man and His Work*, edited by Aaron Steinberg, pp. 41–46. Paris: World Jewish Congress, 1963.

Ginsburg, Shaul. *Amolike petersburg: Forshungn un zikhroynes vegn yidishn lebn in tsarishn rusland*. New York: CYCO, 1944.

————. *Meshumodim in tsarishn rusland*. New York: CYCO, 1946.

Glasner, Peter E. *The Sociology of Secularisation: A Critique of the Concept*. London: Routledge & Kegan Paul, 1977.

Glickson, Moshe. "Ahad Ha-Am." *Ketavim*, vol. 2, pp. 267–83. Tel Aviv: Dvir, 1962–63.

Goldenweiser, Alexis. "Legal Status of Jews in Russia." In *Russian Jewry (1860–1917)*, edited by Jacob Frumkin, Gregor Aronson, and Alexis Goldenweiser, pp. 85–119. New York: Thomas Yoseloff, 1966.

Goldhagen, Erik. "The Ethnic Consciousness of Early Russian Jewish Socialists." *Judaism* 23 (1974): 479–96.

Goldman, Emma. *Living My Life*. New York: AMS Press, 1970.

Goldscheider, Calvin, and Alan S. Zuckerman. *The Transformation of the Jews*. Chicago: University of Chicago Press, 1984.

Goldsmith, Emanuel S. *Architects of Yiddishism at the Beginning of the Twentieth Century*. Rutherford, N.J.: Fairleigh Dickinson University Press, 1976.

_____. "Zhitlovsky and American Jewry." In *Never Say Die: A Thousand Years of Yiddish in Jewish Life and Letters*, pp. 291–95. The Hague: Mouton, 1981.

Goldstein, Yosef. *Ahad Ha-Am*. Jerusalem: Keter, 1992.

_____ (Yossi). "Ahad Ha-'Am: A Political Failure." *Jewish History* 4, no. 2 (fall 1990): 33–48.

_____. "Ma'amado shel Ahad Ha-Am ad bo Herzl be-ri'ee 'mishpat dibah' neged Margalit." *Zion* 52 (1987): 471–87.

_____. "Yehaso shel Ahad Ha-Am la-dat be-aspeklariah ha-historit." *Tmurot be-historiah ha-yehudit ha-hadashah*, pp. 159–68. Jerusalem: Merkaz Zalman Shazar, 1988.

Goodman, Saul L. ed. The *Faith of Secular Jews*. New York: Ktav, 1976.

"Gordin, Jacob." *Encyclopedia Judaica*, vol. 7, cols. 787–89. Jerusalem: Keter, 1972.

Gordin, Robert. "Does Secular Judaism Have a Future?" *Judaism* 30, no. 2 (spring 1981): 228–32.

Gorlizki, Yoram. "Jews." In *The Nationalities Question in the Soviet Union*, edited by Graham Smith, pp. 339–59. London/New York: Longman, 1990.

Govrin, Nurit. *Meorah Brenner: Ha-ma'avak al hofesh ha-bitui*. Jerusalem: Yad Izhak Ben-Zvi, 1985.

Greenbaum, I. "Milhemet ha-sekularizatsiah be-yisrael be-tekufah ha-achronah." *Iyim* 1 (1927): 63–74.

Greenberg, Louis. *The Jews in Russia: The Struggle for Emancipation*. New York: Schocken, 1976.

Grumelli, Antonio. "Secularization: Between Belief and Unbelief." In *The Culture of Unbelief*, edited by Rocco Caporale and Antonio Grumelli, pp. 77–90. Berkeley, University of California Press, 1971.

Gruzenberg, Oskar O. *Yesterday: Memoirs of a Russian-Jewish Lawyer*. Edited by D.C. Rawson. Berkeley: University of California Press, 1981.

Haimson, Leopold H. "The Parties and the State." In *The Transformation of Russian Society: Aspects of Social Change since 1861*, edited by Cyril E. Black, pp. 110–45. Cambridge, Mass.: Harvard University Press, 1960.

Ha-lashon veha-hinukh, neumim be-hevrat "Mefitsei haskalah be-yisrael." Cracow: Yosef Fisher, 1907.

Halevy, Zvi. *Jewish Schools Under Czarism and Communism*. New York: Springer Library, 1976.

Halpern, Ben. "The Disciple, Chaim Weizmann." In *At the Crossroads: Essays on Ahad Ha-am*, edited by Jacques Kornberg, pp. 156–69. Albany: SUNY Press, 1983.

_____. "Exile and Redemption: A Secular Zionist View." *Judaism* 29, no. 2 (spring 1980): 177–84.

_____. "The Jewishness of Secular Judaism." *Judaism* 30, no. 2 (spring 1981): 225–28.

Halpern, Israel. *Yehudim ve-yahadut be-mizrach eropah*. Jerusalem: Magnes, 1968.

Harcave, Sidney S. *First Blood: The Russian Revolution of 1905*. New York: Macmillan, 1964.

_____. "The Jewish Question in the First Russian Duma." *Jewish Social Studies* 6 (1944): 155–63.

_____. "The Jews and the First Russian National Election." *American Slavic and East European Review* 9 (1950): 33–41.

Heller, Yosef Eliahu. "Le-dmuto ha-nafshit veha-ruhanit shel Ahad Ha-Am." *Melilah* 5 (1956): 241–64.

Hellman, Yom-Tov. "Rabi Shimon Dubnov." *He-Avar* 8 (1961): 10–16.

Herder, Johann Gottfried von. *Outlines of a Philosophy of the History of Man*. Translated by T. Churchill. New York: Bergman Publishers, nd.

Hertz, Frederick. *Nationality in History and Politics: A Psychology and Sociology of National Sentiment and Nationalism*. London: Kegan Paul, Trench, Trubner & Co., 1944.

Hertz, J.S. "The Bund's Nationality Program and Its Critics in the Russian, Polish, and Austrian Social Movements." *YIVO Annual of Jewish Social Science* 14 (1969): 53–67.

Hertzberg, Arthur. "100 Years Later, a Jewish Writer's Time Has Come." *New York Times Book Review*, March 31, 1991.

_____. *The Zionist Idea*. New York: Atheneum, 1970.

Himmelfarb, Milton. *The Jews of Modernity*. New York: Basic Books, 1973.

Hobsbawm, E. J. *Nations and Nationalism Since 1980*. Cambridge: Cambridge University Press, 1990.

Horodetzky, S. A. "The Genealogy of Simon Dubnow." *YIVO Annual of Jewish Social Science* 6 (1951): 9–18.

Howe, Irving. *A Margin of Hope*. New York: Harcourt Brace Jovanovich, 1984.

Hundert, Gershon D., and Gershon C. Bacon. *The Jews in Poland and Russia: Bibliographical Essays*. Bloomington: Indiana University Press, 1984.

Hyman, Paula E. "Culture and Gender: Women in the Immigrant Jewish Community." In *The Legacy of Jewish Migration: 1881 and Its Impact*, edited by David Berger, pp. 157–68. New York: Social Science Monographs, Brooklyn College Press, 1983.

"Igrot Ahad Ha-Am." *He-Avar* 5 (1957): 157–65.

"Igrot el Ahad Ha-Am." In *Sefer Shimon Dubnow*, edited by Simon Rawidowicz, pp. 245–85. London: Ararat Publishing Company, 1954.

Jackson, M.J. *The Sociology of Religion: Theory and Practice*. London: Batsford, 1974.

Janowsky, Oscar I. *The Jews and Minority Rights, 1898–1919*. New York: Columbia University Press, 1933.

_____. *Nationalities and National Minorities*. New York: Macmillan, 1945.

Jewish Life Under the Tsars, A: The Autobiography of Chaim Aronson, 1825–1888. Translated and edited by Norman Marsden. Totowa, N.J.: Allanheld, Osmun, 1983.

Kabak, Aharon. "Le-tsurato ha-ruhanit shel Ahad Ha-Am." *Ha-Shiloach* 30 (1914): 231–42.

Kallen, Horace M. *Secularism Is the Will of God: An Essay in the Social Philosophy of Democracy and Religion*. New York: Twayne, 1954.

Kaminka, Aharon. "Le-vikoret shitato shel Ahad Ha-Am." *Ha-Shiloach* 30 (1914): 272–85.

Karklins, Rasma. *Ethnic Relations in the USSR: The Perspective from Below*. Boston: Allen & Unwin, 1986.

Karu, Baruch. "Be-mehitsato shel Dubnov." *He-Avar* 8 (1961): 17–21.

_____. "Hed peraot shnot ha-shmonim be-itonut ha-ivrit." *He-Avar* 9 (1962): 3–6.

Katz, Ben-Tsion. "Ha-yahadut ha-rusit be-shnat ha-mahapekha veha-peraot 1905." *He-Avar* 4 (1956): 3–10.

Katz, Jacob. *Tradition and Crisis: Jewish Society at the End of the Middle Ages*. New York: Schocken, 1971.

_____ (Yaakov). "Yahadut ve-notsrut al reka ha-hiloniyut ha-modernit." *Leumiyut yehudit: masot u-mehkarim*, pp. 111–31. Jerusalem: Ha-sifriyah ha-tsiyonit, 1983.

Kaufman, Yechezkel. *Golah vi-nekhar*. 2 vols. Tel Aviv: Dvir, 1960–61.

_____. "'Yahaduto' shel Ahad Ha-Am." *Ha-Shiloach* 30 (1914): 249–71.

Kenani, David. *Ha-aliyah ha-shniyah ha-ovedet vi-yehasehah le-dat u-le-masoret*. Tel Aviv: Sifriyat poalim, 1976.

Ketavim le-toldot hibat-tsiyon ve-yishuv erets-yisrael. Edited by Shulamit Laskov. Vol. 3. Tel Aviv: Tel Aviv University, 1987.

Klatzkin, Yaakov. "Boker shel tekufah." *Ha-Shiloach* 27 (1911): 259–303.

Klausner, Yisrael. *Be-darkhe tsiyon.* Jerusalem: Reuben Mass, 1978.

_____ (I[srael]. L.). "Literature in Hebrew in Russia." In *Russian Jewry (1860–1917),* edited by Jacob Frumkin, Gregor Aronson, and Alexis Goldenweiser, pp. 364–81. New York: Thomas Yoseloff, 1966.

_____. *Opozitsiyah li-Herzl.* Jerusalem: Achieved, 1960.

_____. *Toldot ha-kehilah ha-ivrit be-vilna.* Vilna, F. Garbera, 1938.

Klausner, Yosef. "Shimon Dubnov u-tnuat 'hibat tsiyon.'" *He-Avar* 8 (1961): 32–42.

Kleinman, Moshe. "Meh hayah lano Ahad Ha-Am?" *Ha-Shiloach* 30 (1914): 297–301.

Klier, John Doyle. "The Ambiguous Legal Status of Russian Jewry in the Reign of Catherine II." *Slavic Review* 39, no. 3 (September 1976): 504–17.

_____. "The Jewish Question in the Reform Era Russian Press, 1855–1865." *Russian Review* 39 (July 1980): 301–20.

_____. *Russia Gathers Her Jews: The Origins of the "Jewish Question" in Russia, 1772-1825.* DeKalb: Northern Illinois University Press, 1986.

_____, and Shlomo Lambroza, eds. *Pogroms: Anti-Jewish Violence in Modern History.* Cambridge: Cambridge University Press, 1992.

Kling, Simcha. *Joseph Klausner.* Cranbury, N.J.: Thomas Yoseloff, 1970.

Kochan, Lionel. *The Jew and His History.* New York: Schocken, 1977.

Kornberg, Jacques, "At the Crossroads: An Introductory Essay." In *At the Crossroads: Essays on Ahad Ha-am,* edited by Jacques Kornberg, pp. xv–xxvii. Albany: SUNY Press, 1983.

Kozlov, Viktor. *The Peoples of the Soviet Union.* Bloomington: Indiana University Press, 1988.

Kucherov, Samuel. "Jews in the Russian Bar." In *Russian Jewry (1860–1917),* edited by Jacob Frumkin, Gregor Aronson, and Alexis Goldenweiser, pp. 219–52. New York: Thomas Yoseloff, 1966.

Kuznets, Simon. "Immigration of Russian Jews to the United States: Background and Structure." *Perspectives in American History* 9 (1975): 35–124.

Lampert, Evgenii. *Sons Against Fathers: Studies in Russian Radicalism and Revolution.* Oxford: Clarendon Press, 1965.

Lederhendler, Eli M. "Modernity without emancipation or assimilation? The case of Russian Jewry." In *Assimilation and Community: The Jews in Nineteenth-Century Europe,* edited by Jonathan Frankel and Steven J. Zipperstein, pp. 324–43. Cambridge: Cambridge University Press, 1992.

_____. "Religious Reform in Russian Haskalah, 1830–1880." Unpublished essay, 1979.

_____. *The Road to Modern Jewish Politics: Political Tradition and Political Reconstruction in the Jewish Community of Tsarist Russia.* New York: Oxford University Press, 1989.

Leksikon fun der nayer yidisher literatur. 3 vols. New York: CYCO, 1960.

Lerner, Daniel. *The Passing of Traditional Society.* Glencoe, Ill.: Free Press, 1958.

Leskov, Nikolai S. *The Jews in Russia: Some Notes on the Jewish Question.* Translated by Harold Klassel Schefski. Princeton, N.J.: Kingston Press, 1986.

Lestschinsky, Jacob. "Dubnow's Autonomism and His 'Letters on Old and New Judaism.'" In *Simon Dubnow, The Man and His Work,* edited by Aaron Steinberg, pp. 73-91. Paris: World Jewish Congress, 1963.

_____ (Yaakov). "Moreshet ha-yahadut ha-rusit mi-lifne ha-mishtar ha-sovieti." *He-Avar* 4 (1956): 11–19.

_____ (Yaakov). "Ha-reka ha-kalkali shel tehom ha-moshav la-yehudim be-rusyah." *He-Avar* 1 (1953): 31–44.

_____ (Yaakov). "Yidishe ekonomik." *Algemayne Entsiklopedie*, Yidn A, cols. 387–440. New York: CYCO, 1950.

Levenberg, S. "The Historian of Russian Jewry." In *Simon Dubnow: The Man and His Work*, edited by Aaron Steinberg, pp. 180–92. Paris: World Jewish Congress, 1963.

Levin, Dov. "Mi-riga ha-sovietit le-yerushalayim be-da'aga: mikhtavo ha-acharon shel Shimon Dubnov le-yedidav be-erets yisrael." *Shvut* 8 (1981): 111–12.

Levin, Mordechai. *Orkho ha-hevrah ve-kalkala ve-ideologiya shel tekufat ha-haskalah*. Jerusalem: Bialik Institute, 1975.

Levin, Shmaryahu. *Forward from Exile*. New York: Jewish Publication Society, 1967.

_____. *Youth in Revolt*. New York: Harcourt, Brace, 1930.

Levitats, Isaac. *The Jewish Community in Russia, 1844–1917*. Jerusalem: Posner and Sons, 1981.

Lieberman, Hayim. *Doktor Haim Zhitlovski un zayne fartaydiker*. New York, 1944, n.p.

_____. *Idn un idishkayt in di shriftn fun Doktor Ch. Zhitlovski*. New York, 1944, n.p.

Liebman, Charles S., and Eliezer Don-Yehiya. *Civil Religion in Israel: Traditional Judaism and Political Culture in the Jewish State*. Berkeley: University of California Press, 1983.

Lilienblum, Moshe Leib. *Kol kitve Moshe Leib Lilienblum*. Odessa: Moriah, 1912.

Lübbe, Hermann. *Säkularisierung: Geschichte eines ideenpolitischen Begriffs*. Munich: Verlag Karl Alber Freiburg, 1975.

Luckmann, Thomas. "Belief, Unbelief, and Religion." In *The Culture of Unbelief*, edited by Rocco Caporale and Antonio Grumelli, pp. 21–37. Berkeley: University of California Press, 1971.

Luz, Ehud. *Makbilim nifgashim: Dat ve-liumiyut be-tnuah ha-tsiyonit be-mizrach eropah be-reshitah (1882–1904)*. Tel Aviv: Am Oved, 1985.

Macartney, C.A. *National States and National Minorities*. London: Oxford University Press, 1934.

MacIntyre, Alasdair C. *Secularization and Moral Change*. London: Oxford University Press, 1967.

Mahler, Raphael. "Ahad Ha-Ams filozofiye fun der yidisher geshikhte un kultur." *Yunger historiker* 2, pp. 5–23. Warsaw: B. Kletzkin, 1929.

_____. *Hasidism and the Jewish Enlightenment: Their Confrontation in Galicia and Poland in the First Half of the Nineteenth Century*. Philadelphia: Jewish Publication Society, 1985.

_____. "Shitat Dubnov u-mif'alo be-historiografiah ha-yehudit." In *Simon Dubow, The Man and His Work.*, edited by Aaron Steinberg, pp. 57–72. Paris: World Jewish Congress, 1963.

Maimon, Solomon. *The Autobiography of Solomon Maimon*. London: East and West Library, 1954.

Malia, Martin. "What is the Intelligentsia?" In *The Russian Intelligentsia*, edited by Richard Pipes, pp. 1–18. New York: Columbia University Press, 1961.

Maor, Yitzchak. "Ha-liberalim ha-rusiyim be-meah ha-19 u-she'elat ha-yehudim." *He-Avar* 5 (1957): 90–103.

_____. "Sh. Dubnov be-'tekufat riga.'" *He-Avar* 8 (1961): 26–29.

_____. *She'elat ha-yehudim be-tnuah ha-liberalit veha-mahapkhanit be-rusyah: 1890–1914*. Jerusalem: Mossad Bialik, 1974.

_____. *Ha-tnuah ha-tsiyonit be-rusyah mi-reshita vi-ad yamenu.* Jerusalem: Hasifriyah ha-tsiyonit, 1984.

Marcus, Joseph. *Social and Political History of the Jews in Poland, 1919–1939.* Berlin: Mouton, 1983.

Marrus, Michael. *The Politics of Assimilation: A Study of the French Jewish Community at the Time of the Dreyfus Affair.* Oxford: Oxford University Press, 1971.

Martin, David. *A General Theory of Secularization.* Oxford: Basil Blackwell, 1978.

_____. *The Religious and the Secular: Studies in Secularization.* New York: Schocken, 1969.

Marty, Martin E. *Varieties of Unbelief.* New York: Doubleday, 1964.

McClellan, James C. *Autocrats and Academics: Education, Culture, and Society in Tsarist Russia.* Chicago: University of Chicago Press, 1979.

Medem, Vladimir. *Zikhronot.* Tel Aviv: I.L. Peretz, 1984.

Meisel, Nachman. *Doktor Hayim Zhitlowski.* New York: IKUF, 1965.

Meisel, Y. (Meisl, Josef). *Geschichte der Juden in Polen und Russland.* 3 vols. Berlin: C. A. Schwetschke & Sohn, 1921–1925.

_____. "Haye Shimon Dubnov." In *Sefer Shimon Dubnow,* edited by Simon Rawidowicz, pp. 24–60. London: Ararat Publishing Company, 1954.

Melamed, Hillel. "Vi azoy di nazis hobn demordet Prof. Sh. Dubnov." *Zukunft* 50 (April 1946): 320–21.

Meland, Bernard. *The Secularization of Modern Cultures.* New York: Oxford University Press, 1966.

Mendelsohn, Ezra. *Class Struggle in the Pale: The Formative Years of the Jewish Workers' Movement in Tsarist Russia.* Cambridge: Cambridge University Press, 1970.

_____. *The Jews of Central Europe Between the World Wars.* Bloomington: Indiana University Press, 1983.

Mendes-Flohr, Paul R. "Secular Religiosity: Reflections on Post-Traditional Jewish Spirituality and Community." In *Approaches to Modern Judaism,* edited by Marc Lee Raphael, pp. 19–30. Chico, Calif.: Scholars Press, 1983.

Menes, N. "Yeshivahs in Russia." In *Russian Jewry (1860-1917),* edited by Jacob Frumkin, Gregor Aronson, and Alexis Goldenweiser, pp. 382–407. New York: Thomas Yoseloff, 1966.

Meyer, Michael A. *Jewish Identity in the Modern World.* Seattle: University of Washington Press, 1990.

Miron, Dan. *Bodedim be-moadam.* Tel Aviv: Am Oved, 1987.

Mishkinsky, Moshe. "Al emdatah shel ha-tnuah ha-mehapkhanit ha-rusit le-gabe ha-yehudim be-shnot ha-70 shel ha-meah ha-19." *He-Avar* 9 (1962): 38–66.

_____. *Reshit tnuat ha-poalim ha-yehudit be-rusyah: megamot yesod.* Tel Aviv: Ha-kibutz he-meuhad, 1981.

"Moscow." *Encyclopedia Judaica,* vol. 12, cols. 36–65. Jerusalem: Keter, 1971.

Mosse, George L. *German Jews Beyond Judaism.* Bloomington: Indiana University Press, 1985.

Mosse, Werner E. *Alexander II and the Modernization of Russia.* New York: Macmillan, 1958.

Muller, Sharon. "The Zionist Thought of Ben Halpern." *Judaism* 27, no. 3 (summer 1978): 364–73.

Munby, D.L. *The Idea of a Secular Society.* New York: Oxford University Press, 1963.

Nahirny, Vladimir C. *The Russian Intelligentsia: From Torment to Silence.* New Brunswick, N.J.: Transaction Books, 1983.

Neusner, Jacob. *The Death and Birth of Judaism: The Impact of Christianity, Secularism, and the Holocaust on Jewish Faith.* New York: Basic Books, 1986.

_____. "From Theology to Ideology: The Transmutation of Judaism in Modern Times." In *Churches and States: The Religious Institution and Modernization,* edited by Kalman H. Silvert, pp. 13–48. New York: American Universities Field Staff, 1967.

_____. *Judaism in the Secular Age.* New York: KTAV, 1970.

Niger, Sh(muel). "Shimen Dubnov—un yidish." *Zukunft* 56, no. 10 (December 1951): 456–61.

_____ (Niger-Charny, Samuel). "Simon Dubnow as a Literary Critic." *YIVO Annual of Jewish Social Science* 1 (1946): 305–17.

Noruk, Mordechai. "Pegishato im Dubnov." *He-Avar* 8 (1961): 22–25.

Orbach, Alexander. *New Voices of Russian Jewry: A Study of the Russian-Jewish Press in the Era of the Great Reforms, 1860–1871.* Leiden: E.J. Brill, 1980.

_____. "The Russian-Jewish Leadership and the Pogroms of 1881–1882: The Response from St. Petersburg." *The Carl Beck Papers in Russian and East European Studies*, No. 308, pp. 1–37. Pittsburgh: University of Pittsburgh, 1984.

Oren, Yosef. *Ahad Ha-Am, M.Y. Berdichevsky vi-havurat 'tseirim.'* Rishon Le-Zion: Yahad, 1985.

Orlov, B. "A Statistical Analysis of Jewish Participation in the Russian Revolutionary Movement in the 1870s." *Slavic and Soviet Series* 4 (1979): 3–20.

"Pale of Settlement." *Encyclopedia Judaica*, vol. 13, cols. 24–28. Jerusalem: Keter, 1971.

Panikkar, R. *Worship and Secular Man.* London: Darton, Longman and Todd, 1973.

Parfitt, Tudor. "Ahad Ha-Am's Role in the Revival and Development of Hebrew." In *At the Crossroads: Essays on Ahad Ha-am*, edited by Jacques Kornberg, pp. 12–27. Albany: SUNY Press, 1983.

Parsons, Talcott. *On Institutions and Social Evolution: Selected Writings.* Edited and with an Introduction by Leon H. Mayhew. Chicago: University of Chicago Press, 1982.

Patt, Emanuel. "Mit gloybn in di folks-koykhes: Zekhtsik yor autonomizm in yidishn gezelshaftlikhn leybn." *Zukunft* 63, nos. 1–2 (January–February 1958): 19–24.

Patterson, David. *The Hebrew Novel in Czarist Russia.* Edinburgh: Edinburgh University Press, 1964.

Pinsker, Leon. *Road to Freedom: Writings and Addresses.* Westport, Conn.: Greenwood Press, 1975.

Pinson, Koppel S. "Dubnovs natsionale teorie in shayn fun unzer tsayt." *Yivo bleter* 34 (1950): 9–20.

_____. "The National Theories of Simon Dubnow." *Jewish Social Studies* 10, no. 4 (October 1948): 335–58.

Pipes, Richard. "Catherine II and the Jews: The Origins of the Pale of Settlement." *Soviet Jewish Affairs* 5, no. 2 (1975): 3–20.

_____. *The Formation of the Soviet Union: Communism and Nationalism, 1917-1923.* Cambridge, Mass.: Harvard University Press, 1970.

"Pogroms." *Encyclopedia Judaica*, vol. 13, cols. 695–97. Jerusalem: Keter, 1971.

Pollack, Allen. "Secularism." *Forum* 46–47 (fall, winter 1982): 177–85.

Pomper, Philip. *Peter Lavrov and the Russian Revolutionary Movement.* Chicago: University of Chicago Press, 1972.

Pratt, Vernon. *Religion and Secularisation.* London: Macmillan, 1970.

"Press." *Encyclopedia Judaica*, vol. 13, cols. 1044–45. Jerusalem: Keter, 1971.

Raeff, Marc. "Patterns of Russian Imperial Policy toward the Nationalities." In *Soviet Nationality Problems*, edited by Edward Allworth, pp. 2–42. New York: Columbia University Press, 1971.

Raisin, Jacob S. *The Haskalah Movement in Russia*. Philadelphia: Jewish Publication Society, 1913.

Reinharz, Jehuda. "Ahad Ha-'Am—In the Eye of the Storm." *Jewish History* 4, no. 2 (fall 1990): 49–58.

———. *Chaim Weizmann: The Making of a Zionist Leader*. New York: Oxford University Press, 1985.

Renner, Karl (Rudolf Springer). *Der Kampf der osterreichischen Nationen um den Staat*. Leipzig/Vienna: Duticke, 1902.

Richardson, Alan. *History, Sacred and Profane*. Philadelphia: Westminster Press, 1964.

Rivkin, B. "Dr. Haim Zhitlovski un zayne talmidim." *Zukunft* 36 (May 1931): 339–44.

Rogger, Hans. "Government, Jews, Peasants, and Land in Post-Emancipation Russia." *Cahiers du Monde Russe et Sovietique* 17 (1976): 5–25, 171–211.

———. *Jewish Policies and Right-Wing Politics in Imperial Russia*. Berkeley/Los Angeles: University of California Press, 1986.

———. "The Jewish Policy of Late Tsarism: A Reappraisal." *Wiener Library Bulletin* 25 (1971): 42–51.

Rosenbloom, Noah. "Ahad Ha-Am veha-yeda ha-histori." In *Salo Wittmayer Baron Jubilee Volume*, vol. 3, pp. 331–52. Jerusalem/New York: American Academy for Jewish Research, 1975.

Roskies, David. *Against the Apocalypse: Responses to Catastrophe in Modern Jewish Culture*. Cambridge, Mass.: Harvard University Press, 1984.

Rotenstreich, Nathan. *Al Ahad Ha-Am*. Jerusalem: Dfus limude yerushalayim, 1956.

———. "History, Sociology, and Ideology." In *Simon Dubnow: The Man and His Work*, edited by Aaron Steinberg, pp. 47–56. Paris: World Jewish Congress, 1963.

———. *Tradition and Reality: The Impact of History on Modern Jewish Thought*. New York: Random House, 1972.

Roth, Leon. "Back to, Forward from, Ahad Haam?" *Conservative Judaism* 17, nos. 1–2 (fall 1962-winter 1963): 20–30.

Roth, Y. "Ha-filosofiyah ve-Ahad Ha-Am." In *Mehkarim be-filosifiyah shel yahadut*, pp. 3–15. Jerusalem: Hebrew University, 1937.

Royle, Edward. *Radicals, Secularists, and Republicans: Popular Freethought in Britain, 1866–1915*. Manchester: Manchester University Press, 1980.

Rubenstein, Aryeh. "Tefisat ha-'kulturah' be-mishnat Ahad Ha-Am." *Melilah* 3/4 (1950): 289–310.

Rubinow, I(saac) M. "Economic Condition of the Jews in Russia." *Bulletin of the United States Bureau of Labor* 72 (September 1907): 487–583.

"Russia." *Encyclopedia Judaica*, vol. 14, cols. 433–506. Jerusalem: Keter, 1971.

Salmon, Joseph. "Ahad Ha-Am and Benei Moshe: An 'Unsuccessful Experiment'?" In *At the Crossroads: Essays on Ahad Ha-am*, edited by Jacques Kornberg, pp. 98–105. Albany: SUNY Press, 1983.

——— (Yosef). "Ha-maavak al daat ha-kahal ha-haredit be-mizrach eropah be-yachas le-tnuah ha-liumit ba-shanim 1894–1896." In *Prakim be-toldot ha-hevrah ha-yehudit be-yeme ha-benayim uvi-et ha-hadashah*, pp. 330–68. Jerusalem: Magnes Press, 1980.

——— (Yosef). "Tahalikhe kituv be-yishuv ha-yehudi be-arets be-machatsit ha-rishonah shel shnot ha-90." *Catedra* 12 (summer 1979): 4–30.

Schafler, Samuel. "Modern Zionism—An Historic Perspective." *Judaism* 30, no. 1 (winter 1981): 111–19.

Schapiro, Leonard. "The Pre-Revolutionary Intelligentsia and the Legal Order." In *The Russian Intelligentsia*, edited by Richard Pipes, pp. 19–31. New York: Columbia University Press, 1961.

Schrey, Heinz-Horst, ed. "Säkulasierung." *Wege der Forschung*, Band 424. Darmstadt: Wissenschaftliche Buchgesellschaft, 1981.

Schweid, Eliezer. *Ben ortodoksiah li-humanizm dati*. Jerusalem: Van Leer Jerusalem Foundation, 1977.

————. *Toldot he-hagut ha-yehudit be-et ha-hadashah*. Tel Aviv: Ha-kibutz ha-meuhad, Keter, 1977.

————. *Ha-yahadut vi-hatarbut ha-hilonit*. Tel Aviv: Ha-kibutz ha-meuhad, 1981.

————. *Mi-yahadut li-tsiyonut: Mi-tsiyonut li-yahadut*. Jerusalem: Ha-sifriyah ha-tsiyonit, 1984.

Scult, Mel. *Judaism Faces the Twentieth Century: A Biography of Mordecai M. Kaplan*. Detroit: Wayne State University Press, 1993.

Seltzer, Michael. *The Wineskin and the Wizard*. New York: Macmillan, 1970.

Seltzer, Robert M. "Ahad Ha-Am and Dubnow: Friends and Adversaries." In *At the Crossroads: Essays on Ahad Ha-am*, edited by Jacques Kornberg, pp. 60–72. Albany: SUNY Press, 1983.

———— "From Graetz to Dubnow: The Impact of the East European Milieu on the Writing of Jewish History." In *The Legacy of Jewish Migration: 1881 and Its Impact*, edited by David Berger, pp. 49–60. New York: Social Science Monographs, Brooklyn College Press, 1983.

————. *Jewish People, Jewish Thought: The Jewish Experience in History*. New York: Macmillan, 1980.

————. "Simon Dubnow, A Critical Biography of His Early Years." Unpublished Ph.D. dissertation, Columbia University, 1970.

Seton-Watson, Hugh. *The Decline of Imperial Russia, 1855–1914*. New York: Frederick A. Praeger, 1952.

————. *The Russian Empire, 1801–1917*. Oxford: Clarendon Press, 1967.

Shapira, Anita. "Herzl, Ahad Ha-'Am, and Berdichevsky: Comments on Their Nationalist Concepts." *Jewish History* 4, no. 2 (fall 1990): 59–70.

Shapiro, Leon. *Introduction to Dubnow's History of the Jews in Russia and Poland*, vol. 1. New York: KTAV, 1975.

Sharfstein, Zvi. *Haye ha-yehudim be-mizrach eropah be-dorot ha-achronim*. Tel Aviv: Yavneh, 1973.

Shavit, Yaakov. "Ahad Ha-'Am and Hebrew National Culture: Realist or Utopianist?" *Jewish History* 4, no. 2 (fall 1990): 71–88.

Sherman, Bezalel Charles. "Bund, Galuth Nationalism, Yiddishism." *Herzl Institute, Pamphlet No. 6*. New York: Theodor Herzl Foundation, 1958.

———— (C. Bezalel). "Secularism in a Religious Framework." *Judaism* 1, no. 1 (1952): 36–43.

"Shimen Dubnov tsu zayn 75-yorikn yoyvl." *Historishe shriftn* 2 (1937), xixiii.

Shochat, Azriel. "Ha-hanhagah be-kehilot rusyah im bitul ha-kahal." *Zion* 42, 44 (1977, 1979): 143–233, 161-65.

————. *Mosad "Ha-rabanut mi-taam" be-rusyah*. Haifa: University of Haifa Press, 1976.

"Shtetl." *Encyclopedia Judaica*, vol. 14, cols. 1466–1473. Jerusalem: Keter, 1971.

Silberstein, Laurence. "Judaism as a Secular System of Meaning in the Writings of Ahad Ha-Am." *Journal of the American Academy of Religion* 52 (1984), 547–68.

————. "Religion, Ethnicity, and Jewish History: The Contribution of Yehezkel Kaufmann." *Journal of the American Academy of Religion* 42 (1974): 516–31.

Simon, Aryeh, and Yosef Heller. *Ahad Ha-Am: ha-ish, pe'alo, vi-torato.* Jerusalem: Magnes Press, 1955.

Simon, Gerhard. "Church, state and society." In *Russia Enters the Twentieth Century, 1894–1917*, edited by Erwin Oberländer, et al., pp. 199–235. New York: Schocken, 1971.

Simon, Leon. *Ahad Ha-Am.* New York: Herzl Press, 1960.

Simon Dubnow (1860–1941): The Life and Work of a Jewish Historian—Catalogue of the Exhibition. New York: YIVO Institute for Jewish Research, 1961.

Slutsky, Yehuda. *Ha-itonut ha-yehudit be-toldot ha-yehudim be-mizrach eropah ad 1881.* Jerusalem: Mossad Bialik, 1971.

————. "Kritikus." *He-Avar* 8 (1961): 43–64.

————. "Sikum agum." *He-Avar* 19 (1972): 5–19.

————. *Tnuat ha-haskalah be-yahadut rusyah.* Jerusalem: Merkaz Zalman Shazar, 1977.

Smith, Anthony D. *The Ethnic Origins of Nations.* Oxford: Basil Blackwell, 1986.

————. *The Ethnic Revival.* Cambridge: Cambridge University Press, 1981.

Smith, Graham, ed. *The Nationalities Question in the Soviet Union.* London/ New York: Longman, 1990.

Spencer, Herbert. *Principles of Sociology.* Edited by Stanislav Andreski. Hamden, Conn.: Archon Books, 1969.

Stanislawski, Michael. *For Whom Do I Toll?: Judah Leib Gordon and the crisis of Russian Jewry.* Oxford: Oxford University Press, 1988.

————. "The Transformation of Traditional Authority in Russian Jewry: The First Stage." In *Legacy of Jewish Migration: 1881 and Its Impact*, edited by David Berger, pp. 23–30. New York: Social Science Monographs, Brooklyn College Press, 1983.

————. *Tsar Nicholas I and the Jews: The Transformation of Jewish Society in Russia, 1825–1855.* Philadelphia: Jewish Publication Society, 1983.

Starr, S.F. "Tsarist Government: The Imperial Dimension." In *Soviet Nationality Policies and Practices*, edited by J.R. Azrael, pp. 3–38. New York: Praeger, 1978.

Steinberg, Aaron. *History as Experience: Aspects of Historical Thought — Universal and Jewish.* New York: KTAV, 1983.

Steinberg, Y. N. "Yidishe kolonizatsie." *Algemayne Entsiklopedie*, Yidn A, cols. 483–532. New York: CYCO, 1950.

Stillschweig, Kurt. "Nationalism and Autonomy Among Eastern European Jewry: Origin and Historical Growth up to 1939." *Historia Judaica* 6 (1944): 27–68.

Swet, Gershon. "Russian Jews in Zionism and the Building of Palestine." In *Russian Jewry (1860–1917)*, edited by Jacob Frumkin, Gregor Aronson, and Alexis Goldenweiser, pp. 72–208. New York, Thomas Yoseloff, 1966.

Syrkin, Marie. *Nachman Syrkin, Socialist Zionist: A Biographical Memoir.* New York: Herzl Press, 1961.

Syrkin, Nachman. *Kitve Nachman Syrkin.* Tel Aviv: Davar, 1938-39.

Tartakower, Arieh. "Le-vikoret shitato ha-sotsiologit shel Dubnov." In *Sefer Simon Dubnov*, edited by Simon Rawidowicz, pp. 77–88. London: Ararat Publishing Company, 1954.

————. "Migration Problems in Dubnow's Theory of Jewish Nationalism." In *Simon Dubnow: The Man and His Work*, edited by Aaron Steinberg, pp. 92–103. Paris: World Jewish Congress, 1963.

Tcherikower, E. "Peter Lavrov and the Jewish Socialist Emigres." *YIVO Annual of Jewish Social Science* 7 (1952): 132–45.

Tchernov, Victor. "Hayim Zhitlovski un der 'farband fun di russishe sotsial-revolutsionarn,' 1900-1903." In *Zhitlovski zamlbukh*, pp. 91–149. Warsaw: Farlag Ch.Brzoza, 1929.

Tchernowitz, Chaim. *Pirke haim*. New York: Bitzaron, 1954.

Tchernowitz, Shmuel. *Bnei Moshe u-tekufatam*. Warsaw:, Ha-tsefiirah, 1914.

Thaden, Edward C. *Russia's Western Borderlands, 1710–1870*. Princeton: Princeton University Press, 1984.

_____. ed. *Russification in the Baltic Provinces and Finland, 1855–1914.* Princeton: Princeton University Press, 1981.

Thalheim, Karl C. "Russia's economic development." In *Russia Enters the Twentieth Century, 1894–1917*, edited by Erwin Oberländer et al., pp. 85–110. New York: Schocken, 1971.

Thon, Yehoshua. "Lo zeh ha-derekh." *Ha-Shiloach* 30 (1914): 211–16.

Tobias, Henry J. *The Jewish Bund in Russia: From Its Origins to 1905*. Stanford: Stanford University Press, 1972.

Trivush, Y. "Partsufah shel odessa ha-yehudit." *He-Avar* 1 (1953): 58–64.

Trotzky, Ilya. "Jewish Institutions of Welfare, Education, and Mutual Assistance." In *Russian Jewry (1860–1917)*, edited by Jacob Frumkin, Gregor Aronson, and Alexis Goldenweiser, pp. 416–33. New York: Thomas Yoseloff, 1966.

_____. "Jews in Russian Schools." In *Russian Jewry (1860–1917)*, edited by Jacob Frumkin, Gregor Aronson, and Alexis Goldenweiser, pp. 408–15. New York: Thomas Yoseloff, 1966.

Trunk, Isaiah. "Historians of Russian Jewry." In *Russian Jewry (1860–1917)*, edited by Jacob Frumkin, Gregor Aronson, and Alexis Goldenweiser, pp. 454–72. New York: Thomas Yoseloff, 1966.

Tuchman, Hyman, ed. *Ahad Haam: The Philosopher of Cultural Zionism*. New York: Jewish Agency Department of Education and Culture, 1967.

Tylor, Edward B. *Researches into the Early History of Mankind and the Development of Civilization*. Edited and abridged by Paul Bohannan. Chicago: University of Chicago Press, 1964.

Ussishkin, Menahem. "Baal-dimyon." *Ha-Shiloach* 30 (1914): 306–8.

Venturi, Franco. *Roots of Revolution*. New York: Grosset & Dunlap, 1960.

"Vilna." *Encyclopedia Judaica*, vol. 16, cols. 138–51. Jerusalem: Keter, 1972.

Vital, David. "Ahad Ha-'Am as the Sage of Zionism." *Jewish History* 4, no. 2 (fall 1990): 25–32.

_____. *The Origins of Zionism*. Oxford: Oxford University Press, 1980.

_____. *Zionism: The Formative Years*. Oxford: Clarendon Press, 1988.

_____. "The Zionist as Thinker: Ahad Ha-Am and Hibbat Zion." In *At the Crossroads: Essays on Ahad Ha-am*, edited by Jacques Kornberg, pp. 87–97. Albany: SUNY Press, 1983.

Wandycz, Piotr S. *The Lands of Partitioned Poland, 1795–1914*. Seattle: University of Washington Press, 1974.

Waxman, Chaim. "'Bitter Almond': Prof. Shaked's Dubious Case for Secularism." *Forum* 48 (spring 1983): 127–29.

Weiler, Gershon. *Teokratiah yehudit*. Tel Aviv: Am Oved–Ofakim, nd.

Weinreich, Max. *History of the Yiddish Language*. Translated by Shlomo Noble. Chicago: University of Chicago Press, 1980.

_____. "Yidish." *Algemayne Entsiklopedie*, Yidn B, cols. 23–90. New York: CYCO, 1948.

Weinryb, Bernard (Dov). "Dubnov veha-historiografiah ha-yehudit." In *Sefer Shimon Dubnow*, edited by Simon Rawidowicz, pp. 67–76. London: Ararat Publishing Company, 1954.

_____. *The Jews of Poland: 1500–1800*. New York: Jewish Publication Society, 1973.

Wengeroff, Pauline. *Memoiren einer Grossmütter*. 2 vols. Berlin: M. Poppelauer, 1913–1919.

Werblowsky, R.J. Zwi. *Beyond Tradition and Modernity: Changing Religions in a Changing World*. London: Athlone Press, 1976.

Wiener, Max. *Ha-dat ha-yehudit be-tekufat ha-emantsipatsiah*. Jerusalem: Mossad Bialik/Leo Baeck Institute, 1974.

Willetts, Harry T. "The agrarian problem." In *Russia Enters the Twentieth Century, 1894–1917*, edited by Erwin Oberländer et al., pp. 111–37. New York: Schocken, 1971.

Williams, Robert C. *Culture in Exile: Russian Emigrés in Germany, 1881–1941*. Ithaca: Cornell University Press, 1972.

Wilson, Bryan. *Contemporary Transformations of Religion*. London: Oxford University Press, 1976.

_____. *Religion in a Secular Society: A Sociological Comment*. London: Watts, 1966.

_____. "Unbelief as an Object of Research." In *The Culture of Unbelief*, edited by Rocco Caporale and Antonio Grumelli, pp. 247–93. Berkeley: University of California Press, 1971.

Wischnitzer, Mark. "Reminiscences of a Jewish Historian." In *Russian Jewry (1860–1917)*, edited by Jacob Frumkin, Gregor Aronson, and Alexis Goldenweiser, pp. 473–77. New York: Thomas Yoseloff, 1966.

Wisse, Ruth. "The Politics of Yiddish." *Commentary* 80, no. 1 (July 1985): 29–35.

Wistrich, Robert S. *Revolutionary Jews from Marx to Trotsky*. London: Harrap, 1976.

_____. *Socialism and the Jews: The Dilemmas of Assimilation in Germany and Austria-Hungary*. East Brunswick, N.J.: Associated University Presses, 1982.

Wohl, Robert. *The Generation of 1914*. Cambridge, Mass.: Harvard University Press, 1979.

Woocher, Jonathan S. *Sacred Survival: The Civil Religion of American Jews*. Bloomington: Indiana University Press, 1986.

Yerushalmi, Yosef Hayim. *Zakhor: Jewish History and Jewish Memory*. Seattle: University of Washington Press, 1982.

"Zamenhof, Ludwik Lazar." *Encyclopedia Judaica*, vol. 16, cols. 925–26. Jerusalem: Keter, 1971.

Zarzuvsky, Avraham. "Mihanekh ha-dor." *Ha-Shiloach* 30 (1914): 294–96.

Zaslavsky, Victor, and Robert J. Brym. *Soviet-Jewish Emigration and Soviet Nationality Policy*. New York: St. Martin's Press, 1983.

Zborowski, Mark, and Elizabeth Herzog. *Life Is with People: The Culture of the Shtetl*. New York: Schocken, 1972.

Zhitlowski, Chaim. "Bimkom tsionizmnun un das sotsiale lebn in erets-yisroel." *Zukunft* 38 (July 1933): 406–11.

_____. *Gezamelte shriftn*. 10 vols. New York: Yubelyum Oysgabe, 1912–1917, 1919.

_____. "Hebrayizm un idishism." *Das Naye Lebn* 1, no. 10 (July/August 1923): 1–9; no. 11 (September 1923): 4–13.

_____. "Der kamf far idish-natsionale rekht (1900–1907)." *Zukunft* 38 (December 1933): 711–17.

_____. "Der mandat oyf erets yisroel." *Das Naye Lebn* 1, no. 1 (October 1922): 1–4.

_____. "Di naye konstitutsie in rusland." *Zukunft* 42 (May 1937): 260–72.

_____. "Di problemn fun dem golus-natsionalizm." *Zukunft* 38 (November 1933): 652–53.

_____. "Shayles un tshuves in hilkhes idishizm." *Zukunft* 36 (September 1931): 570–76; (October 1931): 640–52.

_____. "Tsu dem ershter mai." *Das Naye Lebn* 1, no. 8 (May 1923), 1–5.

_____. "Tsu der krizes fun der idisher natsionaler autonomiye." *Das Naye Lebn* 1, no. 4 (January 1923): 1–6.

_____. *Zikhroynes fun mayn lebn.* 3 vols. New York: Posy-Shoulson Press, 1935.

Zipperstein, Steven J. "Ahad Ha-Am and the politics of assimilation." In *Assimilation and Community: The Jews in Nineteenth-Century Europe*, edited by Jonathan Frankel and Steven J. Zipperstein, pp. 344–65. Cambridge: Cambridge University Press, 1992.

_____. "Ahad Ha-Am as a Leader: Elitism and the Coming of Mass Jewish Politics." Unpublished essay, 1988.

_____. "Ahad Ha-'Am's Politics." *Jewish History* 4, no. 2 (fall 1990): 89–96.

_____. *Elusive Prophet: Ahad Ha-Am and the Origins of Zionism.* Berkeley/Los Angeles: University of California Press, 1993.

_____. "Heresy, Apostasy, and the Transformation of Joseph Rabinovich." In *Jewish Apostasy in the Modern World*, edited by Todd M. Endelman, pp. 206–31. New York: Holmes & Meier, 1987.

_____. "Jewish Historiography and the Modern City: Recent Writing on European Jewry." *Jewish History* 2, no. 1 (spring 1987): 73–88.

_____. *The Jews of Odessa: A Cultural History, 1794-1881.* Stanford: Stanford University Press, 1985.

_____. "Russian Maskilim and the City." In *The Legacy of Jewish Migration: 1881 and Its Impact*, edited by David Berger, pp. 31–45. New York: Social Science Monographs, Brooklyn College Press, 1983.

Zunser, Miriam S. *Yesterday: A Memoir of a Russian-Jewish Family.* New York: Harper and Row, 1978.

Zylbercwig, Zalmen. *Achad Haam un zayn betsiyung tsu yiddish.* Los Angeles: Farlag Elisheva, 1956.

INDEX

Achiasaf, 236, 242. *See also* Ahad Ha-Am

Ahad Ha-Am, 217–91; as editor of Achiasaf, 242, 268; and Second Aliyah, 256, 257; and Third Aliyah, 257; and Alliance israélite universelle, 239; on anti-Semitism, 246, 247, 249, 283; and anthology of Jewish thought, 289, 350 n. 264; anti-social nature of, 337 n. 6; views on Arabs in Palestine, 256–57, 345 n. 155; on assimilation, 254, 274–76, 284; on atheists, 263, 270, 273; as an auto-didact, 227; critique of autonomism, 278; response to Balfour Declaration, 241, 255; reaction to Beilis trial, 250; correspondence with Shmuel Ben-Ami, 291; influence of Jeremy Bentham on, 225; defense of Eliezer Ben Yehuda, 238–39; evaluation of Micha Berdichevsky, 266; and Berlin, 242; birth, 222; and Hayim Nachman Bialik, 232, 250, 251, 253; support of binationalism in Palestine, 257; biological definition of Jewish nationhood, 259–60; and Bnei Moshe, 234–40, 266, 280, 341 n. 63; response to Bolshevik Revolution, 255; and Yosef Haim Brenner, 252, 266, 269–70; interest in British empiricists, 225; dislike of British Jewry, 251; attitude toward British Zionists, 251, 255; in Brody, 227; childhood, 220, 223–28; interpretation of concept of Chosen People, 264; attitude toward Christianity, 252, 269–70, 274; on colonies in Palestine, 231, 240–41; influence of Auguste Comte on, 225; contemporary relevance of, 300; concept of cultural Zionism, 221; influence of Charles Darwin, 225; daughter Leah, 220; daughter Rachel, 252–53, 344 n. 135; death, 258; and dialectics, 339 n. 30; view of Diaspora, 101–102, 205, 206, 207, 262, 276–78, 281, 282, 290, 300; at Zina Dizengoff's salon, 60; and Dreyfus Affair, 249; rejection of presidency of Dropsie College, 245; relationship with Dubnow, 171, 204–5, 228, 248, 256, 257, 258, 278, 287; criticism of Dubnow's writings, 205, 252, 259, 275, 277–78; view of East European Jewry, 263, 275–76; hostility toward East European Jews in London, 251; 1905 elections for Duma, 246; praise of Rabbi Mordechai Eliasberg, 264; elitism of, 217–18, 232, 281, 290; as an essayist rather than a philosopher, 219; 1923 visit to Europe, 257; emphasis upon evolutionary development, 228; relations with his father Isaiah, 220, 223, 226, 242, 273, 338 n. 8; influence of Ludwig Feuerbach on, 225; attitude toward French Jewry, 249; as a candidate of General Zionists party, 257–58; on concept of God, 226, 264, 262, 270, 276; in Gopishitsa, 223, 230; debates with Ha-Poel ha-Tsa'ir, 256; admiration for Yehuda ha-Nasi, 226; editorship of *Ha-Shiloach*, 242, 245, 249, 266, 268; attitude toward Hasidism, 223; view of Haskalah, 224, 288; on centrality of Hebrew, 206, 286–90; use of Hebrew as daily language, 251, 287; support of a Hebrew University, 253; critique of Theodor Herzl, 217, 221–22, 247–48, 282, 283–86, 348 n. 236; reaction to death of Herzl, 252; involvement in Hibbat Zion, 80, 217, 220–21, 228–30, 234–40, 241, 244–45, 279, 280, 282, 283; on historical origins of Jewish people, 260–61; and historicism, 265; indebtedness of Israel to, 300; unknown in Israel today 337 n. 1; influenced by Italian nationalism, 279; desire to write book on Jewish ethics, 253, 273–74; view of Jewish identity, 258–61; theory of Jewish nationality, 265; view of Jewish State, 217; response to establishment of the Jewish Theological Seminary of America, 245; view of Judaism, 193, 260, 261, 262–64, 270, 271–72, 276; influence of Nachman Krochmal (Ranak), 226; attitude toward Moshe Leib Lilienblum, 229, 243, 279; in London, 250–52, 254, 287; correspondence with Rabbi Judah Magnes, 280; veneration of Moses Maimonides, 191, 226, 270–71; response to March 1917 revolution in Russia, 255; marriage, 226; reaction to